I0128027

The Dark Side of the Criminal Justice System

Critical Perspectives on Race, Crime, and Justice

Series Editor: Tony Gaskew, University of Pittsburgh, Bradford

This book series seeks interdisciplinary scholars whose work critically addresses the racialization of criminal justice systems. Grounded within the connective space of history, the nuances of race continue to define the standard of how justice is applied throughout policing, courts, and correctional systems. As such, this series is open to examine monographs and edited volumes that critically analyze race from multiple narratives—sociopolitical, cultural, feminist, psychosocial, ecological, critical theory, philosophical—along criminal justice lines. The Critical Perspectives on Race, Crime, and Justice book series speaks to the significant scholarship being produced in an era where race continues to intersect with crime and justice.

Titles in the series

The Dark Side of the Criminal Justice System: War Crimes & the Black Community, 1960-1990 by Ronald L. Morris

Gift from the Dark: Learning from the Incarceration Experience by John R. Chaney and Joni Schwartz

Stop Trying to Fix Policing: Lessons Learned from the Front Lines of Black Liberation by Tony Gaskew

Race, Education, and Reintegrating Formerly Incarcerated Citizens: Counterstories and Counterspaces edited by John R. Chaney and Joni Schwartz

Law Enforcement in the Age of Black Lives Matter: Policing Black and Brown Bodies edited by Sandra E. Weissinger and Dwayne A. Mack

The Dark Side of the Criminal Justice System

War Crimes & the Black Community, 1960–1990

Ronald L. Morris

LEXINGTON BOOKS

Lanham • Boulder • New York • London

Published by Lexington Books
An imprint of The Rowman & Littlefield Publishing Group, Inc.
4501 Forbes Boulevard, Suite 200, Lanham, Maryland 20706
www.rowman.com

86-90 Paul Street, London EC2A 4NE, United Kingdom

Copyright © 2022 by The Rowman & Littlefield Publishing Group, Inc.

All rights reserved. No part of this book may be reproduced in any form or by any
electronic or mechanical means, including information storage and retrieval systems,
without written permission from the publisher, except by a reviewer who may quote
passages in a review.

British Library Cataloguing in Publication Information Available

Library of Congress Cataloging-in-Publication Data

Names: Morris, Ronald L., 1938– author.
Title: The dark side of the criminal justice system : war crimes & the black community,
    1960–1990 / Ronald L. Morris.
Description: Lanham : Lexington Books, 2022. | Series: Critical perspectives on race,
    crime, and justice | Includes bibliographical references and index. | Summary:
    "Beginning in the Civil Rights era, the American criminal justice system waged a
    campaign of terror and warlike oppression of Black Americans, Ronald L. Morris
    analyzes those dark times, it's cause, short- and long-term effects, and calls for
    change"—Provided by publisher.
Identifiers: LCCN 2021058453 (print) | LCCN 2021058454 (ebook) |
    ISBN 9781793613196 (cloth) | ISBN 9781793613219 (paperback) |
    ISBN 9781793613202 (epub)
Subjects: LCSH: Criminal justice, Administration of—United States—History. |
    Discrimination in criminal justice administration—United States—History. |
    Race discrimination—Law and legislation—United States—History. | African
    Americans—Race relations.
Classification: LCC KF9223 .M67 2022 (print) | LCC KF9223 (ebook) |
    DDC 345.73/05—dc23/eng/20211223
LC record available at https://lccn.loc.gov/2021058453
LC ebook record available at https://lccn.loc.gov/2021058454

An Elegy to Heroes

*This book is dedicated to the countless exemplary
Criminal Justice System agents and law enforcement
personnel who during the period of 1960–1990 tried
to maintain professional ethical standards, personal
decency, and respect for racial justice and tolerance
toward Black (and other minorities) men and women
in their custody. This despite odious laws, regulations, and
draconian policies under which the CJS pursued its
mandate to rid America of Black Street criminals, thugs,
and Black "Super Predators." In a lighter vein, this work
is also dedicated to kindred spirits who inspired me like
my muse, Nomi Waksberg, herr Doktor Professor Graf Frederick
von Kramer, and the wonderful geniuses at John Jay
College of Criminal Justice's sociology department—Alisa Thomas
and Theresa Rockett for providing me with
many years of academic enjoyment.*

Contents

.

Introduction

Rules of Engagement

Who was it that said one benefit of winning a war is the victor gets to write its history? Whoever they were, they were able to identify the good guys and the bad boys. Here lay a golden opportunity for a conniving historian to vilify the enemy to the rafters. Consequently, governments have always found handmaidens willing to fulfill this purpose. Professor of Jewish History, Lucy S. Dawidowicz noticed academics were often chief providers of this service. She wrote,

> The authoritarian and totalitarian societies that flourished in our time have suffered no dearth of historians who have been willing to subvert their craft in the services of political dogma . . . there is a sufficiency of historians who are prepared to falsify history in their national interest.[1]

Such misrepresentations justified all that happened, all that was necessary to win a war. It also allowed for conveniently forgetting or dismissing the full range of crimes and naked brutalities against the enemy in pursuit of heroic victory. For purposes of our story, the enemies in this case were millions of African Americans who have been conveniently allowed to fade into the mists of history; whatever atrocities they endured on an industrial basis at the hands of a fascist government have been mostly forgotten, distorted, or even minimized by the sufferers themselves. As this study proceeds, our intention will be to add sociologists and criminologists to the list of academic subverters who conveniently hide the historical crimes of government.

No democratic government through its policies should cause direct suffering and injury to its citizens. Even the thought is perverse. That's not what governments are for. Nor should they ever pursue policies designed to bring hurt. It may be wrong for governments to intentionally do so, but that's what

1

American governments, whatever the political party, did, actively and deliberately in this period. For this, they should be condemned and are, rightly so,
throughout this book via their enthusiastic connections with an allied and supportive criminal justice system (hereafter CJS). Prominent sociologist Alvin
Gouldner has written:

> All suffering which is unavoidable, tragic and truly part of the human condi-
> tion deserves sympathy but the suffering that is a product of social injustice is
> especially deserving of our attention because it is far less likely to be known and
> more likely to contain much that is avoidable.[2]

Citizens may conduct themselves badly toward their fellow citizens and
do many terrible, unforgivable things. But these are individuals acting on
impulse and emotion, generally alone. They don't pursue a coordinated
policy designed to maximize harm to others around them on a round-the-
clock basis. In this study that's exactly what the American governments
were applauded for doing against its Black and minority citizenry by White
nationalists in the period under study. And for any government to disregard
its constitutional obligation to make the lives better for all its citizens dis-
qualifies it as a legitimate government. It becomes merely a shadow government, an agency of reprehensible terror and illegitimate, no matter what its
staff of elite lawyers say.

The War on Crime that took place in this country between 1960 and 1990
was waged by the various administrations and their proxy CJS personnel
over unsuspecting Black communities. Year following year after 1960, this
obsolete 225-year-old system ratcheted up the pain and suffering of millions of its Black victims under the pretense of waging war against crime.
Allowing for the enormous psychic damage done to the community from
a completely unnecessary War on Crime we raise the question should even
limited reparations be requisitioned for those Black citizens caught up in this
tyranny? The all-powerful apparatus of CJS agencies, spread across the country while under federal control, ruled over the nation's ghettos, exercising a
law enforcement dictatorship over its Black residents.

Invoking the adjective Orwellian seems wholly applicable to this nightmare landscape of totalitarian reality that targeted the nation's Black population. Coincidently, George Orwell's greatest work, *1984*, is a prophetic date
that falls within the years of this study. It seems perfectly applicable then
to use the adjective "Orwellian" for concepts that describe these years for
Blacks: blinkered justice and repressive government for minorities but unseen
by the bulk of the White population, visual propaganda (that told us all Black
males were synonymous with being criminal), minority life that staggered
under Police State surveillance and control, doublethink where racism meant

White patriotism, and research convinced us that there existed without proof inherently negative characteristics of a violent Black personality.

These were years where administrations led by both political parties deemed it necessary for the survival of White society to suppress Black protest and demands for equal rights and criminal justice by clamping down heavily on Black dissent and twisting these demands into warped definitions of urban crime and violent Black criminal behavior. The haughtiness of government demeanor to accept no criticism for their actions made it clear they cared little of the effect their genocidal power exerted over millions of Black citizens. Indeed, University of Belfast professor Ruth Jamieson wonders if criminologists can even spot the difference between a country waging war against crime and one simply committing genocide.[3]

After all, these agents of authority were the victors in the War on Crime though victory was never formally declared and they could leisurely recount their vainglorious individual roles in it as they pleased. But let's not forget: amid all this persecution the institutional goals of human liberty, social justice, and political truth had been compromised. Broken lives and destroyed futures, besides the many physical casualties wrought by this war, were the many sadistic by-products afforded by the defenseless Black men and women of the era. One is mindful of the German occupation of Europe in World War II with the thousands upon thousands of deportations to concentration work camps. In the annals of this period, all this is quite forgotten.

No proliferation exists of memoirs, witness books, plaques, awards, school, and street names celebrating the Black resisters of the Nixon and Reagan's brand of colonial fascism. That may never happen. There is a gaping silence and lack of textual testimony and paucity of sources for what befell America's Black urban class in the War on Crime. Stop and frisk, lockup, fingerprinting, mug shots, appearance before the magistrate's court, severe sentences, handcuffs, leg chains, chokeholds, abusive language, physical pain and facial lacerations, ignoble incarceration, nothing was missing from this picture for many Black men and boys during this period. Law enforcement agents full of righteous indignation and self-importance have won the public relations crime war to tell their story in the media, and were supported by the general public who didn't really want to revisit this phase of the American Police State. But heroes who loathed this occupation did emerge from a long line of persecuted ancestors.

Black people have an undeniable instinct for danger. And for good reason. As *New York Times* journalist T. J. English wrote that many Black people who followed the civil rights events of these years viewed them as part of an "orchestrated reactionary campaign on the part of White supremacists, including the Ku Klux Klan and police authorities."[4] Some were classified as criminal offenders or prison inmates to deflect their harsh criticism of American racial conditions. Some were simply murdered during the casual violence of police arrests, confinement, incarceration, or on the streets when challenging wrongful acts by law enforcement. Even if we refuse to acknowledge or praise this generation, perhaps this study of CJS malfeasance will help place a glow on the heroism of this group while we can still remember them. It was an era when the CJS piled outrage upon outrage. This unprovoked war of aggression by the CJS is herein unequivocally called a crime. The point of arrest has long been understood as an unassailable right of police as a sovereign agent of the government. But used wrongly as this study will document, we might as well call it what the Germans did—*ein kriegsverbrecken*—a war crime by the American State. The sheer waste of Black people through an endless parade of petty arrests, shameless court appearances, and, too often, lengthy violent stays in prison totally destroyed the future of these victims forevermore. This morbid reportage is their revenge. These were all crimes against humanity.

This study intentionally omits certain aspects of the CJS. We choose not to consider the juvenile justice system, the federal prison and parole system, women defendants generally or federal agents (less moments with the FBI and the federal drug authority). Far fewer people were affected by these agencies; punishments were on a different scale as imperial judges had a much lighter docket from which to impose sanctions, and, more importantly, custom and tradition meant federalese left most crime and its pursuit to states and local jurisdictions. The sinister behavior and policies that emanate from all the many juvenile justice systems in and out of the federal government toward beleaguered juveniles in this period deserve its own attention but, as they say in academia, let's save something for someone else to expose.

Finally, and returning to Orwell, in 1940, during a time of national emergency, he published *The Lion and the Unicorn,* a socialistic novel with its famous opening: "As I write, highly civilized human beings are flying overhead, trying to kill me." A quarter of a century later, an American Black person, during this time of emergency brought on by the "War on Crime" might well be forgiven if he wrote, "As I write, all around us, a completely uncivilized beast is trying to kill us." He also may be forgiven for pointing overhead to the CJS as the American version of Germany's Luftwaffe.[5] The following chapters amplify and validate why this view should be seen as necessary and valid.

As the title says I have tried to maintain some rules of engagement to confer decorum on a painful subject matter. As a rule, many Black men may not be perfect citizens (how many Whites are?) but we must dismiss terms as "gangsters" and "thugs" and "hoodlums" to deprecate their status as people owed mandatory justice and constitutional rights. Nor are they "Black" criminals, as if that adjective defined an especially dangerous category of social renegade that deserved special attention at the end of a menacing nightstick. Moreover, while this may be a criminology book, we must refrain from the occupational hazard of seeing all our subjects as anonymous, faceless, and nameless statistics: They are, above all else, American citizens with constitutional rights and allegedly guaranteed legal protections. Sadly, defense attorney Johnny Cochran Jr. claimed he "was never viewed as just a lawyer, he was perceived as a 'Black' lawyer and every decision, every action he made as a professional was still defined by this cruel color lie" as if his skin color was a notable professional flaw.[6] Hopefully, we don't apply such negative distinctions in this report. There is also a collective sense of outrage that permeates the entire Black community so that when one of its members protests against CJS abuse, it can be seen as the communal reaction to the feelings of all Black people, deserving special attention. A final note and as a tribute, warm and collective appreciation should be given to all the suffering Black mothers whose children during this period were savaged and hatefully abused by an unaccountable CJS.

NOTES

1. Lucy S. Dawidowicz, *The Holocaust and the Historians* (Cambridge: Harvard UP, 1981), p. 145.

2. Alvin Gouldner, Jr., "The Sociologist as Partisan-Sociology and the Welfare State," *American Sociologist* 3 (1968): 106.

3. Ruth Jamieson, *The Chronology of War* (Ashgate: Farnham, 2014), p. 77.

4. T. J. English, *The Savage City, Race, Murder and a generation on the Edge* (New York: Morrow, 2011), p. 30.

5. Mentioned in Calum Mechie's essay on George Orwell in the *Times Literary Supplement*, "Still Orwell's England? The writer as 'moral litmus paper.'" 18 December 2010, pp. 30–31.

6. Johnnie L. Cochran, Jr. (with Tim Rutten), *Journey to Justice* (New York: Ballantine Books, 1996), p. 64.

Chapter 1

Ministries of Terror

THE STATE AS CRIMINAL

They were a frightening spectacle if you happened to be an ethnic minority from 1960 to 1990. The American Criminal Justice System (hereafter: CJS) behaved like a rampaging army in all the nooks and crannies of Black America. They invaded and assaulted, particularly the police who went about their business undeterred by constitutional safeguards designed to protect Blacks and other minorities. Applying brutal tactics that dated from the era of slavery, police brought devastating ruin to millions of families by improper and vicious arrests before turning their victims to other parts of the CJS (the court's probation, and corrections) who, in turn, continued the torment and oppression. Why the alarm?

White politicians complained that Black demands for civil rights fed into a criminal state of mind. Senator Strom Thurmond (R-Miss) worried that "civil rights demands for integration of the races would bring a wave of terror, crime and juvenile delinquency . . . and I refer you to New York City as proof." Agreeing was fellow Southerner from the same state, James Eastland (D-Miss.), who remarked "If the Negro is entitled to equal social status why does he not earn equality? Why is he responsible for most of the crimes in this country? It is my belief that Black freedom will require harsher law enforcement." Civil rights activist Patricia J. Williams complained, "The very definition of criminality has been raced as in the causally reiterated defamation that Blacks commit all crimes."[1]

It didn't have to be this way. There were plenty of contemporary calls to change the criminal justice landscape as it applied to Black Americans, such as calls for the abolition of prisons, downsizing jails, eliminating excessive bail, wholesale decriminalization of the criminal law, defanging the police through local community control, apportioning out probation services to local neighborhood self-help groups, creating new leadership and dumping corrupt political appointees in the Black communities, getting serious about helping drug addicts within a halfway house network, downplaying ritual court sanctions at the exclusionary level, and most importantly establishing legitimate police review boards under civilian control and funding these projects with federal government oversight. What were the odds, within the span of a decade, that two authoritarian right-wing presidents (Richard Nixon and Ronald Reagan), each having challenged California's liberal justice system, would revert to a racist anticrime ideology that ignored all opportunities to properly reform the justice system? In the process, law and order Republicans and their Southern allies thwarted civil rights demands using the criminal law and the CJS behemoth as weapons for political repression. Princeton University African American Studies professor Naomi Murakawa writes:

> The notion of a backlash against excesses of Black radicalism willfully ignored historically entrenched opposition to even the most modest civil rights reforms throughout the South and much of the urban North across the entire post WW2 period. Even when crime rates were low and stable.[2]

Add to this a limp Democratic Party (which composed 60% of Congress in this period) that utterly failed to protect their Black constituents against a vindictive White electorate that applauded the hundreds of anticrime bills being pushed through state legislatures as well as Congress at this time. Such bills empowered the CJS to display intolerance and disregard to millions of Black citizens, which was the very purpose of this legislation. Sadly, the CJS seemed only too prepared to act as punitive water carriers. The injustices that will be reported here are much in line with American historian (University of Michigan) Heather A. Thompson's own observations that "injustices were spread over all segments of the CJS during this period."[3]

From 1965 to 1968 congressmen made connections with everyday street crime, which meant Black people labeled "lawless jungle dwellers," striving for equal rights seen in fact as everyday criminals. The result was an avalanche of anticrime bills aimed at using the CJS by equating political protest with criminal intent. In 1967 alone, ninety punitive bills were quickly passed to criminalize political demonstrations and riot incitement. And riot incitement there truly was. Between 1961 and 1967 there were nearly 100 urban riots: the vast majority having been caused by trigger happy and nervous cops using excessive force and brutality to effect order. These only served to incite Black communities to accept violence against the CJS as a logical solution. In the 1967 Watts riots, nearly 4,000 police were arrested and subjected to miserable conditions during incarceration awaiting a court hearing. The majority were released without a formal complaint. After the assassination of Dr. Martin Luther King in April 1968, over 175 cities went viral and exploded into Black rage.[4] The country was in shock. The Kerner Commission in 1967 was less so-admitting that police barbarism was the cause of the many urban rebellions.

Between 1960 and 1990, and as a result of the American government's War on Crime, opportunistic politicians of all stripes managed to audaciously connect civil rights turbulence to street crime. As a result, this belief fostered a series of militarized public policies designed to attack the rising crime rate as the product of Black political activism. African American Studies Professor from Princeton University, Naomi Murakawa, wishes to remind us about this period:

> Senator (R, AZ) Barry Goldwater at the height of the civil rights era traced rising crime rates to Black civil disobedience, Black demands for equality under the law, and Black reliance on the welfare state. He conflated civil disobedience with violence in our streets. Black activists with "bullies and marauders," and in so doing he contended—subtly but undeniably—that Black freedom necessitates a strong "law and order" response.[5]

O. C. Fisher (D-Tx) agreed seeing America in 1967 "as plagued with insurrection, murder, Arson, looting and violence on a scale such as might be expected to occur in darkest Africa."[6]

In a PBS television interview, UCLA criminologist Elliot Curie summarized the frightening trend:

> Crime rates went up very dramatically in the 1960s, scene of many explosive civil rights protests. They had been quite low during World War II . . . up through the middle 1960s and then pretty much skyrocketed. So much so, particularly for violent crimes and stranger crimes, that we had a President (Nixon), who pretty much got elected on a platform . . . of simply going after Black citizens.[7]

This is surely not the function of government. Talk about "law and order" and street crime went hand in hand with White backlash toward Black Power and Republicans were quick to pick up this disillusionment and use it for political electoral leverage. Murakawa traces this theme as far back as 1946 when national Republican leaders were "explicitly and routinely" addressing Black civil rights in criminological terms:

> The U.S. didn't confront a crime problem that was racialized. It confronted a race problem which was criminalized. The battle to preserve Jim Crow in the 1940s and 1950s segued into the battle against crime in the mid-1960s and this

was led by Republicans and Southern Democrats with law and order rhetoric against Black alleged crime.[8]

Barry Latzer, criminology professor at John Jay College of Criminal Justice (New York City), cited some notable statistical thinking about crime and its impact on citizens with make-believe scenarios of fear to shake the most fear-less citizen of the time. He reports that in the mid-1980s the Federal Bureau of Justice (with Reagan appointees guiding the conclusions) calculated, based on the criminal victimization rates from 1975 to 1984, the lifetime chances of being raped, robbed, or assaulted (all speculative, of course, and the assaulter was no doubt Black). If crime rates remained the same (which, of course, they didn't) 83% of all Americans over the age of twelve (presumably White) would, in their actuarial lifetimes, be victimized (which didn't happen) by attempted or completed violent crime of robbery or assault and 40% (how precise) would be injured as a result (that never came about). But this is how crime statistics were politically speculated into frightful human scenarios. America had become the land of rampant make-believe crime scenes spon-sored by government voodoo tactics to keep Whites on edge.[9] But what if the crime being committed was really happening by the country's crime fighters?

This finally brings us to the government's crime-fighting arm, its CJS. These agencies, composed of police departments and sheriff's offices, crimi-nal courts, corrections jails and prisons, probation and allied rehabilitation services, have long been capable of a multitude of crimes of their own. Some were severe, some far less so. But the system's insularity and freedom from surveillance and overview and the belief that they are a quasi-oriental brother-hood devoted to fighting an enemy clan cause this to happen. This study will show how quietly and secretly they account for more crimes against the public than the other way round. Surprisingly few books have been devoted to con-sidering this phenomenon. Henderson and Simon began the foreword of their 1994 review of the system as:

> This book clearly portrays that the high rates of crimes committed by actors working within the criminal justice agencies were remarkably frequent and constant throughout the system. None of this was really new. Police corruption and abuses of authority, members of the courtroom workgroup tampering with juries, taking bribes or just being conveniently incompetent, prison officers engaging in brutality, sexual exploitation or taking payoffs; and prison admin-istrators participating in and/or sanctioning such behavior were all too common features of the CJS in the United States.[10]

Professor R. C. Monk of Coppin State College (Baltimore) called these many examples of occupational deviance by members of the CJS "perhaps the most serious crime problem" of the country, discussing a category of crime that requires far more exploration which this study attempts to address. "The vast majority of wrongdoing within the CJS," he points out, "stems from causes within immediate organizational environments and conditions within the larger social structure" (i.e., racism) of which criminal justice organizations are a part ". . . and violations of civil rights and abuses of authority through the use of excessive force has been a long standing problem across a significant number of law enforcement agencies." Representative John Ashbrook (R-Ohio) added the CJS with his knock-on indulgent government officials, a lax CJS, elite sociologists, and Black civil rights leaders. Murakawa takes up this southern emphasis in observation: "As Black civil rights gained momentum, Southern states deployed their CJS apparatus to combat Black protesters as if they were criminals. This law enforcement mentality soon extended to Northern and Western regions as well."[11]

In this pursuit, we are faced with an insurmountable problem, one which the researchers have faced before us. Ross points us to the inevitable lack of official documentation by agencies who don't want to publicize their crimes or bad behavior for fear of official reprisals or criminal prosecution. Not every CJS war crime was as easy to see as when Bull Connor and his Nazi police force were captured on television unleashing police attack dogs on civil rights protesters in Birmingham in 1963. Without such obvious evidence, the result must induce innovation and creativity and even speculative guesses on the extent of such criminality if we are to proceed into the very nature and extent of these dangerous governmental activities. An early observer of state-organized crime, William Chambliss made the following novel points: "Acts defined by law as criminal and committed by State officials in pursuit of their jobs as representatives of the state are a legitimate topic of criminological inquiry. . .Be open to expanding parameters and not feel constrained by traditional methodological paradigms."[12]

Simon and Henderson detect several obstacles besides the lack of documentation that affects the present study. The CJS fosters racism and reinforces social class bias against the poor—all statistics point to the fact that a disproportionate number of offenders are Black and poor. But it is extremely difficult to assign these motives when assessing many of the severest crimes mentioned in the study. Did CJS agents really do such bad things because the offender was Black? Anecdotes are useful but hardly replace the agent saying "I did that dastardly deed because that man is Black." But that won't happen as no CJS actors took the time to document with exactitude what would aid future researchers on a mission.[13]

Off the Rails

In any event, due to its historical mission of monitoring suspects for criminality, simple daily interactions always kept civilians vulnerable to the whims of cops who employed aggressive street corner tactics, leaving nothing to be written that might indict them. Vindictive judges who ignored constitutional safeguards for defendants were also too wily to let their racism or anger at working-class offenders become obvious in the court renderings or written reports. Nevertheless, it was a period when many criminologists gave the system little praise. W. Sturz claimed the CJS by its very erratic behavior toward communities they served was "off the rails." Former prosecutor Paul Butler said the CJS was premised on controlling just one group—African American men. Professor Angela Davis, who had served time in California prisons, labeled it "dysfunctional" while British professor of criminology and British criminologist Vivien Stern defamed the system as "an inexplicable deformity." Author Leonard Moore, focusing on police malpractice in his study of New Orleans, noted that following public integration in the local schools, police presence increased dramatically as did the number of police murders of Black men with no serious investigation into their deaths. With no indictment by the district attorney nor department sanctioning, all the offending cops involved were back patrolling the streets immediately after the killings. Sociologist Steven R. Denziger claimed the CJS was facing a terrible crisis in credibility. Huntington called police the symbol of White Power and concluded

> police were one of the most reactionary and racist institutions of White society . . . who . . . during the riots acted out of a desire to vent individual hostilities to re-establish police authority and avenge police honor.

One expert on police, with years of experience in their study, believed police officers saw Negroes as culturally and biologically inferior and inherently criminal, disliked the legal technicalities that hampered their work with Black suspects, and carried their negative opinions into their daily work in the Black communities. Cops were easily the main culprits in the CJS war against Black citizens, and they employed zeal and nastiness in a firestorm of brutality and indifference to the human suffering they caused.[14]

President Johnson's hastily called National Criminal Justice Commission in 1969 summed up the decade's long-growing crime problem in its opening words:

> What the Commission found was while rates of crime remained stable . . . one out of three young African-American men are under supervision of the CJS compared to one out of five only five years ago . . . we see little or no change in the capacity of the CJS to affect the rate of crime and violence in (Black) communities. We quickly realized that the CJS had no strategic plans to manage the crime problem and was being held accountable to virtually nobody . . . (in

fact) criminal justice policy was often in conflict with itself. Professor Alfred Blumenstein (Carnegie Mellon), felt the one thing that came of the Commission was in thinking the CJS as a system. Another original member, Sheldon Krantz, reported how police in America were in a very primitive state-what with limited training, lack of education and no real diversity. "It needed a radical revision."[15]

Once on the ground, most CJS abusers should have known the consequences of what they were doing, and that what they were doing was wrong and indefensible. Given the calamitous outcome of many of their actions, best to play dumb and assume nothing. Look the other way and deny being near the scene. Hope no reporter would pick up the scent of a scandal and expand the incident into a full-blown expose. And how many reporters were willing to do this and risk losing all contacts with agents fearful of being drawn into the melee. But here was a tip of the iceberg.

Let's just take the case of criminal court judges. According to experts, from 1988 to 1989 alone, 600 charges of misconduct were brought against Texas judges, 1,100 against New York criminal court judges, and 700 each for those in Florida, Washington, DC, and California. Nationwide, some 6,800 complaints were filed with state agencies to investigate their judges, excluding ten states that refused to participate in the report. This meant that if each judge of the roughly 12,000 presiding judges in 1975 had 25 possible cases a day or over 100 per week in a year some form of misconduct (as discussed in the relevant chapter on the courts), 60 million petty criminal cases might contain some form of judicial abuse, racism, or legal misconduct. Just try and transfer this same type of corruption to the other departments within the CJS. A *Washington Post* investigation reported the number of cops charged with some type of corruption, despite community opinion to the contrary, was infinitesimal. A 1930s study of what the public wanted from its police was not honesty and efficiency. The public showed no concern about how the police did their job so long as it didn't directly affect them. Open season, however, could be declared by cops on marginal groups and there was little interest in how the police behaved toward political radicals, Black men in general and working-class stiffs. CJS crime was ignored in the report.[16]

Not here. In this study, we refuse to overlook criminal and abusive behavior toward citizens, particularly Black men, by the CJS bureaucracies as anomalies or something so secretive it is best left unexplored, or as the just approach to fighting crime by offenders more dangerous than any government agents. Or assume if you highlight so many official offenders, you will have nobody to fight crime or be willing to sign on for the job. Nor do we accept the premise that if agents don't apply excessive force and brutality to bend nasty criminals to their will, the latter will devise ways to reoffend with bravado and make the lives of innocent citizens unbearable. Or will we justify such behavior as being jaded acts from years of working with terrible people and see everyone as a criminal—don't blame the agent, blame the society for producing such criminals in quantity. We instead elevate this high level of ill-considered CJS brutality in all its forms as a war crime. This is especially the case as the government and its rulers and administrators and legislators have called the crime fighting of these years as a "War on Crime." In this context, they sent carloads of money and military equipment to local CJS agencies to conduct campaigns against criminals best found on a rice paddy in Vietnam. Let's face it; these agents are representatives of our government and, as citizens, we all deserve far better.

A Runaway Train of Government Spending

Two sets of numbers tell us all we need to know about skyrocketing CJS costs after 1965. The first is there were over 120 riots in major cities between 1963 and 1968 (especially after the assassination of Dr. Martin Luther King in April 1968). President Johnson's National Advisory Commission on Civil Disorders in 1967 identified White racism as a major cause of Black grievance. His administration took a different view and saw it as a law enforcement problem curable with more police in the street. This view would have major negative consequences for Black residents in the urban riot zones. The other is the resultant Black violent crime rate which in the 1950s stood unstirred at 161 per 100,000. By 1975 and the War on Crime campaigns of punitive law enforcement, the rate soared to 548 per 100,000 and later 663 in 1984 as the Reagan years intensified vindictive CJS activities against the Black population.[17] Both of these trends frightened politicians of every stripe in seeking some sort of resolution to satisfy public outrage. Nixon's eventual War on Drugs plan worked like a charm. It enabled millions of federally funded dollars to flow quickly to law enforcement agencies and quickly led to arrests and convictions to satisfy public demands for vengeance. For over fifteen years, money flooded CJS coffers so that the ghettoes could be invaded by agents seeking to suppress Black antagonisms.

None of this curbed crime but at least the government was seen to be doing something even if much of it was excessive and brutal. Before the War on Crime and the 1960s, making an adequate living in the CJS held little promise. In the 1950s, probation officers earned little and were often tied to specific judges for referrals from whom they derive an income for ensuing reports to the court. Jail guards owned a low-grade job that captured little public respect, so only the worst possible workers could be found for the job; some might say only the most sadistic. Rehabilitation services were mainly for the wealthy and applicants needed to be pretty subservient to be considered for pay that often depended on an agency's ability to raise funds.

Police had a more enviable position as they could shake down suspects and accept money on the spot not to arrest people. Still, in some locales $200-400 might be an average monthly wage. Judges ruled over sleepy courtrooms with dockets made up of ne'er-do-wells, wife-beaters, drunkards, and prostitutes none of whom was in the chips.

Initial costs in the early 1960s were borne by the local taxpayers; after 1968 it was the federal government with deeper pockets, with more urgency to fight crime as a political wedge issue, and more willingness to use the police as the sharp end of the stick against Black offenders. President Richard Nixon and his Republican and Southern Democratic henchmen were willing accomplices. In his 1968 acceptance speech at the Republican nominating convention, Nixon used the "law and order" theme twenty-one times; after assuming the presidency in 1969 he declared a "War on Drugs" which got the financial ball rolling in high gear. Since Nixon's promotion of law enforcement and the unprecedented expansion in all aspects of the CJS, by 1997, the CJS was the third-largest employer in the country.

Come to the War on Crime with its bountiful federal funding through the Law Enforcement Administrative Agency (LEAA) in 1969, money began to flow like wine for those who joined the CJS. Everyone made out like, well, bandits. For Blacks it was just the opposite. Since few agencies would hire Black men for any sort of law enforcement job they occupied the position of being the reason why agencies were being well paid. They were the enemy being associated with riots, drugs, and violence. Index crimes stood at 3.4m in 1960. Ten years later the figure was 10m, enough to shock the public. Two economists (B. Wayson and G. S. Funke) took a look at the CJS in financial terms. In 1989 they concluded: It was financial bingo for official agents in the services no matter how many arrests were made, how much crime was curbed (if much at all), how many human abuses might be sustained to process a defendant, how much recidivism was reduced. Researching the Mid-Atlantic suburban areas, they estimated each arrest cost the public $295m (all expandable figures that would increase over time) regardless of the outcome or whether the arrest was even justified. Imagine millions of arrests that occurred and what those would cost the taxpayer who had little choice in the matter on whether the money might be better spent on more valuable social services. Then there were court costs (up to $800 just for the first appearance), lawyer hearings ($200+ a piece), and so on. Let's not forget jury trials estimated at $4,700, assuming a thirty-day detention factor (which meant an added cost). Wayson and Funke saw the potential costs, without the trial, at maybe $2,500. And we were looking at very labor-intensive work, with upward of a dozen CJS personnel all on the clock. Humana buses and disregard of constitutional safeguards to the defendants were free and at the victim's expense. If the offender was ordered to prison another set of costs would arise. The National

Criminal Justice Commission found "Hundreds of billions of dollars have poured from taxpayers' checking accounts into penal institutions and the businesses that serve them. Several million people have come to depend on the CJS for employment."[18] Let's not forget expenses associated with inflation and unexpected spikes in operating costs, plus regular increased salaries. As a probation officer, I received on every time my union requested the increase at the time of budget negotiations every two years or so. There were also jail costs, courtroom building depreciation, supplies, capital costs, construction costs (in the millions and millions during this time of rapid prison construction), debt service, fringe benefits, costs for assigned counsel, depreciation, fringe rates, life cycle costs, accrued liability, clerical support, well, you get the idea. Metropolitan, big-city rates went up by four to five times. Everything depended on two factors: a cop's desire to stop, annoy, even arrest someone, and a prosecutor's desire to proceed with a court hearing. Was he willing to initiate the costs that followed in pursuit of this concept of justice? Bearing in mind none of the costs and expenses that followed came out of his pocket or that of the arresting officer, nor the judge and the dozens of others who participated in the eventual disposition of an offender's case.

Here are a few additional figures to make the case for not just a runaway train but a gravy train for the CJS in these years. Police made the greatest gains (snagging 75% of the criminal justice expenditures) to employ 125,000 cops as salaries jumped from an average $842 per month in 1971 to $1,500 per month by the end of the decade. Total employment in the CJS in October 1971 stood at 930,000, eight years later it was 1.3m. Criminal justice expenditures rose steadily from $10.5b (1971) to $26b (1979). Professionals in the field weren't the only beneficiaries. Schools also did well. Colleges and universities with criminal justice and police studies departments saw a major increase in students from a mere 1,000 (1966) to over 200,000 by 1977. With more scholars came more articles. Almost 1,000 criminology articles by 2,000 authors were published in eight leading criminal justice journals in the 1970s and 1980s. According to the WashingtonPost.org, in 1960 state and local expenditures for the police stood at $2b. Eleven years later, as crime increased threefold and urban areas underwent riots and violence attributed to Black criminality, the bill for the police shot up to $11b+, an almost sixfold increase and $15b in 1980, a sevenfold increase with the crime rate staying roughly the same. The CJS monthly payroll in October 1971 was $715m, by the end of the decade in October 1979 it was $17b, a 137% increase. someone was profiting from crime but it wasn't the Black resident.[19] How much lower might CJS costs have been if instead of hiring "professionals and experts" with little knowledge of Black culture to be of any value, hiring had been done on a different basis. This would have been the perfect moment to redraft Black communities toward progressive urbanization. It would have been the perfect time for launching a drive for linguistic and cultural education in America's Black neighborhoods, segregated as they were, within each of them. Cultural music, literature, fashion, and even food could have been presented to highlight Black achievement. Locals could also have been hired into CJS administrative positions and given preference over outsiders in law enforcement workplaces. All the CJS services would be staffed by community representatives best poised to know how to resolve local social, drug, and crime problems. I speculate costs and real expenses at a third or less what was actually spent, with a more effective infrastructure to replace the wasteful, highly expensive inefficient agency that was built solely to satisfy political considerations. Surely, with so much money being spent, and some very good minds were at work devising anticrime policies, the CJS might have been rewarded with far better personnel on a much higher plane of morals and intellect. We were willing to pay a lot; we should have got a lot more than we did than just a bunch of tired bureaucrats.

Such exorbitant amounts of money to arrest people and keep them incarcerated for long, empty months seems wasteful and inefficient, also destructive of human capability. But consider it from the perspective of the CJS agent who sees his weekly salary going up (plus fringe benefits) every time his union gets their budget demands approved year after year (no need to strike). That's wonderful disposable income for his community to also enjoy. He and his family can buy big-ticket items as well. And don't forget the three to five times multiplier effect as it makes his expenditures mean even more. Just the reverse for the Black defendant who has lost kills, money, job, family, and so on. But what value has society already placed on him? Whatever a cop does to implant him into the CJS with all its collateral suffering, his value has been minimized by society who considers him as of little value. His only achievement is to be the reason so many other people are paid to keep him down. To this extent, he employs hundreds in the CJS who gain from his loss. In financial terms, how do you measure human ruination? Apparently, fascist politicians of the time had no such hesitation in ignoring moral issues in favor of satisfying electoral ambitions.

Criminology without a Crime

This study has nothing to do with criminal activity or the right or wrong of the criminal law. It has nothing to do with crimes rates, rates of incarceration over time, violence statistics, drug offenses, or defendant bad behavior toward the community and society. It has everything to do with how people are treated once suspected by police on the street all the way through the CJS. What kind of treatment can one expect to receive if under suspicion of some crime? How much respect are they entitled to even if they have committed a dastardly act? That is what we are talking about? And we mean treatment that is extended equally and impartially to all suspects even if later found to be innocent. Treatment means physical, verbal, facial, and body gestures all designed to frame a person as a potential suspect, nothing more. Surely, nothing harsh or vicious in the employment of police equipment or extreme physical restraint. This also applies to judges who don't ignore signs a defendant has been unconstitutionally mistreated at the time of arrest; or a prosecutor the same; or a corrections officer who doesn't use naked force if an inmate is found to have stolen food from the cafeteria.

This study suggests this kind of bad behavior goes on all the time with CJS agents. But it is never treated as a crime. There is no mentioning of criminal activity in arrest reports, the judiciary is tight-lipped on pronouncing human rights violations shown offenders and the staff of a jail or prison will admit to no crime in how they badly treat prisoners. We speak of possibly millions of such war crimes in this report but "crime" is not a CJS product. So if their behavior is ignored, any discussion about Black crime in the streets must also be disregarded to keep the slate clean. Which is worse, a Black man assaulting a police officer or a cop assaulting a local Black resident? Which has greater implications for the safety of the community by failing to deal with it? It is for this reason we have spent little time analyzing the proclivities of Black adult men. Apparently, when dealing with the CJS, crime is beside the point, and unimportant, if committed by its agents or the judiciary or any rehabilitation personnel. We cannot offer fair conclusions to the rate of Black crime during this period if we are unwilling to present what we consider an even worse tale of malfeasance by closing an eye to CJS war crimes. We see these as far greater for the security and integrity of the country and so choose to examine them in closer detail. There are already tons of material to be found on Black crime. We won't be presumptuous to add to it. One consequence of all this is the possible shattering of a myth that violence is a Black thing. Inasmuch as we found so much excessive force and violence being used by the CJS against defenseless Blacks, although lacking legitimate records, the issue must remain unanswered at this time. Future researchers may find better ways of resolving this issue on whether CJS agents are more likely than Blacks to use force and violence as a dominant method of control.

Did Cops Really Hate Black People?

Would you prefer the word despise? Judging by police behavioral manifestations and attitudes of hate toward Black people, I'd say the probability was high. As a probation officer, I spent the late 1960s and 1970s in and around police hearing plenty of invectives but nothing nice about Black residents these men were supposed to protect. Well, maybe a lecherous remark about the women. Despite departmental suggestions, no cop ever wanted to live in a Black neighborhood (not that the officials did). Costs of living were appreciably lower than surrounding White suburbs, much closer to the job, full of inexpensive and tasty ma-pa restaurants, older housing had all sorts of advantages, and freeway traffic wasn't an issue. The schools weren't as good and parks were few but cops living in the area may have helped change all this for the better.

The historian Mary Sacks noted that as Black migrants invaded the western and northern cities from the depressed Southland in the 1930s and 1940s, they became instant targets of police enmity, suspicion, and were constantly being harassed. Why would that be so? Why annoy new people for whom you knew nothing and who held no grudges against you? That they were usually quite poorly dressed, spoke with a different accent, hung about the streets where they could be seen, often begged for money from Whites, and knowing nothing of local resources didn't help their cause. Police found them a nuisance which wasn't the same as a criminal. Cops found they annoyed White businesses and that was a problem; also, the vice and drugs which they came to be associated with meant continuous police crackdowns. White owners considered it bad for business to have Blacks seemingly hanging about causing a visible eyesore.

Consequently, it was up to the cops to do the removal and this they both resented and hated the Black men for having to be enforcers of public codes and protect White businesses and property; this extended into physically restraining, roughly treating, and aggressively arresting Blacks from entering White areas alone, looking for work or just curious. One man, a Texas journalist named John Howard Griffin, wanted to know how Whites felt about Blacks but being White himself he was in no position to find out. Brilliant idea? Paint himself Black in skin color and visit the Deep South to find out. This he did in 1951. What did he learn? It wasn't safe to be Black in Southern America. Within a few months of being there, he found "it was a personal nightmare to be Black." He was threatened by strangers, met with ritual rudeness and constantly denied basic courtesies by Whites he met along the way. Followed by White thugs, trailed by cops, tossed into a cold cell for no reason, told by a prospective employer: "We don't want you, don't you understand that?" even threatened by the KKK who brutally beat him on a dark road one night in 1964, leaving him for dead. "But nothing gnawed at me so much," he recalled, "was the 'hate stare' the unmasked hatred he drew from many White men he came into contact during those months in the South."[20]

But we cannot chalk all this talk of hate and vengeance of cops to violent cultural practices and attitudes learned in the Deep South. Something else is at work here. Blacks everywhere were also treated badly. Let's take the case of Portland Oregon (1970 pop. 835,000). Here was a city with no tradition of slavery, plantations and cotton fields, chain gangs, slave blocks, blood-hounds, or Jim Crow to remind people of antebellum oppression. No history of underground railroads, all White juries or local sheriffs leasing out Black inmates to local farmers. Were cops any different in behavior and manner-isms in Portland than elsewhere? Could they be said, by their more benevo-lent actions toward Black citizens, to be free of "unmasked hatred"? The few Blacks in Portland were themselves confined, as elsewhere, to a small seg-regated area known as the Albina area (less than 5% of the population were Blacks of whom 80% were confined to 2½ square miles, 1940). This made Portland, as everywhere else in the country, an area supervised by police that itself was segregated and bore the pains of injustice in the economic and social spheres. One local resident Rachel James talks of the police brutality in the ranks of which she was a witness in 1974:

> For years Black people in Albina have been bullied and victimized by our so-called lawmen . . . it seems as if anytime a cop gets the urge to punch something they snatch the first available Black man they see and use him to satisfy their savage egos.[21]

This witness tells us something of the spontaneous and wanton brutality on Blacks just because they are available. Is hate a part of this reaction? Another way to determine the nastiness of police is through court documents. In 1981, the Portland Criminal Court actually ordered the police department to desist in using insulting, degrading, and derogatory terms against Black suspects, stop using lead batons and shot-filled "sap gloves during arrests, eliminate lethal sleeper choke holds from their repertoire, make visible their badges and nameplates to citizens, advise citizens on how to proceed with filing a complaint and employ legitimate court-ordered search warrants during raids. This list of prohibitions suggests just how widely police disregarded citizen safety in the Black community."[22] Yes, they were no different.

Portland police believed they sought out Black offenders not because of their color but due to their inherent criminal tendencies. In the early 1960s, before the rise in crime nationwide, of all arrests in the city, 45% were Black (remem-ber only 5% of the population was Black). Eighty-six percent of the police felt the cause was civil rights and the Black Power movement which were "moving too fast," a view traceable to many other police departments of the time.[23] Watching Black men for subversive activities such as plotting riots was number eight on the list of important duties before traffic watch and helping old ladies. It was also found that police were not spreading rumors accusing certain Blacks, especially young men, of terrorism, regardless of evidence, that could lead to arrest and unjustified detention. How much hatred does this show?[24]

Attempts to reform Portland's police, as in so many other cities, provoked a whirlwind of anger by the rank and file whose archly conservative union flatly refused to comply with even superficial changes to police practices and improvements in the best interest of police-community relations. How much hatred of Blacks could be gauged when the whole department chose not to cooperate with local Black leaders? Some of the worst offenders disparagingly called Black reformist efforts mere "ticks on a cow" and met every request with "swift, hostile, resistance."[25]

Blauner broadened this portrait: Black citizens saw police as representatives of a state that delegated the legitimate use of violence to police authorities in the interest of Black subordination. Those who fought back drew hateful responses from cops; "only Negro docility and conspicuous inferiority brought genuine affection from Whites . . . more aggressive Negroes became the object of active police hostility." Reuter, a psychologist, adds an additional layer of psychological shading to the picture of a cop's hatred for Blacks:

An attitude of hate lies at the basis of all crimes against Negroes. The particular offence of Negroes is not a matter of consequence; the racial antagonism is always ready to express itself in overt activity. The occasional calling out of violent brutality is a matter of accident.[26]

Writer James Baldwin put a more literary spin to the hateful police domination of the ghetto he knew all too well from his years of life growing up in Harlem:

The only way to police a ghetto is to be aggressive . . . their presence is an insult and it would be, even if they spent their entire day feeding gum drops to the children. They represent the force of the White world and that world's criminal profit and ease, to keep the Black man corralled up . . . in his place, the badge, the gun and the holster and the swinging club make vivid what will happen should his rebellion become overt. He moves through Harlem, therefore, like an occupying soldier on a bitterly hostile country; which is precisely what and where he is and is the reason he walks in twos and threes.[27]

Hatred of one for the other is the only possible result that could come from such execution of domination of one by the other. We end with a roundup of speculations to account for the hatred of police authorities for the Black citizen of this period. Much of the hatred can be measured not in the words that say "I hate you," but in the many actions which show a viciousness and passion only a trait like hate can summon up. Much of the hatred of cops for Black people can be traced to cops who lacked any empathy to identify with Black conditions and civil rights. Lower-class cops appreciative of their newly gained power and control over Black citizens from LEAA recognition; ability to murder without retribution; guilt for White-imposed centuries of slavery; competition for jobs that Blacks simply don't deserve; belief that Black people have more fun and are less inhibited and thus not serious about crime fighting; feelings of superiority being White with distaste for the Black culture and customs; belief that Blacks cause disorder and are inferior; indeed, a full acceptance of White nationalist thinking that Black people are inherently criminal; that Blacks aren't happy unless doing something illegal; that Blacks are rude and actually hate White people who have done so much for them; that Black men are devious and will do anything to fool a cop; and finally, that Blacks simply can't be trusted. Of course, there is little evidence to any of these preposterous beliefs but that never stopped the ignorant person from hating anyway. Reuter offers a final psychological explanation attributable to hate:

> White police pose a deep fear of Black males. Whites believe Negroes possess behavioral tendencies menacing to White men or his domination . . . which functions to create an external image which objectifies a psychological state where Negroes become a symbol rather than simple social reality. Hatred of the Negro is a perpetual reminder of conduct in violation of normal moral standards . . . the presence of the misused person is a constant irritant so that Negroes become an object of aversion and hatred.[28]

It follows from all these possibilities of hate-mongering among police officers that it's a very small step to aggressive behavior toward Black suspects and the inevitable war crimes. In sum, what we were witnessing was extremely interpersonal racist-inspired violence on Black people. Much of the impetus came from White Supremacy ideology with its historically deep hatred of the Black culture. Police brutality coexisted with unremitting Black Supremacy hatred and over-policing, always in violation of constitutional rights. It is to this factor that we now turn to understand the hatred and virulent brutality that underlay so much CJS activity.

Infiltration of the Klan into the Police Departments (and CJS Generally)

The *White Power* newspapers of the time fixated on the theme of White supremacists infected with Ku Klux Klan ideology joining local police everywhere. This was part of the overall desire to physically prevent the progress of Black civil rights progress. Many cops even without this Klan outlook were in sympathy with such a view and believed Blacks were impatiently pushing too hard for rights that should require decades to grant. The origins were certainly in police departments in the Deep South but by the 1950s such a link could also be found in California and the Northern urban cities with large Black populations. For example, *White Power* newspaper issues for January-February 1971 and October 1972 stress the resistance to Black progress as being too quick, with drawings of police with swastikas on their helmets and White nationalist commentary can be found in numerous articles presented in these issues. Headlines cry out "Race Violence Flares in Schools" (New Jersey, Nevada, Pennsylvania, and New York); "Black Violence of Terror Reaches Epidemic Proportions" reads another; "80% of all violent crimes are caused by Blacks" is matched alongside "Negro Crime Is Going Completely Wild," and "Mindless Black Frankensteins Are Simply Running Amok." Also getting attention are several news articles linking the White Power movement with the Republican Party (see the October 1972 issue, pp 1–2). Another false article mentions "White Victims of Black Atrocities as U.S. Cities face Open Race War." Implications are that only through strong police enforcement and brutal suppression of Black protesters can these trends be reversed. Genie Donley narrows the indictment to the CJS itself:

> Law enforcement must acknowledge its role in racial injustice and include the history of racist violence and denial of civil rights. Police in the past have had to perform many unpalatable tasks. White Supremacy in policing includes racist ideologies, arbitrary violence complicity in terror . . . and under policing of White Supremacists threats toward Black citizens.[29]

Professor Geoff Ward, a specialist on this subject, writes on the political repercussions:

> As White Nationalist and White Supremist groups increased in numbers at every political level after 1950, especially Conservative candidates tapped into these growing movements to build or rebuild their voter base and win political control . . . They aimed to halt African American advancement especially after the 1954 racial desegregation in public schools . . . so that the rallying points for civil rights activists were the same for White Supremists determined to maintain White Supremacy . . . police were a big help in thwarting Black demands for justice.[30]

Local police departments and their civilian superiors (i.e., mayors, citizen councils, judges) did their utmost to increase the ranks of police officers through a variety of means to deputize them, create auxiliary police units, tolerate vigilante and militia organizations (especially in the South) as a means of engaging law enforcement without increasing budgets in an effort to curb

Black resistance and protest. Chafe repeats a Black man's reminiscences in a small Alabama town that all the White men were police in the sense they possessed some degree of policing power over Black lives. "There was always a law officer around and all of them weren't dressed in uniforms. If he had a White face, he was a police officer."[31]

Cunningham enlarges on this theme to include the country as a whole:

> These were years of considerable Klan and other White Power activities in violence . . . the aggressive moves of Federal agents to dismantle the Klan pushed its militant core underground. Members became lone wolf cells while others joined military and police forces where their anger could best be emphasized against minority groups generally.[32]

Vida Johnson, professor of criminal law at Georgetown University, called this infiltration of White Power supremacists into local police forces of the 1960s "an epidemic." He notes this in over 100 different police departments in over 40 states in which despite denials, Klan mentality had taken over large parts of police officer routine including those of high-ranking members. Sikes confirms that

> The real danger from police departments is the right-wing influence in a large number of these agencies (i.e., Denver, Los Angeles, Houston being the most notorious). One report estimates a minimum of 10% of cops in practically every California city were members of Klan-type groups, 500 in the NYPD alone and at least 3% in the Midwest and West generally.[33]

My own estimate is upward of 20% Of police forces nationwide were infected with White Power beliefs and hatred of Black people; enough to stimulate on a regular basis police bully actions and racial intolerance I label war crimes. This attitude ran through all the CJS agencies in greater or lesser degrees depending on the location and historical relevance to Deep South thinking. But if we put all these White supremacist agents together, we would have as dangerous as anti-Black army capable of sedition as rallied behind general Robert E. Lee in 1981.

Who's Training These Bozos?

By 1968 the CJS had become an octopus with ubiquitous tentacles of agencies and services reaching deep into the Black communities to pluck out victims. Incompetent staffing and poorly designed training programs were always the Achilles heel of the CJS, while hiring was another major problem as badly selected candidates (with all the wrong social and psychological qualifications) flocked to these jobs with their alluring guaranteed wages and tempting health and vacation benefits. While many candidates with adequate qualifications signed on to serve, I also believed, in the years when I was in the CJS misfits, macho psychopaths, alcoholics and druggies, illiterates and sadists also easily found their way to the open doors due to low expectations required of the applicants. Southern high-school diplomas filled with sports courses told us nothing about the brain inside the cop's head. And some of them I met seemed only too happy to flash their special gun under my nose or demonstrate their brawn by tearing up a phone directory as if that was a suspect while promising to knock a few heads. Such words echoed mayor Frank Rizzo's advice to his Philadelphia Police Department in the 1970s "Break their heads is right. They try to break yours. You break theirs first."[34] This rag tag army of new recruits spelled danger ahead when the man was given a gun and badge, a license to kill, the right to recommend prison for a lengthy period for some bedraggled offender, the right to torment and harass inmates without mercy, or the right to bust heads indiscriminately. Tests were at a dismal level of sophistication from what I could see in the police, corrections, and probation departments in Los Angeles County, and I know of no internal reports that evaluated how often poor candidates were weeded out during the selection process.

My own evaluation written after my first year claimed I was a decent worker, rather naïve for the job, who might catch on over time. Needless to say, the Black community was given no voice in this process. Theirs was only to suffer from the results of men often holding poor social skill qualities. They casually arrested, bruised, indicted, advised, and imprisoned with an uncaring and irresponsible attitude on the long-term consequences of those under their mitt. Firing a gun might kill the wrong person, maybe another cop, maybe the suspect who hasn't been judged guilty of anything as yet. Killing a man means a devastated family, kids who will grow up without paternal support, lost income for all, just by unthinkingly firing a gun. No training that I ever had or heard about dealt with the after-effects of our work. Or how to think through problems before setting everything in horrible motion by reaching for a gun and shooting willy nilly. In addition, training never attempted to bridge the vast cultural gap between White and Black, what White recruits needed to know before going into the field to cause harm. The end was an endless repetition of social injustice, intolerance, and brutality.

Criminologist Michael Tonry extends this idea of incompetence found in CJS agents. "No reliable case can be made that gross racial disparities were unforeseeable and reasonable people cannot have failed to recognize that policies adopted since the mid-1980s would produce prison."[35] He adds:

It was apparent the CJS was racially biased and influenced by racial stereotypes. It meant that the political climate was long on vindictiveness and short on empathy and that White politicians nationwide (especially Republicans and Southern Democrats who wished to limit the civil rights movement through suppression of the Black vote by disenfranchisement from being convicted) were quick to adopt policies of unprecedented Harshness.

It was these policies we as CJS agents were being trained to enforce. No one I knew in any of the training classes or beyond ever questioned vicious policies set by our superiors. I consciously thought I'd find ways around them to show leniency and ignore or reject the worst abuses. I'll never know how many colleagues thought the same way but I have no doubt there were more than a few. You just didn't broadcast openly. We all lived in secret cells of office efficiency, with occasional bouts of punitiveness, to soften our need for humanity. But there were many who accepted such training as a Nazi might do unquestioningly, fully bent on displaying as much ruthlessness and cynicism as would move him up the greasy pole of career ambition. If war crimes occurred, so be it. Luck of the draw. In the autumn of 1968, three years after the calamitous Watts Riots, while working on my PhD dissertation at a local university, financial troubles beset me and I allowed myself to be hired as a supervising probation officer (adult) for the Los Angeles County Probation Department. That they were prepared to take me to cause a bit of a startle. I knew nothing of criminals, had never seen a jail cell, had shied clear of criminal courts, and didn't know how to talk to a judge who appeared like some distant mandarin of a different country. I didn't watch cop shows on television; cops were never seen in my bourgeois neighborhood. In any event, I was hired. Not only that but told to report to the Willowbrook/South Central office, ground zero to a legion of Black Panthers from Compton an area where the riots actually began! All the vestiges of war were still there: burned out buildings, torched and looted cars, vacant lots filled with clutter and upturned furniture, retail shops some still half barricaded, and plenty of young male adults wandering aimlessly in the barest of clothing looking for prey.

My first day, lacking any training sessions, and with no idea how the whole CJS fitted together, what the inside of a courtroom, much less jail, looked like, with no idea how to fill out forms or get training in the most basic aspects of client interviewing, I was tossed into the melee. A friendly, elderly secretary was shoved in my direction and I was made to understand she would answer any question I had about the processes of the job—she was, in effect, my training officer! My first two probationer clients soon put me straight what life would be like for a young, White novice from a protected Jewish background: One followed the other in quickly taking in my rawness and ignorance and proceeded to yell the worst of names and abuses in my direction. They were both ex-participants of the riot so they didn't mince words with a punk like me. I was totally unprepared for this invective and came to believe the department knew but didn't care about me or these angered men—no training because none of it mattered! I was there as a watchdog as were the nearby police, many of whom had been recruited from Oklahoma, Texas, and Louisiana with all that implies for justice to Black people. I was given no resources and untrained in how to adequately merge local social services with client needs and dependencies. It was a pathetic joke and the probationers from Compton were well aware of this attitude and what the CJS thought of them. Just get out of line a little, bucko, and back to jail you'll go, no free get out of jail cards for you. After several months of this futility, and still no training, I moved after I had received my degree, to the Bay Area where I was quickly able to get a job with the probation department in Marin County. Training there was tedious: a week spent filling out the correct form for the correct activity, great efforts were spent on helping me do adequate record keeping and learning the ins and outs of writing court reports to satisfy the most taciturn judge. The only human contact was with fellow trainees and, of course, the trainer who spun a few departmental anecdotes to keep us amused. Doubtless, he had told these same stories to dozens of classes before us. The stories were stale, the punch lines weak but the intention to take our mind off of just filling out forms was appreciated. Oddly enough I liked working in the CJS and wanted to learn how it all tied together. But doing so meant disregarding departmental training and going it alone by being self-taught. This meant training myself for skills in court writing, interviewing, community liaison, emergency calls, house calls, networking, analysis of rap sheets, law as applied to probation, and family referrals. None of this was taught by the training staff in Marin County.

Police recruits training in the 1960s was even worse. What they received varied by location, official interest, and budget. Training might be a few days, maybe four to six weeks but for some it could be measured in hours. A cop once told me his was "little to none." From the 1900s, political interference on police departments was heavy, more than for any other CJS agency. Expectations from the police were little more than blind compliance to whatever standards and political decisions the higher ups and their political comrades demanded. If problems arose in the streets, brawn was expected to pummel suspects and control the rabble. Patrolmen were often hired with low intelligence, untrained, and where record keeping was not asked of them. Nor did compliance with legal processes matter. This world of ignorance and brutal oppression of the neighborhoods couldn't last forever and by the 1950s reform was in the air. Most police departments sensed they were going to be asked to change their way of doing business. LEAA and federal funding made these departments a deal they couldn't refuse: modernize and streamline your agency, and add more legal processes and less tough guy policies and we'll spend millions of dollars to help in your conversion.

In the 1960s what was taught? YouTube videos of police training in the 1940s and 1960s show us what was considered the curriculum: plenty of self-defense tactics, much time spent at the firing range, a few lessons on the law as it applied to them, exercises to maintain an "iron physique," using the baton as a weapon, use of a cover while shooting, operating a blockade, searching a stolen car, shooting for survival (military music played as background for many of these films), learning the habits of a criminal and how to transport an offender to jail.[36] Cadets were told that once they got in the field, "to forget what they learned in the academy." Plenty of war stories ended with the basic police warning "kill or be killed." Little to nothing on civil manners and etiquette, respect, ethics, participating in community relations, or understanding Black culture not as an enemy, maintaining White privilege in how you ordered people round ("being forceful, loud and decisive in your tone commands respect from citizens and gets instant compliance"). You had a 26" wood baton to do your talking for you.[37] Anyone with a modicum of high-school learning could apply. The highly impressionable age of seventeen was ok no matter how awkward the rookie. As mentioned in one reference, "small police departments would literally take a guy off the street, put him in a uniform and a car and it was all OJT. He was required to buy his own body armor if he could afford it, even his own weapon. That was it. When correctional officers showed up on their first day, they were most likely going to be given a job where they had to interact with inmates. They didn't have anyone specific to teach them or look after them. They were on their own. Sink or swim was the result."[38] Prior to 1960, the sole requirement of correctional officers was to be custody-oriented. Recruitment standards were low or non-existent, training manuals had yet to be written and in many prisons, training just didn't exist so physical demands were easy to implement. The typical recruit had a rural or mid-sized town background, with limited education, very conservative (if not actually White nationalist) political views, with a job resume dotted with casual work and many changes of employment. The likelihood was few, if any, had ever met a Black person much knew how to carry a conversation with one, much less know how to discipline one that didn't border on racist anger while owning a war crimes mentality didn't hurt. Training was on the job and often involved nothing more than a new man being handed a set of cell block keys and told to get on with it. Some jobs required only 20-20 vision with a high threshold for boredom. Security and control were a CO's watchwords, enforcing prison rules his sole directive, not really quite sure what those were. If necessary, he was told to simply accuse and punish inmates as he wished and disregard due process or inmate rights.

Unchallenged power was to be objective and, as a result, public reception of correctional officers believed them to be "simple, brutal, alienated, cynical, burnt out, and either racists or fascists or both. Some claimed it was a job only for imbeciles."[39]

How Many War Crimes Are Too Many?

With the many political allusions during this period to a "War on Crime," it seems only logical to suggest, as in wartime, many of the casualties and victims and collateral damage, if severe enough, could qualify as war crimes. They necessarily flowed directly from the action of a militarized police force on a Black community long seen as the "enemy." War crimes stemmed from the excesses of force and death inflicted on Black people as if they were struggling under wartime conditions. This was founded on the principle of racist suppression as a means of total social control.

No longer was it local or state law enforcement oppressing Black people. The federal government, in Johnson's administration, had entered the fray and brought a wider range of crime-fighting tactics and techniques to bear, supplying the CJS with generous amounts of control mechanisms to thwart Black civil rights ambitions under the guise of fighting crime and incarcerating criminals. However, these mechanisms were so vicious and brutal that we feel incumbent on calling them not crime-fighting techniques but war crimes against an innocent population.

As in war, the vast majority of these crimes inflicted by the CJS went unnoticed by the general public and were undocumented, untried, and thus unpunished. Picture how this would torment future researchers trying to portray the enormity of this vindictiveness on the Black community. They were justified as being any actions necessary to stop crime and rid the cities of criminals by any means necessary. In war, every strategy is deemed valid if it brings victory. And to the CJS agents after 1990, they had won as the public was no longer fearing for their security as was the case in 1965. In keeping with military terminology, these had become "war zones" and ghettoes had been transformed into "battlefields" and cops were the "foot soldiers" in the battle for America's safety. It was only appropriate that perhaps as many as 30% of the police force in the country were composed of ex-soldiers drawing upon recent combat experience from Vietnam. Many of the war crimes perpetrated on Black citizens were so grievous (i.e., murder, false arrest and imprisonment, severe bodily harm, long-term trauma, bloody violence, careless destruction of private property, intimidating interrogation, torture, etc.) they had actually been outlawed by the Geneva Convention of 1949 and should have applied across the board to all CJS agencies. The important elements of the GC, as expanded in a 1996 Congressional Act (HR 3680) as relevant here were simple and easily applicable: victims could be US citizens, war crimes could occur inside the continental United States, perpetrators could be US nationals (including law enforcement), with punishments for such crimes being court-imposed and ranging from fines, imprisonment, to death (if the victim died). Although these sanctions were on the books, and despite the thousands of opportunities to implement them and establish some sort of lawful order within the ranks of the CJS, they were neither tested nor used. Statistics and supporting evidence were neither gathered nor applied to specific cases, human rights violations were never created. It is left to socio-logical studies like this one, incorporating eye witness accounts of war crimes the CJS came to perform so effortlessly and routinely without any official obstruction during this period.

War crimes is a factor in the CJS' end game where long-term consequences of their actions overshadow their thinking. Besides all the physical harm done to Black victims, unnecessary suffering by all members of a man's family, including the children, were never given priority or credence. Detention and enforced incarceration for many months at a time were never seen as some part of the equation that must be considered before consigning an offender to his doom. Human rights abuses were never considered. So much of this stemmed from traditional and deep-rooted White animus toward strangers which is how Blacks as illegals were perceived by society and the agents of law enforcement. War crimes suggest complicity with superiors direct to the commission of these grave acts. Superiors give cover to criminal officers or provide plausible excuses because brutality was necessary. They also draw our immediate attention. War crimes create a special category of barbarism. They also enduce many official cover-ups that make investigation impossible. There is also the stark consciousness of its intolerabilty by the victim commu-nity. Here there is the need for an unmistakable and critical judicial response to this high act of brutality. War crimes by state agents are the utmost infringement upon fundamental societal values of an ordered society that must be viewed in a different, more critical light than simply a bad arrest or a corrupt cop. These must be considered so serious to the victim community that no time limitations should apply in terms of prosecution and sanction. It places certain officials on notice that they have exceeded ethical standards and guarantees no future employment in the CJS with such serious stains on one's service record. We leave appropriate punishment for another time.

What ties all this together is that at the core of these official depredations was a CJS charged with employing ruthless force to accomplish its job, to go well beyond the bounds of decency to curb crime, and to move into forbidden areas of bestial criminality against the Black community to satisfy political demands in how crime should be suppressed in America's inner cities. Right-wing politicians as far up the chain of command as the presidency spent these years in hostile methods of enforcement to appease the White nationalists of the electorate and foreshorten civil rights gains by Blacks. Crime bills legislated by these men provided the necessary perk for police, to use the "peace" end of the nightstick to gleefully enforce draconian laws. In 1981 alone over 350 anticrime bills were floated in the California legislature, and 500 in Texas with comparable figures elsewhere.[40]

This study will reveal the many types of war crimes each of the affiliate agencies of the CJS generated: Not just cops but jail guards, probation officers, judges, defense attorneys, rehabilitation agents, and so on. Of course, these many thousands upon thousands of cases have been undocumented and discarded, and each agency has its own pet ways of destroying evidence or denying responsibility. That's not to say they never happened, that there were no victims, that those lives were not ruined. We need to start somewhere to put this whole shabby episode into a realistic perspective. Where to begin?

Can we estimate with any degree of accuracy the level of war crimes committed by the CJS for this period? Much of it is speculative and only in the case of police, where the crate was the highest and the number of eye witness reactions was greatest that we can make some legitimate effort. There will always be some hesitation since documentation is nonexistence. But with the police, the charges are quite serious. We can try for it is important to gauge some degree of criminality of the CJS as the bedrock of this investigation.

Let's set down a few numerical criteria, keep the range of abuse on the conservative side, compare them to what has already been said by other researchers, do a little massaging of the numbers, and see what we have. Let's always remember we are discussing terrible events being done to citizens for whom there were lifelong negative consequences; many never fully recovered. In 1975, the police force in the country totaled 520,000 of the nearly one million full-time CJ personnel spread over 40,000 separate neighborhood policing agencies in daily contact with the public and any potential offenders. It was a force growing every year since the mid-1960s with overall regulation of their conduct impossible. This was an increase of 20% over 1971, with the NYPD hosting over 30,000 police officers, or two army combat divisions.[41] Let's assume that a tenth of the police officers in the country who patrolled urban areas were racists, and another tenth who held obvious White nationalist beliefs. Adams estimated the range of excessive use of force based on police anti-Black beliefs ranged from 4% to 10%, especially high in Geller and Toch, 9% in the Reiss work, and Friedrich at 10%. For 1970–1978, a Philadelphia study set the figure at 20%.[42]

Thus, upward of 20% of the 520,000 cops were likely to harbor serious anti-Black beliefs that could easily propel them to commit acts of excessive force, or what we label war crimes. Adams agrees: "Observational research suggests police use of force occurs twice as often as suggested by official use of force reports (which may range from 4–8%)."[43] But a single percent-age can have different outcomes depending on different contexts and situa-tions. For example, using the 20% figure as a benchmark, one in five Black citizens witnessed a multitude of physically violent acts by police on a daily basis; or one in every five cops in urban police departments were guilty of committing some kind of war crime on a regular basis; or one in five were sadists who should have been fired; or 20% of all physical incidents between urban police and street people end up brutal and violent; or twenty pedes-trians in a crowd of one hundred will be criminally attacked by police in every Black community on a single day or in a single week. Let's break that down even further. Twenty percent of the 520,000 cops means that 104,000 of them were capable of repulsive behavior toward Black Americans in a single day. Let's say each conservatively committed a violent act or war crime at least twice a week (they had a pool of hundreds of suspects to deal with each week). That makes over 200,000 possible war crimes a week. In a month that totals to 800,000 or possibly 4m in a year! Spread that over a cop's 20-year life on the force, and he might have committed up to 96 a year and possibly 2,000 in a lifetime of injustice without once being investigated and reprimanded much less found guilty of misbehaving with negative con-sequences. 2000 reprehensible acts as a terribly high number? This doesn't include war crimes of varying sorts from other parts of the CJS such as jail and prison guards who are notoriously vicious toward inmates, or proba-tion officers, prosecutors, and judges (who will be discussed in succeeding chapters).[44]

Set these war crime incidents of maybe 4m in a year beside the 10m criminal arrests (arrests do not mean convictions and must be reasoned to be maybe a half of this, property crimes greater than violent, per year for the same period, and we see where our crime focus has previously been misplaced). According to ex-cop Robert Leuci, former member of the NYPD Tactical Patrol Force, as reported in English, "police brutality was not uncommon. Some cops sought out the tactical patrol because they were the kind of people who liked to bust heads." At the time, Leuci didn't ques-tion what he saw was that the street cops were expected to show they had the right stuff.

> I walked in on a lot of beatings and when you walked in on a beating you were
> expected to add a kick or a punch of your own to show you were with the pro-
> gram. Some cops were more brutal than others. Some of this was because there
> was so much brutality around us—it made us feel a kinship that no outsider
> could understand. Few witnesses protested our actions. The police considered it
> their job to keep the colored people in their place.

He also noted that during the 1960s and 1970s "police violence in Brooklyn was even more unfettered. Riot cops in helmets clubbed Blacks indiscriminately. "I'm tired of you niggers," one cop whined."[45] Black cop from St. Louis recalled:

> Occasionally I had to physically restrain White officers who collectively had a tendency to brutally assault Black men . . . and willfully violated the human rights of the people in the communities they served. The union showed nothing but indifference and contempt for victims of cop beatings and had a pathological disregard for Black life. Serving his country in Viet Nam didn't exempt a Black police officer from being Black in the eyes of White officers, nothing did.[46]

Criminologist John Hagan concurs it has taken a long time for this country to address these issues of state-originated crimes against humanity. Sadly, politicians and CJS administrators should have known, as Tonry reminds us, the consequences of such vicious behavior toward Black communities if they had a head on their shoulders. They should have known what would be the outcome if a cop slammed a nightstick against a human head that pain, suffering even death would be a normal result. How stupid were law enforcement not to know, or care what aggressive actions against Black suspects were likely to cause. This constituted a supreme failure of publicly responsible officials to the communities, they were paid to serve.[47]

The Value of Eye Witness Accounts in CJS War Crimes

A seeming defect of this study is its reliance on eye witness testimony to the continuing scenes of police violence and use of excessive force. So little was written down. And no cop or agent of the CJS ever labeled his action as a "war crime." But we have other sources. At least 200 Black residents of Harlem participated in a brief survey of the CJS as they perceived their behavior in the 1960s and 1970s. Individual police have also added their own views on negative police behavior. In 2015 Rosa Brooks, a law professor at Georgetown University, became a volunteer member of the local police reserve corps in Washington, DC. She ended up patrolling a downtrodden section of the city policing the "sad, small crimes of the very poor." Her book reviewer writes:

> Brooks laments her training had "eight units" on vehicular offenses but nothing at all on race and policing . . . she observes that officers are taught to perceive fear and contain the mortal threat in every encounter, however mundane, while knowing that their actions will be scrutinized by Monday morning quarterbacks

. . . attitudes and training itself should change to emphasize acceptance of risk and protection of the public over self-preservation.[48]

I have added my bit of observation derived from the probation departments in which I worked and have written about it during this period. This also enabled me to see contemporary urban police, jail guards, drug therapists and prosecutors, and defense lawyers at work in trying to unravel the complexities of crime, protest, and injustice. Some of the eye witness accounts were deeply traumatic and personal; some produced anger and were obviously unforgettable to the viewer as the impressions were long-term. The importance was made urgent due to the failure of CJS to document its participation in the many war crimes of its making while trying to reduce crime in Black neighborhoods. Undoubtedly the thousands of negative interactions between CJS and citizens should have produced a mountain of written material from which to judge law enforcement during these years.

But this never happen and so we were left to our own devices—which means eye witness accounts were necessary to correct important omissions. Otherwise, we would be left with the impression the CJS were never culpable and the many Black citizen reactions to the brazen brutality that occurred never existed to be recorded. Such transactional incidents had to have impressed onlookers enough that eye witness accounts, with no reason to lie, provide satisfactory corroboration. For these reasons, we stand by what witnesses reported to us and believe they help justify and validate the victim side of the ledger.

Given that cops didn't write down and explain to their superiors all the bad things they did, we are often left with eye witnesses to provide some of the enormity of police officer and other CJS agent crimes. It raises the question: Do eye witnesses have anything to contribute or is it all speculation? Well, let's be clear, many of these war crimes were out there for the public to see. The uproar of a scene in which a cop stops someone and proceeds to administer his own brand of street justice can be noisy, wild, abrupt with unexpected physical movement by all participants including onlookers; yelling with various distractions to make noting the details impossible for everyone involved. Add to this melee, a bunch of gesticulating cops just arrived as back-up and all the ingredients of chaos with a growing and angry crowd to stir it up. The turmoil may well be beyond any cop to record faithfully, much less the witnessing of or participating in a war crime. This is not the scene where actions can be scientifically verified or adequately researched. Recall errors are a possibility by witnesses as is the court haggling over words to describe the action and consider different versions of events. White CJS agents and court personnel may well distrust Black witnesses out of racist beliefs in the inability of Blacks to review accurately and dispassionately. There are also other factors to consider and criminologist Kenneth Adams besides the racist possibility has reminded us of what some might be:

> The Court is often the biggest hurdle to accepting eye-witness reports of CJS brutality. Defense attorneys may be unable to prove force was excessive. How do you evaluate force itself? When was the tipping point reached between simple and aggravated? Then too there are always legal battles over the facts of the presumed wrong or biased on both sides. We must never forget evidence is always seen from the perspective of the cop—his available options and his perception of threats against him. No one in an action scene is likely to consider or perceive outcomes given various courses of action. Then too, precision and completeness in the data of the crime scene is often unlikely. Let's not forget this is not a purely scientific investigation that can be replicated, nor can rank ordering of excessive force be easily numerized.[49]

Police departments and other CJS agencies do not routinely collect data to make violent encounters between agents and victims who are easy to monitor. Not all cops have jobs that bring them into daily contact with criminals where force is a necessary tool of persuasion. This is more the case with probation officers, drug therapists, and prison guards but such agents wouldn't even consider what they are doing a war crime and have no training in how to control their behavior toward victims. Excessive force is based on contacts police have with criminals (which always puts the criminal by classification as the guilty party to force). But not all citizens can be described as criminal suspects—what if the victim who might merely be tangential to the original stop, whether suspect, accomplice, or just onlooker? Which is most likely to be heard if victimized by a cop? Which one, if any, is most likely to exaggerate the incident?[50] There are always nefarious issues at hand. Incidents often occur in isolated, remote locations where besides being unreported by cops are also unobserved by the community. Fyfe tells us the cops he has studied take rational steps to conceal their activities. Then too, these crimes against people often occur late at night, or in cluttered areas, making them hard to observe. In this analysis, we have accepted our colleague Heather A. Thompson (University of Michigan) who, in her own work, used historical examples that were

> not exhaustive . . . and can't be comprehensive because the subject being studied here is so overwhelmingly merely representative and reflects broad practices . . . given the paucity of data use. In this case, eye witnesses can't be ignored or dismissed inasmuch as law enforcement replies are non-existent and never make any attempt at all to examine evidence impartially other than to simply dismiss all charges as false and biased against police.[51]

Let's assert each eye witness interviewed for this study is in a position to see a wide range of "war crimes" due to the nature of American arrests and court disposition. Offenders were not just aware of police misbehavior but, by the very repetitious nature of the arresting process. They also came to know rather intimately, from repeated interaction, criminal lawyers, prosecutors, judges, jail and other correctional personnel, as well as supervising POs, therapists, psychiatrists, and rehabilitation officers. Consequently, not a single punishment, being beaten by a cop was a suspect's fate, but the plurality of pain derived from each CJS department an offender would confront along the way to a final verdict, perhaps ending up in prison. Each department would apply its own flogging, with whatever racist overtones and pathological revenge this might include. To any single offense, then, a multitude of war crimes never recognized as such might occur. Here, then, we have approached the nub of the book. Add to the police zeal and blindfolded judges willing to ignore human rights abuses and a general systemic disrespect for Black people as perpetual defendants, and we are left with the worst consequences of a failing, vindictive system. It is where White nationalism and racism, as I witnessed, infected the minds of law enforcement rookies that became a major impediment to civility toward people without genuine legal redress. Then too, rehabilitation agencies weren't much help, too few of them overwhelmed by too many clients. I was probably affected too, even though I suspect I didn't know it.

Eye witnesses give us context and facts in their review of the CJS. One man surveyed was a sixty-five-year-old Black man living in a Philadelphia housing project in the 1960s (met by one of my students in Harlem in 2014) with a lot of lived commentary. Everyone surveyed had at least one war story they could never forget:

> Police festered throughout South West Philly projects as they watched our every move, harassed, and arrested Black and Latino folks like it was a pick-up season. Especially dangerous was the first of the month for cops on a quota system. They were like crack addicts looking for their next hit. My friends and I could be sitting by the basketball courts in the middle park of the complex, as they drove into the neighborhood, spotted us and hopped out of their vehicle placing drugs on us. This was to issue arrests based on a specific headcount and claim us for possession of illegal substances. Ultimately, my uncle was arrested and spent 32 hours in interrogation about a crime he was not even initially arrested for, before he was released for lack of evidence . . . everybody I knew was a witness to police brutality that had malicious intent and a racist viewpoint toward minorities but no one in administration cared.[52]

Some responses were short but nonetheless pithy in spotting a war crime. This comment was from a seventy-two-year-old man: "Harlem police officers didn't really care about you. One guy I knew was handcuffed to the wall at the police station and not offered food, water or a toilet for more than 36 hours."[53]

Another witness, a seventy-one-year-old Dominican woman described the whole CJS as she knew it:

> I saw tons of police brutality, cops stopping everyone, making unnecessary arrests, beating people and just being nasty. Cops brought drugs into my neighborhood to frame drug dealers. I knew this because I had a couple of friends who were drug dealers who told about getting busted for drugs that weren't theirs but planted on them by the police. They would take bribes from high-end dealers in order to make money on the side from their salary. One was constantly stopped by police, frisked, asked where he was going and what he was up to, this on a regular basis. He didn't protest against this because if you saw the way protest was handled by the government you wouldn't protest. Those that went to jail described them as pure hell. Lawyers and public defenders only wanted your money or didn't care what happened to their client. Some sought out only drug dealers that had just been brought in. These were assumed to have some money and would pay for legal services just to avoid incarceration and be in a position to keep drug sales flowing. It all seemed like a game.[54]

A New York City man (aged seventy-one) provided a sweeping picture of the CJS of the time:

> The police system was a total failure on its own, it didn't need criminals to make it worse. The police who are meant to stop corruption and abuse are the ones who promote it. You would find officers meddling in purely civil transactions that didn't warrant police interference (i.e., citizen disputes). How do you explain a cop arresting people randomly on the street with no reasonable cause except probably to extort those they later arrest? The Courts are not proactive in asserting its authority over police excesses and violations of our civil rights. Jails are filled with Black suspects (not even offenders) who had yet to see the judge, let alone be sentenced. Probation services were merely surveillance and a steady stream of demoralizing sermons designed to destroy a man's will to live. Was this a system to applaud or condemn?[55]

Who's Getting Left Behind and Why

This study has a singular focus: the African American adult male and his relationship and interaction with a vicious CJS during the years 1960-1990. It was during a time of serious civil rights protests against the inhumanity, violence, and injustices of government generally. At the time the government and its law enforcement agencies attacked younger Black men almost exclusively. Throughout the period, they were consistently seen as the most criminal and hence received the main attention.

So, who was left behind and why? The study omits Black women, Black juveniles, Hispanics, parolees, and federal offenders and its prison system. They were ignored because incorporating these groups would have required a minimum of eighteen more months of research and would have increased the book's bulk by 50% without adding any new insights or major conclusions to the study. Diversions of other groups might even have dissipated the strength of argument about CJS abusiveness to Black men. Regarding parole, since the mid-1980s this prison release service to inmates has undergone vast changes and by 1985 had been abolished or were in the process of being eliminated in twenty-plus states. The changes would have weakened comparisons, skewed statistics making a broad overview of its impact difficult to develop. Hispanics were also avoided as being too few in numbers as offenders in big cities of the time and having a different relationship with Whites as having no long tradition of slavery to plague it. The surrounding confusion of Hispanics being computed in statistics as possibly Black or White categories, and the civil rights discussion not being pertinent, left this group without relevance for the present purposes in the discussion of war crimes.

Finally, Black women and juveniles were bypassed due to their fairly low and stable rates of arrests and convictions compared to men in these years plus the availability of a different set of rehabilitational services and enlightened probation casework when dealing with women. Moreover, juveniles are prone to indulge in teenage crimes that cannot be equated with adult crime, nor are court procedures and sanctions the same. There is also a degree of CJS leniency offered to both groups that cannot be found in the case of Black adult men whose punishments are of a higher and much longer degree of punitiveness, family destruction, and political disenfranchisement. Only since the 1980s, leaving a third of the researched time span left to devote to analysis, have arrests, court convictions, and incarcerations risen greatly for Black women and those under eighteen. These groups are best left for a future generation of criminologists, especially women, to review these trends and keep to my themes of war crimes and brutal behavior by the American CJS.

NOTES

1. Heather Ann Thompson, "Why Mass Incarceration Matters: Rethinking Crisis, Decline and Transformation in Postwar American History," *Journal of American History* 97 (2010): 221.

2. Naomi Murakawa, "The Origins of the Carceral Crisis: Racial Order as law and Order in Postwar American Politics," in Joseph Lowndes, Julie Novkov and Dorian T. Warren (Eds.), *Race & Political Development* (New York: Routledge, 2008), p. 234.

3. PBS website New River interview with Professor Elliott Curie, his participation in the Presidential Crime Commission under Lyndon B. Johnson in the late 1960s, host Ben Wattenberg, 2000; Steven R. Donziger, director of the National Criminal Justice Commission, 1996, *The Real War on Crime* (New York: Harper, 1996), p. xi, xii, xv and xvii.

4. Murakawa, op. cit., p. 235; See M. W. Flamm or similar impressions in his *Law-and-Order Street Crime and Civil Unrest and Crisis of Liberalism into the 1960s* (New York: Columbia UP).

5. Barry Latzer, *Rise and Fall of Violent Crime in America* (New York: Encounter Books, 2017), Polls reflected that crime was seen by the public as the country's number 1 problem in the late 1970s; and Michael Tonry, *Punishing Race, A Continuing American Dilemma* (New York: Oxford UP, 2012), p. x.

6. Joel H. Henderson and David R. Simon, *Crimes of the Criminal Justice System* (London: Routledge, 1994), especially chapters 1, 4 and 7.

7. R. C. Monk, *Taking Sides: Clashing Views and Controversial Issues in Crime and Criminology* (Guilford: Dushkin, 1996), p. 11.

8. J. G. Ross, et al., "The State of the State Criminal Research-A Commentary," *Humanity & Society* 23, no. 3 (1999): 273–275; William C. Chambliss's address to the American Society of Criminologists, "State Organized Crime," 1989, p. 184.

9. Henderson and Simon, op. cit.

10. Timothy G. Ash, *The File, A Personal History* (New York: Vantage, 1977), p. 194; Herbert Sturz, Deputy Mayor of New York City, board member of Vera Institute, see Open Society.org, 1993; Angela Davis, "Race and Criminalization: Black Americans and the Punishment Industry," in Wahneema Lubiano (Ed.), *The House that Race Built* (New York: Random House, 1997), p. 265; Vivien Stern, *Failures in Penal Society* (Manchester: Statistical Society, 1987); and Leonard Moore, *Black Rage in New Orleans-Police Brutality and African American Activism from WW2 to Hurricane Katrina* (Baton Rouge: Louisiana State UP, 2010), William A. Westley, *Violence and Police, A Sociological Study of Law, Custom and Morality* (Boston: MIT Press, 1970), p. 3; and Elizabeth Hinton, *From the War on Poverty to the War on Crime-The Making of Mass Incarceration in America* (Cambridge: Harvard UP, 2017).

11. Cheryl Corley, "President Johnson's Crime Commission Report, 50 Years Later," *NPR*, 6 October 2017; also, Richard W. Velde, administrator, *Report on the Task Force on Criminal Justice Research and Development* (Washington DC: 1971).

12. Melvin P. Sikes, *The Administration of Injustice* (New York: Harper & Row, 1975), pp. 123–124; Spencer Parratt, "A Police Service Rating Scale," *Journal of Criminal Law and Criminology* 26 (1938): 105; and Matt Ferner, "Here's How Often Cops are Arrested for Breaking the Law They're Paid to Uphold," *Washington Post*, 24 June 2016.

13. See race riots of the 1960s in Encyclopedia cengage.com, 2014; also, Arthur Ritzer and Lars Trautman, "The Conservative Case for Criminal Justice Reform," *The Guardian/U.S. News*, 5 August 2018.

14. B. Wayson and G. S. Funke, *What Price Justice?* (Rockville: National Institute of Justice, 1989); also, Paul Brakke's study with a similar title, *The Price of Justice in America-Commentaries on the Criminal Justice System, Ways to Fix What's Wrong* (Columbia: Changemakers, 2017); Denziger, op. cit, *The Real War on Crime*, p. 31; and Bob Wells, "United States Police are Killing People with War Crimes Ammunition," *San Francisco Bayview News*, 25 January 2016, p. 1.

15. Rizer and Trautman, op. cit; V. L. Lowe, *Overview of Activities Funded by LEAA* (Washington DC: USGPO), November 1977, p. 62 and 132; Editor, *Who's Who in Jail Management* (Washington DC: American Prison Assn., 5th edition, 2007); Loic Wacquant, *Punishing the Poor, The New Liberal Government of Social Insecurity* (Durham: Duke UP, 2009); Jan Sorenson, "Institutional Affiliation of Authors in Leading Criminological and Criminal Justice Journals," *Journal of Criminal Justice* 30 (2002): 11–13; Bureau of Justice Statistics, Prisoner's Series, 2008; S. R. Schlesinger, *Justice, Expenditures and Employment in the United States, 1971-1979* (Washington, DC: U.S. Department of Justice, 1984), p. vi, 24 and 37.

16. Bruce Watson, "John Howard Griffin Gives Readers an Unflinching View of the Jim Crow South. How Has His Book Held Up?" A record of his adventures in the very successful Black Like Me sociological diary from 1951, in *Smithsonian Magazine online*, October 2011; also, Mary Sacks, "Police Repression of N from 1951ew York City's Black Population in the 20th Century," *Journal of Urban History* 31 (2005): 200; and Robert Stiles, "White Racism, Black Crime and American Justice," *Phylon* 36 (1975): 14–15.

17. Quoted in Leanne C. Serbulo and Karen T. Gibson, "Black and Blue-Police & Community Relations in Portland's Albina District, 1964-1985," *Oregon Historical Quarterly* 114, no. 1 (2013): 18.

18. Op. cit. pp. 16–17.

19. Murakawa writes of this attitude affecting many police departments in the country. See her comments on pages 237–239.

20. Serbulo & Gibson, op. cit., p. 12, 13, 24 and 26.

21. Ibid., p. 15, 18, 20 and 30.

22. Blauner, Robert, "Internal Colonialism and Ghetto Revolt," *Social Problems* 16, no. 4 (1969): 393; Edward Byron Reuter, *The American Race Problem* (New York: Crowell, 1970), pp. 356–357; man respondent, #40, interviewed 13 February 2015.

23. Serbulo & Gibson, p. 26.

24. Reuter, op. cit., p. 358.

25. The editor-in-chief for the *White Power* newspaper was Matt Koehl. Every issue was laced with open hatred for Blacks and Jews, discussing their many criminal tendencies and how they were bringing the country to ruin. See *White Power, the Newspaper for White Revolution*, National Socialist White People's Party, Arlington, 1970–1973; also, Genie A. Donley, *The Gathering Storm, The Role of White Nationalism in U. S. Politics* (Cleveland: Cleveland State University online, 2018), p. 4.

26. Geoff Ward, "Living Histories of White Supremist Policing Toward Transformative Justice," *Dubois Review, Social Science Research & Race* 15, no. 1 (2018): 3–4.

27. William Chafe and William Gavins, *Remembering Jim Crow: African-Americans Tell About Life in the Segregated South* (New York: New Press, 2011), p. 244.

28. David Cunningham, Klansville USA: *The Rise and Fall of the KKK in the Civil Rights Era* (New York: Oxford UP, 2013), pp. 2–5; also, Cunningham, "What Policing Responses to White Power in the 1960s can Teach us about Dismantling White Superiority Today," *The Conversation.com*, 4 March 2021.

29. Quoted in Serbulo & Gibson, pp. 28–29; Reuter, op. cit., p. 358; and Vida Johnson, "KKK in the Police Department, White Supremacy Police and What to do About It," *Lewis & Clark Law Review*, Georgetown Law School 23, no. 1 (2019).

30. Quoted in *The Philadelphia Inquirer* online, 18 June 2021.

31. Tonry, op. cit., p. 67, 78 and 79.

32. See YouTube for the many training videos that pertain to police of the 1940s and 1950s. Larry L. Siegel and John L. Worrall, "Police and Law Enforcement, Introduction to Criminal Justice," *CEOgage* (2018): 174; also, Steven G. Brandel, *Police in America* (Beverly Hills: Sage, 2020), pp. 8–10.

33. Quoted in *Fordham Business Review* online, Regular Training for Police Officers in 1950s, 1960s.

34. Victoria L. Farrell, "The Effectiveness of Training for Correction Officers in the Performance of Their Job," in *Scholars Archive for Criminal Justice* (Albany: SUNY, 2015).

35. Susan Philliber, "Thy Brother's Keeper: A Review of the Literature of the 1960s," *Justice Quarterly* 4 (1987): 9–11.

36. Alexander Chasin, *Assassin of Youth, A Kaleidoscopic History of Henry Anslinger's War on Drugs* (Chicago: Chicago UP, 2017); Henderson & Simon, op. cit.

37. Paul Tagaki, "A Garrison State in a Democratic Society," *Crime & Social Justice* 1 (1974).

38. Kenneth Adams, op. cit. as "Measuring the Prevalence of Police Abuse of Force," in chapter 3 of *Geller & Toch*, pp. 61–62; Albert Reiss in *Communities in Crime* (Chicago: Chicago UP), and Robert J. Friedrich, "Police Shootings in Pennsylvania, An Analysis of two Decades of Deadly Force," Ph.D. Dissertation, Temple University, 1999.

39. Adams, op. cit., p. 71.

40. We have left for a different study the spectacle of police killing Black men. The rate of Black males (aged 9+) killed by police showed a frightening consistency, a trend that began around the early civil rights era, which was symbolic for expanded police oppression against minorities. The rate for Blacks has been placed at least ten times higher than for Whites, peaking in 1973–1974 with about 400 murders a year, or one a day recorded. We can only surmise that this figure should be closer to fifteen times the rate as many murders were ignored or not listed by police, or of people found dead without explanation or Black men killed with reasons unknown. Killings of police by civilians (not always Black) fluctuated for these years between thirty and fifty, a

significant difference in rate. Of these how many police were accidentally killed as part of collateral damage was never cleanly defined or reported. But when police were killed it was headline news; Blacks murdered was hardly newsworthy and few details were ever given. See Sid Haring, Tony Platt, Richard Speigelman and Paul Takagi, "Management of Police Killing," *Crime and Social Justice* 8 (1977): 34–35.

41. Elizabeth Hinton, *From the War on Poverty to the War on Crime: The Making of Mass Incarceration in America* (Cambridge: Harvard UP, 2017); Robert Leuci, *All the Centurions: A New York City Cop Remembers His Years on the Street, 1961-1981* (New York: Morrow, 2004), pp. 3–12; Redditt Hudson, "The Hell of being a Black Cop," *The New Republic*, 31 August 2000; and John Hagan, *Modern Criminology, Crime, Criminal Behavior and its Control* (New York: McGraw Hill, 1987) and *Hagan, Crime and Disrepute* (One Thousand Oaks: Sage, 1994).

42. Michael Tonry, *Malign Neglect: Race, Crime and Punishment in America* (New York: Oxford UP, 1995), pp. 1–22.

43. Adams, op. cit.

44. Binder and Peter Scharf, *The Badge and the Bullet: Police use of Deadly Force* (New York: Praeger, 1983), chapters 2, 3 and 5,

45. Leuci, op. cit.

46. Hudson, op.cit.

47. Tonry, op. cit.

48. Quoted by Eric J. Iannelli from the book under review, *Tangled Up in Blue by Georgetown Professor of Law, Rosa Brooks on Her Volunteer Mission with a Special Unit of the Washington DC Police* (New York: Penguin, 2021), as relayed in The Times Literary Supplement, 10 July 2021, p. 23.

49. Adams, op. cit.

50. H. A. Thompson, *Racial History of Criminal Justice in America* (Cambridge: Cambridge UP, 2020), p. 235.

51. James Fyfe, *Readings on Police use of Deadly Force* (Washington, DC: Police Foundation, 1982).

52. Man respondent, #40, interviewed 13 February 2015.

53. Man respondent, #63, interviewed 16 July 2015.

54. Woman respondent, #6, interviewed 22 September 2015.

55. Man respondent #131, interviewed 13 February 2015.

Chapter 2

Black People under the Gun

THE GRUESOME FANTASY WORLD
OF LAW ENFORCEMENT

Between the years 1960 and 1990, crime surged in this country in rates never before seen by law enforcement officials. There was little crime reported in the years before 1960, and after 1990 the crime rates began to drop sharply. But during this period, street crime and the rate of violence in inner cities (read communities of color) were at spectacular heights. In 1960, records show 3.4m arrests were made in the United States. In 1990 that figure had climbed to 13.9m, over 400% in thirty years despite the national population increasing by 40%. Violence rates had soared from 300,000 incidents to 1.8m, over 600%. Everyday media reports served only to continue to shock and strike fear in its readers. There was no central authority established to control the 50,000 CJS agencies whose aim was to prevent or sanction crime.[1]

Coincidentally, these incidents appeared at the time of major political demonstrations, urban riots, and fierce civil unrest in pursuit of Black equality and social justice. Political Science professor at Colgate University, Manning Marable has called this period "The Second Reconstruction in Black America." He noted it came with a lot of pain:

In May 1961, citizens calling for greater political rights for Black America had been threatened and arrested for contravening Birmingham (AL) Jim Crow laws. The city's unrelenting segregationist police chief, Eugene "Bull" Connor, before national television, brazenly let loose vicious police dogs on children as they knelt to pray. Almost 1000 children were then arrested and jailed. Across the world, humanity was repulsed by the sickening spectacle of American racism, the reality of White democracy.

The battle lines at that moment were being drawn for the next thirty years, to be played out with murderous frequency by the borderline racist forces of law and order.[2]

During these years, the federal government stepped in to take sides. This was a major change in how crime and violence were to be handled. Before all this had been left to individual states to resolve, using whatever abilities they had and in a way which best suited their outlook on civic safety and views of Black people. Beginning in the mid-1960s, the federal government under both Democratic and Republican administrations used their views on crime and Black inner cities to provide bountiful resources (usually funding) to equip local law enforcement and the CJS as a whole to combat Black crime. Blessed with government largesse this meant to many of the CJS a tacit permission to use whatever tactics were necessary, no matter how brutal and unconstitutional, to curb crime at the source: America's Black communities.

Marc Mauer, assistant director of the Sentencing Project and leading expert on sentencing policy, race, and the CJS, contended that race was an unacknowledged issue throughout the CJS, unspoken as it was. This was because the decisions made by police at the point of arrest and prosecutors studying arrest reports to the public were subjectively made on the streets or behind closed doors and not subject to public scrutiny or analysis. The whole system had tremendous leeway on whom to arrest, prosecute, or on which charges. In actual fact, in most cases defendants had no idea why CJS decisions were made as no formal and lengthy explanations were given. Browning was in agreement and even broadened the dangers exposed by CJS procedures to the common defendant. "The legal agencies and courts were utterly inadequate to address all these state-sponsored mass arrests which were often of a racist nature . . . and had considerable discretion to speciously discredit inconvenient truths about egregious miscarriages of justice that passed through the courts on a daily basis." These were without the slightest repercussions or damage to the professional reputation among their peers. America not only had a law problem but also a judge problem. The American judicial community was deeply complicit. It had to choose between massive support for democratic and constitutional principles against fascist police crimes and its wholesale dismissal of such illegalities ever occurred. Conveniently as befit members of a racist ideology, it cowardly chose the latter.[3]

Federal boxloads of anticrime money served a useful purpose for White supremacists in government and in the CJS. It made it possible for millions of dubious arrests to occur throughout this period. No matter the relationship between crime rates and arrests was never proven; that White collar crime surged just as much, especially under a forgiving Reagan administration, but was ignored; that policies of rehabilitation of the past still could help offenders despite being rejected by politicians. Or the draconian drug laws that brought about so much pain and broken lives were part of a big lie.

Why a big lie? Because of what politicians refused to believe that alcohol consumption was far more dangerous to people than cocaine, even crack cocaine, and many other drugs taken from a long list. Yet it was crack cocaine, the drug of choice for many poor Black Americans, that received the harshest consideration when it came to arrests and penalties that could send a man to prison for a very long time. The 1970s and 1980s, in particular, saw many thousands of arrests of Black men for drugs, most of whom were far less likely than alcohol, drug of choice by White politicians and part of an active and legal corporate entity with companies selling on the New York Stock Exchange, to bring havoc to the man's body or community. Alcohol, not cocaine, was found to make people more aggressive and more prone to committing crime and also to become involved in fatal traffic accidents. Not that cocaine doesn't have risks but these are less criminally oriented. All of this was ignored by politicians who saw the advantages gained by conducting a war on drugs with the principal offender, the one most used by Black street addicts, being crack cocaine. Hence the war began and by 1990, when this study ends, is at a high point in arrests and imprisonments. War crimes by the tens of thousands were the end result of this pernicious political rationale to thwart Black civil rights ambitions by diverting attention to a contrived story about Black criminalization of drugs.[4]

Contentious politics is the term used by some sociologists to describe how all this has played out between Black crime and civil disobedience. We refer to Charles Tilley, Sidney Tarrow, Doug McAdam, Clarissa Rile Hayward, and the leading light of this broad perspective Iris Marion Young. Here crime is seen as an unintentional yet disruptive tactic for those seeking social justice while deploring government policy criminal justice policies deemed fascist and structurally racist. In this view, crimes appear as everyday acts of resistance to law enforcement. Agencies operating in an institutional setting of intolerance pursue war crimes against Black people. "Listen to me," "Hear my protest," "Take me seriously," and "Black lives matter" are being said to the CJS in contrast to decades of bourgeois palaver between Black and White peace negotiators weakly attempting to bring human rights and legislative equality to thirteen million Black people. In Haywards view, crime is a by-product of government misadventure: "to correct large-scale injustices like institutional racism where in certain cases crimes are practical resolutions." Dr. Tarrow had his own take on the crime issue where he shifts the focus from Blacks as radicalized objectified criminals to the government mechanisms (bureaucratic agents of the CJS, fascist government policies, and racist institutions) that create these victims during a revolutionary situation, such as the enormous surge in urban crime in the 1960s, 1970s, and 1980s.[5] A final definition of contentious politics of use to this study is from the Cambridge University department of contentious politics where what they have done is explore noninstitutionalized political actions, including revolutions, crime, civil war, cycles of protest, and ethnic conflicts that power political and social perspectives found in governmental bureaucracies, to which we add the CJS.[6]

THE MURKY WORLD OF CJS INTELLIGENCE

For almost 100 years, the bureaucracies that comprise the CJS have been masquerading as a crime-solving, science-oriented branch of government (police, judiciary, corrections, probation services, and rehabilitative thera-pists). But it was never a science nor was it capable of reducing crime on its own. It needed the country's economic prosperity to do that. The modern CJS, as noted by University of Toronto psychiatrist and social activist Don Weitz in studying modern psychiatry, has been driven by unproved empirical assertions, criminological biases about how to prevent crime, and pseudo-scientific statements that underscored its opinions as addressed by its bureau-cratic apparatus.[7] Regarding street crime, there are no laws or testable facts in criminology that are useful in assessing crime activity that does not now delve into the nature of racist theory. In short, the CJS lacks scientific proof or evidence that punishment works most of the time, whatever the sanction and type of offender, that the court system works effectively and judiciously, that corrections rebuild lives, and that the public gets what it pays for in the enormously expensive bureaucratic operation known as the CJS.

Professor Zygmunt Bauman (University of Leeds, UK) repeats the ques-tion already raised: How could an educated, rational modern citizen of a lib-eral White Eurocentric democracy, normal by contemporary psychologically healthy standards, work so easily in an atmosphere of sociopathic racism that still attempted to humanely reduce urban crime of the 1960s and 1970s? From Bauman, we learn how technological bureaucracies such as the CJS led per-fectly normal people to collectively commit racial injustices and even atroci-ties. Mindless political thinking by Republicans and Southern Democrats made the law enforcement atrocities of the War on Crime possible as they were unopposed by any countervailing moral or ethical considerations to do otherwise and verbally protest. Bauman believed the War on Crime was made possible not from a patent form of hatred against Black people but from a more sinister type of routine indifference. An indifference developed through a bureaucratic ritual that smothered serious contemplation of the outcome and dangers of what these bureaucratic agents of the CJS were doing to people on the other end of their misbehavior. As Arendt noted, it was a sad com-mentary of the elitist educated class who ran bureaucracies that there existed little pity or empathy for the victims of what they were doing to somehow curtail crime.[8]

The dean of sociologists on the subject of bureaucracies, Max Weber, saw these governmental organizations as ruling class threats to human freedoms and the normal functioning of bureaucracies as "leading to a polar night of icy darkness in which the increasing rationalization of human life traps the individual in an iron cage." The dangers were obvious: inflexible policies, dehumanizing workloads, inefficient, a rigid division of technical and specialized labor within fixed areas of activity that was inevitably subservient to the totalitarian instincts of politicians. Constas and Meron also pointed to the serious leadership problems, cross-agency rivalries for funding, unhealthy conflicts based on personalities, high turnover of administrators, plenty of red tapes to overwhelm anyone trying to use these agencies, and little regard for comprehensive planning—all common to the federal programs that occurred during the War on Crime years. The worst criticism is of these worker bees, who obstruct basic community human complaints and problems with the CJS are nonelective government officials with no public standing or mandate from the people they allegedly serve. Yet they make policies and decisions that interfere with and paralyze whole urban communities to their detriment. To this effect, the CJS is a perfect system for repressing and keeping the thumb on personal initiative and innovation—either from the agents who work the system or the offenders who are the obvious victims. Merton noted that bureaucracies represented "goal displacement" where strictly obedient, rational conformity to departmental rules and norms led to situations where rules became ends in themselves, inhibiting an agency to achieve its goals. The result led to dysfunctional outcomes that depressed any Black neighborhood's ability to control CJS interference.[9]

The Most Undemocratic of Social Institutions

The nonelective nature of the CJS bureaucracy deserves our attention. These officials have no public standing or mandate from the community (Black or otherwise) they allegedly serve. Yet they make policies, derived from anti-crime legislation enacted by Congress, many of whose members lack any real connection to the communities they serve (especially the White representatives of the many Black communities of the South and Northeast). Yet they make policies and decisions that affect individuals and paralyze urban Black neighborhoods to their detriment. To this effect, the CJS is a perfect system for repressing and keeping a thumb on the community members who are its obvious victims. And what is the result? A bureaucracy with glaring deficiencies compared to European counterparts, flying blind when it comes to fulfilling its mandate.

The CJS bureaucracy lacks social policies that are genuinely accountable for the prevention of crime. It ignores the causes of crime by placing all the blame on the individual with his many personal flaws and views the poor Black as a definite threat to be watched by law enforcement. Complex causes of crime are disregarded. Punishment becomes the sole crime deterrent. Punitive social exclusion of the offender is seen as the best way to reduce crime. This leads to unprecedented use of prisons (to be discussed later) where over 2–4m men were at various times incarcerated during these years. The rate of prisoners is 700–800 per 100,000 in the United States and 80–90 per 100,000 in Europe.

There has always been a refusal within the CJS to humanize prisons and jails, or drastically reduce sentences, or completely redress Court procedures and remove racist judges, or consider wide use of amnesty and decarceration as alternatives, or eliminate victimless crimes, revise hiring requirements, create a climate that keeps political intrusion to a minimum, or vigorously enforce human rights and inject results of criminological research into humanistic legislation. Consequently, even a normal bureaucracy is subject to eternal laws that hide war crimes and waves of terror that make these agencies dominate and persecute the Black community under their charge.

"Like fighting a 'war against criminals'" was spoken in 1982 by an academic describing the bureaucratic functions of the American CJS.[10] Ronald S. Clark professor of criminal justice at Florida State University said so. Not much rehabilitation policy for human resource development is mentioned. In fact, punishment seemed to be the constant theme of each of the agencies which made up this fragmentary, independent system of organizations whose eye was on public safety and outwitting the criminal. Punishment in each case: the cop using his baton, the judge ordering jail time for an offender, the correctional guard throwing someone into solitary confinement, the probation officer placing a strict order of confinement on a probationer. All part of a system where arbitrary and discretionary orders flowed from a system with little supervision and oversight to place restraints on the agent. There are enough catastrophic blunders on the record of the CJ mandarins to suggest that, however brilliant they may be, it is not wise to leave them in control of the levers unattended by checks and balances, not least those provided by public opinion and the close scrutiny of the people who are going to have to live with the decisions of the CJ administrators. This study will indicate how far afield they went in the years 1960–1990 to not providing tolerant services to the Black communities they served.

The phrase CJS implies institutionalized social organizations to deter, correct, or preclude criminal behavior. CJS involves interactional patterns where each agency in turn handles an offender if adjudicated by the court. We have already listed the agencies concerned with criminal justice, each having definite separations and responsibilities between them. But things go very wrong at this point. The public has no input despite living in a democracy, permitting only a potent political faction with decidedly strict views on how Blacks should behave. The CJS is set up in a bifurcated, decentralized way to guard against governmental over-reaching. But in this period the over-reaching federal government, through its CJS components in every state, became a Big Brother monitoring (and arresting) Blacks universally, extending various phases of the CJS deep into their lives and those of their families and communities for the worse. Policies and tactics in this system are designed to be in harmony with local wishes and for the Black community to construct its own organizations and allocate duties to provide for the special needs of the community. This surely never happened.

Clark noted that the management and administration of justice from the CJS required "absolute equality in the treatment of every individual member of the public . . . respecting the dignity of the least trust worthy citizen to build an atmosphere of trust and confidence in government."[11] In the period we are studying, and for Black communities of that period, these things never happened and the concept of fairness was more likely to be met by oppression, intolerance, and general social injustice. So much for the many niceties about the American CJS when it confronted the reality of racism and oppression between 1960 and 1990. Clark took a wide, critical view of the CJS:

> Criminal justice agencies may . . . attract more negative criticism than the average business, perhaps because there is no clear measure of success, such as a business's profit. The success of the CJS appears to be determined mainly by the views of the communities it serves . . . (but if) a justice agency views it members as a special elite engaged in a war against criminals, the ultimate result tends to be bad. It separates the agents of justice from the people they serve, producing a walled-in subculture of *us* against *them* . . . The best measure of the success of a criminal justice agency is the satisfaction of the communities it serves.[12]

The last chapter of this current study, that interviews members of the Harlem community about its own CJS, will reveal how badly these agencies were perceived by a sample of Black Americans of the time.

Despite its intentional flaws as an oppressive bureaucratic institution, the CJS had structural deficiencies that helped to make Black citizens of this period more of a victim of law enforcement than was necessary.

The dean of German sociologists, Max Weber, was pessimistic about what bureaucracies could accomplish for people other than themselves. He called them "iron cages" for the bureaucrats who became impersonal captives to the disciplinary implications of bureaucratic rationality. In so doing, the institution required a special kind of worker personality. He had to be capable of transcending what was seen as mere clerical administrative work and turning its functions into a veneer of professionalism of mock importance other than what was conferred by laws and legislation. What evolved often turned into a formal spider web of oppression by different civil servants and agencies against the needy user of these services.

The result of bureaucratic obstruction and formal delay negates justice and unfairly erodes the rights of minorities with consequences of preventable CJS injustices. This is done by bureaucrats placing blame for legal entanglements, arrests, and low performance of Blacks on themselves rather than the systems that perpetuate the inequalities from which Blacks face. Functionaries thus fill out forms that evaluate Blacks as having low self-esteem, low aspirations, a minimal ability to relate to demands and requirements of the CJS, and an unrealistic cognition of economic achievement.

Red tape is one of many bureaucratic mainstays that work directly against Black clients especially those mired in problems with the CJS agencies. Then too, civil servants feel besieged by clients whose needs are apparent but where bureaucrats are unable to influence policy implementation. The result is two grumpy individuals making any possibility of successful resolution rare. Major reasons:

1. Black offenders bring more difficult problems to bureaucracies especially where police, courts/judges, and jail are involved. This means there is also a sense of urgency that confronts bureaucratic slow, methodical, time consuming with lots of questions and forms that bedraggle Black men seeking action. These along with extreme financial problems of eviction, arrest, loss of work, domestic abuse, and so on require faster and immediate action from workers that is rarely achievable; this is not lost on Black clients who assume racist interference with their predicament.
2. Bureaucrats are unwilling to enforce or call out human rights and legal violations for fear of intruding in areas beyond their ability to change; Black clients are alert to this.
3. Black clients seek active representation from bureaucrats who are steeled in formalistic, orderly procedures and processes aimed at simple casework integrity. This is generally too slow for Blacks who are feeling extreme external pressure from a variety of sources which aim at their freedom and sense of justice.
4. Impersonal passive and lethargic casework angers Black clients who feel their problems should receive candid, personal, intimate attention, where they can speak angrily even vulgarly to best present their case, and where they are seen as individuals and not simply as someone in a long stream of people all unable to successfully navigate the CJS.

5. Black men want immediate resolution in a bureaucratic nightmare where everything takes time, lots of forms must be completed, and various stages of the hierarchical process must be completed and reviewed by senior officers prior to formal approval of the task.
6. Often workdays mean lots of personal problems heard by the bureaucrat, all from people on a mission to get heard. This can lead to antagonism and grumbling when civil servants reach a limit to how much anger they are willing to stomach by a Black client who feels the CJS has harmed him and his family directly and seriously.
7. If this isn't enough, bureaucracies like the CJS present demographic problems that often are the reason clients fail to reach a level of accomplishment or satisfaction in tune with their needs: Black versus White caseworkers, young versus old, men versus women, American-born versus foreign with the usual cultural differences, and where both feel underappreciated and ready to scuffle rather than spend time resolving the client's issues.[13]
8. Over all these issues lies the one big fear by Black defendants that the bureaucratic caseworker, so ready to drag out the case, is really quite incompetent, doesn't really know how to fight for his clients, and is unable to offer much help due to his general unfamiliarity with the many cultural, racial, and economic issues being posed by the client.

In the end, we are only talking about normal men in their role as supermen charged with making major decisions on people they have never met before. Mills was his usual pejorative self when in 1958 he condemned these blind decisions made by bureaucrats.

> The atrocities of our time are done by men as "functions" of social machinery— men possessed by an abstracted view that hides them from human beings who are victims . . . it is not the cruelty that is distinctive; it is the fact that nobody protested these distinctive acts.[14]

War crimes were disregarded and hidden, even perpetrated by the very nature of the bureaucratic structure of CJ agencies. Blacks had many unresolved complaints and grievances by the behavior of cops, judges, and correctional workers but were met with a wall of structural resistance to their needs. To this effect, such obstacles represented a major part of the problem victims faced when trying to seek redress to the many injustices inflicted upon them. At least ten examples come to mind. First, no provision exists in the bureaucratic structure if something goes wrong in the relationship between caseworker and client. The agency assumes nothing can go wrong by being infallible or it doesn't care. Second clients are left hanging and have little recourse to object to the proceedings as strict rules preoccupy all activities. Nor do suggestion boxes exist for clients to make themselves heard. There are no forms that exist to argue against regulations that are set in stone and tell clients their situation is unimportant.

Third there is no way the client can see his chart/record/case file should they wish to correct a mistake or understand why the bureaucracy is fighting their charges. One would think a person is entitled to see why and how his case is proceeding against him for an objection to be raised. Fourth, agencies are closed lipped and files are secret and sacred—as if a war was being fought, which, of course, is actually happening to the complainant. Fifth, the agencies offer no encouragement or reward to show a happy face or be nice to clients or go the extra miles to help solve their issues. Some agencies being so good-natured might feel they are creating a situation where clients come to expect this kind of service, slowing everything down to a snail's crawl. This will jam the works and cause caseworkers to deviate from standard procedure, making the whole process too unpredictable for higher officials to manage and evaluate.

Sixth, there are no ways to make expedient a serious, urgent matter that is respected as urgent throughout the agency by all departments and agents. Somehow, somewhere down the line, the matter will come to a halt and aggravate any already serious problem into an uncurable conclusion. A seventh issue that needs to be addressed is that such CJS agencies are funded in part by the community it serves although caseworker behavior doesn't suggest appreciation or obligation to treat local citizens as anything more than nuisances and earaches. This belief is quickly passed along to anyone applying for assistance so the message is loud and clear—state your problem and then back off; we'll resolve it in our own time. Bureaucratic pencil-pushers cannot deal with arcane issues like ethical behavior, human rights abuses, or legal niceties. Training for CJS bureaucrats is often limited to knowing which forms to use for which complaints, who along the chain of command processes what and when, what referrals to use (if known) in given situations, and what words are best applied to move the client along to some other department, inasmuch as the buck does not stop here. Eighth, witness complaint forms to process displeasing law enforcement behavior (or worse) simply don't exist. Last but one, no way exists for a client to request the intervention of a higher official if he believes the original agent is unresponsive to the demands of the victim. Finally, opportunities do not exist for the client to volunteer his time to help agents follow through on his own case or even be available to offer local advice and counseling in matters where the caseworker is obviously in deep water. All these weaknesses of the bureaucracy doom most victim injuries to failed attempts at resolution, thus enlarging a war crime to even greater proportions of intolerance and social injustice.

Definitely Not in the Public Interest

An example of a CJS bureaucracy gone rogue is the Law Enforcement Assistance Administration (LEAA) established in 1968 as an attempt to provide political and governmental solutions to the rampant crime, violence, and criminal disorders then rocking the country. Black-originated crime seemed to be on such a massive scale; only money, equipment, and technical advice and generous federal resources could possibly come to grips with what was seen as a runaway problem affecting the whole country. The single aim of the agency was to improve the law enforcement effort at curbing crime and violence. The main target was the Black community for it was from them that most crime, violence, and inner-city riots originated.

This we can guess because LEAA was born from the Omnibus Crime Control and Safe Streets Act of 1968. Who else but Blacks were associated with unsafe streets of the time? Money was thrown at the problem. In 1969, $60m was spent by LEAA, rising to $850m by 1973 and $3.3b to be spent from 1974 to 1977, hefty sums at the time (from $4.2b in today's purchasing power to $21b).[15]

From the very beginning there were controversies, very many attempts by police to dominate and control funding and its application, development of a system of block grants that permitted 85% of the funds to be exploited by states and local communities to serve their own personal interests, LEAA failure to control allocation processes, very minimal Black input despite Congress' desire that its community involvement be of paramount concern, overall staff and management incompetence on all levels, research findings that lacked genuine application to community needs, ambiguous and ill-defined programs leading to an assessment that everything "failed to live up to expectations."[16]

As American involvement in Vietnam wound down in these years, many companies active in the defense industry noticed that LEAA money offered a new market for their expansion. Kodak, Bell Company, Northrup, Smith & Wesson, among many others, realized their products of war could easily be adapted by law enforcement to fight crime. Soon federal purchases of previously war-related hardware were refurbished for use against Black Americans: electronic computer surveillance for watching inner-city street life and recording names of suspects, night fighting equipment transposed from use against Viet Cong soldiers to American Black men, and the aforementioned Bell helicopters.[17]

Darrow Smith, associate warden at San Quentin (CA), gave a damning indictment of LEAA:

> The Black community was seen as a pretext for large flows of money into organizations and public officials who were White, often Republican, with White

Power orientation. Much of this did not go unnoticed. "The CJS has been the Black community's biggest enemy. LEAA has not been responsive to the problems and concerns of the Black community and has created more problems by providing funds for unwarranted and repressive police action. The Black community would be better off without LEAA which operates in its own repressive manner."[18]

Even those most likely to benefit from LEAA largesse were extremely critical of the agency. One New York City police official narrated a litany of complaints before the HR subcommittee reviewing LEAA's achievements in 1981:

What I witnessed were erratic funding policies with no certainty of funding, no meaningful planning at the local level, inefficient programs maintained while credible ones were terminated, gadgetry for police, no oversight tools implanted to monitor or evaluate local community groups in any rational or realistic way. There appeared to be no way to stop funding projects doomed to failure, little research propounded to evaluate whether judges of prosecutors, tough or lenient, were actually contributing to crime reduction or possible and viable options to expensive, failed CJS agencies. Yet after ten years and over $10b wasted dollars, what did LEAA give us? Institutional unprofessionalism, an incompetent approach to criminal justice research and a complete failure to meet stated aims, goals and results.[19]

Other officials stood in line to fire their complaints at LEAA conduct. Robert McClory (HR R. Ill.) claimed "By 1978, a decade after its beginnings, LEAA leadership was floundering and the bulk of its anti-crime programs were also failing." Jeanne Vogt claimed in 1976 local CJ allocations were such that 84% of the money went to fund police while perhaps 8% was spent on corrections and a paltry 4% for rehabilitation projects and supervision contacts from probation departments. Courts received less than this. And juveniles—what were troubled youth worth? In LEAA young people were always the lowest priority."[20]

Varon was not without scathing criticisms. "High crime areas never received sufficient resources" . . . "Money was channeled into the wrong programs and used for the wrong purposes" . . . "crime statistics were manipulated for political reasons and wide variances that were reported were often in relationship to the needs of local mayors and contained many discrepancies" . . . and the worse one of all considering the billions of dollars spent: "LEAA had a negligible effect on crime reduction, they just tinkered around in the CJS."[21]

White nationalist ideology surely had a part in how funds were allocated and made sure money went to organizations run by Whites, with the greater percentage of Whites also being employees. Dr. Jeffrey Schwartz, president of Law Enforcement Training and Research Association (CA), appeared before the House of Representatives Committee investigating LEAA in 1967–1968 in its early days to make the following comments:

> The biggest problem with LEAA was staff incompetence. They didn't have the requisite knowledge, experience or education to design or manage or evaluate CJS progress. People were hired for all kinds of reasons . . . people who had six months police experience, sophomores at colleges in the Washington DC area that were simply available for staff research and others for less meritorious reasons . . . A lot of these people are now managers in LEAA making million-dollar decisions and telling State directors of corrections, police chiefs and communities what they should really be doing with their money. We ourselves became discouraged by the lack of change in police agencies in minority and female employment. In fact, LEAA had even less representation of minority employment between 1974–1977 it was simply not representative of any part of the CJS (which itself had its own minority issues). Complaints about contract grant awards to cronies went unaddressed . . . 4% of the funding went to white collar crime issues (which was soaring at the time) and under half of 1% of LEAA funding went into police minority employment and correctional minority projects . . . LEAA had even less minority employment.[22]

Blacks were seen as lazy, inefficient, incompetent, and frivolous when it came to spending the slim allocations LEAA dispersed to Black groups. The CJS had never been able to understand the motivations and aspirations of young Black militants when it came to illegal behavior. To what extent were their "crimes" mere acts of defiance to protest wrongful state conditions and racial barbarism exercised by the CJS willfully against the Black community? But this was never considered a possibility. What if the defiance had been treated in a softer way and seen as acts of bravery and resistance; surely other models elsewhere and at other times could have provided insight?

But this was never considered and the CJS maintained a stodgy, antebellum approach to race relations, and opportunities were lost because the CJS was neither courageous nor creative enough to consider this possibility. In 1996, LEAA ex-officials met in Washington, DC, to discuss the past and rehash some of their old grievances and experiences. Fifty-one high-flying bosses showed up. The list attached to the announcement gave me an opportunity to determine who belonged in this august crowd and what might be their political affiliations? Of the fifty-one I could determine that fifteen (75%) had clear Republican roots and alliances and five (25%) were Democrat-sponsored. This did not surprise me since, for most of the life of LEAA, Republican presidents and their advisers had been in a position to nominate and confirm those who ran the show. Most were lawyers, lobbyists, ex-cops, old-line bureaucrats, and pseudo-advisers to presidents and high-ranking senators. This majority of Republicans also told me why LEAA had failed so gloriously: White superiority attitudes I find in the Republican class, tough views on crime, law, police, and punishment, suspicion of anything to do with rehabilitation, and being "soft" on offenders were views in abundance. Ignorance of ghetto conditions and/or lack of concern with research, sociological studies on poverty, and negative social conditions could be added to the list.

If this view represented 75% of the entire LEAA cadre, it explains why LEAA was such a colossal white (meant as such) elephant. Since its inception, LEAA had been polluted and exploited by the same group of professional grifters and hard-boiled eggs who saw it as a mission while fighting Black street crime and drug addicts to make sure the lion's share of funding, if not almost all it, was earmarked for their needs and into their pockets and purses. This wasn't how President Johnson planned it in the late 1960s when his council, looking into causes of crime felt the public, more specifically the Black community, needed to be deeply and democratically involved if the crime hysteria was ever to be solved. Yet according to Serpas, "citizen participation through LEAA was very muted . . . the program was looked upon by professionals in criminal justice as their province." It took Serpas four years lobbying Congress to get a provision for citizen participation which recognized the local police chief could veto proposals; 150 local, community projects then in existence were subject to this kind of scrutiny, control, and rejection without recourse.[23]

When aid was dispersed to a Black community project, a standard rule was to do it in an arbitrary way, make it dependent on government generosity (which was often arbitrary), dole out a little, never too much; also, establish numerous deadlines and timetables for CJS results and make it nearly impossible to provide answers to complex questions and, of course, have too few advisers and helpers available for completing the job on time. In short, discourage those seeking government help. Do it to a few local Black leaders and they'll tell the rest. This was probably deliberate. Was this a war crime?

LEAA seemed instinctive to know how to remain distant from the people they were supposed to help. It surrounded itself with umbrella agencies where White officials were appointed to combine into one as many low-level jobs as were available. High-paying administrative jobs? Well, you know the answer who would get these treats. According to my studies, perhaps 15% of the better work went to White women, a high percentage in management positions around men at the time.

But LEAA did nothing about police brutality, local CJS repression, or help resolve some of the many social concerns presented to the bureaucracies by Black citizens. Worse, these men always blamed the ghetto resident for his troubles which were standard throughout the LEAA where the financial needs of residents were not their concern. In my experience dealing with LEAA officials interviewing me for probation issues, I found them tyrannical in attitude, imperious with community residents, and incapable of admitting error. They seemed to forget they were mere petty bureaucrats and were fierce with me when I brought this to their attention.[24]

Making Allowances for Operational Misunderstandings

A police state mentality formed the basis of White nationalism; it also was the result of how LEAA dealt with issues of crime, Black displacement and criminality, and urban riot control. It meant that society need not get serious about the root causes of crime to reduce it. Black offenders were the obvious guilty parties and they would respond to obvious LEAA-backed disincentives: more police patrols in the ghettoes, more use of computers and surveillance equipment borrowed from the military to determine prime areas of criminal activity, tougher judges and lengthier sentences, more prison building with more inmates, random shakedowns, increased entrapment policies, show indifference to drug importation which demoralized Black neighborhoods and dehumanized its citizens. Not one cop I ever met recoiled at these restrictions as antidotes. Possibly, it is because LEAA gave every signal how they came to ridicule Black communities.

Such a perspective is consistent with Charles Tilly's analogy between war-making and state-making as reflected in LEAA activities and objectives. He argues that states often develop war-oriented policies that provoke a perpetuating false or exaggerated threat about internal enemies from which administrations then frame their actions as protecting their citizens. To Tilly policing and war-making were seen simultaneously as genuine examples of naked aggression with violence invoked under the guise of "citizen protection." By this process he distinguishes between groups (White) who are privileged and advantaged with the ability to exact violence through coordinated violence against unprotected groups (Black) who are tyrannized to the point of serious injury and much worse hidden from public view while suppressing militant opposition. In this matter LEAA found itself through policies and funding on the side of Whites, combatting who it saw in its policies and studies as Blacks causing the street crime and riots. "Police and the Courts serve to justify external coercion as mechanisms of selective security and protection to the point where . . . State making reduced the protection awarded some classes and communities (i.e., Black neighborhoods)."

Law enforcement during the Nixon/Reagan years of oppression provided the most glaring examples of war crimes on innocent citizens, whatever the misdemeanors of some. Indeed, we might even say the number of undocumented cases was immense. At the same time, LEAA, administered mainly by appointees of these repressive governments, did nothing to look into this matter or produce policies and studies aimed at reducing or altering the commission of such human rights abuses and denial of civil rights.[25]

To mean White nationalist thinking members of the LEAA these stereotypes of the people they deemed the enemy seemed to persist:

1. Ghettoes meant "darkness," New Africa, danger for innocent Whites wandering through, guerilla warfare against the CJS. Communities were known as Jungle Land, Coonville, Darkey Town, Little Congo, and Cannibalville.
2. No well-adjusted Black men would be found here. The lucky ones, presumably saved by a White education and working for White employers who overpaid them, would move to the safe White suburbs and keep out of sight (the ones that would accept them).
3. One should treat inner-city Blacks as though they represent one country (forget state or city). They are all the same and have the same conniving attitudes, lusty behavior, manners, and tendencies toward violence and deceit.
4. Taboo subjects over which urban Blacks knew little: kindness, compassion, domestic bliss, intellectualism, kids with high IQ, and patriotism.
5. An "I expect as much" tone, so don't look for thanks or appreciation for any good deeds or saving of life done for Black people by humane cops.
6. Blacks need to be pitied, controlled, and dominated by Whites or else the ghettoes will be doomed to a fiery, violent, and chaotic destruction.
7. Typical ghetto characters who are endless problems for beat cops include: twelve-year-old drug pushers, fourteen-year-old baby mamas, sixteen-year-old warlords, older Black women watching over the brood of babies their daughters produce out of wedlock, and lots of adult men doing nothing but getting drunk, shooting dice in alleys, and just wandering listlessly.
8. Blacks blame police, judges, and their probation officers for everything including all their personal faults and life's failures due to infantile irresponsibility.
9. Blacks rarely know anything beyond what can earn them a fast buck or how to chase women or create fast alibis when police ask them questions.
10. Well-mannered Black school children can only be found in White districts and these have to be bused in. The rest act like animals for which school is just time wasted and they have to be treated accordingly.

What we have tried to document is an LEAA-inspired American-style holocaust in its war against crime and the Black culture. LEAA proposals to curb crime led to failure and ruin. Worse were the Black men who had learned to distrust their government in Washington as much as their local law enforcement officials and the soaring rhetoric of race-baiting politicians. They had witnessed and experienced too much brutal police behavior. They had watched and remembered the war on drugs as military campaigns in their neighborhoods, talk of more prison building and sentences of men they knew to long terms away from their families in these prisons, academics with hands out for funding about studies that pose prison as a legitimate solution and especially Democrats who failed to take a courageous stand and argue on behalf of the Black constituency which was their voter base.[26]

If any doubts existed on what social improvements, welfare, and jobs were needed in Black areas, LEAA, which employed over 650 personnel at its peak in 1978, delayed so that nothing significant took place. It forced the usual poor resident, as so many other government projects did, to rely only on individual resources and limited assets to advance the cause while federal monies were directed almost solely to the police so that more arrests could be made. LEAA officials had little to no experience in dealing with ghetto issues (many of which were created by the CJS itself). LEAA made sure this ignorance was maintained by hiring its top dogs with no experience who remained aloof, indifferent, and ineffective. Savelsberg (sociology professor at the University of Minnesota) reminds us that LEAA funding for research projects created self-reinforcing tendencies that helped administrators justify their decisions. "Public opinion polls and speeches of politicians reinforced each other once the punitive trend that began at the tail end of Johnson's reign had gotten under way. This meant research funded by political agencies (such as the Department of Justice and the National Institute of Justice as well as LEAA) became academically produced knowledge that followed political demands. It was easy for the LEAA to justify conservative-oriented projects as they had available research findings to agree with their vision."[27]

One of LEAA's biggest critics was Conyers who attacked them at every opportunity in the Congressional hearings into crime, justice, LEAA appropriations, and the Black community. He claimed:

> There seems to be a CJS that is highly partisan . . . where we have a constitutional problem. LEAA is predisposed for certain people, classes, races as objects of prosecutorial attention. It feeds a racial apparatus . . . the whole CJS requires change which LEAA ignores only to feed a corrupt, medieval process not changed since the agency began its operation in 1968.[28]

In addition to its funding function, LEAA chose to create dubious research and planning units, promote police education. If a cop (only) went to college for a brief time his pay would increase. This applied to no other branch of the

CJS and shows the might of police lobbying in securing such benefits. In the end, none of the money spent on research has been shown to have actually decreased crime. Despite the decade of the 1970s with the wild spending by this bureaucracy of failure, President Reagan abolished the agency in 1982 as one more example of the waste and inefficiency of big government. But it did teach us one thing:

> Crime panics and fear do pay. Crime scares promoted by politicians and the media, of good versus evil, and ghettoes seen as violent places to be politicized military fashion . . . where politicians used the racial divide and fear of violence so disproportionate to any real problem that rational scenes that took hold . . . suggest the bloody tip of the iceberg of repression by governmental authority.[29]

The LEAA stood as one such repressive authority. LEAA did nothing to prevent or bring attention to police brutality or harassment of Black citizens or war crimes. This was simply too explosive an issue. It offered no rewards for Black people caught in the maw of the CJS. There was little done to help Black communities achieve any real authority, or have their anticrime projects funded, or have access to funding on any kind of workable scale. It seemed the idea was to prevent communities from asking too much of their government while presenting Black neighborhoods (i.e., ghettoes) in conflict, and always dealing with illegal street activities and drugs. A negative image of these places was presented through the media to White voters that such communities were unworthy of federal funds seen as handouts. Just the reverse: treat local people as if they were intentionally dangerous and stupid, where good federal money goes to die. Make sure good deeds by Blacks organizations were given no publicity while LEAA took credit when it could for local law enforcement successes. In short, the perfect conclusion to White nationalist ideology of Black America.

LEAA was never designed to help Black people. It failed to offer or fund creative new ideas aimed at improving Black lives. It failed to single out Black community leaders and present them with opportunities to help more vulnerable young Black men avoid drugs and prevent misbehavior. It failed to show a soft face, fully aware of the iron-clad racism of Black history in America. All that was left was a "series of penalties with long term disastrous effects on ghetto residents."[30]

Schwartz provided lengthy testimony to the HR Committee considering reauthorization of LEAA funding in 1979 in a lengthy rebuke on LEAA's expert help for communities:

> Technical assistance for LEAA is a euphemism. They supply technical assistance only in areas that they determine are important and they simply can't

respond to most of the problems that people call them about for help with. I believe that the staff at LEAA are looking for some kind of magic answer . . . unfortunately most of them don't have practitioner experience so they are not well grounded . . . what is actually happening in operational agencies is that they continuously look for some new buzz word, some new concept, some magic that's going to, in one fell swoop, solve the country's crime problems in a 3-year, $4m grant . . . and, of course, it doesn't.[31]

When aid was dispersed to a community, a standard rule was to do it in an arbitrary way, make Black communities and organizations wait while doling out a little-never too much. Other macabre bureaucratic annoyances: set numerous deadlines and timetables for results, be inconsistent about how to develop projects or get immediate aid rapidly, keep phone lines busy and hire too few advisers at the local level to discourage people from seeking government aid. When it came to police requests, doors were always open and a happy face was always present to bring confidence to law enforcement, no request was too large or outrageous. Nobody wants crime so any amount sought cannot be too high. White supremacist bias could infect some of these proposals, so reasons other than personal flaws in Black people were rarely stated to get the money. Ann Ginger, law professor and criminal attorney, claimed that while there were plenty of reasons cited why Black men are violent and criminally oriented, there was a paucity of statistics and proposals regarding human rights violations by law enforcement that needed to be rectified in LEAA inquiries. Wrongful arrests, cases of excessive police force, wanton injury to suspects, lack of statistics on police abuse, bad arrests from lack of evidence, abusive interrogations, civil rights violations—generally what we are calling war crimes. Speaking out on what LEAA left out of its overflow of statistics, Ginger noted:

> There is no conception by LEAA of the number of police misconduct incidents . . . It takes an awful lot of instances or violations of police misconduct to get one lawsuit and needs an awful lot of lawsuits before one sticks because lawyers quit clients, clients quit town, somebody moves far away.[32]

Nor did LEAA do anything meritorious for Black life in the Deep South. Life was brutal and filled with racist-inflected terror by law enforcement just as it always had been. Judicial justice was punitive, random murders by police and vengeful Whites on a mission obsessed with thoughts of Black citizens having civil rights amid dire poverty highlighted by the *Fortune Magazine* article previously cited. Top LEAA and CJS officials failed to present oversight, control, and effective policies and programs to propel Southern law enforcement into the twentieth century. Aspects of LEAA ineffectiveness were a part of the Washington, DC, political climate when it came to issues affecting the poor and minorities who were so often charged as enemies of the state with all their street crimes and violence.[33]

In 2010 noted criminologist John Hagan wrote a book in which he surveyed the story of crime policy from the age of Franklin Delano Roosevelt to Ronald Reagan who was elected on a "get tough" policy, from 1933 to 1993. After reviewing street crimes, corporate crime, and politicians who make crime policy in stodgy bureaucracies like LEAA, he asks the question found in the book's title: *Who Are the Criminals?* At the end of page 267, despite cloudy language, Hagan noted that the Age of Reagan's deregulation of America's corporate suites contributed to a massively costly and counterproductive policy response to problems of crime in America's streets, leaving us with the impression the real criminal was the politician himself.[34]

Where Have We Seen This All Before?

In 1922 Roscoe Pound and F. Frankfurter took it upon themselves to evaluate the CJS on the local level and chose the various CJS agencies in Cleveland (OH) for their probe. This was one of the first broad surveys of its kind to include the entirety of the CJS and its size of 725 pages suggested it tried to cover every aspect of the system that they could get access to. And what did their access reveal? It revealed the conditions very similar to what could be found in many unreformed agencies in 1993. The city jail was dark and dingy. Judges put off sentencing people if they knew them, or liked them, or simply wished to just because they could. Drunkards, traffic violations, and violent criminals stood side by side for the usual 2½ minutes of time allocated by the judge before pronouncing a judgment of "rough justice." The Cleveland prosecuting attorney filed no paperwork nor presented a criminal indictment if the defendant "was a good chap" belonged to the society of White men, and/or was known favorably by the department. Then there was the typical long history of police complicity in repressing the Black residents with many local cops' adherents to White supremacy ideology. In making arrests, cops used torture for confessions, wildly unproven hunches to locate culprits, and a whole grab bag of unscientific tactics, in catching their man. Pound and Frankfurter wrote how often they came across political interests interfering with and corrupting the entire system with little noise from the press. Raymond Moley, a social activist and police reformer, wrote that if the English monarch Henry II had paid a visit to Cleveland's CJS, "he would have felt right at home and comforted in finding familiar characters and processes as he knew at home." Many systems remained in this moribund state regardless of LEAA and various reformer actions which spanned the years

1922 to 1992. To improve the entire CJS was obviously well beyond the capability of any government of the time.[35]

Well, how did it all turn out after thirty years of a pursuit on the elusive issue of crime and its reduction? What did the CJS look like in the early 1990s when this study concludes? Not very well, it appears. Despite the fact that US population grew from 249m in 1990 to 263m five years later, about 5% while decades of advancing crime rates were apparent every year, until 1995 when all indices having to do with crime were declining—violence, arrests, property were all on the decrease of 1–2%.[36] Nevertheless, the political need for a fall guy to soothe public anger was still present, which meant the CJS and most of its constituent parts had learned nothing. Thirty years after the vicious police attacks on Black people by Bull Connor in Birmingham, a national audience was again treated to another chapter of excessive police force and brutality in the televised beating of Rodney King in Los Angeles in 1991. When the five cops were acquitted, we witnessed an updated version of the Watts riots which had occurred in that area almost 30 years earlier: 5 days of rioting in Los Angeles, 6,000 arrests, at least 10 Blacks killed by LAPD and the National Guard which again had been summoned. Since the King riot, how many thousands of other incidents of police brutality could we report? As in previous years, CJS bureaucratic documentation about crimes against humanity doesn't exist because that's how the CJS wants it—public approval of a war crime mentality without the annoyance of reportage or legal consequences. Professor Zimbardo saw how strangers could easily punish one another when a few minutes earlier they had a quiet identity. He called this "the Lucifer Effect." From his experiments, we can quickly come to conclusions that apply just as logically to "good" CJS agents dealing with the public. In such matters, they can unconsciously violate the rights of people without batting an eyelash. Here, too, the allocation of immense power which CJS members are authorized to use, in streets, courts, as well as prison grounds, could quickly destroy the rights and livelihoods of total strangers.

After the King riot in 1991, an inexorable law enforcement mentality that we saw in 1967 again grabbed hold. Within three months of the arrival of the 1992 Democratic administration and 116th Congress under Bill Clinton, at least 200 anticrime bills were being legislated in retaliation to keep White nationalist furor at a minimum. Worse was to follow. In 1994, the infamous Clinton Crime Bill appeared. Provisions were very punitive and easily matched some of the worst features of anticrime legislation in the years of Nixon and Reagan. Democrats now stood to be seen as just as horribly cruel, and included such leaders as Clinton, Senator Joe Biden (D. De), and Bernie Sanders (D. Vt). Inmates now had to serve 85% of their sentence before being considered for release; 100,000 new cops were happily authorized with the consequence that thousands of new arrests of Black men were predictable;

massive amounts of federal aid ($12b) were being appropriated for new prison and jail construction all of which accelerated mass incarceration for African Americans. Inmate imprisonments jumped from 800,000 in 1991 to 1.3m by 1998, additionally, there was a 59% increase in the death penalty which was being expanded to include 50 new types of crimes.

Between 1980 and 1995 probation services jumped from 320,000 (1980) to almost three million by 1994. If judges didn't place almost everyone who came before them on probation, they sent the rest straight to prison providing beds were available. In many cases there weren't so prisons had to be built. From 1980 to 1995, 213 new state and federal prisons had been built, increasing bed availability by 46% which were soon filled. Despite the boom, prisons were over capacity by 3%, federals by 24%. One in every four state correctional systems faced Court orders to limit and address specific confinement issues. The system topped one million men at any given time in 1995 (almost 300,000 more than in 1995)! Thanks to the extremely costly prison building campaign which made a lot of money for architects, contractors, and other related vendors, almost 40% of the existing inmates were in prisons built since 1985. Obviously, crime was paying wad making many people wealthy if not the inmates. In 1990 it was 293 per 100,000, in 1995, 427 per 100,000, an increase of over 40%. The wolves were out: Alabama politicians called for revival of the chain gang, Mississippi wished to restore flogging, and other Deep South states instituted caning. The country was running amuck and had learned nothing since 1960. Crime was going down but not the means and willpower to punish the Black community.[37]

Years later Clinton admitted before an NAACP convention "I signed a crime bill that made the problem worse." What made all this so tragic was that crime was at a historic low level—crime down by 22%, violent crime down by 25%. Politicians of either stripe could now be seen as inhumane and uncaring in how these changes would eventually affect Black Americans. Police chiefs were just as block-headed in their unshakable belief that America's major problem wasn't crime or violence or terrorism but drug addicts, presumably Black and inner-city. A 2004 poll of 300 police chiefs found that 67% believed the CJS was unsuccessful in reducing the drug problem which was still the country's most serious social problem.[38]

So it is that reasonably "good" people of the CJS can act irrationally and violently in mindless conformity of rules established by higher ups who see Black men as a fundamental threat to the American way of life and must be removed, forcibly, if necessary, from the community. Tonry provides us with a fresh breath of decency with his decidedly negative views about the CJS's persistent war on drugs:

The drug wars should never have been launched. Costly, harsh, doubling of arrests, tripling of sentences and unnecessarily blighted lives of thousands of Black men. The war was fought from partisan political motives . . . rising levels of Black incarceration did not just happen . . . intellectual dishonesty and political cynicism have long histories.[39]

One would be forgiven for forgetting John Ehrlichman's, Nixon's personal adviser for domestic affairs, comments in 1971 on the true intention behind legislating the war on drugs:

The Nixon campaign in 1968 and the Nixon White House after that had two enemies—the antiwar Left and Black people. You understand what I'm saying? We knew we couldn't make it to be illegal either against the war on Blacks but by getting the public to associate the hippies with marijuana and Blacks with heroin, and then criminalize both heavily, we could disrupt those communities. We could arrest their leaders, raid their homes, break up their meetings and vilify them night after night (using the police as the battering ram and the courts to be legally administering justice on the evening news). Did we know we were lying about the drugs? Of course, we did.[40]

So great was the threat, according to the White nationalist view, that natural human rights and constitutional legalities were suspended and ignored in this pursuit. Security and soothing White citizen fear, no matter how unjustified, was all that matters; the vote was sacred to politicians wishing to hold office at all costs. Agency repression of minorities was seen as good as it showed who was boss. Here, as in the Zimbardo experiments, a sadistic, dark side of the CJS was exposed, by men operating with blind obedience and moral disengagement. It answered the question "What right has the CJS to seize the destinies of Black males?" This was the operative theme that carried forward over the three decades of this war (and well beyond).

Zimbardo leaves us with these simple thoughts. First, a bad system with racist-influenced laws and operators can induce normal people to behave in pathological ways even when contrary to their nature. Second, war crimes will emerge when allowing CJS agents to impose their will in such a system. Third, inhuman procedures and rules will arise from superiors to rectify and justify such bad behavior that overrides ethical standards. Here basic human rights will be destroyed while pursuing the so-called greater goal of White security. Subduing the enemy is crucial regardless of cost or loss of humanity. Even so, most war crimes are not observable to the larger public; so these consequences of fascist law enforcement, whether they be from police, judges, probation officers, jail guards, or therapists, pass unnoticed to remain locked away in history's archives.

NOTES

1. Figures are derived from the U.S. Crime Rates 1960–1990, disastercenter.com /crime/uscrime.html.

2. Manning Marable, *Race Reform and Rebellion, The Second Reconstruction in Black America, 1945-1982* (Jackson: University Press of Mississippi, 1984), pp. 76–77.

3. Mark Maurer and Sabrina Jones, *The Race to Incarcerate* (New York: New Press, 2013), p. 188; Christopher R. Browning (history professor at the University of North Carolina), in (New York: Harper/Collins, 1993), pp. 36–39.

4. References to alcohol as a more dangerous drug than cocaine can be found in David Nutt's UK study for the Independent Scientific Committee on Drugs reported in *The Lancet* and *The Economist*, 25 June 2019; Genievieve Carbery, "Alcohol More Dangerous than Cocaine," *The Irish Times*, 11 February 2010; Abby McKenna, *Is Cocaine or Alcohol Worse?* Raleigh House, Arvada, CO, August 2018; and Kelly Fitzgerald, *Why Alcohol is the Deadliest Drug*, Addiction Center of New Jersey, December 2017.

5. The reader is referred for purposes of reviewing the main ideas of these sociologists to several evocative works: Charles Tilly, *Popular Contention in Great Britain, 1758-1834* (Boulder: Paradigm, 1995); Sidney Tarrow, *Power in Movements and Contentious Politics* (Cambridge: Cambridge UP, 1998); Doug McAdam, *The Political Process and Development of Black Insurgency, 1930-1970* (Chicago: Chicago UP, 1999); Clarissa Rile Hayward, *Justice and the American Metropolis* (Minneapolis: University of Minnesota Press, 2011); and the dean of this concept, Iris Marion Young, *Justice and Politics of Difference* (Princeton: Princeton UP, 1990) and *Responsibility for Justice* (New York: Oxford UP, 2011), p. 52.

6. Clarissa R. Hayward, "Responsibility and Ignorance on Dismantling Structural Injustice," *Journal of Politics* 79, no. 2 (2012): 396; Sidney Tarrow, "Contentious Politics," in Donatella Della Porta and Marion Diani (Eds.), *Oxford Handbook of Social Movements* (New York: Oxford UP, 2015); see the Cambridge Studies in Contentious Politics with Mark Beissinger (et al.) helping edit a publisher catalogue of seventy-three relevant titles.

7. Don Weitz, *Notes on Psychiatric Fascism*, see www.antipsychiatry.org, 2001.

8. Zygmunt Bauman, *Modernity & the Holocaust* (Ithaca: Cornell UP, 1985)

9. Hannah Arendt, *Eichmann in Jerusalem* (New York: Viking Press, 1963); and Arendt's monumental classic, *The Origins of Totalitarianism* (New York: Harcourt, Brace & Jovanovich, 1968). For more on Weber's views see Helen Constas, "Max Weber's Two Conceptions of Bureaucracy," *The American Journal of Sociology* 63, no. 4 (1958): 400; and the important works of Robert K. Merton, "Bureaucratic Structure and Personality," *Social Forces* 18, no. 4 (1940): 560–561 and his "Social Structure and Anomie," *The American Sociological Review* 3 (1938): 672–682.

10. Robert S. Clark, *The Criminal Justice System: An Analytical Approach* (Boston: Allyn & Bacon, 1982), p. 26.

11. Clark, op. cit., pp. 18–19.

12. Clark, op. cit., p. 20 and 26.

13. The reader is encouraged to read John Clayton Thomas, "The Personal Side of Street-Level Bureaucracy-Discord or Neutral Competence," *Urban Affairs Review* 22, no. 1 (1986): 34; or Edward G. Ludwig and John Collette, "Bias in Bureaucratic Decision-Making," *The Journal of the National Medical Association* 65, no. 6 (1973): 487; especially recommended is the master, Max Weber, *Capitalism, Bureaucracy and Religion, a Selection of Texts* (London: Allen & Unwin, 1983); or the classic study by economist Herbert A. Simon, PhD dissertation, *Administrative Behavior* (Chicago: University of Chicago, 1947); Helen Constas, "Max Weber's Two Conceptions of Bureaucracy," *The American Journal of Sociology* 63, no. 4 (1958); and Frank Elwell, "Sociology of Max Weber," Rogers State University website, 1996.

14. C. Wright Mills, *The Causes of World War Three* (New York: Simon & Schuster, 1958), pp. 83–84.

15. Jay N. Varon, "A Reexamination of the Law Enforcement Assistance Administration," *Stanford Law Review* 27, no. 5 (1975): 1304.

16. Op. cit., p. 1306.

17. Op. cit., p. 1308.

18. Smith in *LEAA Reauthorization Hearings before the Subcommittee on Crime,* HR 96th Congress, February-March 1979, Washington, DC, pp. 10–11.

19. Clarence Kelley, *Chief of Police Department*, Kansas City, op cit., pp. 44–46.

20. Frank Serpas, Director of the New Orleans Mayor of Criminal Justice Coordinating Committee, LEAA Reauthorization, op. cit., pp. 60–64; also 46, 61 and 590; Jeanne Vogt was the anti-crime program director for juvenile delinquency in Detroit, op. cit., *LEAA Reauthorization*, pp. 173–175.

21. Varon, op. cit., pp. 1310–1312.

22. Jefferey Schwartz's testimony before the HR Subcommittee on Crime and LEAA Reauthorization, John Conyers, Chairman presiding, 27 February 1979, pp. 602–604.

23. Serpas, op. cit., p. 591.

24. Kofi B. Hadjor, *Another America: The Politics of Race & Blame* (Boston: South End Press, 1995, pp. 95–96 and 101.

25. Charles Tilly, "War-Making and State-Making of Organized Crime," in Peter Evans, Dietrich Ruesch Hemeyer and Theda Skoepel (Eds.), *Bringing the State Back In* (Cambridge: Cambridge UP, 1985), p. 181; and Tony Payan, *A War That Cannot be Won* (Boston: Atlantic Press, 2013).

26. Paul Butler, *Chokehold, Policing Black Men* (New York: New Press, 2018), p. 4; Max Lerner, *America as a Civilization* (New York: Simon & Schuster, 1957), p. 32; Alan Elsner, *Courts of Injustice: The Crisis in American Prisons* (Saddle River: Prentice-Hall, 2004), p. 20; Leif R. Rosenberger, *America's Drug War Debacle* (Brookfield: Ashgate, 1996), pp. 26–27; especially the remarks from John Conyers (HR D-Mi), *Oversight Hearing Before a Subcommittee on the Judiciary and Crime* (Washington DC: USGPO, 97th Congress, session 10–11 and 18 June 1981), p. 542, 544, 556; and Joseph D. Davey, *The Politics of Prison Expansion-Winning Elections by Waging War on Crime* (Westport: Praeger, 1998), p. 109.

27. See Conyers, op. cit. pp. 574 and 581; Joachim J. Savelsberg, "Knowledge, Domination and Criminal Punishment," *The American Journal of Sociology* 19 (1994): 934–935.

28. Conyers, op. cit.

29. Hadjor, op. cit., p. 101.

30. Daniel P. Moynihan, *Maximum Possible Misunderstanding* (New York: Free Press, 1969), pp. 69–70. Adam Walinsky called the various LEAA funded community action administrators "abominable." See his review of Moynihan's book, *New York Times*, 2 February 1969, p. 34.

31. Schwartz, op. cit., p. 600.

32. Ann F. Ginger, expert on human rights law, political activist, and lawyer/professor at many important law schools (esp. Hastings Law School in San Francisco). See her *The Relevant Lawyers: Conversations out of Court on Their Clients, Their Practice, Their Politics and Their Lifestyle* (New York: Simon & Schuster, 1972). She also gave testimony to Congressional hearings into LEAA reauthorization in 1981.

33. Roger Boardman, "The New Negro Mood," *Fortune Magazine*, June 1968, p. 33.

34. John Hagan, *Who are the Criminals? The Politics of Crime Policy from the Age of Roosevelt to the Age of Reagan* (Princeton: Princeton UP, 2010), p. 265.

35. Roscoe Pound and Felix Frankfurter, *Politics and Criminal Prosecution* (New York: Minton Balch, 1922), p. 143, 145, 155, 166 and 245 for the Moley observation.

36. A broad overview of these negative changes was reported by Ed Chung, Betsy Pearl, and Lea Hunter, *The 1994 Crime Bill Continues to Undercut Justice Reform— Here's How to Stop It* (Washington, DC: The Sentencing Project, 20 March 2019), pp. 2–5. Another view come from Jessica Lussenhup, *BBC News Magazine*, 18 April 2016; and Jenni Gainsborough and Marc Mauer (Washington, DC: The Sentencing Project, September 2000), pp. 2–5.

37. Amos N. Wilson (New York: Africa World Infosystems, 1990), p. 180; *The New York Times*, AP, 8 August 1997, Section A, p. 14 and Louis Jankowski, *Bureau of Justice Bulletin on Probation and Parole* (Washington, DC: U. S. Department of Justice, 1990), pp. 1–2.

38. Mathea Falco, *Drugs and Crime Across America: Police Chiefs Speak Out, National Survey among Chiefs of Police* (Washington, DC: Peter Hart Research, December, 2004), p. 1; crime figures from disastercenter.com/crime/uscrime.html.

39. Michael Tonry, *Malign Neglect, Race, Crime and Punishment in America* (New York: Oxford UP, 1995), p. 4, 7, 44, 79, 81 and 123.

40. John Ehrlichman to Dan Baum, reporter for Harper's Magazine, September 1994 in Baum's "Legalize it All."

Chapter 3

Just for That, I'm Gonna
Smash Your Face In

Prominent entry into the CJS War Crimes Hall of Fame must begin with the nation's 18,000 police departments and 400,000 cops (in 1970) all of whom were capable of great mischief—especially those in the large urban centers. Police brutality and war crimes didn't begin yesterday. Marilyn S. Johnson's book, *Street Justice* (2003), traces the stunning history of police brutality in New York City from 1865 to the present and claims, despite changing forms and tactics, "victims of police violence have remained remarkably similar and more often than not they have been minorities."[1] Social scientist Albert Reiss repeats a former New York Police Commissioner Frank Moss', no less, following words made in 1903:

> For three years, there has been through the Courts and the streets a dreary procession of citizens with broken heads and bruised bodies against few of whom was violence needed to effect an arrest. Many of them had done nothing to deserve an arrest. In a majority of such cases no complaint was made. If the victim complained, his case is generally dismissed. The police are practically above the law.

Reiss then goes on in ten pages to highlight some examples of police brutality then occurred in 1968.[2]

The first official documentation of police excesses and other proto war crimes was uncovered by the president-appointed Wickersham Commission of 1927–1931. Their finalized report established the police as the first line of offensive behavior which being conducted on a massive scale. As the report disclosed "the prevailing interrogation of the 1920s and 1930s included the application of the rubber hose to the back of the pit of the stomach with a telephone book on the side of the victim's head. These techniques did not

69

stem the tide of crime nor did the use of illegally seized evidence which most state courts permitted as late as the 1950s."[3]

It took a British criminologist, Ian Loader, to remind us

> Police brutality and killing are part of the Black American experience. So too is the legal impunity, and White denial or endorsement, that attends and facilitates these killings. It is a rare event indeed for a police officer to be prosecuted, still less convicted for violating Black bodies.

To Arthur P. Davis, influential Black author and academic, writing in the *Journal of Negro Education*, "the Negro" as seen by police "was never an individual. He was a threat, or an animal, or a curse or a blight or a joke."[4]

Such brutality and endless war crimes did not go unnoticed or uncriticized by Black urban residents. The final chapter of this study includes a recent survey taken of Black eye-witnesses of the 1960s and 1970s and the failing grade they assign police for their tyrannical behavior toward residents of these years.

Of course, the commission of a crime is often the starting point for the relationship between police and the Black citizen. But not all crime is seen in the same way by all parties. For police the transgression of an act is straight forward and they act accordingly. For many Black people of this era, what is or is not a crime is not that easy to define. And being unable to define it in moral or legal terms that would satisfy a cop make any possible violation a matter of heated debate. Black psychologists make it clear,

> The Black man can never quite respect laws which have no respect for him . . . to break (the White man's law) may be inconvenient if one is caught and punished but it can never have the moral consequences involved in breaking one's own law . . . committing a crime may be a normal device to survive in America.[5]

Even the act of breaking the law fails to entitle a cop to use brutalizing and criminal tactics to subdue a suspect, effect an arrest, or apply personal interpretation of justice to a would-be offender. Fear of such reprisals often causes confrontations with cops to even escalate, as Grier and Cobbs note:

> White Americans (which includes cops) are born into a culture which contains the hatred of Blacks as an integral part . . . (consequently) we submit that it is necessary for a Black man in America to develop a profound distrust of his White fellow citizens . . . He must be on guard to protect himself against physical hurt . . . cheating, slander, humiliation and outright mistreatment by the official representatives of society . . . for his own survival he must develop a cultural paranoia in which every White man is a potential enemy unless proved

otherwise and every social system is set against him unless he personally finds out differently.[6]

This outlook is reinforced by the "them versus us outlook":

A major fear of sophisticated city police chiefs is that contact between ghetto residents and the nation's urban 200,000 policemen has become so abrasive that only force will "keep the peace." It should be pointed out for reformers that fewer than 25% of U.S. cops have finished high school and only four States currently demand much training in police academies. Most police education is taken up in such basics as judo exercises, small arms training and learning how to write tickets.[7]

It is left up to this chapter to discuss a seemingly endless series of police war crimes against African Americans in violation of all existing constitutional and human rights. These objectionable acts were mainly avoidable and unnecessary except to maintain an image of White male superiority, bring pain to hated Blacks, and maliciously thwart civil rights' demands for social justice and economic equality. This study highlights millions of big and little war crimes by police throughout the country committed without real validation other than to disarm, disfigure, or disparage Black citizens. They often led to serious injury, death, or arrest where a man's future was often in the balance. Worse, the hidden iceberg was that the vast majority of crimes were unreported, unverified, and undocumented and, needless to add, went unrepentant. We shall never know the full amount. Only one's imagination can set the limits but it can be presumed they are cosmic.

A chapter such as this one cannot begin to catalog the bestial crimes committed by the nation's police. The best one can do is highlight this continuously nasty behavior for what it was—personal, vindictive, and criminal. Cops knew their victims. They spent years working in neighborhoods where they came to know the men they would occasionally brutalize, injure, arrest, maybe even kill. We remain wondering how many millions of Black citizens had their lives shortened, ruined, and diminished by police who showed little concern about the impact of their arrests on victims forevermore spoiled by such arbitrary injustices.

The Jim Crow system of segregation in the South before 1965 not only relegated Blacks to servile status for whom all rights were restricted; it also denied them adequate government protection from the racial violence used to sustain this caste system. Black codes, racist legislation, and government unwillingness to protect Black families from approaching racial violence allowed members of the many White superiority groups (especially the Ku Klux Klan) to pursue a racist regime of public violence with impunity. Since local officials were uninterested in prosecuting White violence on the Black community, police officers could also avoid culpability as they too abused the civil rights of Black residents.[8]

In the early years of the Civil Rights Division, few convictions of police criminality took place as former Attorney General for Civil Rights Burke Marshall recalled "The problem of police misconduct was totally beyond reach because of little resources, no local cooperation and total exclusion of minorities from juries."[9]

We are discussing war crimes committed during the nation's War on Crime after 1964 with the full acceptance of Democratic president L. B. Johnson. We include the full gamut of illegal and dangerous police behaviors what some called "creative apprehensions": torture for contrived confessions, evidence planting, ignoring due process, false arrest and detention, intimidation, sadistic physical harm, abusive psychological damage, overcharging felonies, wanton disregard of family members during the process of stopping men (especially in front of traumatized children), sexual mayhem on Black women, brutality, general assault and battery, and, of course, inexcusable murder. In this era of alleged civil rights, police were a veritable war crime-producing machine. "If I didn't plant evidence sometimes, I wouldn't be making very many cases against some bad characters and sometimes I'd arrest my informants just to help my quota," one cop recalled.[10]

In 1996 William A. Geller and Hans Toch, old hands on the subject of police violence, assembled twenty contributors in fourteen academic essays (ten of the twenty were professional criminologists, only one was representative of a police agency who continued police tradition by refusing to see the subject as a major attack on human rights and values). Geller and Toch tabulated an impressive bibliography on the subject, totaling 852 references on police violence since 1952 in 328 pages of tortured insights into the subject. Of the 852 references only 26% dated from the 1970s, a mere 7% from 1952 to 1969 when police brutality was arguably at its worst at under no scrutiny of any kind. Sixty percent were written between 1983 and 1995 when the book was published. Not that the 852 references really made a dent in the investigations and reports on the subject, what it did seem to do is provide an epidemic of interest for sociologists and criminologists to develop CJS theories and studies which in initial form were submitted to government agencies responsible for law enforcement policies and reforms, seeking funding that helped assure a good life as long as the reports didn't criticize the agencies for failures or cite individuals responsible for the obvious failures present throughout the CJS. Moreover, many researchers were catapulted into the role of "expert" on the subject, hosting conferences and seminars, participating in collaborative efforts on some law enforcement subjects, and being available for questions by local television stations looking for the pithy remark on the day's news of crime and violence.[11]

By 1995, whether from the writings of these specialists or not, someone was profiting. By then Toch had published ten books on the subject of crime and violence, T. Tyler published eight, L. Sherman published eight, Reiss published nine, Geller published thirteen, Fyfe published seventeen, Bittner published eight, and D. Bayley published seven. Clearly someone was benefiting from the murderous treatment of Blacks by the CJS, but it obviously wasn't the war's victims. Nevertheless, what wisdom can we deduce from this compendium of ideas and references on police barbarism as discussed from the viewpoint of twenty "experts"? What can they tell us while hiding behind almost 900 references? Anything sobering to excuse such assaultive behavior against defenseless Blacks? I'm mindful of the glowing blurb on the rear cover of this book: "The most comprehensive examination of the subject currently available—The authors address the ramifications of excessive force including the impact on citizens." Who is the publisher kidding? None of the essays convey confidence in the research findings as applied to the problem of police violence and citizen punishment. Under sociological causes of police brutality, we get this perplexing assessment from Egon Bittner: "The role of the police is best understood as a mechanism for the distribution of non-negotiable coercive force employed in accordance with the dictates of an intuitive grasp of situational exigencies."[12]

Rothmiller and Goldman's report documents the premier police department in this era, the Los Angeles Police Department, whose excellence in unconstitutional police practices were copied by cop agencies elsewhere, including their dirty tricks with Black people, abusive methods, and out-of-control tactics used to maintain physical superiority and control in Los Angeles' Black communities. The report repeats the words of one training officer of this time: "If you want to last here, if you want to survive, if you want to make probation, all niggers are fucked, don't ever forget that!" Racism was expected and was a part of group persona and racial hatred in the LAPD was a dominating force, especially in the projects which were called "the jungle."[13]

Rothmiller and Goldman narrate a few of LAPD's tactics designed to strike fear and terror in the hearts of victims they were supposed to be protecting.

"If you don't like someone's looks, pull him over . . . you can always find probable cause . . . follow anyone for a block and he's sure to commit an infraction"; "Lying on arrest reports was routine . . . cops decide for themselves who was guilty and then weave a spell over the arrest report to make it match their perceptions—most of the arrest reports were doctored in some way—facts deleted or invented, it wasn't exactly frontier justice or a lynch mob, but it wasn't justice either."[14] "The more proficient the officer, the more sophisticated became his false accounts. Clearly, defense attorneys could rarely shake the testimony of a polite, earnest, diligent lying cop"; and finally, "Officers believed extra-legal procedures were necessary to counter all those constitutional rights guaranteed to the enemy."[15]

The book is filled with examples of war crime and draconian abuses no civilized society should tolerate:

> There were no video cameras so cops routinely beat defendants senseless if they chose to run; duct tape over the mouth if a noisy suspect and hold his nose just long enough to make him think he was dying; in the paddy wagon grind the defendant into a floor mat, brake sharply and see him go flying, spray mace into a suspect's car a/c vents which could make a person miserable all the while the cops laughed; moderate whippings are common, dangle his ankles from the edge of buildings; fill a suspect's mouth with shit and then gag him for several hours—but most of all: never rat on another cop no matter how sadistic or nasty: a whistleblower would be snuffed out before he got his lips puckered.[16]

The authors bring up the infamous chokehold and its use:

> Drag the suspect around, knee him in the back and kidneys before applying the chokehold which they claimed guaranteed the death of Black defendants. This common practice was made much easier because "the brass looked the other way and at worst encouraged so street justice was meted out daily."[17]

Speaking of police-caused homicides (i.e., shooting in the back from suspects fleeing for their lives) was numerous and Black men from every social background were liable to this undocumented practice. How many died in this manner from police brutality each year? Official data on the number of Black men killed by police for this era turns out to be remarkably unreliable and unacceptable. We simply don't have data as police hardly bothered to file it. FBI Director James Comey in 2016 helps us in this regard with his comments about citizens murdered by depraved police:

> Agencies have data about who went to a movie last weekend or how many books were sold or how many cases of the flu walked into an emergency room but I cannot tell you how many people were shot by police in the United States last month, last year or anything about the demographics . . . our leading sources of information are newspapers and that's a very bad place to be.[18]

Journalist Kimberly Kindy gives some idea of the proportions when she claims "Blacks are shot and killed at a rate 2.5 times higher than for Whites.

Blacks are 13% of the population but up to 30% of people killed by police (and that's just for those victims documented)." Added to this point is Harvard University economist Roland Fryer whose study of poor Blacks concludes: "African Americans and Hispanics are substantially more likely to experience force in their interaction with police like having a gun pointed at them, being handcuffed without an arrest, pepper sprayed, tasered, hit with a baton."[19]

In 1973, Paul Takagi first raised the subject of police killings of civilians in the first issue of *Crime & Social Justice*. He examined the deaths of males over ten years old killed by the police from 1950 to 1972 and noted the dramatic increase of Blacks causing deaths by the police between 1962 and 1969, a time of turbulent civil unrest and civilian militancy. The report indicated "The death rate for Blacks was found to be consistently from nine to thirteen times higher than for Whites for this period . . . (yet) police killings of civilians (especially Black men) received virtually no attention, except in the early studies by Robin (1963) and Knoohuizen, et al. (1972)."[20] Knoohuizen's detailed case-by-case study of two years of police killings in Chicago found that fully 33% occurred under questionable circumstances and indicated serious violations of the criminal law and police department regulations. Kobler reported that a similar percentage of civilians killed were not involved in any criminal activity, 27% were engaged in low-level property crimes, and 20% were killed during the commission of some vague domestic disturbance. Police misuse of firearms, indifference to life, and unjustifiable killings were difficult concepts to sneak into the police reports and were not discussed. Takagi's major thrust came in the middle of their report on police killings:

> The management of police violence has to be understood in the context of a police system that is often unreliable and disorganized despite the massive infusion of federal monies. Rank and file patrolmen have consistently resisted innovations (i.e., reallocation of jobs, changing work hours and shifts during high crime hours), the civilianization of police work and the introduction of new computerized command and control technology. Yet the failure of police to deal effectively with crime and their record of wanton brutality during the rebellions of the 1960s have brought them under serious criticism . . . from liberal reformers.[21]

Getting insider information from an ex-cop lends credence to tales of police war crimes. San Diego police officer Norm Stamper opens up a curious line of inquiry with his talk of police "misdemeanor murders" of the 1960s and 1970s. This was police lingo for an officer murdering a Black citizen for which the code was NHI—no human involved—and police batons were called "nigger knockers."[22] Stamper notes cop talk of the time was filled with creative ethnic slurs which he claims were used by 95% of the police force he knew: "niggers, boys, slibs, toads, coons, garboons, groids, sambos, buckwheat rastuses, jigaboos, jungle bunnies, spooks." For those who knew, 11–13 was code for injuring an animal or a Black person. An arrest charge could also be written: "BBN, busy being a nigger."[23] The extent and viciousness of such terms say something about police disrespect for the Black communities they were paid to respect and protect. Stamper estimates 71% of the dysfunctional police with whom he came in contact admitted to using excessive force when they felt so compelled. He estimated this at a minimum three to four times a month, possibly as high as two to three times per officer weekly. His view was that one in four do it on a regular basis, as many as half on "special occasions" such as if the officer was having a bad hair day or had previously had a fight with his wife.[24]

During the 1970s and 1980s, Stamper goes on, even minor verbal encounters with enraged citizens refusing compliance might merit physical punishment for any officer possessing a sadistic streak slam the defendant against a wall or car, ratchet down on handcuffs where blood could be choked off from the hands, twist arms, knee the subject in his nuts (with or without his pants removed), shove a baton up a man's anus or use it for beating his head. None of these or a gallery of similar brutalities required much exertion and could provide satisfaction to those cops with dangerous streaks of psychopathy.

Ex LAPD cop and author Joseph Wambaugh adds his own insights into police use of excessive force around Black suspects.

> Go easy with that grip. You can cause brain damage with that hold for too long a period, you stop the flow of blood to the brain even kill somebody. Never use your fists if someone uses his fists, you use your stick and try to break a wrist or knee like we teach you; if he uses a knife you use a gun and cancel his ticket then and there.[25]

Police made fun and mocked mentally ill persons they encountered in Black neighborhoods, they sang racist songs to those they arrested, goading young Black men to take a swing at them so they can make a clean improved arrest, roust someone by using racial slurs even to the few Black cops in the department or, especially to White women found in the company of Black men. Think of all the fun they could have in incidents such as these. Such was the fun time experienced by those cops who saw this as tension releases while patrolling inner Black ghettoes.[26]

In addition, cops would hassle "targets of opportunity," gays, hookers, pimps, johns whenever they felt the urge and could make life miserable for those groups depending on how far cops wanted to take any single encounter with these street people. I myself have witnessed numerous examples of such

barbarity as cops actively went looking for these people when I was a probation officer in South Central Los Angeles (especially on a Friday which was
when people in the area got paid and proceeded to indulge in whatever fun
they could select). Or they would seek places where youths congregated to
agitate and act as unnecessary disciplinarians. They were deeply hated.

Drugs offered amusing satisfaction for zealous cops: door could be kicked
in, people could be chased around their home or neighborhood, furniture was
often busted searching for evidence, apartments torn apart, people forced to
lie on the ground or floor for lengthy periods of time while police snooped
around often without a search warrant. They could also be pocketed by cops
for resale or consumption. Anything of value in a home be searched could
be confiscated and or pocketed depending on an officer's own sense of greed
and booty. It was a glorious time for grabbing. No judges, district attorneys, media people, or academics would believe such graft but I was there
in 1969–1971 and witnessed some of these misdeeds by the various police
departments I came to work with as a probation officer.

The atmosphere between Blacks and White cops at the time was rife for the
occurrence of war crimes. Stamper believed,

> White cops were afraid of most Black men and became panicky, rude and
> impulsive. Such reactions were dangerous to accompanying police as the shaky
> ones might escalate a situation that involved all nearby cops in bouts of exces-
> sive violence and the predictable cover-up.

Wambaugh concurred:

> Gus watched a young negro strutting across Jefferson Boulevard and he studied
> the swaying, limber shoulder movement, bent-elbowed free swinging arms and
> the rubber kneed big stepping bounce and as Kilvinsky remarked he's walkin'
> smart . . . Gus realized how profoundly ignorant he was about negroes . . . he
> wondered how he would fare if the two of them were face to face in a police-
> suspect confrontation and he had no partner . . . and the young negro was not
> impressed with his glittering golden shield and suit of blue. He cursed himself
> again for the insidious fear and he vowed he would master it but . . . still the fear
> came or rather the promise of fear, the nervous growling stomach, the clammy
> hands, the leathery mouth, but enough to make him suspect that when the time
> came, he would not behave like a policeman.[27]

Who knew the whirlwind that would be created after numerous fascist politicians, criminal justice administrators, police chiefs, even presidents spoke
of the breakdown of law and order and pillagers running wild in the streets of
urban America after 1964? Like manna to police, such statements unleashed

the fury of police vindictiveness against Black demands for equality and justice and migrations from the South to the Far West and Northeast cities. Once
President Nixon legalized no-knock raids for all law enforcement agencies in
1973 as part of an omnibus drug bill, and Ronald Reagan launched the War
on Drugs in 1982, police departments became largely unaccountable paramilitary forces. The War on Drugs led to the signing of the Military Cooperation
with Law Enforcement Agencies Act, in which the military trained and joined
forces with local police to stop the flow of drugs into the country. Next, the
Comprehensive Crime Control Act of 1984 allowed for any local police
department cooperating with federal agencies to take a cut of seized assets in
drug raids. Then, in 1988, the floodgates opened with the Anti-Drug Abuse
Act, which enabled police departments that proved successful at drug raids to
become eligible for billions of dollars in federal government grants to procure
new weapons and equipment. It was a glorious period for war-minded police
chiefs and the game was on!

The result was a hapless Black population caught up in a CJS awakened
to the threat promulgated by these racist statements. Aided by legislatively
designed antidrug laws, the result was police on the lurch in Black neighborhoods focusing on mass arrests to stem the tide of Black resistance.
Wambaugh had his own take on how police saw this trend:

> It's all happening here . . . this civil rights business and Black Muslims and all
> are just a start of it. Authority is being challenged and Negroes are at the front
> . . . Black people were only the spearhead of a bigger attack on authority and
> law. That was surely coming in the next ten years.[28]

Presidents offered their own brand of encouragement to hate groups. A student of the Reagan years, William Kleinknecht, wrote:

> Reagan made appeals to bigotry and race . . . there was never any doubt that this
> was a deliberate strategy. His first speech after the 1980 Republican Convention
> on State's Rights was made in Philadelphia, Mississippi, where 1964 murders
> of three civil rights workers had taken place, and he had audaciously used a
> Southern strategy (of likening black demands to criminal behavior) as a wedge
> issue became an enduring GOP tactic.[29]

One statistic leaps out at us. According to the Department of Justice, for the
1980s alone, a strongly reactionary period of the Reagan years, there were
recorded almost 100 million arrests of which half were bogus and led to no
charges being filed—simply harassment and opportunities for police to rough
up and intimidate citizens. If we assume a factor of three simple stops and
harassments per Black American urban resident per annum, disregarding the

many numerical possibilities for displays of brutality by police and injury of citizens, we are looking at a possible total over these thirty-year period of maybe 180–250 million arrests! Can anyone imagine what this must do to Black family life, relationships, ghetto development, and future lives of men so continually harassed?

Uniform Crime Reports of the period were exercised in futility and surprise. They had limited utility as a tool for scholars much less statisticians. Their accuracy was constantly challenged and each report was replete with errors. They simply couldn't really be used to make broad generalizations on where the whole world of crime fighting was headed. Seedman commented:

> The UCR was a summation of a series of local responses to partisan issues and highly misleading for what they are said to measure. The UCR is useless as a tool for evaluating social policy . . . and unlike social scientists, police administration never sought purity in crime statistics but used them simply for deployment of officers.[30]

Drug arrests were often fabricated, evidence planted (as well as the use of drop guns in cases where shootings occurred). Stamper notes how dozens and dozens of men and boys were put behind bars by a single cop, spread over many months. "There isn't an unscathed police department in the country where drug scandals regularly prevailed and where cops protected drug shipments and extorted dealers besides arresting those who wouldn't comply with extortion." With regard to making such arrests, Stamper notes some police have "hot pens." They can write four tickets in the time an average cop completes one, known as "daily padding" and "creative arrest shakedowns."[31]

War crimes were enacted in staggering numbers during this period. Let's just consider relatively mild but negative police encounters. Assume an eighteen-year-old Black man. It was very conceivable he could be simply hassled, stopped, rebuked, or interrogated for even a trivial offense, much less something truly suspicious on the basis of twice a week (far more if he has no adequate identification papers). Not an outrageous claim considering the outdoor street nature and social ability of some of these men. This totals perhaps eight times a month (without any escalations) infrequent but guaranteed contacts with the police who often bother anyone they take a dislike toward (for no particular reason). This represents 100 contacts, all mild, although you never know, per year. You total the numbers: 100 annually over a 30-year period make 3,000 routine and conceivable stops. If the nearly 8 million urban Black men over age 14 were subject to simple harassment, this totals possibly 2 million such occurrences between 1960 and 1990!! This does not take into account the stops that go awry, get out of control, escalate into confrontations, and use of force or worse. Probably

larger figures when one considers increased rates of stop and frisk in the
Deep South and additional stops and challenges with young Black women
of the same age cohort.

Besides the many brutal, racist, and rude things White cops said or did to
Black men, even worse reports arise of sexual predators in uniform which
Stamper records in his chapter 11 of the mild-mannered San Diego Police
Department. He calculates 5% of the force fondled women prisoners, made
bogus traffic stops on women in all sorts of sexually motivated situations.
Cop traded freedom to arrest Black men or women who were willing to
perform sexual services and favors to these police. Some women were even
required to expose themselves or worse to satisfy lascivious cops. In all this,
he says, there was a "general unwillingness of police department officials
everywhere to acknowledge these sexual mischief makers in their midst" and
who did little to nothing to expose these war crimes for what they were.[32]
Incompetence, lack of accountability, favoritism, and silence in the case of
civil rights abuses with police well-distanced from community discussions,
contacts, or complaints on the many human rights abuses that inevitably arose
when such police behavior was tolerated by those at the top of the police
ladder.[33]

William R. Burwell wrote his 1983 PhD dissertation for the Illinois
Institute of Technology on authoritarianism as it led to police brutality,
here a war crime. In his 87 pages which covered the period between 1978
and 1982, he discovered 124 Illinois policemen who had been charged with
excessive brutality. Unlike most researchers doing academic work on police
brutality, this writer has a seventeen-year career as a police officer in the
city of Chicago. From his original cohort, Burwell studied ninety-two cops
to learn what he could about their attitudes toward force and authoritarianism. A reluctant 35% of the original survey responded to his mailed material
(suggesting suspicion and resistance by police officers to academic surveys).
As a cop himself, Burwell speculated as a trusted fellow officer, his status
probably helped the return rate.[34]

Results? Burwell pointed to local social and national political events creating frustrations for these Chicago cops. Offered as an excuse, they explained
the war crimes acceptance of police whose behavior was conditioned by
challenges to local conservative politics as well as encouragement from top
department officials of bad police behavior toward Black citizens protesting
social and economic injustices of everyday life. The result was constant confrontations with short-tempered police of the city frustrated by the many challenges to the authority itself.[35] Burwell is direct: "It is the author's contention
that all of these events (of the period), working alone and together, created an
atmosphere where beliefs in external aggressive control by police were the
norm rather than the exception."[36]

He estimated 40% of police studied felt constrained by legal restrictions and loss of control in the streets. These he tied to violent behavior and excessive force that helped overcome the perceived impotency of cops in traditional ghetto situations. "I suspect that police are more likely to respond with excessive force when they define the situation as one where there remains a question as to who is in charge."[37]

Another problem for his study was that the Chicago Police Department in the 1970s and earlier used few, if any, psychological measures for personality assessment. Who knew how many police brutes and sadists, plus those war veterans hired with Vietnam combat experience, were singled out and rejected in the early stages of recruitment? Lawyer Johnnie Cochran claimed the LAPD went out of their way to hire a large number of military veterans with combat experience and marines over the years as a buffer against Black citizens.[38] A major failing and difficulty of all police brutality surveys is discussed by Burwell at the end of his study and is worth quoting at length:

> The inability of this writer to examine the files of the police department could be considered a research limitation. Without access to the files, particular situations and forms of aggression could not be identified. A researcher needs to be able to differentiate between instrumental aggression and aggressive drive. Instrumental aggression is conceptualized as aggression that is necessary to effect an arrest (and this is also subject to severe limitations), not an end goal. Aggressive drive relates to aggression with the goal of harming another individual. The ability to differentiate between these two disparate forms of aggression could eliminate a considerable amount of confounding variance. A related limitation of this study was the lack of descriptive detail on the subjects. Data on race, ethnic background and previous disciplinary history also could have reduced the amount of confounding variance. These questions were not asked because it was believed they would reduce an already low response rate.[39]

Westley (in one of the earliest studies of violence and the police) found that for one medium-sized city 37% of the cops interviewed gave "disrespect of the police" as a justification for use of pain-producing force, an opinion that outranked all others.[40] McNamara tested New York City police and found that 39% agreed "some force is necessary and justified when a citizen insults and curses at a police officer."[41] In the late 1960s and early 1970s, a common theme in law enforcement research was study of the police personality and in particular the authoritarian personality capable of producing wanton police brutality.[42]

An obvious explanation that reinforces the term of war crime behavior was grounded in the use of arrest powers. One body of research has consistently shown that arrest and use of deadly force were more likely if the suspect became either antagonistic, disrespectful, or Black, all three combined meant Bingo! "Minorities are more likely to be the objects of police deadly force merely because of their race."[43] According to Worden, the LAPD rewards officers for hardnosed enforcement that is likely to produce arrests and often bring the police into conflict with citizens. In essence police departments fail to discourage the improper use of force, while complaints are ignored and sanctions imposed on cops accused of using excessive force is so slight the message comes through such behavior is of no real concern to higher ups. Hence organizational forces in the LAPD tend to reinforce each other in producing an aggressive style of policing and an elevated probability of the use of force. Worden suggests the psychological theories of police brutality center on the authoritarian personality as originally discussed by Adorno, et al. in 1950.

Was it any wonder such practices and war crimes prevailed against Black citizens when an article from the *Police Chief* expressed benign attitudes toward police brutality by police administrators in the 1960s? Here the International Association of Chiefs of Police's executive director went on record with the following influential comment:

> I know of no period in recent history where the police have been the subject of so many unjustified charges of brutality and harassment and ineptness . . . (I decry) these baseless charges of police brutality made to cover excesses and illegal conduct on the part of some demonstrators involved in the current racial tensions . . . as well as the excesses of "hoodlums" who falsely fly the banner of civil rights.[44]

The same theme was echoed by another IACP official who described police brutality as a "commonplace and almost automatic accusation attached to any physical action taken by a cop to control disorder and, alternatively, as a battle cry . . . used by supposedly responsible Negro leaders to whip up support among their followers." *US News & World Report* listed Supreme Court rulings, civil rights pressures, and cries of police brutality as "signs of an impending breakdown in law and order throughout the nation."[45] At the time, it should be pointed out that a 1974 survey on race relations found that only 4% of law enforcement officers were minority and less than 2% were women cops.[46]

In 1976 a college professor named Nicholas Alex was granted clearance to interview dozens of NYPD officers as part of a survey of views within the department. Anonymity was promised so some cops talked their heads off, many wishing for the great old days when restrictions on police were slight. Many began discussing subjects like corruption but soon wound up talking about race. One quote is notable for its being a commonly held view:

Blacks have more rights than they ever had and they want more. The don't want to be equal to whites they want to be superior to whites! They want reverse position with whites, that's not all they want, they are a different breed of people . . . they have no family life . . . no one is supervising them. They want to do things for kicks and they want more and they don't want to work as its easier to steal. They love to commit crime . . . they love to stick a knife into you, they are ruthless people.[47]

Then there was this view:

Police officers not only believe that most crimes were committed by Blacks but also that any attempt to solve Black violence and crime must come from police repression of Blacks rather than from attempts to solve the economic, social and racial problems facing many Blacks.[48]

Robin cites several distinguishing features of the "working personality" of the police in ghetto neighborhoods: always be alert for danger, view everyone as suspects especially Blacks, treat minorities as "symbolic assailants" and remember that any encounters with them will always spill over into violence and jeopardize a policeman's safety. Remember, too, look upon young Black males as the biggest threat to cop safety. Order and control will result in restraining freedom of action and physical dominance, if you wish to enforce civility toward cops.[49] Police subculture of the 1960s can easily be summarized as punitiveness, aggressiveness, cynicism, and inflexibility characterized by clannishness and aloofness from outsiders, an exaggerated concern for authority, a code of secrecy concerning internal operating procedures and job-coping techniques, reflexive willingness to come to aid of officers, and distrust for all but their own kind. Of course, all of this will inevitably lead to heightened danger, social isolation, and, when in doubt, a fall back to a strict authority role.[50]

Robin recalls the case of a criminology professor he knew who quit the campus scene to become a cop. Overnight, this person started to become punitive toward those he earlier excused, also cynical of people generally, racist as seeing Blacks as natural-born criminals, against rehab, skeptical of constitutional rights of defendants, pro-death penalty, frustrated over any laws in court which spoke to leniency. In short, the police subculture had overwhelmed his previously liberal academic personality and substituted it with a steel-jawed oppressor of minorities.[51]

War crimes from overzealous police was countenanced by those at the top whose own racist bias had begun thirty years earlier, when they were rookie officers, coming at the height of the Jim Crow era. Episodic examples of war crimes against Black citizens in this period is through department policies established which paid little concern for Black rights and interests. In 1960 in Detroit, there were 136,000 arrests on "suspicion" with no specific charges. One in every three arrests in Detroit between 1947 and 1956 was "under investigation" while arrests "stopped for investigation" was often found on police reports. Between 1960 and 1961 only 57% of those Black men arrested were ever charged with a crime and the vast majority of cases were tossed out of court. Robin notes that "at present (1950), too few police departments have meaningful policies, standards and criteria for controlling field discretion. Police chiefs who issue policies along these lines are unfortunately in a slim minority."[52] Police officials were reluctant, as were the politicians, to formally acknowledge patrol officer's bad conduct without witnesses as prompting war crimes. Top brass ignored such behavior, or refused to believe it, assumed no responsibility, produced no written guidelines, created no monitoring system, and rejected the idea of punishing wayward cops—time-consuming tasks not without departmental risks to police morale, officer reprisal, and public reaction which can never be adequately gauged.

Ed Cray brings to our attention in 332 pages his belief that "hatred of police fueled the urban disasters of the 1960s." Continuous brutality of psychotic cops escalated mob scenes into mass violence during the time of continuous civil rights demonstrations and political dissent. With an army of 200,000 law enforcement officers in 3,100 jurisdictions, the end result of constant confrontations was 4–5 million arrests per year (even without considering the injuries and homicides). "Police will themselves violate the law over one million times while making these arrests," Cray concludes. "Yes," he says, "police brutality was as common as the next arrest . . . it was an institutional pattern."[53]

Most of the cops used totally unnecessary violence with a noticeable lack of restraint. This helped define such actions as war crimes. Many just displayed police racism at its worse: in at least 25% of the felony arrests, no charges were ever filed for lack of decent evidence although a man's life might have been altered for the worse by the thuggish experience. Illegal searches prevailed as harassments, rousts, arbitrary detention before eventual release can all be seen as war crimes and never recompensed for lost wages or damaged personal property or punished by senior officers who chose to always look away. In 1964 the NYT polled Harlem residents where 43% believed police brutality was part of an arrest, 85% said likewise in a Detroit Urban League study. In a 1966 survey, 66% of young Black men in Watts had witnessed some form of police violence against community residents. In Boston, a study claimed "up to 25% of Black men are roughed up during arrest procedures" while in New Orleans a study found "at least 18%."[54] In all these cases and the many more unreported, human lives and rights were being sacrificed by zealous, White nationalist-inspired cops who should have known how these actions would lead to grave consequences for citizens the remainder of their lives. Cray and other colleagues studied such police behavior as it existed in the Black ghettoes of the North. Little is known of police treatment in the Southern States where rural violence against Black communities was viral. Police and CJS mismanagement went too far and war crimes flourished on a pace directly related to how local White cops and their supervisors, and the local courts, saw the development of Black resistance and demand for equal treatment in an era of mass civil rights protest.

WARRIOR WHITE NATIONALIST COP

The concept of the "warrior" cop in the guise of SWAT teams was synonymous with war crimes. The very brutal nature and violence against weak often unsuspecting and innocent victims were legion. The idea of brutish and pugnacious photos of SWAT teams bunched together with weapons at the ready musters-up images of supposed heroic military-style assaults on houses thought to contain terrorists or drug inventory. Here a high level of destructive police behavior was not only intended and expected but encouraged by CJS officials. Activities included the use of battering rams, wrongful entries, theft by police of anything desirable found during the raid, enforcing "no-knock" intrusions, verbally and physically abrasive crowd control tactics, and general mayhem conducted during the raid leaving a targeted house in chaos and people dazed and bewildered without adequate legal representation.

SWAT was begun as an antidote by the LAPD for urban riots like those experienced in the Watts riot in Los Angeles in 1965 (and hundreds of others that followed over the next two years), where thirty-six mainly Black unarmed citizens were murdered by frightened White cops in South Central. Since their implementation, the public and media have come to expect sudden unannounced nightmare raids blasting hundreds of canisters of tear gas, blowing up or battering front doors by an army breaching private homes as if in a Vietnam war zone, detonating flash-bang grenades, screaming unnaturally for surrender, destroying property in every room, arresting everyone in sight (as a notorious drug seller or not) all frenzied behavior in a climate of constructed and orchestrated mayhem. Each incident I label a war crime in large letters for the very nature of the theatrical violence and high-risk turbulence where physical injury was part of the game in this highly tense drama as SWAT teams acted as if they were acting in a movie.

Robin reminds us that "since 1964 an emerging and controversial law enforcement tool is the use of tactical squads: elite police teams that rely on an aggressive, overtly military approach to handling exceptionally dangerous situations often provoked by the police themselves." In Philadelphia it was

100-man teams, in Watts 60, and as of 1976 there was an estimated 500–3000 SWAT teams nationwide from 2 to 160 members. "With emphasis on weaponry and toughness, their leaders claimed they knew when not to fire."[55]

Our journalist navigator in this gestapo-like atmosphere is Radley Balko, author of the "Rise of the Warrior Cop" from which much of the following information has been extracted.[56] He begins with this frightening scene:

> Today in America SWAT teams violently smash into private houses more than one hundred times per day. The vast majority of these raids are to enforce laws against consensual crimes . . . wearing "battle dress uniforms" modelled after soldiers' attire . . . they carry military grade weapons. Many SWAT teams today are trained by current and former personnel from Special Forces units . . . aggressive, swat-style tactics are now used to raid neighborhood poker games, doctor's offices, bars and restaurants, and head shops despite the fact that the targets of these raids pose little threat to anyone . . . (but) are used to apprehend people who aren't dangerous at all.[57]

Balko asked, "How did we go from a system in which laws were enforced by colonial citizens, often with non-coercive methods to one in which order is preserved by armed government agents pursuing their own agenda against citizens seen as the enemy?"[58] Collateral damage is often the result of CJS agencies who failed to see the destructiveness this causes nearby homes much less whole neighborhoods, lost home values, unplanned evictions, expensive loans required to make repairs caused by such vandalism, serious trauma to by-standers including children and women, overshadowed by the feeling the entire area is in serious decline.

By the late 1960s, the civil rights, voter registration, counterculture, and antiwar movements would be in full swing, leading governments of both parties to call repeatedly for stepped-up police presence to combat the alleged rise in violence and civilian protest against the resulting injustice and rampant numbers of war crimes. President Johnson even went so far as to call for a "War on Crime" which actually forms the basis of this study.[59] As in the case of the many Black insurrections, anti-demonstration military units, National Guard, and US troops were on the fringes of most Black ghettoes just in case order had to be imposed militarily regardless of consequences to people living there. This was the generation of White nationalist-inspired politicians and public officials who fanned and exploited White suburban fears by declaring a sort of military-inspired war on social abstractions like crime, drug use, and Black political militancy. "The resulting policies," says Balko, "made war metaphors and war zone imagery increasingly real." Even Democrats could be blamed for the resulting oppression of Black people. LBJ created the first major federal agency specifically tasked with enforcing federal drug laws.

He also established the Law Enforcement Assistance Agency that created a stream of federal funding to militarily beef up local police agencies with war mentality rhetoric and weapons previously used in combat.[60]

On July 14, 1969, President Nixon gave his first major address to Congress to outline his amplified antidrug program. He declared drugs "a national threat" and demanded aggressive, confrontational law enforcement strategies to fight drug sales and usage, not as a medical or therapeutic issue but as a particular criminal activity. Severe penalties were imposed for drug sellers through a massive budget to underwrite assertive activities of the Bureau of Narcotics and Dangerous Drugs (as part of the CJS, only too happy to secure this largesse). Scores of Special Forces were mobilized to invade any area in America thought to be a major drug/narcotic outlet dealing in drugs. If we substitute the term drug users for "enemy" then another war crimes tableau is revealed. Borrowing military terminology for a military campaign against American citizens, "he asked Congress to make funding for the agency available so it could fully deploy by 1971."[61] Average American citizens, especially if they were Black, became the focus for antidrug strong-arm tactics that enabled cops to institute brutal and excessive behavior toward people whose only crime was using drugs for recreational purposes.

Since Nixon had campaigned and staked his re-election hopes in 1972 on reducing crime, and since crime policy and police procedures were primarily local issues, he had a strong interest in seeing that the states adopt his war plans for fighting drugs. This was one reason for expanding LBJ's earlier LEAA: local police were seen as prime beneficiaries of the money and would jump at getting free military equipment in exchange for their acceptance of his war mentality that made them co-equal allies in the national fight being waged against Black militants in the guise of enemy drug dealers.

After five years of Black urban unrest against increasingly militarized local police forces, the very first SWAT team raid occurred in 1969. This was the November 1969 raid on the Los Angeles headquarters of the Black Panther Party, providing police officials a brash debut as over 250 police officers surrounded the house during a community meeting. World War II style commando raid, which I view as a war crime, was seen as a "public relations" triumph by Balko and was the principal cause of the later collapse of the BPP under the weight of thousands of war crime behavior by police in every city where they resided. It was no coincidence that FBI Director J. Edgar Hoover had made them a top priority and publicly declared that his agency was in an everyday "war on them."[62]

Law and order legislation sponsored by the Nixon administration won many victories in the 1969–1971 period. House anticrime bills were a series of war crimes legislation that Sen Sam Ervin called a "garbage pail of some of the most repressive, near-sighted, intolerant, unfair and vindictive policies he had ever encountered in politics."[63] Despite his criticisms, both parties worked long and hard in concert to develop and pass vicious anticrime policies that easily gave rise to endless police excesses in enforcement against Black residents for whom they were targeted. Senate Dem majority leader Mike Mansfield said he was so overwhelmed by these many bills he gave up trying to figure out which ones were constitutional, so he voted for all of them and "let the Courts sort it all out."[64]

A crime plan the White House developed was to launch an all-out public relations offensive to scare the hell out of the public about crime and heroin. The intention of the White House was to plant media scare stories and have the President on January 17, 1971, declare drug abuse "public enemy number one" while seeking emergency powers and new funding to wage a new, all-out offensive. A month later a poll revealed Americans named drug abuse the most urgent domestic problem facing the country. Police from various law enforcement agencies were pulled into the fray with LEAA financial inducements to persuade local law enforcement to cooperate. High profile, media-friendly arrests would occur, empty but impressive-sounding arrest statistics would appear, Nixon would tout. With the green light on, the game was afoot. This new War on Drugs put political pressure on CJS agencies, notwithstanding the resultant war crimes which emerged from this massive wave of phony baloney arrests.[65]

Between April 1972 and May 1973, the Drug Enforcement Administration strike forces had conducted almost 1,500 separate urban raids. Demonization of drug offenders soon became a big success and hardnosed paramilitary tactics and weapons as used in wartime against the Viet Cong were being employed in epic proportions against people suspected of nonviolent offenses: military-grade ammunition, AR-15 assault rifles, Kevlar helmets, tactical multi-pocketed vests, bomb-disarming robots, battle fatigues, armored trucks with rotating turrets! Civil rights and humane concerns for civilians went poof! Wrongful attacks, wild botched terroristic invasions on terrified people by gung-ho cops playing war were dismissed as "cops just trying to do their job."[66] Balko noted: "Soon just about every decent-sized police department was armed with military issue hammer and the drug war would ensure there were always plenty of nails around for pounding." Balko estimated: number of SWAT teams in 1970 first year—one; 1975—about 500! Federal narcotics agents in 1969—400, 1979—almost 2000![67]

William French set the tone for the Reagan administration early on. In 1982 one of the first cabinet meetings, the new attorney general declared "The Justice Department is not a domestic agency. It is the internal arm of the national defense." This would be a rough decade for the Third Amendment as Reagan's drug warriors dehumanized drug users and cast the fight as a biblical struggle between good and evil. In the process the nation's cops became, in Balko's words, "holy soldiers."[68] Both Nixon and Reagan had quickly come to realize the people under attack were actually political rivals. As a result, attacking and jailing them as drug addicts, ignoring pleas for treatment for those who needed it, worked to the advantage of Republicans since it gave many opponents prison records which prevented them from voting in future elections.

On April 8, 1986, Reagan signed a National Security Directive 221, which designated illicit drugs a threat to US national security. In addition to adding the drug intervention responsibilities of agencies like the CIA and the State Department, the directive also instructed the US military to "support counter-narcotics efforts more actively" including providing assistance to police agencies. In the planning and execution of large counter-narcotics operations and participating in combined exercises with civilian law enforcement agencies and helping military units conducting antidrug operations, the declaration selected marijuana, cocaine, and heroin as an enemy akin to any other whom the United States had fought in conventional wars.

There were a few other policies enacted toward the end of the Reagan years that cleared the way for mass militarization of civilian police agencies, namely a massive influx of federal money to local police departments solely for the purpose of drug policing. The money could be used to start, fund, and maintain newly formed SWAT teams, to expand in size already existing narcotics units, or to pay cops overtime for doing extra drug investigations. Add to this the potential bounty available in asset forfeiture (property seized by the government agents during drug raids) became government or individual agent property which could be used at their personal discretion! What a windfall for zealous cops in jacking up the unknown rate of war crimes committed during this period.

Police departments across the country were now heavily, even dangerously, incentivized to devote more time, personnel, and aggression to drug stuff and less to traditional crimes. There was no money in investigating crimes with actual victims. Menacing drug raids paid for themselves and were well worth pursuing. SWAT team activities in cities having populations over 50,000 were up by 59% in 1982, 78% in 1989, and 89% of base year in 1995. Moreover, 46% of SWAT teams had been filled with military-experienced personnel.[69] By 1987 legislation set up an office in the Pentagon specifically to facilitate transfers of war-developed gear and weapons to civilian police. Congress even created an 800 telephone number specifically for sheriffs and police chiefs could call to see what was available. The General Services administration produced a catalog from which police agencies could make their combat-tested selections. The resultant law enforcement buying spree transformed local police departments into small army-like forces by placing really intimidating equipment into the hands of civilian officers . . . tactics which raised questions about whether the strategy has gone too far. Had they created a culture with the capability that jeopardized common public safety and disregarded wholesale civil rights?. At the time it was pointed out that "many of America's newly armed cops are ex-military from the front lines of Iraq and Afghanistan who knew well how to effectively deploy these weapons against any supposed enemy."[70]

In such a climate of mutual distrust, omnipotent police power, militarization of law enforcement agencies, and quick trigger-fingers by racist cops who fear being in ghettoes after dark, and we still have all the factors alive which gave us so many war crimes in the 1960–1990 period. And overall, it still remains the indifference or failure to supervise rogue cops and wanton destructive behavior by officials who played a large part in the steady development of such institutional and inhumane criminal behavior.

Sadly, no accurate figures were ever compiled by police departments interested in curbing police malpractice inasmuch as very few, if any, were really concerned that this kind of behavior was running amuck. As the White public made no challenges or asked questions in this regard, or filed complaints and city politicians didn't wish to stir up trouble that might frighten off tourists, police had the green light to do whatever the cop on the beat felt was necessary to keep the lid on Black ghetto resentment. Crime control simply met knocking heads and ruling with the iron fist.

> Police . . . are in a class that no politician wanted to oppose. Law enforcement interests may occasionally come up short on budgetary issues, but legislatures rarely if ever pass new laws to hold police more accountable, to restrict their powers, or to make their activities more transparent.[71]

Arrests were common for most trivial offenses and it was expected that every teenage boy in a Black community would be arrested on the slightest pretext before he reached manhood. Any youthful bravado or silly challenges to the police led to fierce reprisal and severe, unreported injuries gave boys an unforgettable lesson about cops. In this period the mere existence of being stopped might mean a police record that would seriously limit job opportunities far into the future, making as available only the most unappealing, listless work with neither advancement nor career reward.

Once arrested and in a local cop's computer, the word was officially out about troublemakers and who to be on the lookout for to roust. Some would be arrested again and again for having a simple anti-White cop bad attitude. Unfortunately, at some point some citizens, goaded with the constant hassle of unconfirmed suspicion by the police would take the bait, explode, and strike out, raising the level of police violence and arrest to a whole new level of enforcement criminality and ugliness.

Not everyone enjoys the thrill of being stopped by a surly cop who is dismissive of civil rights and proceeds to take his time looking suspects up on his computer with the assumption he had netted a felonious criminal. Our time, too, especially if in a hurry for something deemed important, is wasted on this halt. If there is a dispute, more time is lost while the cop becomes nastier. If quickly handcuffed the rest of the process becomes worse, and indignities soon follow eliminating any respect of human rights. War crimes proceed thusly. Few find any of this, plus the bulky presence of a strange, demanding person in blue wielding threats and a baton, make us feel better about our local police force, if blackness is an issue. That is why our constitutional protections are so important in moments like this when a policeman's pistol on his belt is not very reassuring. And let's not forget: The level of poverty in most of the Black neighborhoods in this period were, according to one Harlem resident, "downright shocking." There were very limited social services, no regular garbage collection, rats were everywhere, and the occasional bitter specter of witnessing a bedraggled homeless person freezing to death from lack of shelter and heat.[72]

While such poverty created a sense of alienation in ghetto residents, "the brutishness of police created anger. They hated us. And you respond to that hatred with a hatred of your own." Italian cops used Italian slang to describe Black citizens; Irish favored the worst of the Americans. One observer noted that,

> "Police brutality was not uncommon . . . some cops sought to join the tactical units because they liked to bust heads," says a policeman who remembered. And it was incumbent on some in these units, when walking in on a beating to add a kick or punch of your own to show you were with the program. Some of this occurred because there was brutality all around us—it absorbed us, inhabited us and made us feel a kinship that no outsider could ever understand.[73]

This unrestricted and unreported wave of lethal police attacks on Blacks, for which none would be prosecuted, we label high war crimes for their very nature: no cop ever thought about what the result of his beating a citizen might mean in the long run. Malcolm X had his own opinion of this collective police lawlessness:

> If we're going to talk about police brutality, it's because police brutality exists. Why does it exist? Because our people in this particular society live in a police state. A black man in America lives in a police state. He doesn't live in a democracy; he lives in a police state . . . Black brothers and sisters who have lived here for over 300 years are brutally beaten daily and imagine their physical and psychological suffering . . . it is not a problem of civil rights but a problem of human rights.[74]

Do we blame individual rogue cops alone for the many war crimes committed on helpless citizens during this period? Do we simply leave it at the solitary White nationalist-inspired bent cop who hated Blacks and refused to accept their civil rights? Or perhaps we should continue up the ladder of command and indict heads of departments, even the Chiefs of Police for widespread tolerance and failure to implement proper investigatory methods when Black citizen complaints arise? Maybe the mayor and his/her council should be fired? Surely the power structure of a city had every opportunity to thwart police activities, especially in Black communities to guard against war crimes. Where does the finger of blame stop when assessing guilty parties for this thirty-year spree of officially sanctioned war crimes?

Another agent to condemn: police unions protected by conservative politicians. Lawmakers have routinely shielded police unions from accountability. One study suggests police unions represent 60% of police officers. And in their capacity since the 1970s they lobby for bloated benefits packages, negotiate for arbitration processes that make it virtually impossible to fire dysfunctional or cops accused of war crimes. Those cops accused of misbehavior are supported by these unions so that cops avoid any kind of discipline. As Robert Carle, a New York theological professor, notes:

> For over fifty years, police unions have created for police officers an alternative justice system by negotiating contracts that defang civilian oversight and prevent police chiefs from discipling or firing officers. Police union contracts routinely contain provisions that mandate a 48-hour waiting period before an officer can be questioned, giving him plenty of time to marshal his excuses after a complaint is made and require arbitration in cases of disciplinary action. A University of Chicago working paper found that violent misconduct among law enforcement increased 40% after a state supreme court ruling allowed the cops to unionize.

Corey Pegues argues "It's a blanket system of covering up police officers."[75] Loader refers us to their importance along political lines as a major cause of worry:

> Across the U.S police funding has spiraled in recent decades, at a time when other public . . . budgets have flat-lined or shrunk. This is a result of the political mobilization of crime fears and the power of police unions (the Fraternal Order of Police routinely support and fund preferred Republican candidates in elections for prosecutors, mayors, senators, governors and the president).[76]

Let's face it. Most of the police perpetrators thrived and lived happy, successful, financially rewarding lives off their pensions once they had retired. Most of the victims did not. They were left with the stigma of shame and nightmares of police brutality and concentration camp life forever. Perhaps the real perpetrators were the public itself. What didn't they know about how Black people were treated in America? Why did they choose to do nothing to alleviate this in elections, civil rights demonstrations, volunteer self-help organizations, and complaints to their political representatives? The public always trusted the police and accused the Black community as the barbarians. Whites plainly saw what police in the South were doing to Black citizens on peaceful marches and kept silent. Photos were vivid reminders. Whites knew of such collective violence against Blacks from the news media in their own cities where front-page photos showed Blacks manhandled by cops leering at the camera. Whites may not have known the full extent of what went on in police stations, courts, jails, and inside prison walls. But plenty of crime movies and books of the period gave some idea. Powerful vested interests from the Republican Party helped support, collude with, and protect thousands of police and CJS perpetrators while few ever-helped Black victims. Human rights violations meant nothing, to be overturned whenever it suited White supremist leaders and fascist police unions. Claims, assertions, charges, and demands by Black survivors of CJS war crimes were dismissed while cops were constantly turned into heroes by an indulgent media. At least here in this study, they can't evade censure: this report condemns and indicts this large body of criminal assailants of the CJS for all their maliciousness and ability to evade prosecution as war criminals.[77]

In a paper appropriately titled *Psychopaths Don't Care if They Hurt You, This is Why* by Amherst University psychologist Susan Kraus Whitbourne, this is her response:

> Most of us learn early in life to prefer to avoid making other people sad or afraid. Those who are psychopathic though, do not, and therefore are less likely to base moral decisions on their potential to cause suffering to others . . . and they lack empathy . . . they have the least emotional responsiveness to causing harm in others . . . and they feel less anguish when they have to do so.[78]

Author Paul Colaianni notes "narcissists are people who are just very selfish and act solely to get their own needs met. What they want may just you feeling bad . . . it is when someone is so selfish that you don't matter."[79]

Lastly, we have questioned why police show little interest in the future and dire consequences of their arresting or brutalizing a suspect. Cops may well be like the rest of us except they are in a position where their actions may not be forgivable as when we show little interest in the future. Jane McGonigal writes:

> (To most people) Your brain acts as if your future self is someone you don't know very well and, frankly, someone you don't care about . . . the less

self-control (as in situations shown by some cops) you exhibit today, the less likely you are to make pro-social choices, choices that probably will help the world in the long run . . . according to our studies this is a widespread phenomenon: In our study 53% of respondents say the future crosses their mind almost never. A common response she heard was "I don't expect to be alive thirty years from now so I don't think about it."[80]

Let's leave the last word to criminologists who had seen this kind of cop behavior as early as 1951. In his study, Dr. William A. Westley said he had found a small number of cops "who are clearly sadists, who frequently commit brutalities repugnant to the rest of the police." Yet it was difficult to determine what he meant by "small" because of the "general acceptance of violence and the extreme emphasis on secrecy by the police." Dr. Nelson Watson, a criminologist on the staff of the International Association of Chiefs of Police, noted: "The very fact that police are the only group authorized by the State to use force tends to attract the occasional men who like to use it." Hans Toch, professor of criminal justice at the State University of New York (Albany), cautioned: "I doubt you'll find many real sadists in any police department. What you will find is a substantial minority of men whose reactions to certain situations tend to involve the use of force."[81] Does that make sense, Hans, "a substantial minority"?

NOTES

1. Marilyn Johnson, *Street Justice: A History of Police Violence in New York City* (Boston: Beacon Press, 2003). See especially pages 121–276 which discuss the NYPD from World War II and the rise of the new Black militancy when cops were seen as "an occupying army to keep Blacks in their place and discourage racial mixing," p. 197.

2. Albert J. Reiss, Jr., "Police Brutality-Answers to Key Questions," *Trans-Action Magazine,* 5, 1968, St. Louis.

3. Yale Kamisac, "When the Cops were not Handcuffed," *New York Times Magazine,* 7, November 1965.

4. Ian Loader, "To Reduce the Harm," quoted by Douglas Field in "Hurling the Ink Well," *The Times Literary Supplement* (UK), 14 August 2020, p. 10.

5. William K. Grier and Price M. Cobbs, *Black Rage* (New York: Basic Books, 1968), p. 33.

6. Ibid., pp. 177–178.

7. Peter Henig and Randy Furst, "Cops: Same Role, New Tactics," in Arthur Niederhofer and Abraham S. Blumberg (Eds.), *The Ambivalent Force-Perspectives on the Police* (New York: Ginn, 1970), pp. 318–319.

8. Sylvia Winter et al., *Long Road to Justice, Civil Rights at 50* (Washington, DC: The Leadership Conference on Civil Rights, Human Rights, 2015), p. 1.

9. Vera Institute of Justice staff, *"Prosecuting Police Misconduct, Reflections on the Role of United States Civil Rights Division (pdf)* (New York: Vera Institute, 1998).

10. William A. Westley, "Violence and the Police," *American Journal of Sociology* 59 (1962); Gresham Sykes and David Matza, "Techniques of Police Neutralization," *American Journal of Sociological Review* 22 (1957).

11. William Geller and Hans Toch, *Police Violence: Understanding and Controlling Police Abuse of Force* (New Haven: Yale UP, 1976).

12. Ibid. pp. 22–67.

13. Mike Rothmiller and Ivan E. Goldman, *Los Angeles's Secret Police: Inside LAPD's Elite Spy Network* (New York: Pocket Books, 1992), p. 27, 29 and 35.

14. Ibid., p. 31.

15. Ibid., p. 33.

16. Ibid., pp. 39 and 42, 48–49 and 85.

17. See Donald Black, "The Social Organization of Arrest," *Stanford Law Review,* 23; Richard J. Lundman, "Routine Police Arrest Practices: A Commonweal Perspective," *Social Problems*, 22; Douglas A. Smith, Jody R. Klein and Christy A. Visher, "Street Level Justice: Situational Determinants of Police Arrest Decisions," *Social Problems*, 29; David A. Klinger, "Deference or Deviance? A Note on Why 'Hostile' Suspects are Arrested," paper presented at the *Annual Meeting of the American Society of Criminology*, 4–7 November 1994, New Orleans; Catherine H. Milton, Jeanne W. Halleck, James Lardner and Gary L. Abrecht, *Police Use of Deadly Force* (Washington, DC: Police Foundation, 1977); James J. Fyfe, "Geographic Correlates of Police Shooting: A Microanalysis," *Journal of Research in Crime and Delinquency* 17 (1980); also Fyfe, "Race and Extreme Police Citizen Violence," in R. L. McNeeley and Carl E. Pope (Eds.), *Race, Crime and Criminal Justice* (Beverly Hills: Sage, 1981); William A. Geller and Kevin Karales, *Split-Second Decisions-Shootings of and by Chicago Police* (Chicago: Chicago Law Enforcement Study Group, 1981); and Geoffrey P. Alpert, "Police Use of Deadly Force: The Miami Experience," in Roger G. Dunham and G. P. Alpert (Eds.), *Critical Issues in Policing: Contemporary Readings* (Prospect Heights: Waveland, 1989).

18. James Comey in *BBC News Magazine (website)*, 18 July 2016, p. 2.

19. Kimberly Kindy, *Washington Post*, mentioned in BBC program of #18; and Roland C. Fryer, "An Empirical Analysis of Racial Differences in Police Use of Force, *Journal of Political Economy*, May 2016.

20. Sid Haring, Tony Platt, Richard Speigleman and Paul Takagi, "The Management of Police Killings," *Crime and Social Justice* 8 (1977): 1, 3, and 7; Gerald D. Robin, "Justifiable Homicide by Police Officers," *Journal of Crime, Criminology and Police Science* 54 (1963); and Ralph Knoohuizen, Richard P. Fahey and Deborah J. Palmer, "The Police and Their Use of Fatal Force in Chicago: Chicago law Enforcement Study Group," 1972, p. 2.

21. Ibid; *United States Department of Justice Arrests*, 1980–2009, September 2011, p. 142. Washington, DC.

22. Norm Stamper, *Breaking Ranks: A Top Cop's Expose of the Dark Side of American Policing* (New York: Nation Books, 2005), pp. 160, 204, 217–218.

23. Ibid.

24. Ibid.

25. Ibid., and Joseph H. Wambaugh, *New Centurions* (Boston: Little Brown, 1970), p. 8 and 11.

26. Ibid., Katheryn Russell-Brown, *The Color of Crime: Racial Hoaxes, White Fear, Black Protectionism, Police Harassment and Other Macroaggressions* (New York: New York University Press, 1998, p. 84; Stuart Henry and Mark Lanier, *What is Crime? Controversies Over the Nature of Crime and What to do About it* (New York: Rowman & Kittlefield, 2001), p. 159.

27. Ibid., p. 89 and 136.

28. Ibid.

29. William Kleinknecht, *The Man Who Sold the World, Ronald Reagan and the Betrayal of Main Street America* (New York: Perseus, 2009), p. 220.

30. Stamper, op. cit.

31. Ibid.

32. Ibid.

33. William R. Burwell, *Police Brutality and Authoritarianism-A Locus of Control* (Chicago: Illinois Institute of Technology, 1983), p. 38.

34. Ibid.; M. Parten, *Surveys, Polls and Samples* (New York: Harper, 1950).

35. Ibid., p. 59.

36. Ibid., p. 60.

37. Ibid., p. 64.

38. Ibid., pp. 67–68; A. J. Reiss, "Police Brutality," in R. J. Londman (Ed.), *Police Behavior* (New York: Oxford UP, 1980), p. 293; Johnnie Cochran Jr. and Tim Rutten, *Journey to Justice* (New York: Ballantine, 1997), p. 64.

39. J. B. Jacobs and S. B. Magdovitz, "At Leep's End," *Journal of Police Science and Administration*, 5 (1977): 17–18.

40. William A. Westley, "The Police: A Sociological Study of Law, Custom, Morality," unpublished PhD dissertation, University of Chicago: Department of Sociology, 1951.

41. J. H. McNamara and Dennis Jay Kennedy (Eds.), *Police and Policing-Contemporary Issues* (Westport: Praeger, 1999); J. H. McNamara, "Uncertainties in Police Work: The Relevance of Police Recruits' Backgrounds and Training," in D. Bordua (Ed.), *The Police: Six Sociological Essays* (New York: Wiley, 1967), p. 178.

42. Ibid; D. H. Bayley and H. Mendelson, *Minorities and the Police* (New York: Free Press, 1969); H. Carlson and M. S. Sutton, "The Effects of Different Police Roles on Attitudes and Values," *Journal of Psychology* 91 (1975): 63–64; J. Lefkowitz, "Psychological Attributes of Police," *Journal of Sociological Issues* 31 (1975): 3–26; P. Chevigny, *Police Power* (New York: Pantheon, 1969); and C. E. Teasley and L. Wright, "The Effects of Training on Police Recruit Attitudes," *Journal of Police Sciences and Administration* 1 (1973): 241–248.

43. Worden, Robert E., "The Causes of Police Brutality: Theory and Evidence on Police Use of Force," in William A. Geller and Hans Toch (Eds.), *Police Violence-Understanding and Controlling Police Violence* (New Haven: Yale UP, 1996), p. 25,

27 and 29; and Theodor W. Adorno, Elise Frenkel-Brunswick, Daniel J. Levinson and R. N. Sanford, *The Authoritarian Personality* (New York: Harper & Row, 1950).

44. Toch, op. cit. pp. 30–31.

45. David Stahl, Frederick Sussman and Neil Bloomfield, *The Community and Racial Crisis* (New York: Practicing Law Institute, 1966), p. 120.

46. Reported by Victor Navasky and Darrell Paster, *Law Enforcement-The Federal Role, The 20th Century Fund Task Force on LEAA* (New York: McGraw-Hill, 1976), p. 126.

47. Nicholas Alex, *New York City Cops Talk Back-A Study of a Beleaguered Minority* (New York: Wiley, 1976), pp. 129–130.

48. Ibid., p. 129.

49. Gerald D. Robin, *Introduction to the Criminal Justice System* (New York: Harper, 1980), p. 59.

50. Ibid., p. 60.

51. Ibid., p. 61.

52. Ibid., p. 66.

53. Ed Cray, *The Enemy in the Streets-Police Malpractice in America* (New York: Anchor, 1972), pp. 2–3.

54. Ibid., pp. 4–7, 176 and 266; Michael Harriot, "White Men Can't Murder. Why White Cops are Immune to the Law," *The Root* (2017): 1, 4–9; and Gregory Lewis and Rahul Patkak, *When Warriors Put on a Badge* (Athens: Georgia State University, 2017).

55. Robin, op. cit., p. 70.

56. Radley Balko, *Rise of the Warrior Cop: The Militarization of American Police Forces* (New York: Public Affairs, 2013), pp. xi–xii.

57. Ibid., p. xiv.

58. Ibid., pp. 41–42.

59. Reported in *Time Magazine*, March 1965

60. Balko, op. cit., p. 65.

61. Richard Nixon, "Special Message to Congress on Control of Narcotics and dangerous Drugs," 14 July 1969, available at http://www.presidency.ucsts.edu/ws/indexphp/pid, accessed 1 October 2012.

62. Balko, op. cit., p. 76; Catherine Ellis Smith and Stephen Drury Smith (Eds.), *Say it Loud! Great Speeches on Civil Rights and African American Identity* (New York: New Press, 2010), p. 70.

63. Balko, op. cit., p. 85.

64. Herbert J. Packer, "A Special Supplement-Nixon's Crime Program and What it Means": *New York Review of Books*, 22 October 1970, p. 17.

65. Michael J. Sniffen, "Knock at Door Strikes Terror into These Families," *Associated Press*, 26 June 1973.

66. "Agents Indicted for No-Knock Raids," *Associated Press*, 25 August 1973; Andrew M. Malcolm, "Violent raids Against the Innocent Found Widespread," *New York Times*, 25 June 1973, p. 3; Balko, op. cit., pp. 133 and 136–137.

67. Balko, Ibid., p. 139.

68. Balko, Ibid., p. 157.

69. Ibid., p. 175.

70. *The Daily Beast*, "Cops Ready for War," 2 February 2011, p. 1 and 3; Balko, op. cit., pp. 334–335.

71. Robin, op. cit., p. 70.

72. T. J. English, *The Savage City: race, Murder and a Generation on Edge* (New York: Morrow, 2011), p. 72, 73 and 157.

73. Ibid., p. 74.

74. Ibid., pp. 182–183, 201.

75. Robert Carle, "Police Unions and the Conservative Conscience," *Americaninterest.com*, 2020; Corey Pegues, *Once a Cop* (Dallas: Atria Books, 2016).

76. Marilyn S. Johnson, op. cit., pp. 206 and 210.

77. Deborah Lipstadt, "The Triumph of Deaths. How Nazis Escaped Prosecution," *The Times Literary Supplement*, 1 March 2019, p. 12.

78. Susan Krauss Whitbourne, "Psychopaths Don't Care if They Hurt You, This is Why," *Psychology Today*, June 2017, p. 31.

79. Paul Glaianni, "Dealing with Selfish people that Don't Care if They Hurt You," *The Overwhelmed Brain Workbook (website)*, private, 2013.

80. Jane McGonigal, "Our Puny Human Brains are Terrible Thinking about the Future," *Future Tense*, Arizona State University and New America, pp. 1–3.

81. Quote taken from journalist David Burnham, "Police Violence and a Changing Pattern," *New York Times*, 7 July 1968. Nelson A. Watson, "The Defenders: A Case Study of an Informal Police Organization," *Social Problems* 15 (1967): 127–132; the Westley quote is from his *The Police: A Sociological Study of Law, Custom and Morality*, op. cit.; and Hans Toch, *Violent Men: An Enquiry into the Psychology of Violence* (Chicago: Aldine, 1969).

Chapter 4

Criminal Court Judges Have a God Complex

Should one human being have society's blessing to send another human being to prison? Should he have that right knowing the assigned could be raped, injured, tortured, tormented, maimed, lose his skill set, develop serious psychiatric problems, lose his family, health, credit standing, assets, and self-esteem? Why not simply employ a computer to fulfill the dirty work, or a three-person tribunal, or the seniors in a man's own community? No chance you'll find a Sophocles, Aristotle, Plato, and Terence all rolled up into one privileged White male patrician. Because this is what follows when one human being sentences another to a future of living hell (even assuming he's on death row). Consequently, in the final, sentencing stage of the criminal court process we label a war crime in its most sophisticated form.

Recent scrutiny of this land of mystery dovetails with our own impressions made many years ago about the criminal courts. "The criminal courts are the crucial gateway between police action on the street and the processing of primarily Black and Latino defendants into jails and prisons," writes Professor Gonzalez van Cleve, who spent 10 years and over 1,000 hours observing the comings and goings in Chicago's largest criminal court, "and are portrayed as sacred, impartial institutions shrouded in secrecy to the majority of Americans even while a world of punishment is determined by race not by offence."[1] She noticed judges asleep on the bench, district attorneys behaving like frat boys in a judge's chambers, and public defenders weighing the fate of defendants as to who they would try and save from who they would have to sacrifice during a long days' roll call of punitive sentencing in the court.[2]

There were over 3,000 separate judicial systems in this country, judges in command in each one (larger cities might employ a dozen or more judges to handle either felony or misdemeanor and traffic) cases. Money mattered even when it came to justice. Various forms of funding (or underfunding as in many locations) determined how many public defenders could be handled, what conditions would prevail in the county jail, and how many judges could be afforded. While reforms were proposed and occasionally instituted in various jurisdictions since the 1970s, assembly-line justice was the norm, trials were slow, due process violations pervasive, courtroom practices ritualistic and dysfunctional while their evidence was lacking that reforms had reduced racist disparities or signs of White Power attitudes when sentencing minorities. Nor could reformers do much about judicial incompetence, much less tell judges how to run their courtrooms.[3]

Judges were the mystery men of the CJS. They occupied its most coveted position and were invariably and automatically assumed to have high integrity, wisdom, a belief in fairness, incorruptibility, and high moral regard for civic responsibility. This was without a shred of proof. They were, in fact, mystery men. Their legal mistakes went unseen, their errors of judgment were overlooked or excused and their sentences of men to long terms of confinement were seen as the right thing to do since judges made no errors of judgment. Many of them occupied the bench for life which proved dangerous to minority groups they might despise as derived from their belief in White superiority. They were often aided by their staff who were experts at shielding or concealing a judge's personal flaws and weaknesses (i.e., alcoholism, vulgar language, womanizing) from the public. They were beyond reprisals and being labeled a "hanging judge" was often seen as an unjustifiable commendation for being tough on the city's low life. Worse, over time, and through repeated use of excessive sentences, many judges became inured to the pain they inflicted on vulnerable and poor families and lose themselves in frigidity, cruelty, inertia, disregard, and even hatred of human frailty and obsequiousness often played out before the bench.

Judges were the final arbiters in the long drawn-out CJS legal process. Robin, a professor in the Department of Criminal Justice at the University of New Haven, called them "the front line of Democracy."[4] He strengthened their importance by listing what they were required to consider during the adjudication process of offenders charged with crimes: they needed to consider constitutional rights of each defendant who appeared before them; they needed to conduct hearings so that while the public's protection was foremost in their minds (and how could we ever really know that?) broader human rights of these defendants were to be respected; they had to assess the veracity of a police arrest report which could be filled with lies and deceit; and consider implications of the district attorney's heavy-handed judgment on sentencing and the probation department's sketchy report that mixed a social study of the defendant with weak-kneed recommendations on punishment; plus consider which kind of therapy might be suitable; and weigh the pros and cons of a sentence to the big house.

Until 1994, criminal court judges in cities like Los Angeles were free to appoint any lawyer they chose in cases where conflicts of interest were obvious. In this way, many young lawyers advanced their careers at an early stage and built practices in a system rife with such cronyism. Accepting these appointments at $100/hour locked lawyers into deferential behavior to not upset the court routine in any way, being forevermore banned for using radical speech or calling the police "racists." Needless to say, judges kept appointments to Black lawyers to a minimum and no women. In a summary of their duties, Robin has thus concluded "it was to the Courts that everyone turned to see that justice was done."[5]

The US Constitution says nothing about judges being members of the Bar or even being lawyers knowing the law, much less have any sympathies for the endless stream of offenders brought before them on a daily basis to dispense justice. This is by national design. Yet these are the men who dispose 90% of all criminal cases often without transcripts being kept unless the defendant is prepared to pay for them. By design, this also reduces the chances of poor defendants having their convictions reviewed and reversed by higher courts that rely on complete transcripts to detect and correct lower court errors. Does not each court have a responsibility to the citizens who march before them to provide such records to allow pursuance of dubious justice on a higher level? There appears plenty of money to pay judges and court personnel plus maintain the courts and jails for this to be a poor excuse for the failure. Lack of adequate legal consultation, police use of excessive force, prosecutorial errors and unethical behavior, racism within the CJS, inadequate analysis by the probation department in their reports to the court, and just craven basic hostility to the offender cause grievous harm to one and all but most especially to the ones least able to defend themselves. In all these matters the CJS stands guilty of juridical war crimes against which the defendant is afforded no compensatory justice.

Since approximately 90% of criminal cases are handled locally, this clearly makes crime a community rather than a national issue, one requiring local solutions to affected neighborhoods exploiting whatever resources they have for rehabilitation purposes which they chose or not to fund on the basis of local prejudices, racism, and political conservatism. Local courts mean local judges. Patterson tells us "The fundamental problem is this: a judge exercises more power with less accountability than any other official in our society."[6] Let's agree that it is virtually impossible to do anything about judges who are incompetent, corrupt, senile, unethical, legally ignorant, or political hacks in a local party system. "Traditionally, the selection of judges has been guided by political considerations, a matter of who applicants know rather than a strict choice of the best person for the job."[7]

Whatever can be said about the criminal law, the courts, the prosecutors, and the judges in general, for this period, I can truly say justice was not done, it wasn't even half attempted. Forget the respect for human rights, I saw defendants being condemned to serious invasions of privacy, atrocities inflicted by the police, a life of violence being incarcerated in jail or prison, loss of personal life as judges and prosecutors, and probation officers participated in stripping men of their existence all to prove they were guilty of some infraction, often just a trivial drug charge or petty crime. I was there to see twenty judges and the courtrooms in the space of eleven years as PO in five jurisdictions. What I saw by way of judicial mannerisms tailored to fit White supremacist attitudes of the irresponsibility of Black people. It was an antebellum form of justice obsolete in all aspects. There was application of harsh unjust criminal laws and a too-ready acceptance of police officer investigations that seemed filled with holes and human rights violations; the motto seemed to be "never prosecute a cop for acts of violence." I saw war crimes being committed on an industrial basis. As I sat in court before uncaring tyrannical judges in ominous black robes, they appeared blank to the long-term negative consequences their ill-considered verdicts had on a sad stream of poor and minority characters who marched into court each day. Indeed, the odds were heavily stacked weighed against these ubermenschen. Crime was seen as a political act and the individual to the state seemed unimportant. I smelled judicial fascism all over the place and regard these twenty as falling into that category. The early 1960s was dominated by conservative values of the White establishment that the town (Los Angeles) to the exclusion of other ethnic groups, and I do mean exclusion.[8]

During this period while I squirmed in my courtroom seat, I saw the nasty side of the judicial cadre. In my discussions with judges directly, I felt they rarely bothered to learn whether the final outcome of their judgment had helped or made the defendant worse. They never asked what became of so and so, they never kept notes on those who came before them to refer to later. They never spent much time in private chats with any of these men to learn their objectives in life or concerns about family.[9] It was simply a legal assembly-line process. Black offenders were seen as passive, with a high risk of homelessness, addiction, unemployment, and bouts of violence, articulating remote dreams of a job they would never attain. Such views gave judges little confidence these men would succeed and were just wasting the court's time. Judges had better, more civic responsibilities to follow than these men through life. Judges showed no interest that defendants, too, deserved to enjoy happiness, peace, safety, or security . . . that while their decisions focused on the common good, defendants should be included. The worst kind of judicial decisions were those that caused offenders to become worse or have a miserable life and economic death. Perhaps this was because judges never visited the jails, lockups, and concentration camps where their oppressive sentences had sent the doomed. Nor were they concerned with police misbehavior. Cochran wrote:

> Basically what you have in Los Angeles is a police culture addicted to heavy-handed exercise of power unrestrained by judges or district attorneys. Given the propensity of judges to take the word of virtually any police officer against Blacks little could be done except seek lesser charges to speed things along as judges all too readily accepted police lies.[10]

Did they not want to see the end product of their meanness or were they too mousy squeamish? If this form of fascism wasn't a visceral war crime, nothing would be.

What was crucial was to maintain cordiality and high morale with the police department by accepting whatever they said. Human rights violations were swept under the carpet despite the objections raised by defendants and their attorneys. When judges read probation office reports on the offender's background, they dismissed the report's inadequate premises, its inherent racism and inability to understand Black culture, failures in asking pertinent questions, errors in reviewing a person's criminal record, presenting too limited a series of demographic and sociological variables to better explain a man's attitude and world view. Judges incuriously asked little of these reports and rarely went in depth on what they were reading. POs had little worry unless the defendant's attorney made a fuss that their report was scrutinized and found inadequate. Repressive punishment was the usual outcome. To what extent do judges really seem aware that a sentence to prison would guarantee a newcomer to a life of danger, fear, noise, loneliness, violence, and capricious guard commands? Defense attorney Cochran sounded the alarm:

> At some point I learned that judges, prosecutors and law enforcement officials in dealing with Black defendants and convinced of their own righteousness would do anything to make things yield the "right result." To be a defense lawyer then meant being very skeptical and not unhesitatingly trusting my client's fate to the system's basic fairness.[11]

Distinguished Harvard Law School Professor Derrick Bell also commented on the dark side of this legal system:

> At every stratum of the system—as client, law student, even—the Black man is aware of racism in the administration of criminal justice. Though not as blatant as in the past, its effects remain sufficiently obvious to vitiate the court debate on whether a Black man can receive a fair trial. What every Black knows about

racism and the courts is not a mere manifestation of group paranoia. So many studies support this perception of the data . . . but these findings come as no surprise to Black people who still regard the judicial system . . . and racism in the courts as a (subject for legal scholars) consigned to the shadows where it remains today . . . some judges combine seemingly unlimited measure, qualities of arrogance, ignorance and bigotry.[12]

Other observers had darker views of the broader American criminal court system. Alexander said it simply existed to manage the potentially unruly African American community. Hayes noted its ability to herd Blacks together for the purposes of watching them and keeping order. Issa Kohler-Hausmann (Yale Law School) called it a management technique to mark angry Blacks to identify and detain them and apply increasingly greater degrees of punishment as this handful of defendants became greater troublemakers. Feely, law professor at UC Berkeley, likened it, as did Franz Fanon, to a colonial administration. The system is designed to maintain order in ghetto areas but allows enough business to carry on to make local merchants make sufficient income to pay taxes and rent to property owners.

Officials are not so much concerned with even-handed enforcement of law as they are to keep the peace, to "manage mayhem" so as not to infringe on White men in pursuit of their own reasons for wanting a quiet ghetto.

The great American writer of major influence, James Baldwin, called the criminal courts a social force for oppression which manifested itself as an abuse of power within the American legal and judicial systems.[13]

A Black lawyer who has spent many years defending people in American Courts, Paul Butler, looked at some of the same wretched features of the US criminal-legal and said these were all about Black men. African American men were not only the subject of those processes but were the very people that they were developed for . . . various actors in the legal process target Black men to fail. Who were the people who did this? Butler named all of the actors in the CJS including police, prosecutors, and lawmakers. He believed when people complain about police killing and beating up Black people and ask why these cops aren't disciplined, he feels White society doesn't get it. The problem is not bad apple cops. The problem isn't a problem—the system is working the way it is supposed to. The law is not supposed to punish these cops, the law (and judges who stand behind them) authorizes bad behavior . . . and this goes as far up as the Supreme Court. The Supreme Court has been expanding police powers over the past fifty years with the design of controlling Black men. To Butler this was "an intentional racialist project."[14]

Criminologist Robert Staples felt discriminatory judges pervaded the justice system. He said the legal system was made by White men to protect White interests and keep Blacks down. The system he characterized was filled with second-rate jurists, a weak legal defense team for Black defendants, biased jurors, and second-rate racist judges.[15] A Rand Corporation Study from 1983 was no less critical of these judges. It found that Black defendants were treated more harshly at key points in the legal process especially at the end of it all with sentences considerably longer than for Whites. "POs, judges, and parole boards de facto discriminated against Blacks while PO reports harped on deprived backgrounds, years of joblessness, school disciplinary problems, and family issues that judges who largely come from upper-middle class and elite cultures cannot fathom which often affects the severity of sentencing."[16] According to journalists Adam Liptak, Alma Cohen, and Crystal S Yang, Black defendants received longer sentences from Republican-appointed judges (3 months or more) while a similar group of men were found to get longer sentences from a study of 1,200 federal trial judge verdicts over a 15-year period.[17]

I found similar judges innocently blinded to all the CJS abuses Blacks faced as they inhabited a refined atmosphere in an imperious, aloof, biased, and completely myopic manner. Judicial attitudes and behaviors seemed to befit Black robe mandarins who spent a lifetime bestowing dubious verdicts on men for whom they knew absolutely nothing about (save for a few paragraphs of commentary by equally aloof POs providing amateurish insights into client eccentricities with whom they too had nothing in common).

The list of judicial problems was often of their own making and suggested how poorly trained they were for the onerous job of passing capricious judgment on others. This was soon translated into a precious loss of liberty, overbearing fines, pain of prison confinement, banishment from the labor market, and destruction of normal family relationships so that a police, prison, and conviction record would guarantee the worst possible outcomes.

The list? Oh yeah, I began with that. Here are a few aversions of justice I liken to war crimes that I witnessed during my tenure in the CJS: five-minute trials, judicial tongue lashing, and verbal disrespect to defendants (not to mention judicial euphemisms—in California an IBM defendant meant an "itty bitty Mexican") by one Marin County judge who reigned over hapless Mexican immigrant farmworkers who drank too much to offset miserable conditions of work; or other judges who often used the N-word in chambers while discussing defendants due to come before them after lunch. Then there were hasty sentences that seemed arbitrary and aimed to fit judges' perceptions about the men standing before them—straggly, unshaven, smelly brutes who went through the system on minor charges without representation, social reports, or access to family help. These lasted less than a minute each, offenders arbitrarily fined whatever they had in their pocket. In a single year, three judges in Atlanta had disposed of 70,000 cases and it was seen as common for the average urban criminal courts to handle as many as 30,000 cases annually.[18] If I figure correctly that comes to almost 100 cases daily (assuming each judge takes a month's vacation) which was standard in my courts. What judge would have the time to minutely examine particulars of a case or have time to reflect on alternative punishments to jail. My beef, as I saw it was given this overload—which was not the fault of the defendants but of too few courts or too many arrests and too many prosecutorial indictments and the petty legal squabbling over plea bargaining—greater leniency could have been shown and appropriate allowances made for inadequate court attention paid these miscreants. But after all that's all they were, a poor bedraggled bunch and White nationalist thinking from the courts saw them in no better light: hence the hard end of the stick at all times. Plenty of war crimes to go around from this failure of the CJS.

According to the *New York Times*, in South Carolina, up to 85% of the defendants were tried by judges with the weakest of legal training, where courtrooms might in somebody's kitchen, barn or porch, by "judges" some of whom had never opened a law book and where it was an acceptable qualification for judges to adjudicate cases with but a tenth-grade education.[19] In thirty-two states judges' income depended on the number of cases handled or their outcome (i.e., guilty) or received a percentage of the fines and court fees collected. Occasionally, they were paid only if the person was convicted and able to pay the fees. This often meant jailing the man and then contracting him out to a local farmer or plantation owner who would work the skin off the man and pay a pittance to the courts over time to settle the arbitrarily established court amount. Of course, all this had been declared illegal by the Supreme Court in 1927, but who locally took them seriously in 1970?[20]

As a probation officer, I was called upon to produce presentence reports for court-ordered investigations with maybe three weeks to amass whatever I could gather nationwide. I was allowed to invade whatever school, police, church, social, detention records he had amassed in his sad life. Was this in itself a war crime? On lesser offenses, could not the act itself stand up to whatever sentence might be inflicted? Did we have to tell everyone in view this guy was a hapless, pathetic schnook and lessen whatever bonds people might already have had with him? Rarely was I presented with enough time to meet his peers and advocates, most of whom would view me with suspicion and distrust and say little even in a man's defense. That's because no one on the street or in the ghetto trusted the CJS, the courts, or its PO representatives. Forty percent or more of the defendants whom I interviewed disagreed sharply with the cops' version almost entirely and some even told how brutal the cops had been to secure the arrest and confession, none of which showed up in the police version of the incident. Who was I supposed to believe? Were defendants always liars and cheats because they were alleged offenders? Did cops always have the right version of events? Did they never participate in cover ups, bad behavior, or actual crimes when going about their business to apprehend criminals? If I wrote these things in my report, what would be the judge's reaction? How long might I still have a job? It was a tough spot to be in as I wanted judges to accept what I believed was the true take on this guy. But rarely and as a matter of routine cowardliness, did judges and district attorneys stray away from the sacrosanct police report which pretty much sealed the fate of the hapless in 85% of the cases, as I saw it. A defense attorney could lose a case because a majority of jurors couldn't accept the fact that police could lie, make mistakes, and were sometimes grossly negligent.[21]

Cochran continues:

> I had seen how skilled LAPD officers were in testifying, how well schooled they were in concocting innocent explanations for the harm they did, even when they clearly were wrong or negligent. More importantly, I had seen first hand that they never, ever would admit they were wrong. That refusal was the foundation of the stone wall their siege mentality had led them to construct between their department and the entire community (Black and White). In their minds it was "us versus them" every moment of the day and night.[22]

Caseloads were always a bottleneck—too many were arrested by over-anxious cops who failed to employ intelligent use of discretion, caution, and latitude on marginally illegal activities. District Attorneys on the whole were self-gratifying partisans who couldn't be counted on for fairness. They were preoccupied with the notion of guilt in all its forms and potential punishments, and an illusory "conviction rate" concept to certify their value to their superiors: how many convicted, what kinds of convictions, how tough when it came to sentences, how they scrupulously avoided costly jury trials (which every defendant was guaranteed by the Constitution), how they hated the poor—especially if they chose to run for office. Law Professor Michael Scances noted that

> district attorneys almost always take the conservative, tough on crime position even in more liberal electorates and are, contrary to belief, not hypersensitive to local public opinion. They do not really represent their voters but are more inclined to tout their conviction rates. Yet locally elected DAs hold significant influence over criminal justice outcomes. They decide when to file charges, how severe these should be, how judges would react, what punishment to seek, what evidence to suppress.[23]

Inscrutable judges too often depended upon the police and prosecutor for all their basic mechanical information. And this was mostly negative toward Black disliked defendants who were usually seen as community irritants. Still, judges had other means of deriving social data and did not have to be in the position of rubber-stamping racist police versions that would necessarily exclude bad police behavior or overlooking war crimes and acts of brutality toward the defendants. Plenty of reports existed with broad-based observations by social workers, psychologists, psychiatrists, mental health workers, probation officers, and drug therapists plus reports from families, schoolmates, friends, former teachers, and witnesses. More importantly, they had their two eyes especially when it came to PC 148 cases. In California, 148 of the penal code charges defendants with a violation if they prohibit resisting arrest or interfering with an officer in the course of his duties. Cochran (who was then a prosecuting attorney) discussed how this all played out in a courtroom:

> Every Monday I would arrive for work and confront a courtroom filled with men who were there to answer to one or both of these charges. Defendants invariably displayed visible injuries ranging from cuts and bruises to fractured limbs. Officers with whom they had allegedly struggled never had so much as a visible scratch. The defendants all had something else in common: they were African American men. Everyone in the courtroom knew what was going on. LAPD referred to 148 as an "attitude test." If Black men resisted with a "bad attitude," they would be administered "curbside justice" or a little "wall to wall" interrogation. Cops would beat the hell out of them and some showed they were very badly beaten. How badly they were injured (or even killed) told everyone that a man's life was in the cop's hands.[24]

Despite such obvious use of excessive force and denial of a man's constitutional rights to being allowed safe conduct by cops, judges never asked questions and never chose to reprimand or charge vicious police much less toss out the cases. Here, clear violations were ignored and war crimes by the hundredfold were allowed to stand. Bogus cases with criminal charges against these battered men were compounded by the expected extraction of guilty pleas which then made it virtually impossible for them to file civil suits against the city to obtain compensation for their broken bones and bodily injuries. Cochran claimed as a result of the failure on the part of judges and prosecutors, "police had become accustomed to exercising all that power virtually unchecked by any higher authority, certainly not by Das, judges or other lawyers."[25]

The few judges I knew who let it be known they were receptive to critical reports on the system's failures, or to positives about the defendants, did receive data along these lines on an occasional basis. But you had to know your judge. You avoided sending harsh reports on the CJS lest you put yourself in a firing line; simply ostracized from those who mattered. Yet by what I saw in court hearings, procedures, and sentences, judges rarely strayed far from the original views of arresting officers, if only to keep peace between agencies.

Judges should have known better about the results of all that punitive sentencing, all those jail terms, and the obvious harm it brought to the lives of thousands of poor souls. Common sense and what they saw with their own eyes on family destruction as it happened in the courtroom should have told them that. How many times did I see a judge wince whenever a woman with a toddler in tow showed up at his court to plead that her husband not be sentenced to a concentration camp? Tell me, how does one burglary that took fifteen minutes of victimless time to complete and net maybe $200 in used property equate to three to eight years loss of life? Presumably, judges reminded themselves, if these offenders were Black, they would eventually return to their ghetto neighborhoods and only victimize other Black families of the future. No great loss to the court or to the judges who lived many miles away from harm and who held these people in low esteem anyway. Surely there was enough published documentation of failures of the correctional system for judges to think deeply and carefully about whether incarcerating a man for even a short amount of time would be a rational form of punishment. Judge verdicts were unfettered and sanctions were never reviewed as most states allowed judicial decisions wide latitude. Criminologist Marvin E Frankel, in his examination of the courts, tells us of the many bad yet unreviewed judicial decisions he had cause to review.[26]

War crimes could be seen at every judicial turn. Could judges have tried to use their time more wisely? Say no to the endless stream of petty cases, 10% of which may have led to felonies (which might still have been thrown out for limited evidence)? Police called these "bread and butter" arrests, minor drug sales or usage, prostitution, petty theft, refusing to obey police demands or resisting arrests, dubious searches, taken by police as a suspicious character, and so on. How many human rights were ignored, how many police lies were accepted, how many "confessions" were wrongfully extracted, how much errors were created by using informer testimony to make an arrest? Judges should have known all this. They had to know since they discussed such matters whenever they convened as a body. They knew but didn't care. They abetted in the commission of war crimes. Word was always out in the community whenever cops used brutality and excessive force to make an arrest. I heard about it and I was far down in the food chain. But judges didn't bother to sift through local gossip to uncover these injustices. Judges were too strict, too cautious, too afraid a defendant might reoffend, unwilling to stand up to vindictive public leaders and prosecutors.

They may have taken the time to explore witness testimony for obvious errors in judgment. They could have spoken to defendants in private and taken probation sentencing reports lightly for the many errors they contained. They could have personally inspected jails for abuses and violations (spend some time there incognito). They could have made spot checks of therapy houses to which they have referred defendants to assure they satisfied a judge's view of their value. In addition, they could have issued more community service orders for good deed work activities rather than jail sentences, fines, or supervised probation. Or work with Big Brothers groups? They could have reprimanded police where rights violations at the point of arrest were obvious, even sentenced cops in some cases. They could have reduced jail sentences to hours, employ house arrests or ankle bracelets as a form of containment if this was absolutely for public safety.

I had another bone to pick with judges of this period. It concerned their complete absence of interest and reform of bail. Lack of bail which led to the inability to get out of jail for most Black arrestees meant predictably harsh results. Judges seemed to assume letting one out on low bail or own recognizance was tantamount to the man reoffending, doing violence to some innocent party, at risk to flee, or seek to harm witnesses. Since he had no obvious family resources, so the juridical thinking went, as the man spends all his time on drugs he was a risk on a number of levels, especially criminal. This, of course, was all speculation. Even so, as White nationalist theory went, Blacks can do with severe living conditions and survive the worst of a situation no White would tolerate and anyway he has a legitimate home to go to so is at better risk for bail. The 1960 figures for New York show the inevitable result of men being unable to make bail, languishing in jail, and being unable to work on their defense until sentencing.

Data also suggested 35–40% freed on bail received milder sentences to those sad characters caught in the maw of the CJS where prison was their inevitable fate due to judges who stood in the way of release pending trial.[27]

Judges might have helped organize community forums to learn community needs and help develop resources and community leaders to refer to when assistance and advice (use seniors in this regard) were warranted in certain cases. They might even have used ex-offenders in areas of judicial practice and benefit from advice and suggestions in helping reform defendants now in court prior to sentencing. They might have dismissed district attorney overreach and bundling of charges, informally act on complaints of police brutality where police departments and higher officials failed to respond to local concerns. They could have visited ghettoes to learn of living conditions and better understand the cultures of men who comprise the vast majority of people who come before judges in court. Finally, they might have disposed of courtroom theatrics of gloom and doom by creating a friendlier environment—plants, posters, pastel walls, community art, children's objects: disregard of ominous black robes, no high benches, keep everything eye level, comfortable seating, cats and dogs allowable, and so on.

Prosecution had absolutely unrestricted discretion in the performance of their duty in screening police arrest reports without challenge.[28] Indeed, prosecutors and judges abetted in the way people were arrested and charged as if in a Coney Island shooting gallery. Defendants' rights meant little and few judges that I saw in criminal courts seemed to show concern in this regard. The entire despotic process from arrest and detention in police stations to fettered stays in jail prior to hearings was designed to isolate the subject and deprive him of any human rights. Burns is quite caustic and repeated what we have already concluded:

> American courts almost always found police lying during interrogation (which sadly) doesn't render a confession involuntarily . . . Courts were no more than a formal means of making it legal for police to pass and execute a sentence upon the prisoner.[29]

Implicit in all this was the steady drumbeat of the predatory court process: ambiguity and majesty of the criminal law where rules and regulations existed to contain every quirky ghetto behavior; a public prosecutor dedicated to "the common good" in part but more particularly to heavy-handed treatment in each case so as to advance his political career. Defendants appeared dazed by the bewildering number of hearings. Probation reports that I felt were little read by the judge or district attorney except for the litany of negatives to see if it fitted in with their deal. Then there was the marginalization of the defense attorney who seemed to have no real power to demand human rights or gain funds to conduct a proper investigation; his job seemed to be to only challenge the prosecutor at the edges of each case. Facts were less important, human rights a secondary consideration, negatives of the offender were all that mattered. The result led some defendants to demand some degree of human worth and protested loudly, challenging the proceedings or attacking the court officials to little consequence. Rest assured, judges remembered these unhinged performances when it came to sentencing: how poorly behaved so many Black ghetto defendants were in the brace of the court.

Plea bargains were surrounded by secrecy to even other professionals in the court process. I was never allowed to sit in on how these were conducted, who took the lead, what options were presented, or to what degree compromise intervened as a useful tool. Burns believed 95% of the cases could be placed without any dog fights, mere procedural quietude, and an effort to avoid defendant refusal to comply with the deal and thus up the ante for a lengthy, tiresome, costly trial that might reveal police skullduggery and even get the defendant off.[30]

Between 1950 and 2000, the imprisonment rate for Whites increased by 184% while for Blacks the increase for incarceration was over 350%.[31] It was a great period for zealous, White nationalist-influenced district attorneys who enjoyed absolute sovereign immunity for violating the rights of offenders. Prosecutors were fully aware of what it meant to have basic legal rights in court. Law schools had trained them on this subject and required that they commit themselves to follow such standards. But their misconduct in the courtroom on this subject was almost never subject to disciplinary proceedings and no one in any official capacity bothered to criticize them for ethical misconduct. Nor did they bother to attack police search and seizure techniques or the complete ambiguity surrounding violent arrests and unreliable police confessions. It was Kafka's trial in an American context.

Sitting in felony, misdemeanor, traffic, and family courts as a probation officer, I occasionally wondered how the crazy quilt of sentences was actually played out in the minds of judges. Easy cases got stiff punishment, the more trivial they were the more disparate the final decision; some really serious cases often received short shrift as if little was at stake, and defendants were given bypass jail passes. This didn't happen on a regular basis but it did occur. What, I thought, proceeded through a judge's mind at the time of sentencing besides the standard plea bargain agreement? Judges didn't have to adhere to these if they felt compelled to act otherwise, like more leniently. But they did so generally just to keep harmonious relations between prosecutors and police even when they differed.

Many of the judges I met privately said they didn't like pleas bargains as it took away from them their own alleged wisdom and humanity, court experiences, and haughty awareness of the Black condition. It was their court and they wished to preserve its authoritarian fascist nature. All else got in the way. So, I wondered, what was the mental process, if that could be determined, regarding their decisions: did they in the final analysis simply copy each other for uniformity in sanctions or did they actually decide cases with an eye to compassion?

University of Nebraska criminal justice professor Cessia C. Spohn answered my question in a 2002 book she wrote on this very topic titled simply *How Do Judges Decide—The Search for Fairness in Justice & Punishment*. Spohn brought her the results of twenty years sniffing out judicial results. In a word, she called the whole thing a "mystery." Continuing, she stated:

> I can't tell why or how judges make decisions or their purpose in punishment . . . yet ultimate responsibility for punishment rests solely with the judge . . . and how he decides directly effects sentence severity, from a simple fine to a

ticket to a (concentration camp). Not a very comforting feeling especially if you seek social justice from a CJS wracked by racism and White nationalist, fascist ideology.[32]

Spohn's study concluded that 94% of the judge cohort she studied were predictably White, male, upper middle class, with an enviable higher education, possessing deeply conservative values regardless of the political party. Why not, it was their world? Consequently, very few had any idea about the background of who they were sentencing, the culture of the criminal class, the financial problems they faced each day, or the racism and stress they encountered on a daily basis that caused many to buckle to pressure and commit a crime and/or sell illegal drugs. Nor as I saw it, did these mandarins really care. So judicial war crimes were bottled and manufactured under the judicial fear that without severe sanctions, the offender's probability of recidivism, which he would shamelessly do it again, was guaranteed. This explains, says Spohn, why the prison rate for Blacks was "much worse than in the days of Jim Crow." Criminologist Alfred Blumenstein took this a step further believing 80% of the racial disproportion in prison could be explained by racial differences beginning at the point of arrest through the process ending with the judge's predictable sentence to the big house. Blumenstein found that Blacks overrepresented in prison at increasing rates in this period due to drugs and, especially, because of intolerant judges 6% of the total prison population made up of drug cases in 1979 was, by 1991, increased by 400% when vastly increased chances of arrest meant quick passage to a court docket.[33]

Radley Balko, *Washington Post* opinion columnist, focusing on civil liberties, the drug war, and the CJS explained:

> This is all to say that there was a certain bias in the way the court attempts to administer justice which favors the CJS . . . It means that no matter how impartial the courts try to be, their search for justice will inevitably favor the White nationalist influenced prosecution because they are both trying to uphold the values and traditions of a White-oriented center . . . the closer and stricter the courts hold to the law, relying on only a minimum of lenient interpretation, the likelihood is the more it will favor the position of the prosecutor.[34]

With the supportive help of judges, Balko claimed "no policy since 1980 has contributed more to the incarceration of the African American than the war on drugs." Increased targeting of Black neighborhoods by discretionary drug enforcement and the major contribution of judicial vindictiveness ultimately increased the prison rates. The drug wars were a man-made disaster, planned by White legislators and abetted by White judges to be executed by White law enforcement who cared little for how the life outcome evolved downward for sentenced Blacks or other minorities and so "equity before the law was a social fiction."[35]

Judge Learned Hand wrote in 1953 that to keep our democracy, one cannot ration justice, it should be freely dispensed. Lawyer Arnold Trebach replied that for this period, this was "violated daily." Courtroom justice, in his view, was rationed for the defendant accused of crimes by wholesale violation of his constitutional rights kept secret as the case ensues, especially for poor Blacks. "Police invasions of individual rights left unchecked by judges and methods used by some prosecutors to obtain guilty pleas again found judges turning a blind eye."[36] He noted that a key fact for the defendant is that a "large number of cases are won by the police in the first few days" following the arrest when defense lawyers were often unavailable or too few in number to take on limited paying defendants. When such a defense attorney did present himself "he frequently finds that no legal defense was possible. A large number of cases were won in court not by prosecutors but by police who used primitive measures of threat, violence and illegal detention" to achieve their version of courtroom success.[37] Trebach noted at least five major deficiencies in the rationing of justice in his 1964 book, for example: (a) Independent investigations of a defendant's case don't go beyond a man's jail cell interview. Money dictates how much a lawyer will invest in a case and very little is awarded to the defense counsel. Little time is spent beyond the amount routinely agreeing to a plea bargain. (b) Attorneys often tell their clients that judges tend to give lighter sentences if they plead out; to demand a trial is to venture into unknown territory where severe sanctions are possible. Yet this was a fiction to speed cases along, not jam the court docket and avoid lengthy trials before sympathetic jurors. (c) For every assigned counsel who took time from his practice to aid a "criminal," there were several whose roles in the sentencing process was almost entirely passive. (d) A high percentage of people brought before the criminal court judge were highly stressed and not their best friend in pleading their case; many suffered mental disorder which was also not a positive factor for case success. But without an expert to take the stand for the defense, the word of a psychiatrist, be it soft or hard, in the employ of the state (who often review each case for a defendant's tendency to violence), went substantially unchallenged. Indigent defendants received no expert witness. (e) The role of counsel in the sentencing process was severely limited by the presentence probation report. These are written by probation officers often under pressure by the judge to speed it up, with recommendations about sentencing already preordained. In such a gathered hurry POs were apt to bend to the tough side and present barebones mercy for fear of getting caught in a situation where being nice actually hid a serial criminal (a rare case, indeed).[38]

Defense attorneys combatting the repetitious civil rights violations inherent in the criminal cases before them told us much about the prevailing war crimes mood of justice in the courtrooms. The editor of a series of conversations out of court on the system is Ann Fagan Ginger. By her judicious count, socially conscious activist lawyers numbered fewer than 10,000 of the 350,000 American lawyers in 1970 (maybe, just maybe 2–3%), and maybe as few as 250 proudly fighting the good fight against a fascist system of vindictive legal proceedings. Black attorneys represented only 4,000 (11%) and 8,000 women (23%), spread thin in trying to save clients in the face of courts whose own appointed lawyers saw these as mere menials attempting to save low-achieving Blacks.[39]

Cochran wrote about his experiences with the court when he was asked to help represent thirteen Black Panthers in 1971 in Los Angeles, a trial that lasted for eleven days. He later learned of the many dirty legal tricks employed by prosecution, of evidence suppression, and worst of all that the FBI had informants as part of the defense attorney team furnishing trial tactics to the prosecution while using surveillance techniques on Cochran and his team. The state was obviously prepared to do anything to win, resorting to reproachful extralegal activated to accomplish their intent to win at all costs.[40]

Superior investigative resources available to the prosecutor made most cases silly to fight. In Chicago, for example, the state's attorney had 93 investigators compared to the 6 public defenders; in Massachusetts 10 defense attorneys had average caseloads of 400. A national survey found that 60% of assigned counsel had no money to hire outside investigators to seek crucial evidence for clients. One report claims "in no city studied was the number of public defenders equal to the number of investigators found in the prosecutors' office." As a result, "in the majority of jurisdictions the defendant goes into court at a decided disadvantage." This all has a purpose in limiting justice to those the CJS and society are worthless and bad and this means Black males. In 1963 there existed only 3% of the country with public defender services serving 25% of the population. In 1973 this was up to 28%. One study claimed the average criminal court had virtually no contact with 90% of the defendants who pled guilty and the court/trial process provided "minimal opportunity" to learn enough about the defendant, especially those who were young and Black, to provide a basis for fair and intelligent sentencing.[41]

Unchecked judicial discretion, unwarranted disparity, and excessive sentences derive from the structure, content, and racist practices of the Penal Code translated by prosecutors and judges. States, especially in the South, provided a broad range of penalties for most cases with the choice from leniency to severity being left to the dubious inclinations of individual judges. In a racist environment, this left little doubt that White judges would interpret their mandate to sanction all crimes through the prism of potential slave revolts. As one observer put it:

> Everything that was done for Black people in the State of Mississippi that was worthwhile was done through a Federal Court order. This was because Blacks were meanly treated by local courts as "dumb driven cattle" and hard-core racist judges openly referred to them in their courtroom with viciously racist language.[42]

Getting inmates from local Southern jails and plantation road camps (i.e., Parchment Farm) to talk to their counsel was not easy. Complaints of the system meant retribution and penalty at some point in an inmate's career and intimidation was routine. Of course, courts and judges looked away or did nothing about this situation. Convicts who were brought to see their lawyers were often brought to undersized, unventilated squalid interview rooms in chains with armed White trustees always present and suspicious of any undue movement by Black prisoners. Under such conditions obvious tensions were always high between guards and inmates and any suspicion would earn offenders prompt and extreme injury for their efforts. It was customary, without judicial complaint, for inmates to endure deplorable conditions and be deprived of human rights guaranteed by several constitutional amendments. Indeed, the very CJS throughout the South was witness to broad-based war crimes within the CJS that did nothing to investigate this barbarism.[43]

Few bigoted judges conceded their rulings were made on the basis of racist attitudes. They didn't see themselves as racist. How could they be? It was for them alone to define what it meant to be racist and their definition always allowed plenty of room and scope to pronounce obvious racist sentences without seeing their own war crime. "I am filled with wonder at the power which comes with the black robe," noted an indignant and accusatory African American New York City judge Bruce Wright, "that these men could imprison, impose fines and deliver lectures on morality . . . while simultaneously referring to Blacks as 'urban insect life.'"[44]

Wright condemned a judicial system that its proponents, who he agreed were intelligent and educated men, should have recognized arrest reports, courtroom procedures and police witnesse in court gave birth to war crimes against Black defendants:

> No person called upon to judge the residents of a society so long scorned and held up to contempt because of color stereotypes deeply ingrained in American thinking and emotion should dare come to the bench as ignorant of Black circumstances as most now are and where Black defendants are no more than detested grist for the country's judicial mills.[45]

Receiving plenty of hate mail and continuous death threats, Wright was unrelenting in his criticism, producing a roll call of judicial complaints. They mark the rare critical voice during these years of the CJS and their interrelated crimes against humanity. Here were some: American judges had more in common with Russians than Black Americans, the CJS was broadly racist as well as being a sheer waste of taxpayer money, prisons had neither been a satisfactory answer nor did useful solutions to crime arise within our learned criminologist class, "Black defendants who write me believed they never had a fair trial and that none was possible," short-term rehabilitation programs cannot undo lengthy prison life spent in inhumane conditions and idealists and academics continue to attend conferences, seminars, and research conventions about crime yet perpetuate blindly a system of crime and outmoded forms of punishment. Continuing in his book, Wright claimed the vast majority of judges and prosecutors were all quite unsuited to their job and should have known they were out of their depths, "Typical White judges were power-hungry, egotistical, uncritical of the system affluent, clubby, stylish, hardworking, above scandal, dark suited and, lastly, let's admit it blindly, unequivocally racist."[46]

Despite his legal background and innate ability to argue, criminal court judges were divorced from the Black man's life on the streets and agreed with Wright's premises. One judge recalled: "It was not our way of life and we were shocked. We became angry. We realized that we were really Society's security force and keepers of a peace that had been lost."[47]

Wright again: Judges were chosen from the most conservative segment of a well-behaved society. As a result, radical lawyers who tried to understand the plight of the Black Americans were seldom if ever able to reach the bench. "They were seen suspiciously as destructive of government. It was a badge of infamy to be a radical lawyer or judge." The best judges were better off being ideologically numb and simply good expeditors. Judges of a large urban court system had to dispose of the most cases in the shortest period of time whatever the outcome. Known as "good calendar people" they were rewarded with special treatment and promotion. Moving cases along would have allowed judges to minimize sentences and allocate simple solutions although this did not happen.[48]

Few law schools placed their students in a Black slum or in an environment where the majority of the population was Black. To do so would have allowed would-be White lawyers and future judges to taste a humbler kind of existence. It would have been free from taints of superiority and belief in natural White privilege that blighted the perspective of criminal court judges in their War on Crime. According to Wright, "Black judges kept a low profile. Few felt entitled to belong to any exclusive club composed of White judges and rarely spoke out on militant issues, wearing the mask of mute and well-behaved dignity at all times."[49] Well-dressed like funeral directors, they remained unresponsive to Black concerns and just as regularly failed to rescue constitutional safeguards for Blacks during prosecutions. By so doing they held to a White value system that ensured political survival, financial security, an envious standard of living, and better judgeships as they ascended the political ladder.

In a 1971–1972 study of Black judges undertaken by a judicature society, it was discovered that of 475 federal judges fewer than 10% were Black, of 21,300 national judges only 255 (10%) were Black, almost none in the Deep South or the middle Western states, a surprise, in litigious New York of 35,000 judges only 2.5% were non-White. It bothered Wright, if no one else that White judges never seemed to notice or even care why so few Black judges sat on the bench when in the face of a sea of Black defendants where the need was obvious. These men specialized in assembly line justice where offenders were simply Black digits without worth being sentenced by men with neither interest nor understanding of the need for a top-down redesign of his community. The result was that the Blacks received the harshest sentences lacking constitutional safeguards from a truly racist system.

> Judges had the power to do otherwise but they simply didn't care to do it out of their own policy decisions, they weren't trained for this in law school and they personally had no intention making examples of themselves by challenging the CJS itself.[50]

One flagrant series of power moves that discounted human rights and constitutional safeguards for prisoners could be seen in the Chicago Narcotics Court, one of the first courts of its kind and seen as a progressive move in dealing with drug addicts. Yet war crimes prevailed. Our expert witness was Alfred R. Lindesmith, a social scientist who cataloged the abuses emanating from courts like this as to how addicts were mishandled and oppressed in the larger cities.[51]

He discussed the common police practice in the mid-1960s to arrest known addicts who loitered (there were many local statutes that sought to prevent this), stopping subjects to scan their arms for needle marks, not carrying identification cards, or not registering as an addict. Result for same: instant arrest. Not represented by counsel, 90% of the Black males whisking through Narcotic Court could face either a $5,000 fine (few had such money) or a 5-year prison sentence, whichever the judge preferred, depending on his attitude towards the offender. Having no counsel present also meant any future right to appeal was duly eliminated. The daily docket was a scene of whirlwind confusion, 8,000–9,000 cases per year per judge represented 100+ cases in a single day with all dispositions hopefully resolved by 1:00 p.m. before lunch. Inaudible judges convicted men on the basis of scant evidence and the sole word of a cop with questionable intentions—where the main charge was group loitering. Legal niceties, Lindesmith claims, rarely surfaced, excessive even brutal force at the time of arrest was adjudged part of the job, family members were routinely ignored, and defendant legal rights completely disregarded. After all, who really cared or objected to the unconstitutionality and illegal impositions of it all? Only a few attorneys were present and wished to argue on behalf of their clients during court time past lunch. To spare himself legal debates and just wanting an end to arguments between district attorneys and lawyers, judges would simply arbitrarily dismiss the case.[52]

All of the foregoing highlights the distressful failure of the criminal court system especially located in most of America—and its acute failure to support human rights as they applied particularly to the thousands of Black offenders over the course of the War on Crime. It certainly did not apply to the Southern brand of justice as found in Old Dixie. Here the brand of courtroom justice infused with White nationalism and basic dislike of Black culture within the local CJS were perfected. The War on Crime era was no different from what came before: incompetent judges, insecure lawyers who refused to fight local power structures, all White juries, absence of social services or rehabilitation practices, unhealthy jail and prison conditions, violently racist cops, dangerous and medieval conditions imposed by frightful environments which Black families had to endure in the face of local White violent gangs. Flagrant war crimes were endemic and predictable yet undocumented and ignored throughout the South. Friedman introduces us at the beginning of his study to the worst aspects of Southern justice: "In the South the law owes its allegiance only to hate and fear of the White community which governs the daily existence of Southern Blacks." In May 1964 Mississippi senator Collins (chairman of the senate judiciary committee) exclaimed: "This bill before us may be unconstitutional in stifling civil rights protest but it can't do us any harm and it will keep the streets clean."[53] In many Southern states, laws were passed by legislators with acceptance of local judges that served to strengthen nearby police and permit roundups. Curfew laws were increased, civil rights demonstrations were attacked, jail term punishments were increased, and criminal fines were jacked up. Local media were kept low on these issues. These laws, it was said, "passed with much laughter by Whites." One politician justified the consecutive passing of these laws "as the only way I know to stop this Black tide which threatens to engulf us all."[54]

No local judge or even legislator made any attempt to challenge the tenor of this legislation and judges obviously felt no compunction but to enforce such repressive legislation. In such a climate, unconstitutional behavior and dubious discretionary enforcement by Southern sheriffs, their accomplices, and judges as part of the arrangement perpetuated criminal behavior from the CJS far worse than practiced by local impoverished Black citizens. Vindictive White repression determined and shaped the Southern sense of justice which the courts did nothing to contradict. Such justice was central to the economic reprisals, arrests, threats, costly bail, and police atrocities in this total violation of the constitutional rights of every citizen in the South. Judges appeared determined to do nothing to prevent or criticize wide-scale police roundups and mass civil rights arrests with usual excessive force employed but were notoriously sluggish in seeing any violation of federal law in the pursuit. The sole objective was to cause enough arrests and jailing those Black citizens attempting to register to vote who couldn't afford the risk of losing their jobs while stuck in jail or absorb whatever physical abuse might ensue. Judges were bent on showing potential voters that arbitrary police and judicial power that always went beyond the law could not be opposed by a CJS that had little interest in chastising members of the CJS itself who were flagrant abusers of constitutional rights.

It cannot be stressed strongly enough that American judges within the CJS played a great part in creating war crimes that arose from the War on Crime political campaigns. They refused to accept responsibility to condemn police brutality and wrongful enforcement of the law, ignored abuses by prosecutors in how criminal cases were presented in court, and took little interest in the many alarming crimes that prison and jail officials created in the pursuit of repressing convict life under reprehensible human rights violations that arose from such confinement. Judges did not visit riot zones, jails, prisons, rehab centers, or even homes and communities of the people who appeared before them. As a probation officer, I never saw a judge in our department asking questions, snooping, talking to clients, reading office visit notes. I never had one ask me anything about my job, my concerns, how I viewed the system, how I rated his court and others like his. This must have been maybe a dozen all told, but no one showed any curiosity or wished to hear any complaint.

I have no idea how they viewed the obvious racial disparities in court or within the CJS at large. That they might be a part of the problem never occurred to them, at least in conversations, meager as these were, with me. That their sentences may have been too harsh, or inappropriate, or completely disregarded the men that were being harshly sentenced; or that their use of incarceration was perhaps too quickly decided. Who were these men before them? I never saw a judge take one aside or bring him into chambers for a general chit-chat. Might they have asked these men questions totally differ-ent from the ones normally posed by probation officers and lawyers? I never believed any of them cared enough nor that they wished to get close enough to any of these men that maybe some deep, dark inner question they had har-bored for years might be revealed through a mature discussion with anyone in a jail suit.[55]

I never saw families or relatives engaged with judges or prosecutors unless they were tearfully pleading for leniency. The CJS in its entirety showed no instinct for kindness or curiosity or wished to take a chance on this group. There was no inclination in curbing crime and rebuilding lives by helping start an innovative community program with the judge and CJS personnel taking on volunteer roles. Judges and prosecutors could not have cared less. Politics and upward mobility were their game. This is why we lump them as part of the series of war crimes for which this period in American history brought to intolerant fruition.

In actual fact, I never met a prosecutor or district attorney I liked. Echoing the words of Scances: "They were systematically out of step with their constituents despite the heterogeneity of voter preferences. They almost always took the conservative of nationalist position on criminal justice issues."[56] This is the conclusion I reached in the nine years (1970–1979) in which I was closest to eleven of them to understand how they thought. I knew their job normally puts them in the bad guy role, having to prosecute for alleged crimes police claim these defendants had committed. My frame of reference was Marin County in Northern California during this period, just north of San Francisco. All prosecutors were White, 15% of the defendants were Black or Latino who lived in a small enclave (i.e., public housing) near Sausalito. They may well have been on the moon separated as they were by the rest of the world by a nearby freeway which acted as an invisible wall to enclose them. Prosecutors I spoke with acted as if Black Marinites were a race apart, known only for their community hostility and penchant for committing crimes. After all, this was the county where a shootout with Black Panthers trying to rescue a jail prisoner had occurred in 1968, resulting in one of the prosecutors being shot and crippled (later awarded a judgeship as one of the four in the county). While local Blacks played no part in this event, their very presence on the streets of San Rafael forever sealed their fate and reminded Whites of what they were capable of doing. Consequently, they were stigmatized and remembered by prosecutors (who were elected) when it came to deciding the fate of a Black suspect in court. Vindictiveness is a word that comes to mind and prosecutors liked to boast of their conviction rate.

The local liberal voting public wasn't affected by any local crime issues so they didn't care; prosecutors in Marin County didn't seem to pay any attention to them anyway. Worse, the public appeared unmoved by the trends toward mass incarceration taking place, oppressive drug laws, constant court referrals for prison, or out-of-control police. Just the opposite, except for the ultraliberal, hippie element that infested the county, most preferred district attorneys who exceeded their legal restraints and devoted their time to "racking up convictions with little fear of going too far." The profession was always susceptible to misconduct and the crime wave of the period under study gave them plenty of reason to cheat. The list of possible corruption and illegality was large and disfavored defendants with easily obtained guilty pleas: failure to disclose exculpatory evidence, false confession, over-charging, falsified evidence, intimidation, repressive sentencing, perjury, racial profiling, malicious prosecution, abetting police brutality, and disregard of human rights abuses. The courts and bars failed to hold prosecutors accountable so the problem during these years was full blown and full of war crimes.

Whenever I had cause to visit one of them in their office, I found that among themselves they were jovial, chatty, easy going, and even charming. In the presence of defendants and their families, I saw a different face: scowling, impersonal, obsessed with the law, even punitive, arrogant, and mounting a superior tone. As a result, the defendants recoiled from them. Was this the reaction they sought? They didn't seem to pay much attention to the views of the defendants. From the standpoint of harmonious relationships between two groups of strangers, I wasn't impressed. I don't believe the prosecutors, most of them quite young, saw themselves as obligated to social obligations among these wretched of the earth. Perhaps they weren't altogether ruthless at pursuing right from wrong, but I always felt queasy in their company. Being holier than thou certainly opened one up to charges of hypocrisy and worse. In 1991, the Chicago Tribune ran a 5-part series on corrupt prosecutors, documenting 381 cases back to 1963 over misconduct and corruption. Yale University Law Professor Edwin Borchard wrote a book *Convicting the Innocent* which spelled out many gross injustices by prosecutors being studied that nonetheless enhanced the reputation of the guilty prosecutor.[57]

Once I asked men just placed on supervised probation what their experience had been at the hands of local prosecutors. The answers were not good even though everyone admitted they had no proof of the volume of charges they could lay at the feet of the prosecutors. All they could do was repeat what their own defense attorneys had shared with them during post-mortem evaluations of their case: district attorney failed to disclose exculpatory evidence, indulge in witness tampering, inadmissible evidence, defense attorneys who encountered difficulties gaining access to all available information, and the need for cooperation between defense attorneys and prosecution at all stages of the criminal process, refusal to dismiss or reduce penalties; if new evidence became available to the defense, the planting of false and misleading evidence, threats on increased punishment, failure to abide by earlier plea bargains, use of jailhouse informants known to be lying, extracting false confessions, providing bad eyewitness testimony, and so on. My guess was that for every probationer who was convicted rightfully of all charges, four, maybe more, had serious complaints and doubts on the way prosecution handled their inevitable conviction. What view could they take about a system which operated without humanity or attention to offender family needs? As E. M. McCann, a prosecutor in Milwaukee, WI, since 1969 put it:

> The burden of proving that a district attorney has abused a case is difficult if not impossible to prove . . . it is impossible to know when they break the rules as discretion of a prosecutor is so broad it is subject to almost no control or judicial review.

Further:

> There is little known how this group makes decisions that determine a defendant's future, there is no judicial review, no public inspections, no right to be present when such decisions are made, no right for decisions to be made available to the public.[58]

The ability to create war crimes in these court cases is derived from the failure of the CJS to examine the nature of prosecutorial decisions and the obvious bureaucratic, conveyor belt, unconstitutional, adversarial nature of the CJS process.

NOTES

1. Nicola Gonzalez van Cleve, *Crook County: Racism and Injustice in America* (Stanford: Stanford UP, 2016), pp. 1–6.
2. Op. cit.
3. Malcolm M. Feely, "How to Think about Criminal Court reform," *Boston Law Review* 98 (2018): 673 and 725.
4. Gerald D. Robin, *Introduction to the Criminal Justice System: Principles, Procedures, Practices* (New York: Harper & Row, 1980), p. 168.
5. Johnny L. Cochran, Jr. and Tim Rutten, *Journey to Justice* (New York: Ballantine, 1997), p. 117; Robin, op. cit., pp. 192–203 on judicial problems of the period; Robin, op. cit., p. 217.
6. Lyman Ray Patterson, "Should Lawyers Judge the Judges?" *Judicature*, May 1976, p. 457.
7. Cochran, op. cit., p. 71.
8. Ibid., op. cit.,
9. Ibid., p. 88.
10. Ibid., p. 74 and 87.
11. Ibid., p. 140.
12. Derrick A. Bell, "Racism in American Courts-cause for Black Disruption or Despair?" *California Law Review* 61, no. 165 (1973): 200.

13. Chris Hayes, *A Colony in a Nation* (New York: W. W. Norton, 2017); Michelle Alexander, *The New Jim Crow: Mass Incarceration in an Age of Colorblindness* (Seattle: New Press, 2012); Issa Kohler-Hausmann, *Misdemeanorland: Criminal Courts and Social Control in an Age of Broken Windows* (Princeton: Princeton UP); and Feely, op. cit., p. 689, 691 and 711; and D. Quentin Miller, *A Criminal Power—James Baldwin and the Law* (Columbus: Ohio State UP, 2016).

14. Paul Butler, *Chokehold: Policing Black Men* (New York: New Press, 2018), p. 85.

15. Robert Staples, "White Racism, Black Crime and American Justice," *Phylon* 36, no. 1 (1975): 14–22.

16. Joan R. Petersilia, *Racial Disparities in the CJS* (Santa Monica: Rand, 1983), pp. 1–3.

17. Adam Liptak, Alma Cohen and Crystal Yang, "Black Defendants Get Longer Sentences from Republican-Appointed Judges," *New York Times*, 24 May 2018, three months more on average.

18. Frank R. Prassel, *Introduction to the American Criminal Justice System* (New York: Harper & Row, 1975), p. 141.

19. *New York Times*, 30 October 1974, p. 61.

20. *New York Times*, 2 June 1975, p. 16; and CBS TV Sixty Minutes, "Rural Justice," 22 February 1976 transcript.

21. Cochran, op. cit., p109.

22. Ibid.

23. Michael W. Scances, "Do DAs Represent Their Voters, Evidence from California's Era of Criminal Justice Reform," in Bedrosian@usc/edu/mp-content, 2021, pp. 1–3.

24. Cochran, op. cit., pp. 82–83.

25. Cochran, op. cit., pp. 84–85.

26. Marvin E. Frankel, *Criminal Sentences: Law without Order* (New York: Hill & Wang, 1973), p. 297.

27. David J. Freed and Patricia M. Ward, "Bail in the United States," *Vera Foundation, Department of Justice*, Washington, DC, 1964, p. 47.

28. Robin, op cit., p. 180.

29. Robert P. Burns, *Kafka's Law: The Trial of American Criminal Justice* (Chicago: Chicago UP, 2014), pp. 5–6, 39 and 99.

30. Ibid., p. 65.

31. Ibid., p. 66.

32. Cassia C. Spohn, *How Do Judges Decide-The Search for Fairness in Justice and Punishment* (One Thousand Oaks: Sage, 2002), p. vii and 69.

33. Ibid., p. 101, 116, 119 and 157, 173; Alfred Blumenstein quoted in M. Tonry, op. cit., page 176 and the *Journal of Criminal Law and Criminology* 73 (1982): 1259 and 1283.

34. Balko, Radley, "Exposing Corrupt Prosecutions," 9 January 2014, p. 1.

35. Ibid., op. cit., p. 177.

36. Arnold S. Trebach, *The Rationing of Justice: Constitutional Rights and the Criminal Process* (New Brunswick: Rutgers UP, 1964), pp. 235, 243–264 on the percentages.

37. Ibid., p. ix., 57–58.

38. Ibid., op. cit., p. 122, 138, 161, 171, 172, 187, 172 and 179.

39. Ginger Ann Fagan, *The Relevant Lawyers* (New York: Simon & Schuster, 1972), p. 20, 27, 30, 33 and 37.

40. Cochran, op. cit., p. 125.

41. Robin, p. 198 and 200.

42. Stephen R. Bing and Stephen Rosenfeld, *The Quality of Justice in the Lower Criminal Courts of Metropolitan Boston* (Boston: Lawyers Committee for Civil Rights under Law, September 1970), p. 31; Lawrence A. Benner, "Tokenism and the American Indigent: Some Perspectives on Defense Services," *ACLU Newsletter*, Spring 1975, p. 675; Paul B. Wice and Mark Pilgrim, "Meeting the Gideon Mandate, A Survey of Public Defender Programs," *Judicature*, March 1975, p. 404.

43. See President's Crime Commission (Corrections), Commission on Law Enforcement and Administration of Justice, 1965, p. 18; Robin, op. cit., pp. 337–339; Francis Stevens, Francis and John Maxoy, "Representing the Unrepresented: A Decennial Report," Public Interest Litigation in Mississippi," *Mississippi Law Journal* 44 (1973): 339–337; Tony Dunbar, *Delta Time: A Journey Through Mississippi* (New York: Pantheon, 1990), p. 46; and Ronald Welch, "Developing Prisoner Self-Help Techniques, The Early Mississippi Experiment," *Prison Law Monitor* (1979): 118–122.

44. Bruce Wright, *Black Robes, White Justice: Why the Justice System Doesn't Work for Blacks* (Secaucus: Lyle Stuart, 1987), p. 154, 163, 185. It should be noted that Wright had a difficult time trying to offer the manuscript of this book to leading publishers who declined to publish. He was left to a publisher with limited distribution and publicity resources to accept this important work.

45. Ibid., p. 190, 197, 199,

46. Ibid., p. 201, 204, 208, 213.

47. Bing, op. cit., p. 77, 79 and 87.

48. Wright, op. cit., p. 87.

49. Ibid., op. cit., p. 236.

50. Ibid., op. cit., pp. 88–92.

51. All these indictments of criminal court judge bad behavior or war crimes can be read in Alfred R. Lindesmith's *The Addict and the Law* (Bloomington: Indiana UP, 1965), pp. 90–94.

52. Ibid., p. 91.

53. Leon Friedman (Ed.), *Southern Justice* (New York: Pantheon, 1966), p. 6; reported in the *Greenwood Mississippi Commonwealth Newspaper*, 12 May 1964, p. 3; and Friedman, op. cit., p. 21, 23.

54. Reported in the Jackson (MS) *Daily News*, 21 May 1964.

55. Friedman, op. cit., pp. 57, 59, 78–79.

56. Scances, op. cit., p. 2.

57. Edwin Borchard, *Convicting the Innocent: Errors of Criminal Justice* (New Haven: Yale UP, 1932), p. 3, 19 and 111.

58. See McCann, E. Michael, "Don't Exempt Political Corruption from Effective Prosecution," *Wisconsin State Journal*, 19 October 2015, p. 15 and 17.

Chapter 5

No Convict's Story Ends Happily

The correctional component of the CJS is the easiest to label a "war crimes" industry. Indeed, that was its very essence, to inflict gratuitous pain, to damage an individual's psyche as to self-worth, and as much as possible to reduce their inherent commodity value as it applied to their community and to their family. This took place so that their contribution (while alive) would be as near zero as possible. With so few assets and skills, and little help received from their previous stay in prison or jail, they made for perfect repeat offenders. Men with nothing purposeful to offer was the incumbent tale of the prisons' war crimes rationale. What kind of people does it take to rule such a realm?

And this was an era when prison life came to greet (and grieve) many Black men. Between 1973 and the early 1990s, America's Black inmate population shot up by 332%. In their infinite wisdom, researchers at the American Civil Liberties Union estimated that the figure was really 700%. One in thirty-one Black adults were then under some form of correctional supervision during these years; four to six men were sleeping in a cell built for two, some sleeping in hallways. Incarceration figures had outpaced all other kinds of criminal indices during these years.[1]

This is an easy chapter to document for all its banality. American prisons, jails, confinements, prisoner of war camps, concentration camps in their normal setting with daily routines which overrode human rights spawned infinity of war crimes. Georgetown law professor Judith Lichtenberg called the American prison system "over flawed, racially biased, inhumane and ineffective, a system that breaks up families and raises the poverty rate by 20%."[2] We're only left to present some of the worst abuses this institution was capable of producing. But all the entities that made up the corrections industry were guilty of what they did to living souls. As the chapter title right-fully says, "no convict's story ends happily."

In 1946 in the aftermath of World War II, the Texas Council of Methodist Women, concerned by an apparent increase in crime before their eyes, concerned that so many criminal court convictions led to prison sentences, willingly adopted the cause of prison reform. Unclear what this meant, they beseeched the liberal Governor B. H. Jester to create a report on conditions in Texas prisons to determine what was needed.[3]

In agreement with the idea, Jester summoned twenty-two state assem-blymen and assigned them the task of visiting various prisons and writing up what they saw. The eventual eight-page report appeared in April 1947. Having visited Darrington, Retrieve, Wynne Farm, and Huntsville's peni-tentiaries, the shocked politicians described them as a mixture of clean and filthy facilities, that on average treated the inmates terribly. Many parts of the report made for sober reflection if not deeply disturbed reading as conditions at all locations were but a litany of abominations. A few examples will sup-port this view.

Inmates were often left in solitary confinement buck naked for hours, often handcuffed with their hands behind their backs, creating a bodily posture that inhibited sleep altogether. Convicts were kept dirty, made to wear ill-fitting, old shoes which cramped walking, and, of course, made escape impossible. Blisters that festered or bled openly were common. Then too, men were found to have been refused food for upward of thirty-six hours and com-munal talking at night was prohibited under threat of tear gas attack (the standard retaliatory punishment used on a daily basis against the inmates). Some cells were intentionally shrouded in darkness causing cellmates to feel their way around; the medical doctor at Huntsville was a plodding eighty-year-old incompetent hated by inmates and staff alike. Guards regularly beat their charges with rubber hoses, cursing them in the process. Linen was filthy and rarely substituted—conditions and policies which were well known to administrators at Huntsville (and elsewhere) but preferred things as they were. This was what prison life was supposed to be like for Black enemies of the state.[4]

Raw brutality was a common feature where "men were treated worse than animals." The manager of Darrington brazenly informed the visiting Committee, many of whom were women, "it did not make a damn bit of difference what the Committee thought of how he was running the Farm, he was the manager and would do as he damned pleased." This seemed to be the opinion of all prison administrators throughout the state which no one on the Committee thought of challenging. One inmate serving a life sentence since 1988 described correctional officers he had witnessed as "minimally literate, culturally unsophisticated and lacking a normal adult level of logic or reasoning skills." Most lived in small, rural towns with a fleeting education as kids and little experience working with other men, much less urbane Black men.[5]

Professor Andrea Armstrong, law professor at Loyola University (New Orleans), provides an account from her research on the influence of race on prison staff decision-making:

> Minority offenders were more likely to be perceived as a disciplinary threat by correctional officers regardless of an offender's actual behavior and good conduct. For example, a CO might be more likely to perceive contraband in a Black offender's hand than in a White's. A prison guard might also decide more quickly that a Black is a significant threat as compared to a White offender, leading perhaps to increased citations from Black inmates. It was also possible that this threat was exaggerated for minority offenders and therefore Black inmates might face more serious conduct reports than their White counterparts for the same type of behavior.[6]

The Governor's Committee report acknowledged "that there is no effort being made to remedy conditions, and the ladies were shocked" as was the Governor to the extent that the 1949 Legislature appropriated 4 million dollars to upgrade guard salaries, insert very few rehabilitation programs, and make a modicum of superficial changes with regard to living conditions. What was seen as abominable here, and Southern correctional facilities were the worst, there was not much difference in conditions presented to inmates elsewhere.[7]

According to Wikipedia Encyclopedia while Louisiana State Prison at Angola was the nation's worst prison there were others that followed closely behind: San Quentin and Alcatraz (CA), Attica and Sing Sing (NY), Cook County Jail (Chicago), and Joliet State Prison (IL), and Eastern State Penitentiary (PA) where scientific experiments were openly conducted on hapless inmates. Eleven of the worst dozen had links to the old confederacy. This list could easily stretch to the wall, so many were the abusive American institutions that misused men in these unnatural and confined settings.

All these known violations within prison settings were challenged soon after when the United Nations, chaired by the deceased president's wife Eleanor Roosevelt, issued a bilingual document titled "The Universal Declaration of Human Rights" adopted by most countries including the United States in December 1948. It should be noted that this report set rules on how humans should be treated whether they were confined in jails, prisons, and detention centers or not. Certain rights existed simply because the inmates were human beings and were entitled to recognition as such. Governments, state or local, had an obligation to treat incapacitated men and women humanely by virtue of this universal law. Resistance to this new way of looking at prisoners, political or otherwise, met an official stone wall. The processes of CJS institutions by which such situations would be charged with documentation and enforcement were noticeably absent making such existence of these human rights toothless. How well did that ray of humanity work out?

Over the last several decades of the twentieth century, beginning in the early 1970s, as part of the War on Crime, a combination of forces transformed the CJS and modified the nature of vindictive imprisonment. Over the past twenty-five years, penologists repeatedly described US prisons as "in crisis" and have characterized each new level of overcrowding and inhumanity as "unprecedented." By the 1990s, as this study closes, the United States had incarcerated more persons per capita than any other nation in the modern world and it has retained the dubious distinction every year since.

During this time, California's prisoner population increased by eight to tenfold (from roughly 20,000 in the early 1970s to about 160,000 by 1990); elsewhere it was fivefold. According to Wikipedia in a given year 2 million or more men rotated in and out of confinement centers during this historically unprecedented expansion of prisons on all levels of government (see Wikipedia online for the history of prison systems in America). Contrary to public expectations, this was not the result of any increase in crimes of violence but of the nation's War on Drugs, pursued so methodically in the 1980s during the Reagan administration. As part of a collective hostile mentality, there was no remotely comparable increase in funds for prisoner services or inmate programming, just increased misery for being a prisoner of the system.[8]

In line with this, there soon followed abandonment of rehabilitation as a tool designed to help improve skills and education to a man while in prison. Instead, many correctional systems openly embraced the punitive approach with cheaper, poorly trained guards who arbitrarily resorted to extreme forms of prison punishment to maintain a military-type regime (i.e., inmate isolation, extended sentences by administrative dictate, withdrawal of family visits, denial of phone calls, restrictions on recreational privileges) that had especially corrosive effects on inmates all the while administrative resolution of complaints were habitually ignored. So much for human rights proclamations of the time.

Since 1954, in keeping with Mrs. Roosevelt's best efforts at prison reform, the American Correctional Association developed a lengthy series of standards for the treatment of American prisoners embodied in a code of prisoner rights: namely those having to do with safe environments, prisons operating on a lawful basis, attention paid to inmate post-release planning and reintegration into society, physical and legal protection from harm (especially rape and excessive force by guards or inmates) by watchful authorities, health care guarantees, continuous inspections of prison conditions from appropriate independent state agencies, convict freedom from staff harassment, removal of all forms of racial discrimination, permission for inmates to enjoy political rights and freedom of expression, humane living conditions, proper investigation of inmate complaints, and, most importantly, ability to maintain frequent and healthy relationships with families.

Sadly, and as a portrait of the violations of human rights, these well-intentioned objectives were disregarded wholesale by persecuting prison officials and guards everywhere. With little concern for the fate or outcome of inmates under their control, correctional personnel saw kindness as weakness and refused to modify obsolete rules that were so inefficient in transforming prisoners into better men. Nor did the CJS, except for a few reforming lawyers, police chiefs, and judges, who made minimal progress challenging the endless violations contained in daily confrontations with Black men either inside or outside of prison and jail. All of this was abetted by fascist and White supremacist Republican and Southern Democrat politicians who regularly underfunded convict-aid programs while jacking up draconian punishments that swelled the flow of men into these institutions.[9]

Most observers agreed that these conditions and punishments, along with the more extreme, harsh, dangerous, and otherwise psychological damage, led to unnecessary and counterproductive suffering to convicts. Craig Haney, professor at the University of California @ Santa Cruz, briefly summarized the damage incarceration brought to men especially in the sentences lengthened and the conditions inside prison: "institutional dependence, heightened suspicion, interpersonal distrust, alienation, social distancing and withdrawal towards isolation, diminished sense of self-worth and post-traumatic stress (as found in war)."[10]

The result didn't wait long to happen. It also gave us a peek into how CJS sequenced war crimes that occurred during the episodic battles with the Black community. Perhaps the worst single war crimes campaign committed by the CJS outside the 1965 Watts Riots (when 34 Blacks were killed and 3,400 arrested), and the continuous ambushes by police on the Black Panther Party members between 1969 and 1971, was the September 9, 1971, Attica (NY) Prison massacre (when 60% of the men rioted over four days, and forty-three Black inmates were killed by an all-White New York State Police). The prison riot is worth examining for the sequence of events and the attitudes of the negotiators for the many war crimes that were so much a part of the massacre and the thirteen other prison riots which followed in the wake of Attica. To begin the war crime, the CJS must play an active part in the following sequence of events:

1. Establish and maintain within the Black community (in ghettoes, neighborhoods, even prisons and jails) terrible conditions, unlawful CJS behavior, and unjust legal treatment. Oversight by external organizations to monitor prisoner rights will later be found not to have taken place.[11] War crimes will be central to Black victimization.

2. Once conditions become too unbearable, Black men will challenge the system and seek reforms—New York State inmates were paid fifty cents a day, rehabilitation programs were nonexistent, violence from guards was persistent, visitation rights were minimal, designed for 1,200 it held 2,200, 14–16-hour days in a cell, no narcotics treatment programs, censorship was universal, reading material was often banned, inmate funds were empty, and so on.[12]

3. Requests for reforms will be categorically denied by the White Power structure and CJS (government) and will provoke Blacks to attack the system, often violently, for much-needed relief. Serious criminality could occur on both sides once the battle lines have been drawn and battles enacted. War crimes will be many.

4. Retaliation by the CJS will overcompensate Black violence using greater violence and excessive force by the CJS who will blame Black men for aggression said to be inherent and racially characteristic (police will generally display crude racist beliefs to stifle Black protest). Again, there will be many war crimes enacted by the CJS in its righteousness.

5. Government politicians and administrators (in this case New York State Governor Nelson Rockefeller) will sidestep responsibility and intentionally permit violence to happen. They will openly show little understanding of the issues which stem from generations of government thinking along certain traditional lines of belief in Black people. Wicker quotes Rockefeller doing a sidestep: "I am satisfied that these men (NY State Police) in their best judgement used what they thought was necessary to maintain lives . . . and to save to the maximum degree possible the security and well-being of the hostages and the prisoners." Over thirty were killed, several shot in the back.[13]

6. Negotiations between members of the Black community and government agents will eventually occur and drag out but ignore root causes. War crimes will continue unabated.

7. Blacks will be the ones found guilty, Whites not. In this case, 61 Black men were indicted for 1,400 actions and 40 separate trials; no law enforcement personnel who were White were found guilty of anything, none found guilty of failing to give medical attention where needed. Yes, war crimes are in the extreme here as all sense of equality is gone.

8. Alternative peaceful methods by the government of dealing with the riots are available but there will be little desire to resolve the riots quickly and

harmlessly. Three years after the attack, Nelson Rockefeller, nominated by Gerald Ford to be vice president, during the confirmation hearing, was asked what lessons had he learned from the Attica massacre? Rockefeller thought a minute, "that if this would happen again," I would think that the proper way to proceed would be to "go ahead . . . without weapons."[14]

9. Police officials will find it extremely difficult to negotiate with men seen as terrorists, animals, and bloodthirsty. "The blame lies with the revolutionary tactics of militants and the outside forces who played a role bringing on the violence" was the opinion of one negotiator.[15]

10. Higher government officials (i.e., Rockefeller) will find little to complain about CJS operations despite the ruthlessness and casualties with which the riot was handled. Again, Rockefeller walks away from blame. "The best thing any well-intentioned civilian political personality can do (he graciously refers to himself) is not try and impose his judgement on professional matters but to pick good people and back them up . . . these men were all there, had been there 14 years and served with me . . . with their dedication."[16]

11. Months later a revisit to Attica found that few reforms had been successfully implemented.

12. Refusal to admit racism infected any of the personnel or political decisions made during the battle where the police and the government agents were all White. Rockefeller is quoted as saying with little shred of truth: "I have done a great deal to encourage the recruitment and membership of the police to reflect the broader base of our community make up but when it comes to the deployment of personnel this is a matter of responsibility of the people in charge . . . and any questions about racial attitudes affecting the capacity of police actions—that is irrelevant."[17]

So much for prisons. How decent were the nation's jails in this period? In a word, terrible. Let's listen to the words of Gerald D Robin, professor of Criminal Justice Studies at the University of New Haven who discussed the various aspects of corrections (jails and prisons) in chapters 13 and 14 of his *Introduction to Criminal Justice*. Here are some of his collected observations from research and findings regarding these two correctional institutions. What did he discover on the prevalence of human rights and abuses and war crimes in the nation's correctional system? Bear in mind he is not treating these incidents as war crimes which is where he and I diverge. The chapter opens on a less than optimistic note when he discusses a serious defect in correctional procedures: "For the foreseeable future, jail and prison personnel had their hands and cells full, simply trying to safeguard lives of 363,000 inmates on a daily basis." He then goes on to approximate the scope of the problem in statistics for jail detainees: excluding stays of less than 48 hours, an estimated 3–5 million persons spent time in the nation's jails . . . 10–15 times the number of inmates handled by all states and federal prison annually. In 1933, there were 31,000 men in jail; 1970, 161,000 men; and by 1983, 224,000 or an 8 times explosion.[18]

Recent comprehensive information on the nearly 4,000 jails (1972) suggests most held less than 21 inmates while there were 113 jails housing 250+ inmates. Leading states were California, New York, Texas, Florida, Pennsylvania, and Georgia (about 50% of all inmates nationwide) with most jails having multiple occupancy cells—30% were over fifty years old and 75% failed to separate mere detainees from convicted; 41% had no heat, 38% had toilets that didn't work, 16% had adequate shower provisions, 40% had no recreation areas, and only 16% of the jails had an exercise yard, 86% of the jails had no medical facilities of any kind, and 90% had no educational facilities—all clear violations of human rights requirements.[19]

Of the total labor force employed in jails, 46% were guards (20,000), 27% administrative staff, 17% clerical, and 7% were professional (i.e., social workers, psychiatrists, educators), of which half of these were part-time! 20% employed doctors in varying categories. Inmate-staff ratios from 1972 accounting were: academic teachers: inmates 385:1; psychologists 1,033:1; nurses 189:1; physicians 133:1; but guards to inmates 7:1. On average 9% of all jails had a professional staff of some sort. (The nation's jails, a report of the census of jails from the 1972 survey of inmates of local jails, Washington DC, USGPO, May 1975.)[20]

Robin comments: "With good reason the country's jails have been described as the 'ultimate ghetto,' 'festering sores in the CJS' and cesspools for crime." The dehumanization of inmates begins at intake, a status degradation, ceremony in which both accused and convicted are stripped and frisked given one minute "medical examination (if any) . . . forced to relinquish their personal identity for numerical anonymous and then left to learn the ropes of survival from 'barn bosses' the stronger and more hardened criminals who are the self-styled leaders."[21]

It is reasonable to deduce that war crimes and psychic injuries occurred to the vast number of inmates given their inability to complain to authorities who ignored what was taking place: cell confinement, overcrowding, shower rape, racial strife, lack of privacy, pervasive idleness, lack of jobs or vocational training, poor food, antiquated facilities, filth, disrepair, neglect and poor sanitation, limited access to personal hygiene commodities. "Even such basic items as soap, towels, toothbrushes, showers, clean bedding, and toilet paper are often in short supply and await dispensation by an overworked, underpaid, lethargic custodial staff. Indeed, a handful of jails, especially in the South, still rely on waste buckets rather than flush toilets."[22]

Who was at fault? "Most authorities on the subject," says Robin, have attributed the dehumanizing treatment of inmates and deplorable jail conditions to the local authorities of the institutions by county sheriff and city police management and other law enforcement personnel who are obsessively concerned with security issue that dominate the operation of jails.

Harry H. Woodward, director of the Correctional Project of Chicago, believed that White guards almost everywhere had a complete lack of sympathy for an inmate's plight, no knowledge or desire to learn of Black life, especially where belief in racism and White nationalism were strong components of the local CJS scene.[23]

Who were the victims of these intolerant staff? The usual 42% Black (much higher in urban jails), 60% with no or minimal work record, over half aged 18–29 (principal productive working age), 95% male, 66% with no high-school diploma, 50% below the poverty line, and 75% serving time for a previous conviction (see inmate survey, pages 3–4). Other complaints by Robin also point to CJS' disregard of inmate living standards and rights. There's the $1.55 a day for food as a starter, ineffective state and local standards for inspecting jails (twenty-three states had none), lack of authority to compel jail jurisdictions to maintain proper standards, court indifference even hostility to endless inmate complaints about deplorable conditions, refusal to observe human rights, and prisons whose managements willfully maintained an exclusive orientation and acceptance of guard brutality and abuses.[24]

Angela Davis, witness to her own captivity as a political prisoner in California's Soledad Prison recalled pitch dark strip cells, the smell of excrement and urine everywhere, a hole in the floor for a toilet unseen in the dark, screams, metallic keys forever clinking, and a most unpalatable breakfast of powdered milk Thorazine and stale white bread. Banned were cigarettes, matches, books, writing materials, combs, toothbrushes, shoes, even underwear—all quite unconstitutional but seen by an anxious administration as contraband. When given candy she supposed it to be poison.[25]

While America lacked the morbidity of slave labor camps like Buchenwald, Sachsenhausen, Flossenburg, and Kaiserwald, for any envious dictator there were always Attica (NY) scenes of murderous inmate mutinies, Angola State Prison (LA), former slave plantation, Idaho Correctional Center (ID) with its "gladiator school" (these quotes can be located in the appropriate listings found on Wikipedia for America's worst prisons) and epidemics of gang violence, Walnut Grove Youth Correctional Facility (MS), "a cesspool of unconstitutional inhuman acts, Pelican Bay State Prison (CA) notorious for its twenty-three hours a day spent in windowless cells," Julia Titwiler Prison (AL), where rape was common, education was not provided, and inmates were treated like animals, and Ely State Prison (NV) "with its shocking, callous disregard for human life." Hard to pick a favorite worst prison from this list. And the list hasn't been exhausted! And what about the American public who applaud these barbarities. One poll claimed 75% of public opinion felt CJS was too easy on convicted criminals and 70% felt that for these men probation and parole were not the answer—only confinement. One expert explained: "The public is largely ignorant of the facts concerning the efficacy of the correctional system or the number of defendants actually caught up in imprisonment. Or even the traditional nature of a positive-oriented rehabilitation program."[26]

Baseball historian Bruce Chadwick reminds us that prisons were not always places of intense pain and misery. He writes:

> Prisons in the 1930s entered a new era. Direct punishment was being downplayed and rehabilitation stressed. Classes were offered, convicts were given productive jobs (including that old reliable—making license plates) and athletics were considered to be a useful part of rehabilitation. A main prison yard was the size of a baseball field, and it was very easy for prisons to erect temporary backstops and bleachers from which convicts could watch prison teams play one another. To spice it up, wardens at many prisons invited semipro, minor league and even major-league teams into the prison to play the convicts. San Quentin's warden would make a whole day of it, with a game followed by an elaborate dinner for visiting teams, with printed programs. Several wardens allowed the players out of prison to travel, with a bevy of guards, to a nearby town for a game.[27]

If you're looking for a poster child for the most inhumane of American prisons and concentration camps in the 1960–1990 period, one need go no further than the Parchman State Farm stuck deep in the bowels of the Mississippi Delta. Since 1901 its birth, it has been infamous for committing war crimes, crimes against humanity on prisoners practically every minute of their captivity. Its biographer provides a litany of sadistic details and facts that magnify the nastiness of guards, in which civil rights lawyer Fay Stender likened to the case of Jews under the Gestapo. Nor should one exclude the administrators, judges, and the state legislators who saw the farm as a money-making operation so long as kindness and empathy were kept out of running a slave labor camp. Before a Congressional Committee, Stender, who had represented many Blacks as political criminals, gave some of her impressions made while visiting clients in jails run not by a violent Southern culture but by the California Department of Corrections. She came away with five deeply felt impressions about that system: (1) Guards cared little for inmate needs over whom they have total power. (2) Administrators often lie to reporters and researchers looking into prison conditions. (3) Administrators do their utmost to keep reporters from interviewing inmates. (4) Political prisoners are disciplined, punished, ignored, and wear a "Soledad" jacket which indicates to guards and officials everywhere these men are agitators and militant revolutionaries who will start trouble at any time and attempt to smuggle material out for publication and press coverage. (5) CDC will fight all lawyers or reporters who were seen as destructive to prison rules and counterproductive to their attempts to maintain strict control over facility security.[28]

Robin lists 400 prisons ranging from maximum to minimum depending on the seriousness of the offender's crimes, to near country club settings and amenities for white-collar crimes. What the latter lacked was extreme overcrowding which Robin claims affected at least 44% of the former during the War on Crime years of 1974–1977. The worst was always found in the South where conditions and services—especially for Blacks, the dominant inmate—had been notoriously substandard, brutal, and bordering on the inquisitial for generations.[29] Wikipedia lists fifteen of the most punitive prisons by state. Would you be surprised if I told you ten were from the South and one from a border state—otherwise eleven of fifteen with links to the old confederacy. So much for twentieth-century cosmopolitan living and the Deep South.

It was a period when the governments of both parties and their fascist political representatives in every state acted in an unbridled manner to thwart every means of satisfying African American demands for social justice and equality. As the scene moved from the early 1960s of passive and temperate diplomacy by Black leaders to achieve a better life to the late 1960s, all-out war seemed to have been declared by both sides to either achieve or resist recognition of Black demands. The Constitution itself seemed virtually suspended and inoperative to citizen's demands, for justice and equal treatment, and all sorts of state-directed examples of naked and brute force were condoned as the two sides squared off. The harshness of the CJS was in this way exposed for the vicious nature which was contained barely beneath its surface.[30]

This was no more apparent than in the overuse of prisons and lethal enforcement by police forces and the FBI to either kill or arrest for purposes of long-term imprisonment as the war was declared against Black protesters. The next twenty years saw an American government and all its supporters fully prepared to use whatever tactics were necessary to eliminate the aggressive tendencies of Black militants. It was an unfair fight and hundreds of Black militants and political leaders soon realized that death at the hands of the police and the FBI was a daily possibility. This superiority involved a government without consciences and a state willing to suspend human rights to oppress Black militancy. But this occurred not before hundreds of thousands of citizens had been seriously injured, their lives imperiled, and other hundreds of thousands grew comprehensively familiar with the inside of prisons where disregard of humane standards was standard.

What then constituted an American political prisoner of war was best understood within the larger historical context of repression of Black rights and civic demands and resistance to injustice. It was in the trajectory of rebellion that various types of political prisoners emerge, each citing war crimes perpetrated by the CJS, and demanding accountability and decent treatment under international laws. It was here where men imprisoned should expect a degree of civility and humanity during their imprisonment that the CJS refused to provide. Professor Joy James, political philosopher and professor at Williams College, takes a long view about this interconnection:

> Throughout American history "criminals" were racially invented in the public mind; thus, entire communities are "criminalized." Criminality is considered to be non-conformity and nonconformity is often determined not merely by behavior but also by biology or appearance. Bodies that fail to conform to "whiteness" are treated differently under State or police gaze. Greater obedience is demanded . . . and greater violence is used against those whose physical difference makes them as offensive or threatening racially driven policing and sentencing for both social crime and political rebellion mean that Black men don't do "White time" Compared to their European counterparts, Black inmates disproportionately serve longer sentences under more severe conditions.[31]

These we label war crimes. Criminals may not start out as revolutionaries or political prisoners but in their intellectual rage against injustice, civil disobedience, and rebellion through criminal acts (presumably against the state), they share the same progressive desires to end military racism and sexual domination. The problem was CJS agents (particularly defense attorneys and probation officers) either didn't know the right questions to ask on the ethical and political issues, or refused to engage in this kind of dialogue for fear of frightening a judge into a harsher punishment, or tempt repressive jail guards these defendants would meet later in lockup to employ harsh treatment ignored by administration, or simply didn't know how to phrase probation reports so that a certain kind of treatment could be requested while this person was on supervised probation. This limited the number of potential people considered for this category. CJS agents, as I came to realize, didn't seem to take kindly to this kind of prisoner as shown by their nastiness and failure to offer such inmates basic physical security or figure out a way to discourse with them while indentured.

Throughout this chapter, I have tried to convey the appalling inhumane conditions shown by various correctional departments within the CJS. This current section, aided by Dr. Joy James, wrote about imprisoned intellectuals, *American Political Prisoners write on Life, Liberation, and rebellion.*[32] She provided actual names and specific incidents to the otherwise silent and faceless series of victims generally presented in books on prison violence as mere common criminals, lessening the political content of their activities.

Quite probably many agents of the CJS didn't see Black men as intellectuals or critical thinkers capable of placing the CJS under intense philosophical scrutiny, noting its many serious flaws. Such writers were treated as whiners, dummies, apologists, and pawns to larger, communist ideas from foreign sources. I have borrowed generously from her document regarding prison oppression by twenty-three who felt the sting of incarcerated life under the CJS (page numbers provided). It may well have been 2,300 or 23,000 or more but, in most cases, classification of these men and women was reduced to considering them as common, violent, psychologically damaged street thugs, predatory criminals, and nothing more. This name-calling lessened their importance and what they had to say about a repressive fascist system. In summary, this group provided us with their unique take on how the CJS appeared to someone actively engaged with capitalistic criminal law and a judicial system that aimed to fully brutalize ghetto communities seeking self-determination and economic independence.[33]

Many used the additional protocols of the Geneva Convention and the UN General Assembly resolutions of prisoners of war status so as not to be tried as domestic criminals. Professor James listed two dozen of these representatives and the deeply hostile reactions by the CJS. It was quite common that the worst possible punishments were relegated toward this self-appointed group of "liberators" viewed as common criminals with attitudes. Nevertheless, there must have been many thousands of Black convicts without compatible militant inmates with educational insights or with access to available radical reading material or living in a reactionary confined environment that stifled radical speech; devoid of proper legal representation to realize that they too qualified for this category of prisoner.[34]

The names of these former prisoners ranged from very well known to those forgotten over time. But their attacks on the system for which they were punished attract us by the nature of war crimes the CJS used against them. Martin Luther King and all his many followers were jailed and sentenced to prison for challenging the Constitutions' provisions for free speech, assembly, right to demonstrate and protest, and right to challenge CJS racism. Other dissidents included George Jackson, Huey P Newton, Safiya Bukhari-Alston, Angela Davis, and the many jailed protesters who challenged "the vicious circle linking poverty, police courts and prison as an integral element of ghetto existence . . . . a path leading to jails and prisons that was deeply rooted in the imposed patterns of Black existence."[35]

Dr. Davis clarified the definition of the political prisoner by repressive ideology from members of the CJS:

> The ideological acrobatics characteristic of official attempts to explain away the existence of the political prisoner do not end with the individual criminal

act. The political act is defined as criminal in order to discredit radical and revolutionary movements. A political event is reduced to a criminal event in order to affirm the absolute invulnerability of the existing order . . . as the Black Liberation Movement and other progressive struggles increase in magnitude and intensity, the judicial system and its extension, the penal system, consequently become key weapons in the State's fight to preserve the existing conditions of class domination and therefore racism, poverty and war.[36]

The overlap between crime, political prisoners, and activists occurred in seven different ways. First, contact with the repressive nature of the CJS (whether by police activity or pronounced racist injustice in court) leading to political activism which promotes criminal activity (stealing to support radical causes); second, arrested for committing an alleged crime leads to awareness of conditions in jails and prisons and growing political awareness of CJS racism; third, being arrested creates an arrest record where eventual and continual criminal charges led to incarceration; fourth, arrest by police for no particular reason other than police harassment escalated into physical resistance that resulted in court appearance (and whatever injustice followed); fifth, being personally injured from wanton police activity that caused a reaction against the system; sixth, becoming educated from college campus, rallies, or reading subversive literature that induced an individual to support civil rights and challenged police activities during moments of arrest of others in the community; lastly, being labeled a terrorist by the government or court system to which an individual created a self-fulfilling criminal activity that adheres to the position set for him/her by the CJS. Black convicts who fit into these categories might reasonably expect to endure, in addition to the usual sufferings of inmates, a special brand of inhumane treatment as a reprisal. Professor James cited eight common examples:

1. Being confined in a management control unit (i.e., Trenton NJ State Prison) created for political prisoners for lengthy periods of time; isolation cells smaller than required by law or the Society for the Prevention of Cruelty to Animals for a German Shepherd.
2. Arbitrary transfers without notice from low-level prisons to maximum (Marion Control Unit) and locked down for twenty-three hours per day in a strip cell. Cited by Amnesty International for excessive human rights abuses.
3. Shot and killed by unrestrained, unpunished, vindictive guards unaccountable for their actions.
4. Institutional misadministration and continual abuses leading to riots from abominable conditions, inhumane treatment, and governmental refusal to negotiate (i.e., Attica in 1971 but there were many others in this

period)— "we are men not beasts and will not be driven as such when demanding asylum in another country," refused by Governor Rockefeller.

5. Lengthy periods of incarceration (i.e., fifteen years) by all-White Georgia juries, constant movement every two years to different prisons around the country, and frequent stays in solitary confinement for political activism.
6. Prosecutorial judges pronouncing severe sentences and reprimands for political activism.
7. Hundreds of thousands of illegal arrests, entrapments, unconstitutional treatment of police detainees, endless injustices by all parts of the CJS undocumented to prevent inquiry.
8. Politicians who chose to make available funds for the War on Crime recipients (police, corrections, and refused moneys for anticrime programs in prisons and Black communities).

The Geneva Convention of 1929 ratified by forty-seven countries required that prisoners of war (which many American inmates fighting for civil rights and humane treatment believed they were) be personally assured of safety and protection while incarcerated; provided appropriate food and housing; allowed physical exercise and play and intellectual diversions (access to books, newspapers covering every political perspective which was also the case for magazines). Also, the ability to spend time in artistic pursuits, given the right to elect spokesmen to present complaints to prisoner administrators all with the oversight of the International Red Cross which was required to make periodic investigations into these camps to verify if human rights are being respected. So far, I have found no evidence that contemporary corrections and otherwise concentration camps issued such camp policies or chose to observe them across the board. The US Army ironically, in handling prisoners of war, clearly pursued humane treatment that could never be expected from administrators in the CJS correctional establishments.[37]

In 1964 Malcolm X spoke before the Organization of African Unity charging the United States with genocide against African Americans. But he wasn't the first to do so. Genocide, as a concept, was originally brought before the United Nations on behalf of Black people on December 17, 1951, by William L. Patterson and Paul Robeson who organized and delivered a petition titled "We Charge Genocide." In 1976 members of the Black Liberation Army launched a national campaign to petition the United Nations concerning the plight of political prisoners of war and conditions of the US penal system on behalf of a coalition of several Black human rights groups. The call was for an international investigation into the conditions of American prisons and a fervent demand that these entrapped prisoners be granted transport to any anti-imperialist country willing to accept them and their status. Amnesty International was especially concerned with prison operations in Marion

Control Unit Prison (Ill.) which were said to happily violate minimum rules for the treatment of prisoners; Amnesty found this to be so.[38] In 1966 the UN International Covenant on Civil Rights and political rights was elaborated and presented to the United States for prisoner exploitation, unconstitutional injustice, police brutality, and failure to allow for Black self-defense. By the end of the 1960s political activists deemed criminals were being imprisoned for their radical challenge to the status quo and immediate protest against war crimes of the AM CJS.

As Marilyn Buck, a White prisoner in 1989 wrote: "By the early 1970s, a debate began on who was or was not a political prisoner." In all such matters, the United States refused to neither obey any of these international humane requests nor acknowledge that political prisoners were an inherent part of the country's inmate population. War crimes came from such refusals inasmuch as guards were poorly paid and untrained, the administration pursued a strict military mentality on how complaints were to be treated. Many prisons had been built in the nineteenth century with internal environments unchanged from 1960. Many were badly sited in rural areas far from inmate families and close to low-income employees who were repelled by Black prisoners and a culture that irritated them. Here daily life was a dull routine of deprivation, guard threats, instantaneous violence, disavowal of international standards, and requirements in safety and conditions. Prison work was demeaning, rough, dangerous, and paid little. Nor did income from work leads to adequate savings. Take a man with a ten-year sentence working five days a week @ 25c a day. This calculated to $600 without considering money sent home or for necessities of human maintenance (i.e., soap, phone calls, toothpaste, socks, etc.) Not much to lean on whenever a man was discharged to face a raw society.[39]

Perhaps the biggest war crime of all as it applied to the field of corrections was the sheer loss of crucial time out of a man's life with appropriate time spent in a nurturing family setting, participating in birthdays and moments of family grief, or behaving like a decent marriage partner. Inmates accomplished nothing during their time and so life behind bars snatched a man below the surface of life, dooming most to a future deprived of the basic ingredients of usefulness. Gresham M. Sykes's monumental study of the mental withering of a prisoner was well established in his pioneer study *Society of Captives*. It's hard for anyone to imagine spending years of captivity in a small confined space, with a narrow routine where terrible things occur all around without warning.[40]

Let's take an example of this sheer acknowledged waste. The prisoner is sentenced to four years in prison without the opportunity for early release. Let's say this is to make a point. If we calculate his 16 hours per day with Sundays off, he will have at his disposal to make himself a better person almost 400 hours per month. Multiplied for 4 years yields 19,200 hours available to do something besides eat, play cards, lift weights, and shoot dice. A college student, on the other hand, requires 1,000 hours per semester taking 5 classes and using much time for study and research. This gets him 5 classes for 4-year college degree he utilizes 8,000 hours. Thus, the student can obtain two degrees in the same amount of time allocated to the prisoner who leaves prison with very little money, loss of certain liberties and rights, possible loss of family and other social connections, no obvious job waiting, no new skills, and perhaps a diminution of the skills he brought with him, and little awareness of the real world that has technologically leapfrogged four years from the world he has lost. The fault for this lack of ability to comprehend the new world around him is immense and creates a temptation to lose himself in drugs and reoffend in the same neighborhood (that has also not advanced) he knew when first convicted.

A government panel researching rehabilitation techniques was plainly pessimistic about ex-offenders easily refitting themselves back into society once released from prison. It concluded:

> The current state of knowledge about rehabilitation of criminal offenders is cause for grave concern . . . the entire body of research appears to justify only the conclusion that we do not know of any program or method of rehabilitation that could be guaranteed to reduce the criminal activity of released offenders.[41]

Flying to the moon and exorbitant cost we can do, helping a concerned man get his life back in order is beyond us. Is there a monstrous war crime on human beings luring here?

The ability to help provide extra skills and induce special talents of an incarcerated person so he has a reasonable chance of survival, if not good prospects upon his release, was grim. "The techniques that have been tested seem rarely to have been devised to be strong enough to offer realistic hope that they would rehabilitate offenders, especially imprisoned felons."[42]

Worse, the Panel concluded that the Lipton, Martinson, and Wilks study, which found "nothing works," was reasonably accurate and fair in their appraisal of various rehab programs for inmates. "Where they erred," said the Panel, "was almost invariably from an overly lenient assessment of the methodology of a study or a failure to maintain an approximately critical set in evaluating statistical analyses."[43]

The body the findings from the Panel study offered no encouragement for inmates.

> The research literature currently provides no positive recommendations when it comes to rehabilitation of offenders. Or, to put it more broadly, "given our

current stage of knowledge about rehabilitation of criminal offenders, no recommendations for drastic or even substantial changes in rehabilitation efforts can
be justified on empirical grounds," and "Given our ability to measure phenom-
ena of vital interest . . . rehabilitation is still very limited at best," and "Given the
amount of money spent on the Corrections system, let alone the CJS as a whole,
the amounts of money that have been spent on research for positive results are
miniscule in almost all areas."[44]

Resistance to the nothing works, let's defund all rehabilitation projects
came from a long-time researcher in such projects, Ted Palmer had a great
belief in their efficacy.

Everyone agreed that the cost in money and lives in pursuit of increased prison
capacity had been tremendous. By some estimates, 30% of all young Black
males were incarcerated or under other correctional supervision (probation). I
challenge the nothing works idea . . . 25-35% may do so...continued attention to
rehabilitation is warranted.[45]

Perhaps the wrong people were in charge; visionaries with positive out-
looks on human betterment and creative thinkers that can go beyond the
worn-out traditional approach to the subject were simply not there, not wishing to be hired for this kind of grunt work. Lacking capable planners, we were
left with racist politicians, and those who preferred to avoid public scrutiny
for any ideas regarding leniency to offenders or broad concepts on how to
reconfigure the neighborhoods from which so many prisoners emanate. It
seemed the corrections field throughout this period under study lacked the
wisdom, the administrative capabilities, and the desire to see men's lives
improve. And the responsibility for the unimpressive and inconclusive body
of work on offender rehabilitation that then existed belonged as much to the
many governmental agencies associated with LEAA that funded it to the
investigators, researchers, and CJS practitioners who accepted funding willingly yet prevented many potentially valid interventions while carrying out
failed policies that didn't disturb the status quo of leadership.

Many researchers have studied this problem with harsh critiques of the
system itself. Numerous reports had been circulating for years with bad
news of official ineptitude, financial waste, and inefficient programs. The
finger pointed to general and consistent failure on the part of the CJS to
develop and initiate new ideas that might help these men to whom, having
taken away their freedom, might well feel responsible for creating significant
community-related aftercare services that would do more than simply doom
ex-offenders to broken, empty lives upon release. Bailey (1966), Waldo
and Dinitz (1967), Gibbons and Hassebaum (1971), Robinson and Smith

(1971), Bennett (1973), Martinson (1974), and Lerman (1975) were a few of the studies that come to mind challenging the CJS to do better at providing adequate aftercare treatment having robbed these men of precious years of productive labor simply sitting in prison without incentive to improve their lives.[46]

Princeton University sociologist, Michele Phelps, recently wrote:

> There were no major changes in investment in specialized facilities (prisons) funding for inmate services, related staff or program participation rates throughout the 1970s and 1980s and despite the dramatic increase in correctional population in the period and in length of sentences pronounced, my findings suggest a large gap between rhetoric and reality in the case of inmate services.[47]

What does this say about the vicious deterrent effect of harsh punishment, institutional war crimes, and suffering from lengthy prison sentences? Or the relatively few rehab programs offered convicts with the purpose of bettering their lives after prison? Doubtless being in prison and jail and subject to their negative influence resulting from the institution's war crimes on inmates, these venues were likely to be "crime enhancing rather than crime reducing over the long run." What of the thousands of wasted lives when such men were relegated to rubbish heaps of inactivity upon release, further destroying any chances of a successful life? This could all be seen then, as it is now, as inevitable, the product of a systematic war crime mentality. As was the deliberate intention of its hardened, racist-oriented administrators and its army of correctional personnel. These very actions and the refusal to develop adequate aftercare programs were systematic of widespread disregard of Black men having been caught up in the maw of the CJS. In 1946 fewer than 25% of the nation's jails were judged fit for human habitation (by Jim Crow standards) and by 1970 conditions had hardly improved. An Ohio Supreme Court found its Corrections system often tolerated twenty men in a single cell with standards varying widely from unacceptable to dangerously unforgivable.[48]

The work slave picture of American jails and prisons draws remarkable similarity with Emanuel Kingelblum's Warsaw ghetto-inspired eighteen signs of modern slavery which he discussed in so far as they approximated Nazi slave work camps. At least ten from his list of warnings can be discerned: numbered and stamped inmates (most wore tattoos to indicate gang affiliation or some warning threats to other pioneers); overcrowded, miserable accommodations judged unconstitutional; disregard of inmate families; random beatings by guards, reprisals for inmates who chose to join political organizations; banned from protesting or seeking legal redress; forced labor with minimal pay; precarious living arrangements with deaths and suicides and a reduced life span for all men committed; terrorization by unrestrained guards; and lack of proper health conditions, harsh treatment of those who challenge the system.[49]

Rehabilitation seemed to be a dirty word in this period. In 1971 before a Senate Committee on Corrections, one state attorney general was heard to exclaim:

> Most of the nation's correctional institutions are correctional in name only . . . most State prisons and jails have no program . . . conditions exist which virtually assure further prison deterioration . . . most facilities are antiquated and most are overcrowded. For 1970 NYC's CJS spent $843 million to fight crime of which 75% went to the police. A mere 10% was earmarked for rehabilitation and service programs. Worse, no audits were performed to see whether any of this money were successful and cut crime or made police services better.[50]

New York City prisons were found to be operating at 140% capacity with the Bronx House of Detention even higher (174%). $25 a day was spent on inmates, 69c for food. It was a time when judges were processing up to 283 arraignments daily (most of them for drug offenses that cluttered the dockets and allowed no time to properly assess a defendant's needs). Correctional officers received two days of human relations training which the NAACP said would realistically require four to five weeks to make a significant impression on the trainees. NYC's Board of Corrections proposed a total overhaul of a system they labeled "failed."[51]

Social activist Jessica Mitford was even tougher when pronouncing her views of America's correctional administration when she testified at a 1971 hearing of an Oakland (CA) facility she had visited in the late 1960s. She ran through the usual litany of corrupt practices and war crimes: exasperating bureaucratic roadblocks that prevented her investigating or questioning of staff, lazy but uncaring officials who held arbitrary despotic power over all aspects of inmate life, guard tyranny over inmates was universal where one complaining word from an inmate could cause loss of liberties for years, rampant and arbitrary lawlessness by all who worked in these facilities. She summarized: "Cruel, vindictive and dangerous prison officials and employees on all levels." This indictment was broadened by Melvin Rivers, President of Fortune Society an aid group for ex-offenders by claiming the vast majority of the 4000 local jails could best be likened to dog kennels with administrators "totally irresponsible." By the 1980s, prison "served no social purpose whatsoever except to be a form of welfare payment for CJS personnel."[52]

Sociologists Paul Gendreu and James Bonita took the time to assess many quantitative studies on the effects of imprisonment and associated restrictive cruelties. Their report includes seventeen significant and lengthy studies of uncontrolled prison violence (between 1975–1984 alone) and thirty-two other reports that cite CJS facilities (1958-1987), citing their destructive tendencies and total disregard for an offender's psychological stability and skill set ability to improve his life upon his eventual release. Prison administrators couldn't have cared less about this serf population. They may be war crimes to us but to "staff they were simply part of the functions necessary to keep inmates in check."[53]

A 1970 report from Pennsylvania's 100+-year-old Holmesburg Prison provided additional evidence of mistreatment and war crimes on a daily basis. As found in most US prisons, the following conditions were noted—inmates treated in subhuman manner by vindictive guards, leaking roofs, inadequate and dirty beds, lack of towels, poor medical facilities (only 2 doctors for 1,000 inmates), severe overcrowding (in 1850 the daily count was 750, in 1970 with the same size measurements the intake was 1,300!), inmates laid about 24 hours daily doing nothing as work was unavailable. There was pitifully little effort to provide rehab facilities (inasmuch as 97% of state operating funds went to security guards and administration, a paltry 3% for rehab). Guards were ill-trained, a few minutes each week convicts were allowed yard exercise, guards ran the show as they wished, the warden was rarely seen and unresponsive to inmate complaints, censorship of mail—in short, a firestorm of war crimes perpetuated on innocent inmates every day of their beleaguered sentence. And one wonders why prison riots begin.[54]

Professor H. Schwartz of the University of Buffalo added more misery to this bleak period in CJS history:

> U.S. prisons have survived for over 150 years with few attempts at reform. Many prison administrators continue to claim laws and rights have no place in a prison setting. Defendants are entitled to nothing. There is an axiom security drives out rehabilitation. The function of the prison administration is to keep the lid on and run a totalitarian police state as much as possible.[55]

Consequently, there is a remarkable similarity in conditions found in American prisons with those in the German concentration camp system of the 1940s as revealed by sociologist Anna Pawelczynska. This is further underscored by Stender who noted: "working with the prisoners as I do, as their lawyer, is like being present at Dachau."[56]

Stender gives us an overview of the CJS she witnessed at Soledad prison (CA): "I had to work through a legal system which is almost completely stacked against Black defendants. In the prisons, convicts were literally at the mercy of an arbitrary system that was almost completely above and beyond the law. Prisoners had no recourse whatsoever to the courts of law for most of the charges which were brought against them for offenses they were accused of committing."[57]

Her findings:

"All prisoners in Soledad prison's O Wing were shackled and chained when they left their cells for visits; perhaps 33–50% of all inmates at one time or another did some time in the hole, some for years. At any one time, there were about 700 inmates in the hole of a total prison population of 25,000. I have seen cases where two men per cell were forced to live in 4′ × 9′ space, 16 hours a day although the California Health and Safety Code demands a gorilla be given 1,065 square feet to habituate. Then too, visits were a major issue. The visiting hours at CDC are from 10:00 a.m. to 3:00 p.m. daily. Yet many families after driving hundreds of miles to see an inmate have to wait as much as two hours or more for an officer escort to bring a man to the visiting room. In addition to losing that precious time, another forty-five minutes was cut off at the end of a visit in order to get the inmate back to his cell for supper. At Soledad inmates had very little of value to do to bolster their work skills. What they could do to pass time was play card games, crap games, shoot dice, indulge in amateur fights, and, of course, indulge in frivolous sodomy—all illegal thanks to administration who looked a blind eye. As if this weren't enough, she goes on: "Beatings by guards of prisoners whose hands are tied behind their back plus cases of strangling, kicking and torture were seen as very common at the Adjustment Center at Folsom State Prison where assaultive guards "moved in like a pack of wolves to their victims." She also fell prey, as did many women visitors to crude sexual advances by guards during the visits whenever attractive women, spouses, and sisters appeared for the inmates only to have suggestive remarks (or worse) thrown at them during the process."[58]

None of these misdeeds, misbehaviors, and lethal force practices by guards could have occurred if not for the complete awareness and full complicity of correctional administrators and prison officials. What were these men thinking? Was compassion simply not a job requirement? What did officials think such brutality could achieve in the long run? Under this CJS blanket of secrecy, since very little of both staff and managements disregard for human rights was ever recorded might not all of these suppressed acts be branded war crimes? What kind of persons were these that could impose such pain, grief, and suffering without concern? Simply because inmates were minorities? How different was this from the Nazi persecution of Jews and other minorities? Was Black culture seen as so meaningless with so little to offer White society that its destruction by White nationalist guards was seen as acceptable by administrators? That they had the right to control events and make such broad judgments on others? Could reform be fashioned through personal racist staff vindictiveness?

How do you rank in terms of severity to human dignity war crimes perpetrated by each guard over dozens of unprotected inmates held captive in thousands of prisons and jails? We rank severity of crimes committed by criminals when they appear in court for sentencing. Violent and personal crimes hold far greater sway and receive far harsher punishment than crimes of property or traffic offenses. If done for street criminals why not for guards and other CJS personnel? Surely the war crimes they regularly administered deserved their own sort of ranking by degree of viciousness and indifference?

This chapter concludes by taking a lengthy look at proceedings and findings of 1975 conference on utopian alternatives to prison that offered hope to inmates everywhere. Sponsored by the National Task Force on Higher Education and the National Council of Churches of Christ, the focus was strictly on innovative alternatives to prison (as a countervailing force to the growing trend of mass incarceration) which was spending to the tune of $33–50b yearly.[59] The conference was the culmination of two years of brainstorming for this critical problem. One happy note was the wide variety of concerned and inspired advocates brought together: community organizers, legal aid society members, university law students, social activists, radical attorneys, plus a large number of defensive-minded correctional officials (to challenge attacks on their preserve). In addition, there was an omnibus of academic researchers to help point the way with the usual contradictory findings.

There were plenty of workshops, plenary sessions, and intrapersonal discussions on every scintilla of the subject. An innovative touch was that nearly one-third of the participants were inmates and ex-offenders to present their own intimate perspective (15% of this group supported the need for prison, most wished for its abolition). The conferees expected 600 people to attend; actually 1,600 showed up from 43 states. The whole conference was a beehive of activity and noise and plenty of small group debates in the corridors! The outlook for something important evolving from the conference on mass incarceration was optimistically high.

What evolved was nothing of the sort. The usual chaos and reactionary control of the conference by CJS agents and reactionaries prevailed and the conference terminated abruptly after two weeks. Results were nil. As the final report mentioned:

> Throughout the conference inevitable tension took place between CJS reactionaries and the reformers and political radicals including the inmates. Suggested alternatives were challenged all along the line by prison officials who brought with them basic Establishment-thinking They just went along with bureaucratic shams and frauds, was how one observer put it.[60]

At the close of the conference, social activist Jessica Mitford scoffed at the results, "I see no solutions ahead." Judge Charles R. Richey (US District Court, Washington, DC) was similarly disillusioned.

> The Conference was an abject failure and merely repeated the usual failures of prison life—untrained staffs, inconsequential rehabilitation plans, unrealistic job training, inadequate diets, constant violence, limited access to family and friends, lacking elemental security for the inmates' serving sentences that were way too long.[61]

All that was left was for the more leftist attendees to complain about how the whole conference was bundled together, beginning with the meeting place itself—an expensive hotel to markup food and lodging, an unwieldy program (150 workshops alone), too many verbose speeches, domination of the meetings by CJS officials with not enough attention paid to racism and class issues, and stifling of inmate participation and criticism. As in so many other conferences with high hopes during these years, according to prominent inmate speakers,

> We felt the Conference was too patronizing, didn't give us a prominent role despite our numbers, kept us off Chairs and minimized our place in the prevailing agenda. There was too much emphasis on simply softening radical ideas.[62]

Another attempt at reform, another bevy of utopian ideas, another failure.

I can't believe for the entire period 1960–1990, the era of the War on Crime, men were, on average, dangerously racist, spiritually indifferent to human suffering, and easily capable of inflicting their own brand of White nationalist harm without concern. Did they not know the inevitable consequences of these acts waged on those unable to properly defend themselves? Did they forget these victims had families like their own and that eventually they would be released? Some must have had religious values to challenge these actions? Some guards were ex-military (maybe 30%) from the wars 1939–1956, and surely army regulations forbade torture and disrespect of the enemy. Wouldn't these have been part of an ex-military Code of Ethics? Or were they? To what extent did the ideology of White nationalism infect the CJS as they viewed concentration camp residents? They couldn't have been empty-headed and prepared to do whatever was asked of them by their superiors? Or were they?

And what of the administrators? Surely with a better education, more training in correctional management, experience working with others, officials would have been less susceptible to harsh and vindictive treatment of prisoners if only because this was so counterproductive? But White nationalism during the civil rights era was quite infectious. It relied on a White superiority belief that such a thing as Black criminality existed brought on by the civil rights movement which needed to be destroyed. White nationalists sought to infiltrate government service and subvert, restrict or limit multicultural social welfare policies especially those that aided young Black offenders with assistance aimed at curbing crime.

The ideal candidate for prison and jail work seemed to have possessed certain attributes and a psychological temperament suited to work which could not be matched elsewhere: super suspicious, quickly prone to use force to achieve narrow goals, lacking in empathy, and possessing an education of such limited scope few other competitive job opportunities existed. They needed to do as they were told by their superiors and this they did or lose a job where few other career opportunities existed. A vile racist nature helped, one that had little regard for African Americans as a people let alone individuals deserving decent treatment whatever their crimes. Maybe religion entered where right and wrong were simplistically understood and a transgressor of the law deserved no pity. Toss in supplication before authority in situations of conflict, where peer approval was crucial and negotiation a non-starter. Thus, were unreported and unpunished war criminals born.

CJS officials, politicians, jurists, and correctional staff looked the other way rather than pursue documentation for any war crime that happened against UN Human Rights regulations. Proper training, adequate disciplinary forms, process of admonishing, and punishing for war crimes might have been set in motion by CJS senior officials but I am unaware of anything like this happened to minimize war crime behavior. Reforms were also blocked and resistance by old-time officials were widespread to block reporters and researchers as well as academics from interviewing inmate war crime victims so how much information and statistical data could really be developed to support my contention of universal war crime behavior by the CJS during this period? I guess on a sliding scale of harm to the Black community and the economic futures of inmates, heaviest indictment should be placed on the politicians (especially Presidents Nixon and Reagan) for unleashing the madness called WC and the hundreds of thousands of victims this state-controlled barbarism exuded.

Lack of government interest in convict aftercare success meant that any efforts to address the problem, then and now, would be enfeebled and assuredly ineffective. A primary reason was that the "Black prisoner" status was peripheral not central, as it surely should have been, to the concerns of the vast majority of correctional agents and CJS courts in the process. Minuscule inmate achievements in prison under harsh, inhumane, and brutal conditions with few resources was never perceived by dinosaur officials, politicians, or judges as creating a formidable crisis needing major efforts and tons of money to resolve. As long as 30' high walls existed these people weren't concerned. It's also clear to any objective bystander that attempts at radical reforms to eliminate war crimes had to come from the top of the political and correctional ladders. But there was no one with concern at the top rung of that ladder. And slow-thinking dinosaurs occupied all the other rungs in between. The CJS was in all its ideological parts ill-equipped to break through traditional log jams imposed by the core of the conservative CJS hierarchy. War crimes were thus inevitable.

NOTES

1. J. Pizarro and U. N. K. Stenius, "Supermax Prisons-Their Rise and Current Practices and Effects on Inmates," *The Prison Journal* 84 (2004): 248–249.

2. J. Lichtenberg, *The American Prison System Is Inhumane-here's Why*, 2016. https//theweek.com/articles/651722/Americas-prison-system-inhumane-hereswhy.

3. This document was known as the Austin MacCormick Report, *Committee Report on the Investigation of Penitentiary Houston, Texas, 1947*, reviewed by the noted criminologist who leant his name and written with the authorization of Senator Warlow Lane, House of Representatives.

4. Op. cit.

5. Op. cit., bid., p. 11; also, Lori Lynn Mcluckie, "Correctional Officers Fail to Live Up to Glorified Billing Inmate Says," *The Denver Post*, 1 November 1998, p. 33.

6. Andrea Armstrong, "Race, Prison Discipline and the Law," *University of California Irvine Law Review* 101 (2015); and her more recent *Prison Conditions* (New York: Oxford UP, 2017). Jerome G. Miller, *Search and Seizure, African American Males in the CJS* (Cambridge: Cambridge UP, 1996) and Luana Ross, *Inventing the Savage: The Social Construction of Native American Criminality* (Austin: University of Texas Press, 1998).

7. McCormiick Report, op. cit.

8. Pizarro, op. cit., p. 329, 337.

9. An excellent political account of these years of Black demands for equal rights and justice can be found in Manning Marable's *Race Reform and Rebellion, the Second Reconstruction in Black America, 1945-1982* (Jackson: University of Mississippi Press, 1984), especially chapters 2–5, pp. 12–128.

10. Craig Haney, *From Prison to Home: The Effect of Incarceration and Re-Entry on Children, Families and Communities, The Psychological Impact of Incarceration with Implications for Post-Prison Adjustment* (Washington, DC: United States Department of Health and Human Services, 2001), p. 3.

11. Oversight for New York's prison system had been given to the Correctional Association of New York in 1924. According to their charter, this group of private bankers, lawyers, and businessmen, working pro bono in the public interest, were assigned the task of periodically visiting the state's prisons to verify they were

providing inmates with humane conditions. In all the years not one visit was ever made and not one word of official rebuke to condemn their neglect of their charter provisions.

12. Attica Prison conditions were reported in Tom Wicker's *A Time to Die* (New York: New York Times/Quadrangle, 1975), pp. 306–308.

13. Quoted in Wicker, op. cit., p. 304.

14. Remarks found in the Senate Rules Committee transcript, pp. 199–201, 24 September 1974.

15. Wicker, op. cit., p. 306.

16. *The New York Times*, 4 October 1971, pp. 44, 48.

17. Wicker, op. cit., pp. 305–306.

18. Gerald Robin, *Introduction to the Criminal Justice System-Principles, Procedures and Practices* (New York: Harper & Row, 1980), pp. 322–324.

19. Margaret W. Calahan and Lee Anne Parsons, *Historical Corrections Statistics in the United States, 1850-1984*, produced for Westat Inc, Rockville, MD, 1986, pp. 79, 97–99.

20. Census of the Nations Jails from *The 1972 Survey of Inmates of Local Jails* (Washington, DC: USGPO), May 1975, pp. 8–12.

21. Robin, op. cit., p. 325.

22. Ibid., p. 327.

23. Ibid.

24. Ibid., p. 329, 337.

25. Angela Y. Davis, "Political Prisoners, Prisons and Black Liberation," in Joy James (Ed.), *The Angela Y. David Reader* (New York: Wiley-Blackwell, 1998), p. 73. This was written while Davis was imprisoned in Marin County Jail (CA) in 1971. Davis and James worked closely while both were on the faculty at University of California, Santa Cruz; Angela Davis, *An Autobiography* (New York: International Publishers, 1974), p. 23, 31, 33 and 61; and Adam Fairclough, Martin Luther King, Jr. (Athens: University of Georgia, 1995), pp. 71–72; and Martin Luther King Jr., *The Autobiography of Martin Luther King, Jr.* (New York: Warner, 1998), p. 172.

26. Marilyn Buck, "The Struggle for Status Under International law," in James, op. cit., p. 202; Donal E. J. MacNamara and Fred Montanio (Ed.), *Incarceration: The Sociology of Imprisonment* (Beverly Hills: Sage, 1978), pp. 26–27.

27. Bruce Chadwick, *Baseball's Hometown Teams, The Story of the Minor Leagues* (New York: Abbeville Press, 1994), p. 110.

28. Fay Stender, *Congressional Hearings, Part II* (Washington, DC, 1971), pp. 32–41.

29. Robin, p. 342, 344.

30. Marable, op. cit., p. 128.

31. Joy James, *Imprisoned Intellectuals Write on Life, Liberation and Rebellion* (New York: Rowman and Littlefield, 2003), p. xii and 32.

32. Op. cit., James, p. 66 and 68.

33. Op. cit., p. 136, 145 and 148.

34. Op. cit., p. 177.

35. Op. cit.

36. Ward Churchill and Jim Vanderwall, "Prisoners of War": The Legal Standing of Members of the National Liberation Movements in their book, *Cages of Steel: The Politics of Imprisonment in the United States* (Washington, DC: Maison-Neuve, 1992).

37. See George Breitman's coverage in *Last Years of Malcolm X, Evolution of a Revolutionary* (New York: Pathfinder Press, 1970), p. 1.

38. Amnesty International notes this as AMR 51/26/87; also, Department of the Army Field Manual FM 19-40, USGPO, November 1952, pp. 14–15.

39. Marilyn Buck, "The Struggle for Status under International Law," in James, op. cit., p. 202, 215; and Adam Fairclough, Martin Luther King Jr. (Athens: University of Georgia Press, 1995), p. 72; also Lee Sechrist, Susan O. White and Elizabeth D. Brown (Eds.), *The Rehabilitation of Criminal Offenders: Problems and Prospects, a Panel Discussion on Research and Rehabilitation Techniques* (Washington, DC: National Academy of Sciences, 1979), p. 3, 22.

40. Gresham M. Sykes, *Society of Captives* (Princeton: Princeton UP), pp. 3–5.

41. Joan Petersilia, *When Prisoners Come Home, Parole and Prisoner Re-Entry* (New York: Oxford UP, 2003), p. 102 and 105.

42. Op. cit., p. 102.

43. Op. cit., p. 105; Allyson Ross Davies, "Assessing Outcomes of Medical Care: Some Lessons for Criminal Offender Rehabilitation in Sechrist," op. cit., pp. 151–152.

44. Petersilia, op. cit.

45. Ted Palmer, *The Re-Emergence of Correctional Intervention, Developments Through the 1980s and Prospects* (Beverly Hills: Sage, 1992).

46. W. C. Bailey, "Correctional Outcomes: An Evaluation of 100 Reports," *Journal of Criminal Law, Criminology and Police Science* 57 (1966): 153–161; L. A. Bennett, "Should We Change the Offender of the System?," *Crime and Delinquency* 19 (1973): 332–342; D. C. Gibbons, "Differential Treatment and Delinquent and Interpersonal Maturity Levels Theory: A Critique," *Social Sciences Review* 44 (1970): 22–33; G. Kassebaum, *Prison Treatment and Parole Survival* (New York: Wiley, 1971); Don Martinson, "What Works?" Answers About Prison Reform," *The Public Interest* 35 (1974): 22–54; J. Robison and G. Smith, "The Effectiveness of Correctional Programs," *Crime and Delinquency* 17 (1971): 67–80 and G. P. Waldo and Stanley Dinitz, "Personality Attributes of the Criminal: An Analysis of Research Studies, 1950–1965," *The Journal of Research in Crime and Delinquency* 4 (1967): 185–202.

47. Michele Phelps, "Rehabilitation in the Punitive Era—The Gap Between Rhetoric and Reality in the United States Prison Programs" see Phelps online library, Wiley.com/DOI, 2011.

48. Petersilia, op. cit., pp. 33, 102–103, 137, and 245–246.

49. Emanuel Kingelblum, *Eighteen Signs of Modern Slavery* (New York: McGraw-Hill, 1958); and Lise Pearlman, *American Justice on Trial* (New York: Regent Press, 2016), p. 104; Drury M. Oshinsky, *Worse Than Slavery: Parchman Farm and the Ordeal of Jim Crow Justice* (New York: Free Press, 1997), p. 137, 139; and Dr. Elie A. Cohen, *Human Behavior in the Concentration Camp* (New York: Grosset & Dunlap, 1953), especially chapters 2–4.

50. Congressional Hearing Before the Subcommittee, 92nd Congress, First Session, May/June 1971, Chairman Emanuel Cellers, USGPO: Washington, DC, p. 1.

51. Ibid., pp. 5, 6, 18, 21, 76–80.

52. Mitford testimony before the Subcommittee (see #28), pp. 76–84, 184.

53. Scharf, Peter, "Empty Bars, Violence and Crisis of Meaning in Prison," in Michael C. Braswell, Reid H. Montgomery, Jr., and Lucien X. Lombardo (Eds.), *Prison Violence in America* (Cincinnati: Anderson, 1994), pp. 28–29; and Paul Gendreau and James Bonita, "Re-Examining the Cruel and Unusual Punishment of Prison Life," in Braswell, op. cit., pp. 167–200.

54. David Rudovsky, *Impressions from a Lawyer with the Defender Association of Philadelphia*, pp. 133–135, 145–151.

55. Herman Schwartz, professor of law at American University, *Ring-Wing Justice: The Conservative Campaign to Take Over the Courts* (New York: Basic Books, 2004), pp. 160–161; and Anna Pawelczynska, *Values on Violence in Auschwitz-A Sociological Analysis* (Berkeley: California UP, 1979), pp. 11–16.

56. Comments by social activist and attorney Faye Stender reported in Eve Pell (Ed.), *Maximum Security: Letters from California's Prisons* (New York: Dutton, 1972), p. 9.

57. Ibid., p. 35, 52, 65 and 73.

58. Ibid., p. 80.

59. Summary report on *The Alternatives to Prison* (Boston: Sheraton Hotel, National Conference on Alternatives to Incarceration, 19–21 September 1975), p. 5.

60. Ibid., p. 9.

61. Ibid., p. 18

62. Ibid., p. 25.

Chapter 6

Snoops and Snitches

Beloved is not the word. But of all the CJS agencies under review, the probation department received some of the kindest evaluations from its clients. That is if you consider D+ (2.61 out of 5) as a high mark on a report card. To most, this is hardly an overwhelming vote of confidence and earns little in the way of bragging rights among CJS personnel. But the War on Crime years were great ones to be a probation officer. I was part of those glory years after 1970 when it seemed like every week, I got twenty new low-grade cases to supervise, and the department hired another virgin probation officer, the occasional uptick in salary didn't hurt either. But don't listen to me. Here is what a chief supervising probation officer in a suburban community near Denver said about his career in the 1980s:

> Business is booming. Cops and courts are supplying us with a steadily increasing complement of crooks. Caseloads are swelling. Expectations continue to remain high; everyone assumes that the time and energy possessed by the selfless and dedicated probation officer (hereafter PO) are infinitely expandable. Or perhaps it's just that he's seen as expendable faced with (at best) static levels of staffing and other resources. But in-service training, if and when available, is often so irrelevant and/or so theoretical as to defy application to our daily operations. During my tenure in this business, I've heard few of my colleagues complain about being over trained and overworked.[1]

Probation came into the field whistling the virtues and nobility of probation service as applied to youthful offenders. It was perhaps the only branch of the CJS that was mandated to advise, sympathize, and help shoulder the load of responsibility of young male offenders who had run afoul of society's laws, seen as lightweight predators in their own communities, and/or consumers of too much dope.

POs were surrounded by noble principles and charitable objectives charged to do something for these pathetic lads. It thus might come as a bit of a shock if I suggest that the probation service and its practitioners also engaged in a wide variety of department-specific war crimes. No, not the genocidal stuff coming from the police departments; nor the various methods of torture and gang rape located throughout the country's prison system; nor the unreasonably traumatic fears and punishments inflicted on the thousands of bent reeds facing an irate judge or vindictive prosecutor.

These kinds of war crimes which themselves in their own way left deeply bitter wounds and scars on offenders both physically and mentally. But war crimes on a lesser scale in the guise of a dicey probation department crusade to help marginal men pursue better objectives in life than days being criminals. Probation always offered little and was always underfunded, so it consistently did very little for those they promised to help. But to act as Captain Courageous it might at least could have stood up, fumed, and protested to government funding agencies (i.e., LEAA) about being engaged in a wasted crusade. It could have made efforts to pursue innovative forms of community-based rehabilitation along different lines, and drop the harsh and bitter punishment angles of probation that encouraged snitching and snooping.

Cooper was wary of its mission:

> Probation officers will not as readily recommend probation for individuals from the social periphery because it is believed that the people from such environments make a habit of being deviant (as perceived by White nationalists) and contesting the established structures of authority by nature of their social position.[2]

Historically, society's patrician elite have not been very creative when it came to punishing the poor and Black. Suffering mattered most. And make it lengthy. Create some hideous form of public shame or, if necessary, condone murder. Early American offenders were simply subjected to long bouts in cold cells with minimum food supplies. Silence and no socializing could cause reflection even insanity. Hanging was also a possibility. But by the progressive era, a belief for citizens to watch public hangings (and lynching) and torture of offenders was fast growing out of style and the probation service as a social charity emerged for the government of both political parties to combat crime with a happy face.

According to Piven and Alcabes in 1965, there were almost 27,000 POs in the country. When I entered the Los Angeles Probation Department in 1970 supervised 124,000 probationers but had no actual data on whether they were successful or not. One study called their victories "thin."[3] Despite the fact that the department was supervising 124,000 probationers, it had no actual data on the number of successful outcomes; or why clients recidivated.[4] In 1970, 2,100 positions were budgeted but unfulfilled with appointments. The need for 1967 was estimated at 45,000 (never reached due to budget cuts) with shortage estimated at 27%. "The manpower shortage was of a sufficient magnitude" they wrote, "that there was a serious concern because the pool of social work graduates was too small to narrow the appreciable manpower gap in probation and parole."[5] Projected numbers were going through the roof as all college disciplines were being affected by CJS recruitment over the alleged crime wave. "At current rate of recruitment, it is necessary to train 260,000 traditional social work graduates to produce 18,000 probation officers for 1967."[6] This pressure affected departments of sociology, police science, psychology, social work, and criminology. (It should be pointed out there were no schools of probation during this period.) Instant proof that it hardly existed as a recognized profession and thus professional leadership and an approved code of ethics were lacking. All the humanities on notice-crime were giving potential students the best chance of a good-paying job so long as you could twist your priorities and assume a tough, authoritative, aggressive personality. It also meant turning a blind eye to obvious Black demands, supporting ensuing violence and police brutality, and unsuspecting war crimes if jobs were open. Consequently, 838 academic institutions were prepared to accept this challenge and consciously enrolled nubile students in career work while unconsciously preparing them for participation in undefined war crimes. Did anyone put them on alert? No one saw this coming.

By 1975 it was reported that persons on daily probation at the state and local levels averaged 1.3 million under supervision with an additional 412,000 in prison, 210,000 in local jails. There were almost 2,000 adult probation agencies, 2,100 for juveniles. The budget costs for 1979 were estimated at $385m and climbing. In 1974, there were 46,000 POs expected to rise to 96,000 by 1985. Correctional personnel in 1974 was 106,000 in 43,000 adult institutions. By 1985, it was a steady evolutionary expansion at odds with the trend in the 1920s to abolish probation altogether.[7] Even Deep South states like Texas had entered the twentieth century. In 1968, almost 50% of the Texas counties were served by a PO, a meek total of 120 POs in 55 departments with caseloads running from 199 to 352. There was little value to what was happening in states like Texas but at least some men stayed out of jail and it was a start.[8]

In this War on Crime period was probation seen by the greater CJS as a legitimate mode of punishment? Lemert claimed police saw POs as "unduly lenient," lobbied to withhold federal funds for probation services, denied POs access to police records, and avoided any kind of buddy relationship that could be used to support the client. Only when POs became punitive toward clients did the police show pleasure.[9] For most, probation service is seen as constituting a free pass to thug behavior and another chance for offenders to reoffend and beat up the elderly while laughing at the credulity of the CJS.

Not that probation was a sweetheart deal between judge and defendant. A survey conducted by the National Council on Crime and Delinquency's national probation study, 94% of 1,300 state and local POs who responded to the survey verified they used some form of incarceration with probation in their reports to the court. McAnany, officer of the Department of Justice, University of Illinois, believed "probation is a penal sanction whose main characteristic is punitive" while another report claimed "it only seems non-punitive when compared to being sent to jail or prison. Of all probation sentences, 25% at least end badly for whatever reason, and men were sent to prison whatever the help they receive from their PO. In 1965, such requests were ratified in between 88% and 95% of sentences."[10]

Thus, conservative political perspectives, especially of the "law and order" kind, represented maybe 50–60% of the probation officers I knew and worked with (especially the older ones jaded by all the petty criminals they had dealt with), and who disliked the humanitarian side of probation as namby-pamby social work for exploitative criminals.

Well, is a PO supposed to be a bonafide buddy? In my years in the service, I have found no official tally of which departmental techniques are best for improving the lives of the probationers, treating them altruistically, or treating them as a herd of bison. In fact, I have failed to prove in any direction. One wondered cynically whether these benign services constituted a waste of taxpayer money but were justified simply because it was far cheaper than prison by a ratio of 1:20? Was this the sole reason for keeping it alive?

There were inherent dangers at the core of the probation assistance program. Most POs were allocated few resources unless you count words of comfort and sympathy to help. Most of the probation for the client was admittedly verbal, occurring through interviews that can't be statistically rated, home visits that tended to be breezy and short, and brief street meetings that were also seen with suspicion by passersby. This is a major problem because most defendants are generally uncommunicative and have deep suspicions about bourgeois POs who scrutinize (fantasize?) all areas of their lives. How much of this relationship could really be said to have been effective as helpful to defendants? I found that many of these men didn't really face the implications of their misdemeanors, or pay much attention to what I was saying, or follow through with my recommendations and demands I painstakingly set forward as a prescription for better living. The job was too big and too laden with booby traps. Rather the opposite: they didn't belong there to have a PO tear down their lives and suggest a radically different way of living beyond their scope of acceptance. Roughly 80% of the probationers I met in my thirteen years as a PO believed themselves not guilty of original charges with ample excuses or reasons why they were caught and convicted. Many see themselves as victims of a racist system that had provided them with nothing in which to earn a decent living to support a family. Seeing themselves in the guise as martyrs and victims, how likely would they accept all the claptrap of a probation officer to become a better man. Only lip service prevailed. And well beyond them was any understanding and application to their lives of human rights since no lawyers or community activists or radical POs brought this to their attention on behalf of the community?

Let's not forget the mind-bending process of rehabilitating an offender during this period was basically dead since few resources were available. Sustaining a serious effort at self-improvement might look good in probation officer files and notes, but the likelihood of this accurately reflecting upward mobility for the client was nonsense. Only coercion and threats of returning men to court on a revocation of probation order held them to the terms and conditions of their order to stay clean. If 25% of a caseload was visibly taking baby steps, did this represent a good return on public monies expended? If human rights abuses by POs in the terms of probation were also required to get a probationer to stay clean, was this also justified?

Let's bear in mind, many of the Black clientele after 1965 were composed of drug addicts labeled as criminals when the War on Drugs surged during Nixon's first term. Addicts of this period were either hopelessly unable to be monitored or sought nonexistent treatment. Chicago Tribune journalist Michael Tackett spoke of enormous strains placed on the probation system by drug wars where 90% of the caseloads were composed of street dealers and drug addicts. POs were on the defensive and the Los Angeles Probation Department engaged 1,000 officers by 1986 as clogged court dockets, bloated jails while POs wrote complex, time-consuming presentence reports that tripled the time needed to absorb their recommendations. For POs it became a matter of policing not counseling. Reports now ignored social history aiming at court leniency as POs no longer had time, given 1.2m drug arrests in the 1980s, to know a person well enough to know if they were amenable to treatment. Result: for every 100 defendants being placed on supervised and intensive probation, by my calculations and experience, 15% were simply unamenable to help, for 15–20% it was a tossup, while for the remainder they would have to sink or swim on their own.[11]

Probation officers were not health experts able to advise clients on drug matters. There was simply no money in the budget to provide for a proper ongoing training regimen. Nor could POs prevent clients from taking drugs without embarking on a combat zone mentality. This would translate into constant surveillance as the key PO tool in a cat and mouse game that led to unscheduled home visits, repeated demands for office visits at all hours, need for written and visual verifications of work, incessant contacts between POs and the few relevant drug rehab agencies, constant urine testing, and, of course, talks with mom who would be the only one really interested in seeing her son improve. Was the danger of human rights abuses always being forsaken to satisfy PO suspicions? Because refusal to comply with any of these demands by the client might find him back in court on a trivial violation where referral to a lengthy jail or prison sentence was a likely outcome.

Alarm! If POs weren't health experts, they surely had no technical skills dealing with psychiatric issues possessed by many clients. POs were not trained in this regard. Nor could clients be helped if POs were hampered and confused by bizarre behavior that cannot be adequately explained in rational, man-in-street terms. What percentage of a caseload did this include? Difficult to say due to the long-term damaging effects of drug and alcohol addiction which affected so many. But I speculate perhaps 25–35% of my caseload over time fell into this category. Again, hard to say, because initial social investigations by the department tended to treat the behavior of most prospective probationers going to court as volatile, antisocial, and erratic in behavior, especially if a minority—quick to apply racist labels by nonexpert investigating POs. These may well be considered war crimes as the judgments were often flawed and the harsh treatment meted out was based on these accumulation of errors in initial judgment that led disinterested judges to opt for jail terms and lump in a slew of terms and surveillance orders following the advice of these pretended PO experts. Here again, we border on departmental behavior I label war crimes against human dignity because nonexperts have been making tyrannical decisions over the lives and futures of people who are perhaps less criminal and more mental.

Probation services as I perceived them for this period represented a kind of White paternalism that said to Black clients, you're going to do it this way and like it, or else! Granted, this must have been a sort of nirvana to White supremacists who occupied many of the chairs in the probation departments I encountered. They seem to draw pleasure by castigating and humiliating Black clients, making them do trivial things to prove their inferiority at the hands of racists without disguise. Here the courts become involved in the imposition of bourgeois values and pressuring people to accept them unquestioning despite the resistance that leads to confrontations with POs and eventual returns to court for greater punishments where the blame will rest squarely on his shoulders. Numbing time in jail will be seen as a logical decision as such people haven't the skills to improve their status and jail is something they can handle easily—war crime mentality.

Probation supervision plans were filled with a sense of empathy from the top down toward the poor and misguided. They were highly structured but with little connection to a man's own community or ability to follow through with PO demands. Each court-ordered step was planned in detail and few contingencies were overlooked except the main one: the man hasn't the desire in a brutally racist society to want to comply with demeaning impositions from courts and POs alike. Despite the reforming character of probation programs, few could be directed to a fundamental change in his status as a probationer. You only hope he won't offend before his time on probation expires and you're rid of him.

The one great fear of all POs, senior on down, was the probationer would commit some heinous crime on your watch that commanded maximum notoriety in the local newspaper and set off bells and whistles throughout the community that pointed to you as the chief culprit. The shame! The office looks and quiet murmurs of fellow POs as you walked by.

Norman E. Long, professor of politics at Brandeis University, was critical of the concepts of probation supervision in economic and political terms since it requires that probationers be their own success stories:

> (The probationary advisory aid of POs) assumes some kind of bootstrap magic by which individuals . . . can solve their own problems . . . (from) the magic of efficacy of unaided human will. It seems doubtful in the extreme whether local communities (of these clients) can make up for an inadequate national growth rate (at their level of accomplishment) and, in many, if not all cases, the local economy itself is a reflection of factors beyond . . . the control of individual probationers.[12]

Sometime in the summer of 1974, I became aware of Thomas Holmes and Richard Rahe Stress Scale (1967)—the most stressful life events. I read where these two psychiatrists, after examining 5,000 patients, drew the conclusion that a connection existed between illness and the most stressful life events. They found a strong correlation. This was replicated in 1970 with research into the same subject using 2,500 Cornell University students. The correlation was so strong that they ranked stressful situations on a scale from most to least stressful. These could indicate which life stressors put people at a higher risk of becoming ill. What about also a higher risk of getting into trouble? Could their scale have a useful application for the probationers on my caseload? If I gave this same test, what would I find with ex-offenders? I chose forty-two White probationers and twenty-two Black, eighteen refused to participate.

What would I find that related to the H/R test? I took the test and found my stress level at the time was seventy-two. Both groups of probationers scored well over 225, a few in the 300+ range where there was an 80% likelihood of illness (could this be interpreted to mean the possibility of becoming so disengaged they might commit a crime or harm someone)? The conclusion reached, based on such sketchy testing, was that most of the probationers tested had a 50% chance of having a life event occur to set them off, with Blacks showing about 15% higher scores than White. It suggested that this was an area that offered some clues and suggested paths toward treatment and awareness on the part of the CJS (especially judges as directed in the probation social report) that could tell us who might be more at danger while trying to live their everyday lives. The most stressful events that kept reappearing were the death of someone close, marital separation, imprisonment, personal injury, loss of job, and serious health issues of client or family member. More needed to be done to attempt to establish a correlation between how our probationers lived their lives, the stress they were under on a daily basis, and the extent to which any activity or demand of the art of POs or law enforcement might set off the person to commit an offense.[13]

Were we, in short, contributing members to an offender's bad behavior? "By participating in the punishment process, even as a healer, I loaned a certain credibility to the existing correctional system . . . my very presence makes it easier to rationalize oppression within the CJS." This is how Dr. Halleck interpreted my behavior toward clients.[14] When I presented my preliminary findings and thoughts to my chief PO at the time, I was told the concept might have merit but only in an academic setting; I was a PO and I should keep such ideas to myself. That the probation department presented a perfect place to follow through with some of these ideas made no impact on him and ideas along these lines clearly led nowhere. The idea was abandoned. Routine indifference to offender needs continued apace, and PO demands on their private lives intensified.

So far, my experiences suggested that the threshold of potential significant changes in the status of probationers was rather low for judges who didn't believe offenders could actually improve their status; only slightly better but not particularly high for middle-class POs charged with the responsibility of slotting clients into a woefully few community action groups. This was reluctantly aided by POs who smelled competition for probationer allegiance and thus often did little to assist, join, advise, or encourage community action agencies to help offenders get on their feet. Despite limited LEAA suggestions to work to build community-effective nongovernmental social agencies, probation departments failed in this regard, also seeing such alternative groups as competition for clients who are valued as money chips to departments fighting to keep caseloads high and manage costs. I had also seen probation department heads show little cooperation in the meeting of community groups to fight crime due to their fear that other organizations would beat them out for money to run their programs. The result tended to maintain the status quo of options to an offender in the restriction of local projects, thereby severely limiting the potentiality of change for the poor probationer.

"An inescapable present fact is that the poor are powerless . . . " which means they cannot plan, regulate, or determine their own fate, much less community action programs . . . they must depend for any advancement in life on PO surrogates. To paraphrase Clark:

> The poor have not been educated to confront (POs) in any rational way . . . even when there is flagrant evidence that the interests of the poor probationer have been subordinated to the maintenance of the status quo. The poor can be exploited flagrantly or subtly even by those programs that are designed for their benefit and even by programs designed to protect them from the abuses of governmental personnel and agencies.[15]

The many urban riots of the late 1960s were a godsend to lifeless probation departments across the country. I know, I was affected. I got a well-paying job with generous health benefits from the Los Angeles County Probation Department. The mood of anxiety was in the air. I had no real experience working with criminals or those with anger issues although I had been a social worker for welfare families a few years earlier. I had worked in the ghetto with welfare women but at no time did any agency prepare its workers to learn about the Afro-American's culture, concerns, or aggravations with a distant White society. I was hired so long as I was willing to tell my interviewer I had the backbone to recommend sending someone I knew nothing about to prison based solely on a charge courts seemed appropriate, but where the facts of the case made justice appear to be millions of miles away. Just say yes, I was urged, by someone who didn't seem to care otherwise. I did, I told a fib, I was hired, everyone was happy. The department could sigh relief as they had just employed a college graduate, never mind his major (business) or his outlook on life. One Black probationer later confided in me:

> The probation department has appointed POs for years now that had no business at the helm. It's the equivalent of seeing a dog at the controls of a plane. You're shocked at the hiring and know it's going to end badly for the Black probationer.

My cohort of 1968–1969 was given no race relations training, no insights into the Black experience (my class was all lily white), nor was there an effort made to acquaint me with my future working area (this was the Watts Compton area-scene of much violence, firebombing, police warfare, and the toppling over of Black resentment in 1967). We met no community leaders, knew no community resources, nor was I given local agencies who might be of assistance if I asked. My meager list was amplified by a few suggestions from Black secretaries in the office who perceived I was sincere in wanting allies to help in the rehabilitation process: I got names of a few barbershops,

Baptist church leaders, and a playground director or two. Three months later I met my first members of the Black Panther Party. They set about putting me right on many of the big questions I had about the Black community and their police harassers. Little did I know that by following department guidelines and unwritten street rules that I was being taken down the path of marginal war crimes behavior. Eventually, the Panthers wised me up.

Within six months or a year of exasperated trying, failing, and getting no appreciable results from clients, resources being as miserable as they were, it was easy to abandon hope, leave, or do one's job quietly, take the bimonthly paycheck and benefits, and say nothing. Was this a war crime being paid to stay out of the way? On my first day on the job, I withstood a blistering shower of verbal and racial abuse and intolerance from my first three Black clients who had little regard for the feelings of a White boy. But it was a firestorm of rancor to cause tears to well up and for me to ask what had I got myself into? I never did quite rid myself of the belief few clients wanted me there but put up with me because perhaps I was the least miserable of the bunch of POs they had to confront. Clark wrote his own analysis:

> Ghetto social and community services must come from the citizens of the ghetto (for both adults and juveniles in the form of grass roots activists) who are disciplined and politically sensitive—they just need to be organized otherwise . . . reforms only amount to benevolence from outside the community and vulnerable to control . . . tending to encourage further dependence.[16]

Yet after years of phenomenal growth and cost probation still seemed unable to present a favorable picture of its self to the public and Black communities: what were needed, it was said, was a much improved public image, more realistic and effective programs that encompassed the talent of the ghetto, less destructive fragmentation, greater professionalism, insulation from political interference, and push toward punitive behavior toward clients and aggressiveness in suppressive attitudes toward urban client lifestyle, consideration of creating effective research findings to aid in the rehabilitation and what works, improved fiscal support and better ways of utilizing money, attempts at creative service, and far greater use of community volunteers while yet projecting a ten-year plan calling for, of course, more money.[17]

Some of my colleagues, as well as I, eventually came around to Clark's observation: "The futility and unreality of the present probation system as it relates to reality of the offender's predicament is beyond debate." He spoke of the scarcity of helpful facilities and community programs to benefit local citizens. We saw it alike.[18]

After a few "no's" and "it can't be done" and "Morris, that's not why you're being paid," "don't let the judge hear you say that," "be sensible, young man" from my supervisors who always had their thumb on my neck when it came to community liaison work, I soon gave up openly trying to form contacts in Watts. I knew whatever I did in this regard had to be under the table, and hush-hush and preyed nothing got back to my bosses. Putting trust in someone you don't know and for whom the stakes are high if he fails you is something most young POs are not willing to attempt. An avalanche of rejections, protests, and laughter from fellow POs also doomed my volunteering to create ideas for the benefit of my clients. After my Watts debacle, I soon left Los Angeles to accept a better-paying job (doing even less work) in a beautiful part of the Bay Area (Marin County), working in a streamlined architectural beauty, the civic center building of Frank Lloyd Wright. Later came the NYC Prob Dept and I let probation slip by to just did the basics. I was a casualty of the War on Crime. Outside a girlfriend or two, no one seemed to mind my departure—just another PO transfer. Probationers were used to that; no tears were shed.

After nearly four years in the bowels of the city's inner zone, I found White probationers in Marin County a very quirky lot. As part of a Wild West atmosphere, one slept in a coffin in an upper bunk bed, another wanted me to nurse his dying Doberman with a sinister scowl, a third, on our first meeting, offered me his sister while another slept with a tarantula. Then there was the probationer who walked across dark streets at night hoping unsuspecting drivers would hit him and the guy who lived in a house populated by geese who pooped everywhere; the smell was overwhelming. This crowd made me drop my Black experiences and attempt to add on a new series of weird exposures. POs have to be ready.

What were probationers' views on all this? How did they interpret what I was trying to do for them? Only PO perspectives are generally recorded; few cared what clients thought. We assume they will complain and whine whatever the topic and hate the CJS beyond rationality. I made suggestions from time to time that the department should want to know and pursue active means at interviewing our clients. I was told to "keep my place and let higher ups do the thinking." If the probation department wanted to know, some mister big at central HQ would design the project. For me, "just keep quiet." Because of my initiative and curiosity and belief that we needed to work closer with clients if we were to be of any use to them, these bits of my personality indicated an agitator and I never got promoted. Surprised?

Probation officers talk. They talk to each other. In this interactive process, they talk about their caseload customers. They talk about themselves and their pet peeves with supervision. Sometimes a few even discuss tricks and gimmicks they use to get by and make the job easier and keep off the backs of their clients. Regarding this gossip I was all ears, invisible paper and pencil at the ready. So it is that came to learn very early in my own career how to cut corners, ways of being benevolent, as it were, by keeping out of a man's hair. Keeping people from being jailed, I soon learned, was the best thing I could do if I wanted to be helpful. Giving clients a positive view of themselves and how their artistic or musical skills (which many of them had) might be a stepping stone to a better life did reach more than a few ears. In this way, I even brought a few smiles. Maybe that was the best I could expect from a mean CJS that continually warped my ethics as well as those around me.

Being so charitable and cooperative to client needs often tend to push me into the direction of a whole series of learned tactics and tricks that decreased my involvement with probationers. If I knew little of what they were doing I couldn't exactly actively make harsh demands on how they were living. If they were caught in the commission of a crime, the CJS had its own systematic, bureaucratic, even fascistic way of tossing them into the courts with immediate jail sentences without me saying a word. It kept me out of the picture, otherwise absolving me of intervening in a man's life to make it worse. I could justify this as a clever withdrawal from the scene lessening my guilt but my crime was in not putting up a major sociological defense to prevent jail altogether. But to do this meant placing the limelight on me as the local Marxist, deadening the impact of future benevolence. Doing so was sheer lunacy like going over the top into a battle zone filled with land mines. There was another angle to all this. The more I involved myself in the life of the probationer, the more I felt I was trespassing on his more important civil rights which kept me aloof from meddling. Probationers didn't need reminders they were on probation and always subject to the whim and vagaries of the CJS regardless of my plans. It thus happened that certain tricks were devised to give him space, doing nothing to really help him, as I had no resources at my disposal, but at least not acting as the mean witch of the West.

Such tricks took the following forms to execute:

1. Don't contact them, wait for them to contact me. Don't look for trouble. Perhaps 80% of the caseload could be left in this untouchable status. It worked until one of the 20% went virile and the whole case exploded into a serious local criminal matter; then expect long hours of case management, stress, and tedium. The upside? Plenty of free time to indulge your hobbies. Meet women.
2. Keep a low profile around office staff. Not too loud, not too blustery, don't boast, don't dispute endless stupid office procedures, and avoid volunteering to help in office emergencies which translated into being part of a collective war crime at suppressing client enthusiasm. I could also avoid it all by making a spontaneous home call to a client who was always home due to health reasons and could never present a threat. Bring lunch and all was well.

3. Discover a respectable hiding place in your building where it is unlikely you will be located—some lounge somewhere, a niche in a nearby library, a scruffy coffee bar in town. If you cannot be located, you can't make decisions and someone else will have to be Mr. Tough guy and commit the war crime. Find a grove of trees maybe, or better yet, a fountain or babbling brook. This tactic is usually initiated by cryptically telling the department secretary "I'm going out in the field."

4. NB: A senior PO advises to avoid the local porno movie house (remember this was 1990) where you might unceremoniously discover a judge before whom you usually appear.[19]

5. Look the part of the overburdened PO who is endlessly busy and unable to deflect from the pile of papers and reports crowding your desk due in court always "within two days." It is appropriate to play into this drama by turning your room/desk into a rat's nest of manuals, procedural reports, case files, fat technical books, pink call-back slips, and so on. Clutter is the key here in playing the role of overworked, faithful, and serious civil servant. "I need to read much of this if I want to better help my clients" you say when questioned on why you aren't really seen to be doing anything. Leaving a half-eaten sandwich and open bag of chips on an open case file lends itself to the idea of vast amounts of energy being expended without being able to finish lunch, all in the noble pursuit of helping one's fellow man.

6. Sit around during chinwags with fellow POs, discussing personalities and backgrounds of colleagues, of romantic alliances or cross-agency rivalries or corruption with the administration at the upper levels, spending disproportionate amounts of time harping on the industrialization and politicization of conflict between different local helping agencies.

7. POs have the ability to make life miserable for any client they dislike no matter how innocent or trivial the offense. Reprisal is a personal thing and endless petty punishments are always available to the PO should he be so inclined and able to dismiss these as war crimes. It is one of the lesser war crimes that POs have the authority, without supervision getting in the way, to be nasty and vindictive. In such cases, "gotcha now" is the objective to all personal contacts sent forward to make one's life miserable. With some POs, perhaps 10–15% treat their clients in this cavalier manner-harsh, mean and puritanical, let alone racist and pathological. In the most troublesome client relationships, POs can manufacture nasty comments that judges will accept if what is wanted are more court reprisals (I think roughly 85% of judges), to maintain harmony with the probation department as they do with police, in submit to the demands of the PO and uncritically punish clients as a show of CJS solidarity that clients should always remember if they wish to satisfy their betters in days

to come. In this regard probation department regulations can be found to be lengthy, ambiguous, vague, conflicting where even for a client to go to the toilet may be interpreted as a sign of an aggressive attitude toward PO commands. Seek police insistence to put him on a watch list. Hint you suspect him of unpleasantries with underage children at the playground. This will get police attention and they will watch him to distraction. Give him the idea you are overlooking his activities and one night swoop down while he's alone at home and hang him on some petty infraction. And do as police do, exaggerate. It makes the charge look more serious. These may be possible war crimes but they do tell the client who is the boss in a job where POs have little power except to make the lives of the lower class and minorities miserable.

8. The PO knows it's his word against the clients who are generally without support and alert legal representation and most judges defer to PO wrath (which is how they want POs to perform anyway) rather than risk loss of departmental morale in a tough on crime climate. Rarely, too, will defense lawyers challenge or snarly POs who in the near future they may need for support toward one of their more important defendants. No one wants an antagonistic PO prepared to take it out on an otherwise positive investigative report sought by the attorney. A belligerent war criminal Erickson remarks: "Whenever my charge seeks me out for advice, assistance or interpretation of Court rules, I counter by passing the buck. When he begs permission to travel ten miles outside the geographical boundaries specified in his Court order to visit his elderly, terminally ill father for Christmas, I tell him I will first have to consult with the judge, prosecutor, police chief, makeup a title. I tell him not to hold his breath as a definitive answer may not be forthcoming. If he persists, tell him to use his own judgement and be prepared for possible nasty consequences. I let him know I'm not to blame for unpleasant decisions—it's the 'system' and I'm only a mere cog. I plead the obedient, powerless functionary and I wring my hands for effect. I let him know I'd hate to revoke his probation on such a trivial matter but it's for his own good . . . a convincing application of this technique is crucial if I want to keep him continuously submissive."[20]

9. A dilemma can occur: I want him to be able to get along without me, do it all, think for himself, act on his own since this is our own subliminal message to all clients for their own good. But most will only get in some narrow scrape, minor trouble, or get arrested for a cheapo drug purchase. Then our world of solitude and quiet comes crashing down on us and we have to report to the judge or the DA or our supervisor and explain how much we have been doing with him, how bright his prospects looked, how involved we are in his life so that the current problem is a fluke, a

surprising turnabout from a relatively calm existence being my "best" probationer. All this to cover my own tucas.

10. I confess; some POs experience a wretched kind of exhilaration in possessing extraordinary power over the lives of these pathetic reprobates. There is comfort in knowing life's miseries and slew of arrows slung at one-meaning me can be erased by taking it out on some poor bastard trying to minimize his own slew of arrows. In such cases, I can always kick the cat (proverbially the probationer) and set up stricter rules on his private life, annoy him with repeated home calls, flirt with his girlfriend, or inform the secretary to prepare the usual "ghetto report" which is a boilerplate template report that cites continuous routine misbehavior of the client (name withheld to be filled in later) that might warrant further terms and conditions imposed by the judge in a court hearing.

11. We know all druggies and alcoholics will celestially recidivate, so don't waste too much time on them. Just keep ears open for re-arrests. Clients if on welfare really don't work (for mainly menial slavish work) and avoid searching with any degree of effort so why should I invest time searching on their behalf-time wasted when maybe one or two clients are at a point they will make me look good with their own success story being highlighted in court, credit to me and a praiseworthy comment by the judge who I hope doesn't forget my face when I need a favor.

12. What's that criminological theory about labeling? Once the court and probation department have pinned on a subject the label "criminal," "thief," "addict," "wastrel," "social predator" it is likely he will manage to fulfill the worst expectations with little prodding from the PO.

These twelve strategies might not represent the most extreme examples of war crimes like shooting someone in the back fleeing a traffic stop but they have their purpose in continually humiliating and chastising the offender without doing the least good to make his life better. The belief of superiority through timely use of tough talk, threats, and the occasional returns to court for stern warnings from hateful judges or the occasional arbitrary use of jail presents a series of war crimes that result in a daily disturbance of client's life that adds a separate injustice to the disregard and contempt already found in the supervising probation order. Neutral observers are harsh in their criticism of probation services. Eduardo Mundo spent thirty years with the Los Angeles Probation Department. In 2019, upon retiring, the veteran said:

"Probation is not just 'troubled' and 'beleaguered' it is broken and requires transformation. Aside from changing practices like hiring, training, promoting and assigning of staff, the department need to extract itself from a self-preservation mode." "The current system of probation and parole is an ineffective waste of criminal justice resources and a driver of incarceration rather than as an alternative to it."

Vincent Schiraldi, senior research analyst at Columbia Justice Laboratory and former commissioner of the New York City Probation Department, rebuked the system:

> There are thousands of probation and parole departments in America. These places reek of apathy and neglect. While I was in the department, I encountered distrustful judges, POs with low expectations, an unchanging environment of older POs known as "lunch pail people," (men and women just waiting for retirement by keeping low and keeping things as they are . . .).

A 2015 Report from the Minneapolis Law Review claimed probationers must comply with at least eighteen to twenty different daily requirements and commands just to remain in good standing with their probation officer. Victor St. John, adjunct professor at John Jay College, did a study of the late 1980s where he found Black probationers were 270% more likely to be rearrested for a felony while on supervised probation compared to White probationers. Being on probation seemed to signal to suspicious cops that this person was a community threat or crime-oriented and needed immediate attention with an arrest as the easiest possible solution.[21]

How did POs spend their time? One recent study written in 2002 showed how little PO duties had changed in the over twenty years since I had been doing this kind of work. It made for depressing reading; open-ended and lengthy interrogations and time spent in random questioning of clients took 52% of a PO's office time, written referrals to rehabilitation agencies took 21%, practical help took no more than 7%. Human rights advocates take note as at no time was a client allowed outside help while being interrogated by a PO. No one else was there to present his side of the story; no one know what rights he had in these circumstances. Few POs and defendants identified the same obstacles or how to confront them, few worked together, and 60% of the clients said all they received from POs was cheap advice. POs efforts on their behalf were as likely to fail as succeed, a 50–50 chance. What did the probationers want from their POs? Shelter in dire times which was impossible to obtain, mundane but helpful telephoning other agencies for servile work in an effort to spare shoe leather (the chance that no job existed when they got there was about 90%); and meager resources for carfare and lunch money which clients had to beg to receive. Farrall believed all these requirements were well beyond the efforts of the average supervising PO.[22]

With costs of prison confinement running at perhaps $25,000 per cell per person, costs of traditional supervision were by 1970 a bargain at $150 per probationer per annum. If one saw a client once a month in the office, for perhaps thirty minutes this drove costs down to maybe $5 a session, 25c a word in quick sessions. Even less if bundled into a larger caseload—possibly $84–$113 or pennies per customer. Not that humans were the sole attention of POs. One estimate was that 25% of the workload of a PO was devoted to interviewing and writing reports for the courts which consumed maybe one to two days a week.[23]

In 1975 it was estimated that over one million empty-worded probation reports had been written by possibly 20,000 POs. Caseloads themselves range from 50 to 150 per PO. Mine varied from 85 to 135 which allowed maybe 10 to 19 minutes per week per client. Not much time to rebuild his life but certainly enough time to annoy and pester him while withholding assistance because I had none to give. Almost 25% of a POs time was estimated to be spent behind the wheel of a car as caseloads increased after 1968 and POs were left with the unenviable task of chasing after clients on home visits, job interviews, agency liaisons, and collateral contacts.[24]

Burnout figures are suggestive: A 1983 PhD dissertation suggests a significant percentage of POs report experiencing unhappy or negative feelings about their job. The numbers were telling: 13% experienced burnout feelings on a daily basis, 17% weekly while 47% believed they made a positive difference in the lives of their clients only a few times a month at most. Why? Blame the White support systems—rigidity of rules, massive caseloads, lack of departmental support, their own personal life whenever they took client troubles home, social distancing whenever they tell strangers what they do, pay issues (62%), lack of promotion (85%), and feelings of impotence from being unable to make much difference in the lives of their probationers.[25]

In 1976 I conducted research into the attitudes, opinions, and complaints of 100 probationers gleaned from the caseloads of six POs in the Marin County Probation Department who were willing to participate (I had nine refusals). Marin County is just north of San Francisco in a wealthy enclave; a small Black community living in 1940s World War II public housing tucked away near the Sausalito yacht community. Marin City was a home to 35% of the County's Black population; another 26% of non-White were Mexican scattered here and there directed north toward rural, agrarian regions beyond. It was a glorious, attractive area that supports a counter-culture population of young dissidents living between the main city of San Rafael going west to Bolinas. Police enforcement was rather lax although they did spend most of their weekends dealing with drug dealers, motorcycle gangs, and peripatetic alcoholics in the many local bars.

The question put to this group was a simple one: What complaints, if any, do you have with your present PO? I interviewed them privately in a conference room unbeknownst to senior staff who I reckoned would have apoplexy to learn of this as they had been to two previous polls I had prepared in the past (need not concern us here). Results are as follows.[26]

Few saw their POs as a resource helping them to integrate (or reintegrate) into their community; 60% felt POs knew very little about services available for assistance and thus little was extracted from any outside agency to enhance personal development. In actual fact, few resources were actually funded for use and these had to be explored diligently by POs who had to take time to create relationships of some personal nature to get ready help. Many POs lived outside the area, especially in the East Bay where rents were much cheaper, or San Francisco where I lived for the cultural and artistic attractions. One lived in Fairfax and knew from personal contacts how to connect clients with helping agents but the rest were at sea in this regard. Black probationers (32% of the survey) believed White POs knew nothing of their culture and rarely came to visit the ghetto or meet on a personal basis; about half felt very uncomfortable around White women POs who they felt held antebellum beliefs about nonstop womanizing behavior of its younger members.

When asked whether they felt their civil rights were being properly respected by law enforcement, the courts, or the probation department itself, 75% hedged and avoided direct replies. I believe many of them had no clear idea what were their civil rights and the need for explanation and clarity was surely a function the department might have explored as an aid to young Black men being approached by police, threatening, surly, and otherwise. I later put this suggestion to higher ups who scoffed at the notion as a legal or academic issue best left to other agencies, especially the local schools but not the department, having the potential for being divisive between radical and conservative POs. About the same percentage, White and Black felt POs had no useful legal knowledge when approaching the court. POs were always warned by the administration to leave the legal stuff to lawyers to avoid placing themselves in jeopardy; never did defense attorneys or judges make it their business to give us crash courses on basic rights and courtroom strategy that we might pass along to our clients. No intruding on their cherish preserved tolerated. Respondents believed this was subject matter POs might consider if they wished to help clients without endlessly whining about lack of gelt to help satisfy client needs.

The department was always obsequious when it came to working relationships with judges, district attorneys, or the local business power brokers where they buckled to pressure to what these groups wanted in offender punishment. Overworked local courtroom lawyers viewed this as an infringement on their power and status and duties. It also occurred when POs, especially the newer recruits, planned to advocate for their probationers by proposing leftist opinions or radical solutions that drifted afoul of standard sentencing procedures worn thin by decades of CJS spineless capitulation to faulty judicial decisions.

Roughly 40% of staff, clients believed, lacked proper training to deal with their family and personal issues and didn't really know how to talk to them without leaving their arrogance or surliness behind. This was especially the case for Black probationers (60% of this group) who felt Whites were either afraid of Black people, treated like they were children, found them a mystery, or thought each was secretly involved in some conspiratorial criminal activity that POs wanted to flesh out. Transfers, promotions, ill health, departures for unknown reasons decimated 40% of the staff while I was there during turbulent years 1971–1979 which also caused disruption in client relationships. A few fell afoul of illegal drug dependency and had to resign. All this turmoil meant office stability and attempts to impart a consistent educational program (my input to the department) generated chaos for many clients. Within two to three years of the probation supervision order, it wasn't uncommon for a client to experience the disruption of dealing with four or five newly assigned POs each having their own set of techniques, personality, and degree of punitive nature for clients to make necessary adjustments.

Eighty percent claimed POs solved none of their most immediate problems, usually related to lack of money, jobs, or shelter. Resources given to the department for such purposes were always slender and an embarrassing topic for a frontline organization in the people helping business. Without money what good was it? Even if available I doubt the POs, without local opportunities available to them, would have been able to do much about it. At no time did the department attempt to send POs into adjoining neighborhoods and among nearby institutes and commercial organizations to stoke fires and generate useful contacts for the client's best interests. Without these, little was accomplished and we all fell into lassitude, apathy, or chagrin passing these moods onto probationers who proceeded to waste the time given them by the probation order to possibly improve their lives. The time spent on each of these "customers" was just time devoted to supervision. Some of this was intensive and these men, with nothing being offered to them, merely constituted a pool where POs paid to do little more than annoy and bother and threaten with jail and prison.

We shall get to a study of PO characteristics shortly but in conjunction with this, 85% of the respondents felt POs placed too much faith or emphasis when interviewing them on feelings ("how do you feel about . . .?), or asked speculative questions ("what could you have done differently . . .?) or incriminating questions ("how much dope were you using at the time . . .?) that clients felt ill-equipped or ambivalent about answering. They also disliked PO refusals to interview or consult with defendant's peers, allies, or local homies who might present a different take on the offender's behavior and status in the community. These are the people who might speak up on their behalf and present a different view from that of anonymous law enforcement. Certainly, the negatives were always there in the rap sheet, arrest report, victim statement, and DA's complaint. These always put offenders in an unfavorable light and directed how POs saw them upon first contact.

Seventy-two percent of the respondents claimed POs were hard to find, locate, telephone, or otherwise contact when truly needed in an emergency or in need of paternalistic advice about women. Much of this "need" occurred at night or over weekends when POs were living their own lives. In many cases I had the belief that POs avoided being anywhere near a phone in these moments so they had a second unlisted number of their own calls. This left defendants to their own devices which was a scary thought as they often made the kind of stupid errors in thinking that got them in their mess in the first place. Calling into the department hotline only enabled clients to leave their name and message which would be followed up the next business day but never during perilous moments of absolute need.

The charge of racism came up often when talking to Black clients but examples excluding their gut instincts were not much to verify. Perhaps for the time (1976) no one knew where to take this complaint since agencies were themselves in total denial, unwilling to accept this charge as applicable to them as a legitimate injustice. A few suggested the PO's failure to understand "Black street life" as it was put, pitted the young male Black lifestyle with a White bourgeois upbringing and no department training on the subject led to everything Black being interpreted by Whites bordering on extreme racial ignorance.

A few final complaints come to mind although numbers were small and came as asides or comments once the interview was over. They are recorded here only for the completeness of the study. (1) Many POs just wanted clients to tell good lies and make up traceable addresses and names to corroborate the story and allow POs to keep it short. It meant less follow up, less work, and a quicker report to court to complete the assignment, making POs look efficient and eliciting warm praise from the bench. (2) Terms and conditions by courts were often very many and seemed to set clients up for failure. Probationers were often quick to see this and sought PO help on how to evade some of them, an often-significant part of the relationship that kept clients happy enough with POs. (3) POs seemed not to really care about the client's predicament because POs themselves had never been exposed to such dilemmas and had no practical working knowledge on how these might be resolved. The result often meant the man behind bars. As more than one client told me "to POS, it's just a job."

Earlier I mentioned a study that looked at personality types of POs. When correlated with the previous outpouring of defendant complaints, a quick awareness emerges of how easy it was for the majority of POs I encountered to support recommendations for punishment, lengthy incarceration, extended supervised probation, and expanded terms and conditions. This analysis comes from a 1992 rare study into this matter which we shall now address.[27] Sluder and Shearer studied traditional hierarchical bureaucratic structures and claimed that "much seemingly random variations in behavior are actually quite orderly and consistent." They went on to explore the strengths and weaknesses of POs using scales for introversion/extraversion, how they acquired socially relevant information, how opinions/decisions were formed, and for which different categories. POs from a Southwestern state were used—53% being male, 66% White, 24% Latino, with a mean age of thirty-four (twenty-two to seventy-four) and 60% having less than two years of adult level probation service, 14% possessing five to ten years of service, most were POs on the lower levels of job status, and caseloads averaged a containable seventy-five. So what strengths were found in this group?[28]

The vast majority (70%) of these POs were rated as practical people who could handle court-imposed deadlines, were logical in their reasoning about sanctions, seldom made errors of fact (also useful for judges), completed tasks assigned, fitted well in bureaucratic structures, didn't normally allow personal values to intervene in reports (based upon my work with a similar group, I disagreed with this finding), wrote reasonably concise reports, possessed a deep interest in "justice" (no way to know how that was measured), and periodically displayed an authoritarian streak to maintain client control of interview sessions.[29]

Splendid attributes for probation department demands as they relate to court/juridical requirements. But there was another component missing. Liaison with their clients, placed under their control with strict court-directed guidelines, on how to live. Here limitations, flaws, character weaknesses of POs provided danger signs and clear warnings on whether clients would be positively affected or not. Impersonal demands of the job were easily handled by POs. What was less enticing were weaker social skills and a shaky relationship with people of lower social standing. Racism was not explored, a serious deficiency in the evaluation. POs also showed a dislike for spontaneity, flexibility to alter tactics with clients as events dictated, they preferred to be tied to a plan carved in stone; there was a general dislike for new problems which a client might bring, need for fast decisions to breaking events, and realistic appraisals of probationers which some judges would seek in court peremptorily. Clients were seen by these POs as irritations and nuisances with their recurring problems that interfered with PO's office duties. Nor did they care to search out knowledge on community resources to offer alternatives to jail sanctions. These flaws and weaknesses, as applied to men with no ability to challenge, question, or redirect often draconian orders, led to poor relationships, overuse of incarceration as a tool for rehabilitation, and a

clear lack of justice and human rights for clients with war crimes being the
end result.

US civil rights lawyer based in London, Clive Stafford Smith, recently
noticed what I had seen for a long time. Writing in the TLS he discusses "why
the US Justice system is not fit for purpose." His answer? In not upholding
basic concepts of justice, "the players suited to each role (in the CJS, here the
probation officers) begins with how we choose the players. Instead of tolerance, liberality, and empathy, we appoint the wrong people to almost all the
relevant positions."[30] If we truly wanted the system to achieve its stated goal
of social justice, we would vigorously recruit kind people to become members of the CJS; instead we do the opposite. We need recruits, Smith goes on,
who are skeptical, wary of mistakes and rights abuses in the arresting process
to mitigate sanctions based on lies and deceit. Instead the CJS selects people
who strongly believe in punishment, hard police tactics, tough love, and no-
nonsense therapy tactics. Painting the worse possible picture of an offender
is the usual result.[31]

So where do I see war crimes occurring within the ranks of probation?
Where does the harshness of POs in trying to "improve the lives of the clients" begin to fall into the category of war crimes no matter how slight the
damage to the probationer? One place often overlooked is the defendant and
the Fourth Amendment. His constitutional right of privacy. POs can legally
(?) invade a client's house or room without a warrant (unlike the police) at
any time and stay for three hours if they wish. In effect this might be seen
as an unofficial form of incarceration as the client could not go out while the
PO remained. Parts of the residence could be observed and noted for a report
on articles not belonging to the probationer but connected, making a case for
perhaps contraband. And what if it's a 3:00 a.m. visit?

In effect all POs did this, as did I, although I tried to minimize visits to two
every four months, letting the man know when I would appear. A few POs
took it upon themselves to visit a certain client possibly three times a month
under the suspicion something nasty was going on. Was this the POs job? I
think not. If something is found, are police called in or contacted? Does this
make a PO an agent, a stalking horse of the police? In this the PO is going
places not even police are allowed. Is this harassment, intimidation, good
probation work? Does unlimited power to commit indiscriminate searches
fall into a category of war crime that keeps the community safe? The trauma
of never knowing when also comes to mind. Is this how rehabilitation works?

Several major concerns bother me about the fairness of justice that origi-
nates within the probation sanctions. Is it fair to sentence one offender to a
minimum of three years supervised probation with several provisions to get
a high-school equivalency without evidence is related to the goal of reducing
future crime? I am bothered that offenses that don't warrant incarceration

allow revocation of probation and subsequent jail time for a person failing to abide by conditions that have nothing to do with criminal behavior (i.e., leaving the state, being with old friends, not getting a diploma, getting caught drinking alcohol). In my experience, roughly 50% of all probation sentences over a three-year period eventually lead to a court-requested revocation or jail reprimand. Nor does it seem just to punish minor infractions by modifying probation conditions to create more severe pressure where a small crime could activate a major punishment, always keeping an offender in the shadow of a noose that places too much tension in a man's life, a war crime for being more than the sentence alone.[32]

Harris believes offenders are seen as less than responsible persons by requiring their "consent" to a probation order before imposition knowing not what's at stake in terms of limitations placed upon him for which he had no choice.[33] Should clients fail to follow all demands, even those unrelated to the crime or potential criminality, any future return to court could find such dismissive behavior seen in purely negative terms by POs who will ask courts for jail time just because of refusal to comply, not for a crime itself. I am also bothered at the restrictions being imposed on clients on the basis of unsubstantiated theories and studies to what specific behaviors or associations as they apply to any single probationer are conducive to criminality. Such distortion of fact or attempts to use fake statistics to punish offenders implies a degree of war crime that warrants awareness.

Harris provides policy considerations in such cases that are designed to seek least costly sanctions with rough cost figures discussed to help judges, keep out of court as much as possible, bear human rights always in mind, require POs to acquire training and education on ethnic issues, and assess the real role of the PO as it assures probationers they are getting the best possible consultations. That these are put forward suggests serious gaps in PO–client relations that cause rise of these suggestions and may, in fact, be hiding war crime behavior.[34]

Probationers don't generally begin the probationary sentence feeling genuinely remorseful. If they pled guilty it is for the benefit of significant others to show contrition they often don't feel. Many have told me they don't like hearing details of their crime repeatedly recited with all the errors the police made at the point of arrest and they quickly redefine themselves as but a temporary criminal, and so probation begins badly. In fact, all appearances in court including revocation hearings were seen by probationers as a status degradation ceremony designed to humiliate them publicly.

Most of the probationers I met were pragmatic or fatalistic about their role in the probation process: simply another reminder this is how poor men live. Rather than whine about it, which is seen as wimpy, some in a survey I took felt completely innocent of all charges (maybe 12%), but said their lawyer conned them. Some said they followed their lawyer's advice and now regret it. Many were defiant and felt framed; some attributed their situation to a racist system. Of the ones who accepted their guilt, 50% believed the prosecutor should have shown more charity and presented a more enlightened deal.

So it is that with these attitudes and beliefs in mind, the average PO greets the new probationer who is filled with suspicion, defiance, confusion, overstressed, feeling the system and its workers are rigged against him, that revocation hearings are inevitable and that the PO is simply waiting for the right moment to get rid of him rather than help lift him out of the hole society has placed him. Perhaps 50–60% are of this belief at the beginning which doesn't make it easy to initiate a helpful relationship; but then perhaps that's what the system is designed to create.

Offenders in such a proceeding of the questionable due process never get a jury trial, have court time spent to determine if the hearing is justified or reveals some malice in the PO. Hearings last five minutes. The PO must write a critically negative report to justify this hearing which has its own financial costs and requirements of time wasted by the court professionals—judge, lawyers, and bailiffs. If he has a lawyer there may be a deal afoot with the DA and the fight is minimal and soon over. It is just a means to fill a court's day and just be seen to be doing something. A sort of assembly line justice emerges if other revocations are scheduled at the same time and each offender is but a cypher who is easily expendable in this war crime process.

Result? Longer probationary supervision, harder terms and conditions, jail for a week, loss of human rights which are easily overlooked by the judge, maybe even a quick trip to prison. The whole process may end up with minimal punishment but as a result of this particular hearing woe the offender who may have to come back to this same court a few months down the line. Then this minimal sanction will be sharpened into a nightmare the offender will not soon forget. Speculate on how the future rounds of supervision will turn out as each side becomes increasingly antagonistic toward the other.

Did rehabilitation transform during the 1960s into simple punishment? Has a White nationalist attitude critical of minorities helped shape probation intervention, the net widening tactic that ensnared more clients to help defer increased CJS costs caused this to happen? Can offenders tell the difference? Can any single punishment in the PO's repertoire lead to war crimes? Endless visits, too few minority POs, self-improvement techniques that clients don't want, referrals for jobs and rehabilitation agencies for positions that don't exist but provide POs with the fulfillment of quotas, new definitions on what it means for success on a case, refusal to develop community resources for use by the department, "dubious expertise" by POs with no real skills at helping clients improve their lot beyond espousing platitudes and phony leads, failure for the creation of department support groups (i.e., sports, chess, fishing, movies, acting/arts), computer training as part of a broadened rehab program that avoids just discussing how to stop criminal tendencies, reduced caseloads, widened options to serve as recommendations in court cases, increased editing by a special service to keep PO errors in a report to a minimum, awareness of new ideas found in other probation departments globally suitable for absorption.

Interviews constituted special truth tests. How much of the PO's report was invented? How much made up of innocent little fragments of gossip and hearsay? How much voyeurism and dubious details were being played out with the defendant in attempting to get him to reveal something negative about himself? Who was there as his support, his corroborator, and verifier? Many POs took on a decidedly adverse attitude toward clients and had boilerplate reports resting on their desk just waiting for the simple insertion of key names, a place set aside for demographic social factors with space open for generalized information, a form repeatable in 75% of the cases without much erasing, making report writing relatively easy and fast.

Historically, probation departments have always paid lip service to their idea of community service, providing treatment within a community setting, calling themselves a major cog in the community corrections system, verbally reaching out in local meetings for recognition from the neighborhoods in which they serve. They tend to give them high scores in the aptitudes and service delivery they provide the local population in need. Senior POs who met in Albany at a LEAA-sponsored conference in 1969 flattered themselves on the subject of community attitudes toward this particular service. "Probation officers show a very high agreement . . . which states that our policies should place greater emphasis on community treatment (than presently)." A determined belief was also cast in a survey of these men during the conference which agreed: "We should place greater emphasis on community . . . programs and less on sending offenders to prison." "My department has the respect of most poor people in my community" and "I feel very much that (we) belong in (our) community."[35] It should be noted that this was part of a conflict resolution meeting with high-ranking police to test the validity of this technique of promoting greater harmony between these two CJ agencies. Sadly, no one saw the obvious transfer of this approach to resolving community problems involving probationers, POs, and staff and members of the community representing private nonjudicial agencies aimed at offender rehabilitation.

Despite all the desires by probation departments to strengthen ties with community groups, little evidence suggests that any legitimate effort bore fruit. It is one of my greatest complaints against the service, to the point of it being a war crime for being so resistant to taking this path and making every effort to amalgamate the two branches into meaningful aid groups aimed at helping probationers with realistic opportunities for social and economic growth while on probation under a POs supervision. Yes, both sides would have competed for necessary funds and a mutually envious budget to get the job done but I know of no case where an effort was made to see if such a splitting up of LEAA funds could have been attempted for the benefit of both parties. Jack Williams Spencer noted,

> A review of the literature in the area of probation since 1960 reveals two major themes: (a) a concern by POs and their superiors for possessing the salient explanatory and predictive factors in decision-making by POs when it came to how to dispose of criminal offenders yet were never found to be statistically valid and (b) a search for the major determinants of probation outcomes good or bad. A third might be added efforts to determine the best methods to reach interpersonal discourse preparatory for report writing.[36]

What is not seen as a top priority, despite previous kudos for agency involvement in the community, is an expanded role by probation departments in encouraging local extralegal groups to sit at the table when the issue of probationer assistance comes up; also, how best to be able to incorporate local services not already available from traditional sources. That this could be very helpful arises when Spencer, who gathered his PhD data in an Indiana probation department noted when writing reports for the court: "These cases tended to last five to ten minutes (which included) small talk about the . . . weather, deer hunting and the like." When it came to more serious matters, meeting initiated by the probationer, "the vast majority of interviews . . . to spend a half hour or more seeking advice for major problems where defendants could spill their guts."[37]

Various commissions encouraged experimental, innovative projects by local community groups and criminal justice agencies to bring to bear new ideas required by a generation of Black men who had been deeply affected by Black Power movements, militant rhetoric of civil rights groups, and failure on the part of brutal CJS agencies to observe human rights when attempting to stop crime and make arrests.

In chapter 12 of the *Challenge of Crime in a Free Society*, the commission recommended that CJ agencies "develop their own research units, staffed by specialists and drawing on the advice and assistance of leading scholars and experts in relevant fields pertaining to crime in the community."[38] I knew of no such units being formed in probation departments (excluding NYC) nationwide to forge stronger links with Black communities and when I tried to initiate or implement such a proposal in the several probation departments for whom I was employed, I got a sharp whack on the back of my neck and a resounding slam of the door. I was ridiculed and laughed at, "go back to your desk," "not what you are paid to do," "stop being a pest." This despite my PhD and work in departments both in United States and London. In 1977 I met with a similar rejection by the NYC probation department's Family Court section which was then starved of resources and ideas for community development projects for its probationers. I was told "either to confine my work to doing as told in the field office or expect to be booted out of the department within six months!" Naturally, this was the final boot, and I left happily never to return.[39]

Sociologists have regularly written of the value and importance of the development and social life of its members. George Simmel, Robert Park, Ernest Burgess, Herbert Gans, Louis Wirth, Philip Slater have spoken of the integrative possibilities of a healthy community. Karp and Yoels sounded a positive note when they spoke of the rediscovery of the community in the 1960s by persons owing less allegiance to a particular territory and more to a network of social relationships that POs were capable of generating.[40] But few sociologists applied these ideas to CJS agencies and what they could do to stimulate local resources to aid community rehabilitation projects and personnel. Such ideas as comrade courts, dispute resolution boards, leadership training for residents, social activism, and ways of making the neighborhood better. There was no CJS support. I faced indifferent agencies who had an aversion for creative ideas and were incapable of innovation to help their probationers, supposedly the core of their mission. Here I believe are the war crimes committed in thousands of ghettos by agencies tied to past traditions of social control, deflated by White nationalist thinking that saw Blacks as inferior and unable to resolve any of their self-made problems that required the White man's touch to resolve.

In neighborhoods that have insufficient political influence and lack organizations to offer rehab services, we can expect probation departments, as was the case, to operate with impunity from immediate environmental constraints despite community support or acceptance of legitimacy. As was usually the situation, POs offered but surveillance custodial, simple verbal intervention and monitoring functions plus contacts with police to control clients. Here the offender was prime focus and community resources unappealing and ignored. PO relationships, as I found them, were superficial and infrequent except after escalation or revocation episodes or confrontations with police. Many POs elected not even to enter a disorganized ghetto district, requiring clients to meet them in neutral zones or in the protective cocoon of the office. This situation may permit POs to operate informally, utilizing dubious tactics in supervision and investigation not condoned elsewhere. War crimes in the office can be suitably hidden from public scrutiny.

Whether the probation department is developed and organized to be community-run or community based, as discussed by Duffee,[41] the crucial factor is to free up this agency from its standardized, uniform, structural resistance with its White supremacist ideology among staff to attempt to complement local non-profit agencies as advised by numerous councils in this period.[42] If one looks carefully then at the many of the social policies constructed in the 1970s and 1980s one sees that the underlying themes of correcting flaws in personal behave by promoting more personal resp and blaming the offenders for their circumstance are inherent in the rationale.[43]

Probation departments as part of the CJS failed to take responsibility and bring about any sustained fundamental social change except in the case of the rare Black PO hired, which wasn't common in this period. Top PO administrators were simply locked in stone and simply unable to make changes this would do more for clients at the loss of power and function for the department. Neither Black probationers nor the communities in which they lived gained little from the millions of dollars government spent on the agency short of simply staying out of jail. All funds and expertise flowed into the ghetto and were not transferable to Black activists and leaders.[44] Dr. Kenneth Clark, one such leader activist and educator in Harlem pointed to the effect probation departments everywhere had on the ghetto—simply reinforcing its colonial status and dependency on White man direction and sympathy when it came to funding. All this simply added to the subservience and inferiority of Black probationers notes Clark, expressing this viewpoint to the meager funds allocated for job training, legal services, housing, educational stipends, or leisure activities. He adds, "How could any single probationers, confronted by this racist hegemony hope to make a life for himself and family once over-burdened with terms and conditions and impositions placed in his path by the local probation department composed almost exclusively of Whites who did little to aid the cause of Black redemption."[45]

Clark's notion that the public school system held a critical place in the ghetto, an institution from which probation departments, with their concentration of juvenile offenders and problem children, might offer lending, guiding hand. No such luck.

> As long as the ghetto schools continue to turn out thousands and thousands of functional illiterates yearly, Negro youth will not be prepared for anything other than menial jobs or unemployment or dependency . . . and the tragic waste of human resources will go unabated.[46]

Probation departments offered no assistance, rather they were clear recipients of these unstable, neglected, and uneducated children who as they grew up formed the basic caseloads of the average Black community probation department. Without this influx, POs who had nothing to offer but cheap advice would go out of business. Here we see war crimes being committed on unhappy Black clients on a daily basis. To my reckoning, 95% of the Black clientele were poorly educated, giving POs a quick response why nothing could be done for the offender—his lack of education doomed all PO efforts to nothing. Why even try? So the table was set for failure and another reason why Black self-esteem was so low, a war crime perpetuated to entire caseloads. If I had a job lead to offer my clients, I had to make sure I could translate the location to numbers, like 135th or 144th because letter addresses could not be understood by many clients—Lexington, Madison, Southern, and so on.

There was one community institution that stood out in these years at helping offenders get their lives together. They were neither governmental nor beneficiaries of government funding: The Nation of Islam, a Black Power institution. Successful as they were at rehabilitation especially of young Black men it was the rare White PO who dared make contact with NoI and meet with its representatives. I know of no White power structure agency which attempted to take them seriously (the same suspicion and distrust and anger of White government agents could be found with them as well). By the military and disciplined tactics they used and the rhetoric they employed, their rate of success rehabilitating criminals, despite enormous police and FBI harassment, arrests, and intrusions, was well established. That CJS held them in contempt represented another war crime in refusing genuine assistance to advance the goals of the CJS by reducing recidivism in crime.[47]

Robert S. Weppner, a community therapist with many years of experience in the field, offered his prescription for an effective client-based probation department, where the offender assumes an active role in treatment, where authority is flattened into staff and clients, where there is a client government that acts as a personal adviser against CJS arbitrariness, where an open community exists with directives or ideas coming from offenders as well, attention is paid to realistic costs of sanctions demanded by judges and where relationships between client and PO must resemble real-world support as closely as possible.[48]

This varied on departmental policies and degree of conservatism and belief in White nationalist ideology which disparaged Black clients. This whole period was testimony to such beliefs and practices. War crimes, even on a lesser scale, continued and eroded the belief in the Black man's belief in himself and what he accomplished. Probation thus served no purpose other than to extend war crimes and violations of human rights into another agency of the CJS. The reign of the dinosaurs was sustained.

NOTES

1. Charles L. Erickson, *The Perils of Probation* (Springfield: Charles C. Thomas, 1980), p. 196.

2. Ibid., pp. 198–200.

3. Edwin M. Lemert, *Offenders in the Community* (Lexington: Lexington Books, 1978), pp. 192–194.

4. N. S. Timasheff, *Probation in the Light of Criminal Statistics* (New York: McMullen, 1949), p. 38; Stephen Farrall, *Rethinking What Works w/Offenders and Probationers-Social Context and Resistance from Crime* (New York: Willian Publ., 2002), p. 77, 83, 92, 141 and 143; Herman Piven and Abraham Alcabes, *"Pilot Study of Correctional Training and Manpower," Department of Education and Welfare, Office of Juvenile Delinquency and Youth Development* (Washington, DC: USGPO), 1969.

5. John O. Smyicka, *Probation and Parole-Crime Control in the Community* (New York: Macmillan, 1984), pp. 35–36, 69; James Galvin, Jane Maxwell and Frank Hellum, "Shock Probation and More," draft report from the *National Probation Reporting Study, National Council of Crime & Delinquency*, 16 June 1981; Patrick D. McAnany, *Doug Thomsen and David Fogel, Probation and Justice-Reconsideration of a Mission* (Cambridge: Oelgeschlager, Quinn and Hain, 1984), p. 52 and 57, funded by the Department of Justice; and David Fogel (Washington, DC: The Emergence of Probation as a Profession in the Service of Public Safety: The Next Ten Years, 1980), p. 31 and 84.

6. Stephen Stanley and Mary Baginsky, *Alternatives to Prison-An Examination of Noncustodial Sentencing on Offenders* (London: Peter Owen, 1984), p. 4, 133, 145 and 147.

7. Smyicka, op. cit., p. 5.

8. Alfred L. Havenstrite, "About Probation Practices in Texas," *Criminal Justice Monography, Sam Houston State College Institute of Contemporary Corrections and Behavioral Science, Huntsville*, 1969, p. 3, 9, and 30.

9. Lemert, op. cit., p. 193, 195.

10. McAnany, op. cit., p. 55.

11. Michael Tackett, "Probation on the Defensive in Drug Wars," *Chicago Tribune*, 4 November 1990, p. 1.

12. Norman E. Long, "The Politics of Social Welfare," paper prepared for the *Columbia University School of Social Work, Arden House Conference*, 18–21 November 1965.

13. Thomas Holmes and Richard Rake, "Stress Social Readjustment Rating Scale-43 Life Events," *Journal of Psychosomatic Research* 11, no. 2 (1967): 213–218.

14. Seymour L. Halleck, *Psychiatry and Dilemmas of Crime: A Study of Causes of Punishment and Treatment* (New York: Harper & Row, 1967).

15. Kenneth B. Clark and Jeanette Hopkins, *A Relevant War Against Poverty, A Study of Community Action Programs and Observable Social Change* (New York: Harper & Row, 1969), pp. 251–252.

16. Ibid., p. 53.

17. Ibid., p. 54.

18. Op. cit.

19. Erickson, op. cit., p. 198.

20. Ibid., p. 200.

21. Edwardo Mundo, A 30-year veteran of the Los Angeles Probation Department says "Reform of the LAPD Is Urgent and Must Be Youth Focused," *Criminal Justice Journalism in the Public Interest*, 15 March 2019, pp. 1–3; Isidoro Rodriguez, "Does Community Supervision have a Future? *TheCrimeReport.org*, 3 January 2019, p. 1, given at the 14th Annual John Jay College Harry Frank Guggenheim Symposium on Crime; and Victor St. John. "Probation and Race in the 1980s—A Quantitative Examination of Felonious Rearrests," *Race and Social Problems*, 2019.

22. Stephen Farrall, "Rethinking What Works with Offenders and Probationers," in *Social Context* (New York: Willian, 2002), pp. 77, 83, 92, 141–142.

23. James Dahl et al., "Improved Social Services, City of New York," *Workshop Executive Training Program* (Washington, DC: Department of Justice, 1978), p. 47, 51 and 56.

24. Robert L. Smith, *A Quiet Revolution: Probation Subsidy* (Washington, DC: Department HEW, USGPO, 1970), p. 21.

25. John T. Whitehead, "Burnout Among Probation and Parole Workers," *School of Criminal Justice*, SUNY, Albany, NY, PhD dissertation, Albany, p. 293.

26. Ronald Morris, "*Survey of 100 Probationer Complaints about Their Probation Officers*," unpublished study, San Rafael, CA, 1976, pp. 1–3.

27. Richard D. Sludden and Robert A. Shearer, *An Examination of Probation Officer Ideologies and Personality Types* (Central Missouri State College, 1992), pp. 3–5.

28. Ibid.

29. Erickson, op. cit., p. 206.

30. Clive Stafford Smith, "Judge Dredd, and Why the United States Justice System is not Fit for its Purpose," *The Times Literary Supplement*, 1 December 2017, p. 30.

31. Ibid.

32. Andrew von Hirsh and Kathleen J. Hanrahan, *Abolish Parole? Summary Report* (Washington DC: National Institute of Law Enforcement and Criminal Justice, September 1978), p. 18.

33. M. Kay Harris, "Rethinking Probation in the Context of a Justice Model," in McAnany, Thomsen and Fogel, op. cit., *Probation and Justice: Reconsideration of a Mission*, 1984, pp. 19–21.

34. Ibid., p. 31.

35. Vincent O'Leary and Edward Ryan, "A Study of Conflict Resolution in Criminal Justice," *School of Criminal Justice*, SUNY, Albany, NY, 1969, National Council on Crime and Delinquency, p. 10, 11 and 23.

36. Jack W. Spencer, "Discourse and Textual Processes in a Probation Department: An Analysis of Written and Interactional Communication," PhD dissertation, Indiana University, Bloomfield, 1983, p. 12. His bibliography records several references to Aaron Cicourel and his work in this regard.

37. Ibid., pp. 57–58.

38. Nicholas deBelleville Katzenbach, et al., *The Challenge of Crime in a Free Society, President's Commission on Law Enforcement and the Administration of Justice* (Washington, DC, 1967), p. 273 and 275.

39. John A. Conley (Ed.), *The 1967 President's Crime Commission Report: Its Impact 25 Years Later* (Highland Heights: North Kentucky University, 1994), p. 41.

40. Robert M. MacIver and Leon Bramson, *Community, Society and Power* (Chicago: University of Chicago Press, 197), esp. Ch 3.

41. David E. Duffee, "The Community Context of Probation," in McAnany, op. cit., pp. 353–354, 361–364.

42. Stan Stojkovic, "The President's Crime Commission-Recommendations for Corrections: The Twilight of the Idols," in Conley, see note #39, p. 52.

43. Eric Lincoln, *The Black Muslims in America* (Boston: Beacon Press, 1973), pp. xxvii, 62, 84, 190–191.

44. Mitchell Duneier, *Ghetto: The Invention of a Place, the History of an Idea* (New York: Farrar, Straus, Giroux, 2016), p. 116; and Clark, *Dark Ghetto*, op. cit., p. 171.

45. Clark, Ibid., pp. 59–60.

46. Ibid., p. 148.

47. Lincoln, op. cit., p. 26.

48. Robert S. Heppner, *The Untherapeutic Community: Organizational Behavior in a Failed Addiction Treatment Program* (Lincoln: University of Nebraska Press, 1983), pp. 39, 221–224.

Chapter 7

Ivory Towers Are White for a Reason

In other chapters we have looked at the war crimes of the CJS as predominately physical, deadly, and highly personal—directly aimed at individual Black Americans in the War on Crime, 1960–1990. In this chapter the concept broadens to apply to cerebral and intellectual manifestations of racism and White supremacy as it pertains to the "subordination of the achievements of Black sociologists."[1]

We see it blossoming in two forms. First, where academics carelessly develop sociological studies that depict the Black culture as heathenistic, inherently violent, lazy, and immoral. From this perception, it's an easy road to criminality and dangerous behavior. Such a profile feeds into criminological reviews and is, in turn, picked up by CJS officials who use it to justify severe punishments against alleged criminals. Second, it diminishes the value and product of Black sociologists in how they perceive the whole subject of racism and injustice in academic work. Third, the failure of White sociologists to support, defend, and encourage greater Black participation in the fields of sociology and criminology, while simultaneously lending a hand to boost Black candidacies whenever they occur. Bhambra laments: "U.S. sociology has been historically segregated at least until the 1960s . . . but while this period saw many breakthroughs . . . Black sociology has been largely displaced from standard histories such that even the significant challenge mounted in the 1960s has been largely forgotten."[2] As far back as 1900, the professional White description of Black people used such words as childlike, petty thief, liar, unreliable, suspicious, sexually loose, gambler spirit, exaggerated idea of personal rights, lack of thrift, wayward childhood, deceptive with a predilection for alcohol and drugs.[3] Of course, Black social scientists had no part to play in how these descriptions were unfurled.

This is a relatively new field of study which we intend to explore on both dimensions. Far too many badly researched academic studies and probation reports for judges have been written to highlight Black deficiencies and stereotypical portrayals. One of the most obvious and odious of the first form was Simon H. Tulchin's 1939 report for the famed Sociology Department at the University of Chicago funded by its equally famous director, sociologist Ernest Burgess.[4] This study of penitentiary offenders at an Illinois prison went on to produce deeply disturbing findings of Black offenders in residence. Tulchin found that the intelligence distribution of inmates at the Illinois State Penitentiary suggested 24.2% of Northern-born Blacks rated "inferior" in intelligence, 47.5% for Southern-born Blacks, while 8.5% for Whites of native parents! When he looked at crimes committed, the Black inmates were more likely to be imprisoned for repeated sexual crimes, murder, robbery, and burglary as contrasted with lower rates for Whites in all but fraud and burglary. Blacks were more likely to be younger and single. Hence, the perfect Frankenstein-modeled stereotype took shape of a feeble-minded, dangerous, mainly Southern-born young Black criminal repeatedly copied in hundreds of forthcoming academic studies.[5] This wasn't much different from the professional White's description of Black people in 1900, using such words as childlike, petty thief, liar, unreliable, suspicious, sexually loose, gambler spirit, exaggerated idea of personal rights, lack of thrift, wayward childhood, deceptive with a predilection for alcohol and drugs.[6] In 2006, a poll found that in a word association for Black people, two words kept being repeated: failure and evil. If Whites use these terms, they are uneducated and loutish. If academics impart these terms in their studies, they are racist and have invalidated their work. The real danger is when CJS believes these traits exist: police suspect every African American as being a criminal to be arrested, prosecutors wish to raise penalties for confinement, judges disbelieve Black men can rehabilitate, and probation officers feel they are dealing with children. These are the real dangers such terminologies imply.

As far back as 1928, remarks by the renowned criminologist J. T. Sellin told us all we needed to know about academic racism, negating as superfluous many of the monographs which appeared in criminology and sociology journals of the 1960s–1980s. "The conclusion seems obvious," he wrote, "that if the material presented in this study on the American Negro criminal can be regarded as typical, there is a decided discrimination against him on the part of our agencies of CJ, especially the police and courts . . . on the basis of the available statistical evidence (found in his survey), it cannot be concluded that the Negro's real criminality is lower or as low as that of Whites. Nearly all writers discuss the existence of an apparent higher crime rate for the Negro race rate than for Whites. No indictment of the Negro race can be made if they possessed a higher rate of real criminality. The responsibility lies where power, poverty, and discrimination have its source, the dominant White group. He factored in twenty bibliographical references to address this point."[7]

It seems hard to imagine criminologists and social scientists being accused of war crimes. They carry no guns and even on students they don't use physical force as few might wish to. They rarely traverse the streets of the inner city for purposes of research. Few even know what the inside of a jail looks like. Fewer still a crack house or a prison. We normally picture them in some spacious campus office, crammed with books in bookcases and citations on the wall and a desk piled high with graded papers. Or else chumming around with their buddies in the faculty lunchroom or rathskeller. Their only known crime being that pile of library books in the corner of their office that needed to be returned six months ago.

"All right," you ask, "What would constitute a sociologist's typical academic war crime?" Certainly, research and conclusions which had a hateful racist undertone. But to be more specific I have listed twelve situations in which a piece of sociological/criminological research, departmental racist behavior, and ideology would warrant the accusation of academic war crime. We can't prosecute what some academicians were thinking about inner-city crime but I have spoken to a few who, off the record, shared antagonistic views about the ghetto and its citizens. They mixed the complicated science of empirical sociological constructs with subtle racial views that present innumerable complexities of thought for the reader.

Burning of the offending literature? Albert Murray complains: "These works demonstrate most American social scientists don't mind a bit what unfounded conclusions you draw about us Negroes or how flimsy and questionable your statistics or how wild your conjectures so long as they reflect degradation."[8]

So how can it be that in this chapter criminologists and sociologists became bad guys accused of war crimes, even if we address studies by social scientists like Tulchin and Burgess? What we mean by war crimes here is not on the police level of bashing someone's brains in but of a different sort of cerebral misconduct in the 1960s–1990s. To wit these twelve offensive racial injustices:

1. Writing reports and studies depicting Black offenders in derogatory terms.
2. Repeating stereotypes of the Black criminal for use by CJS agents (especially judges).
3. Refraining from using positive terms to describe Black offenders (as if they had none).
4. Rarely using Black student scholars as interviewers (being paid) on issues related to crime or urban problems.

5. Disregarding Black protests of police brutality, White nationalism, or CJS war crimes.
6. Avoiding sponsorship for Black-directed or led projects and academic studies.
7. Subordinating achievements of Black criminologists.
8. Not standing with colleagues to fight injustice and racial cruelty.
9. Recognizing that the Black community is not criminogenic.
10. Failing to gain views, suggestions, and complaints from ghetto citizens about and for whom basic research is being conducted but before being released.
11. Failing to judge African American traditions, customs, and neighborhood mores on their own terms rather than imposed by White colonial officials.
12. Failing to support Black involvement in academic and local political affairs.

White criminologists have long avoided the subject of race and crime so as not to be labeled racist. The scholar Michael Tonry tells us the end result:

> "Several times from the late 1970s onward I tried to commission research and policy essays on race and crime for a book series I was editing for the University of Chicago Press. Most qualified academics turned me down cold. Two took on the subject and later withdrew because it was just too controversial. Serious writing on race and crime resumed only in the mid-1980s and continued at a trickle."[9]

The social scientist P. A. Sorokin also had sharp words for the profession: "The social sciences suffer from several ailments, including sham scientific slang, testomania, quantophrenia and sham objectivism . . . an overemphasis on quantitative methods that may significantly undermine the quality of the knowledge generated in the field."[10]

Getting back to the original question of this chapter, is there a connection between academics (here: criminologists, researchers, government fund applicants, professors, and PhD candidates) and war crimes they might be capable of committing? Indeed, for this period under study, are there times, moments, and ideas that we can say are racist to the extent they might precipitate war crimes only by academics themselves? Can quiet ivory tower bourgeois scholars, mostly men, be accused of promoting White nationalist thought that it inflects their conclusions and recommendations on criminal justice issues imbued with racist ideology? To what extent was scientific racism inherent in the studies and intellectual by-products for the period 1960–1990? Did they fit with the current common, unimaginative, and punitive ideas on crime that did little to advance the social justice and tolerance toward the Black community? In such a way Debro and Taylor see differences between Black and White social scientists regarding the CJS: Whites see these agencies as somewhat unjust but not really discriminatory while Blacks see them as both unjust and racist.[11]

Who are these academics of which we speak? They are a disparate group of university-trained researchers whose principal work sites are American colleges and universities. Their profile is consistent and hardly diverse: White men, with two or three advanced degrees mainly in the social sciences and humanities, generally urban born from the larger cities. Many of the sociologists were middle-aged men born in the Jim Crow era with what that meant for determining one's views on race. All parts of the country produced this cohort whose background showed a normal trajectory of four-year degree work plus advanced degrees. I would guess their transcripts reflect a consistent pattern of similar subjects taken, again in the humanities, with few electives and little outside, fieldwork dealing with minorities, local law enforcement patterns, and slum analyses. Speed was the essence as these men were ambitious and, in a hurry, to cash in on their excitement to teach and research and earn a decent living, although I suspect the latter seems more important than the former for their future efforts to renown, advancement, and promotion. Let's be fair, some just wanted to teach.

Few that I have been able to determine, from looking at short biographies attached to textbooks and online reviews, had no military background, possessed little familiarity with working for social service agencies, and had no awareness of what ghetto life meant for its residents. In short, no life experiences related to the studies and problems they were analyzing beyond an early marriage and/or divorce (with the raising of kids). A large number were Jewish (maybe 40% by my reckoning) with foreign-born parents (the holocaust parental experiences are no doubt a motivation for the work they pursued with obvious implications). Additionally, their resumes show little arduous proletarian factory work or mindless shopkeeper experience. We know nothing of their leisure pursuits and areas of artistic/aesthetic interests of which I would give a right arm to know.

Not that I didn't try to dig deeper into this profile. In 2008, I created a short biographical questionnaire asking these and other undramatic, noncontroversial questions, perhaps twenty, to the sociology/criminology full-time faculty in the university in which I was then working. There were 35 staff, 80% of which were older White men. I tried to indicate I wasn't interested in exposing their limited knowledge of work outside the academy, and the diverse crowd of people (other than White) they may have been exposed to in their life. I wished only to develop a glimpse of the social and work background of the department's collection of talents, how close they were to criminal environments from which they drew material for books, articles, and seminars. I hoped they would participate in large numbers.

Returns? Of the thirty-five, I received three, one of which was incomplete. Not a very meaningful return. Did I detect indifference, hostility, fear of exposure? And of what? A minimum of extracurricular life's experiences, or a few moments of deviance where they stepped outside society's conventional demands and gained access to a different culture's view of the world? I could only guess that none of these men chose only a straight, non-swerving path of conformity (although some indicators suggested a brief flirtation with anti-Vietnam sentiments and demonstrations and an occasional tip of the hat to civil rights activities with nothing definite mentioned).

Again, a very sparse background when it came to life's little nuisances: no awareness of jail or prison life, or skid row dropouts, or discussions with criminals to get the low down on the CJS as they saw it. I never saw a researcher or academic in any of the probation offices where I worked. I spent a decade in the Bay Area which was home to radical, militant academics as well as mild-mannered ones, but no one poked around to learn more. I made myself available to academics wanting to know something of the stark issues in a probation department with an introductory letter to department heads in the universities but without curiosity or reply. Let's not forget: many of these academics have fine-tuned the art of the social survey or poll and have engaged this method of research for many of their projects, seeking the opinions of others (for free) to further their own interests. Yet here, when asked by a colleague to participate for research purposes where there would be no disclosure other than legitimate sociological findings I would present in a lecture to the department, their active receptivity was nonexistent.

My belief was these men of introversive characteristics had basically formed ideas, attitudes, dispositions, and suggestions for the improvement of the CJS that had arisen out of thin air and rarely from direct experiences gained by contacts from street life and strolling through ghetto backwaters. They were simply exploiting, taking advantage on their own terms of what they saw superficially without asking why this was so. In my own case, this wasn't easy. As a PO who was required to enter ghetto backwaters (Harlem, East New York, Potrero Hill, Compton/Watts), districts, jail settings, drug addict zones, and darkened hallways in the projects in the pursuit of my clients, I encountered stiff opposition: people who glared at me defiantly and angrily; teenagers attempting to loan their sisters to me for a two-hour price; drug sellers hoping to make their quota by unloading bad stuff on me; and others who viewed me as simply another undercover cop. Even police viewed me suspiciously as a criminal type entering the ghetto for some nefarious purpose. These were decided barriers trying to understand and I can see why academics would avoid these dangerous entanglements and isolate themselves in their happy, secure, and comfortable offices, asking minority students in their classes to do their sociological dirty work. In the process they gained little insight or appreciation of the community which they would write about, knowing their reviewers would accept their comments with little challenge as they too rarely visited these areas from which knowledge would provide challenging comments to the studies they were reading.

Criminologists and sociologists don't just research their brains out. They also teach. And this was a great period for teaching classes in criminology and criminal justice. According to Morn, in 1970 there were just 55 criminal justice college programs, a decade later there were over 600. John Jay College (NYC), the premier criminal justice college in the country, went from 1,000 students in 1955 to almost 4,000 by 1970. Three-fourths were White, generally liberal and radical in perspective while teachers were often liberal and those who were CJS agents who came taught off duty were conservative.[12]

But what if these professors were spewing racist tripe, infecting students with the wrong side of science? One good example of what could go wrong can be seen in the career of Edward Byron Reuter, once president of the American Sociological Society and writer of four books on race. The main theme of his life's work was study of the mulatto. Born in the Old South (Missouri) in 1880, his teaching jobs spanned many colleges: University of Illinois, Goucher College, Tulane, State University of Iowa, Fisk, Universities of Michigan, Iowa, and Colorado to name a few where his ideas were given flight. It was here that he had the chance to influence many students on the subject of race and crime. And his ideas?

"Some part of the crime rate," written in 1966, "lies without a doubt in the social traits of the Negro people themselves. In very considerable part they are still ill-adjusted to the impersonal and highly individualistic nature of present-day American life." And "There are of course numerous Negro criminals . . . who are criminals in the sense of being especially predisposed to certain behavior . . . the percentage of Negro individuals with defects likely to bring them into conflict with the criminal law may be higher than the percentage of such individuals in other groups."[13]

About the mulatto his observations were just as ludicrous:

While the bulk of the Negro race in America is yet not many steps removed from African (i.e., primitive) standards, some intellectual Negroes are successful in coming within measurable distance of the best models of the European (by having some Caucasian blood) . . . The dozens of Negro men everywhere having attained some degree of eminence are, in all but one or two cases, men of more Caucasian than Negro blood. Of 139 best known American Negroes there are not more that four men of pure Negro blood . . . mixed (White) blood is the significant rule among the professional class of the race the mulattoes outclass the Blacks 10:1.[14]

Given such remarks by Reuter or indeed by any other sociologist/criminologist of this period, how many caused their students to simply retire or quit their studies rather than listen to these views, to reject the program, and thus deprive the CJS the opportunity of hiring but very conservative, possibly racist, graduates as a result? This would certainly limit or diminish the group from becoming agents and mean whoever did get hired and inculcate this exposure to racist teaching could only bring bad relations with the Black community in the future.

Such academics used the classroom to dispel their views to young minds who may have used these views to see Black people improperly. There was a great need for these scholars to "challenge criminology's violently constructed conceptions of human nature, society, crime, law and justice," not subscribe to it. Professor Coyle put out a call to abolish criminology![15] The same may have occurred in the journal articles this group published, which rarely confronted outside rebuke from militant, radical, or disenfranchised sources regarding the textbooks and commercial books which might quietly have imparted punishing racist or White nationalist views in how Black communities were seen as dangerous and promiscuous. The aim here is to produce a thorough interrogation of criminology's relationship to White supremacist, heteropatriarchal, and imperialist/capitalist institutions, cultures, policies, and practices while dealing with policies that directly engage with and confront criminal justice violence and oppression in direct opposition of CJS power.[16]

Could scientific racism have been infused into this field by criminologists who would suggest it never occurred to their sense of equality, and fair-minded justice dispositions to think in such negative terms? There is little in the literature of criminology to document the policies, practices, and culture that the normal run of scholars had imposed and legitimized, avoiding direct engagement with those most impacted by the CJS (i.e., imprisoned people and families affected by their men being incarcerated). Nor do they indulge in direct engagement with communities and community organizations participating in the many phases involved in abolishing the functions of the CJS. Black professionals in the field were slim on the ground in 1977. Debro and Taylor claim there were only seven Blacks who had PhDs in criminology (all from the University of California, Berkeley), only one was teaching at a Black university, and there were but thirteen doctoral candidates in criminology and criminal justice. Had all minority students been turned off by racism they found when they entered criminal justice classes? Teachers and CJS practitioners saw the current civil unrest as a law enforcement issue and that many urban Blacks were criminogenic. Black students saw it in greater political terms and as a struggle for freedom and justice. This disconnect prevented any real growth in Black enrollment in criminology. Then too, opportunities were certainly too few to guarantee a stable job. Only fifteen books had been written by Black academics between 1951 and 1978. Again, Debro: "People who have tried to explain Black crime have always been White as Black authors traditionally have been excluded from journals. Thus, the riots of the 1960s were completely misunderstood by Whites in the way they were being presented." Not that jobs in the field of law enforcement were any too plentiful. In 1977 of forty Southern cities, only nine had Black cops.[17]

Bhambra points out that in the 1970s sociologists like Blauner and Wellman looking at the legacy of colonial impact on institutional racism in America were in a minority among White sociologists. "The majority failed to adequately address issues of race or make space for discussion of such themes within sociology departments in historically White universities."[18] Since Whites never knew racial mistreatment how would they know what it was and when it was happening to them? How could they be sure they knew how best to deal with the evils of racism in their era if this same idea was believed a generation earlier when that group of scientists thought they were astute in fighting racism?

To this extent senior members of the departments enabled scientific racism to bloom by its total indifference to the way Black residents were lost in nameless oblivion under CJS injustice; or stayed uncritical when some junior researcher, sitting in a cushy room at college, extrapolated from cold statistics, sketchy notes, and book bibliographies. A quiet war crime this may have been as such research gave false impressions of the criminality of Black life that. It also failed to advance tolerance through understanding or producing ideas of direct social benefit to community offenders and their families.

While White criminologists might have eschewed reports and writings of Black colleagues, this was a golden period to read the inspired ideas and concepts that drew on the Black culture from many great Black literary figures: voices of resistance like Richard Wright, Chester Himes, Roland Jefferson, Ralph Ellison, James Baldwin, Donald Goines, and Iceberg Slim (Robert Beck) with his pimp stories. Criminal activity and police repression were always on their collective minds. Omar Fletcher wrote of a man killed by NYPD (Hurricane Man, 1977), Chester Himes wrote of his prison experiences, Mike Davis of Black migration to Los Angeles in the 1920s and the resultant police oppression. According to Gifford, Goines used the Black criminal as

Mirror to view the persistent forms of White containment and police oppression . . . Black fiction expressed a national consciousness of the population where individual acts of violence against Blacks were used by cops to restrain the Black revolution . . . with the Black offender branded as a terrorist subjected to the full force of the American militarized police force.[19]

I have yet to meet a White criminologist or sociologist aware of this part of the Black literary experience with its many realistic presentations of police subjugation; none of this seems to have crept into their studies and surveys that would have been better grounded had these men spent time talking with the likes of Baldwin or Goines (who wrote sixteen novels on oppressed ghetto life in this time). Beck believed there was very little Black literature to draw from in this period because the White market was small. Blacks didn't buy books that told them how badly they were living, none were reviewed in major publications, the commercial book distribution network was poor and the one major publisher, Holloway House of Los Angeles, liked to portray the confined space of the ghetto as swarming with housing projects infested by drug dealers, street hustlers, gang members and pimps, and other sleazy exploiters of women.[20]

How do I see the scientific literary racism being portrayed? Detection should be rather easy by asking a few questions. Does the academic study develop its thesis, or conclusions, or body of knowledge based on personality flaws of the offenders—too impulsive, unremorseful, violent in nature, indifferent to events around him, confrontational toward the CJS and law enforcement agents in general? Do such studies demonstrate Black predilection or tendencies to commit crime, by men who are simply unfit to participate in a democratic open society? For the benefit of White society must they be shepherded behind high, closed walls where we can watch them, assign them simple projects, counsel them constantly, while diminishing their skill levels for the moment when they will be released? Keep them from voting for as long as politically possible. Do conclusions reached by criminologists conclude they are studying an urban human plague by men who need years of restricted life for the safety of the rest of us? In my opinion, such reports deserve the label of war crime for how Black offenders are also seen by academics as not worth investing in them.

Another element of racism derives from a brief glance at who gets published. Quite frankly, there is a paucity of African American reports in this period. The majority of semi-trained Black sociologists lacked basic encouragement from department heads and were rarely considered for publication by editors of the professional journals. I would guess by my reading, the percentage of articles by Black, Marxist, or critical culture scholars is less than 5%. The journals themselves merely reproduced unjust research findings that sought to promote a harsh treatment of Black offenders. A glance at the editorial boards of these journals, how many Blacks were on the boards? Or Marxists or critical sociologists that brought fresh new ideas and insights on the crime problem by attacking the CJS with suggested reforms.

Scientific racism occurred whenever White scholars and researchers found it unnecessary to visit and spend significant time in Black neighborhoods (especially barber shops, churches, and playgrounds), local jails, and other locations that form the natural boundaries of a sizeable Black cohort before beginning their crime project. Failure to learn about the complexities, strengths, complaints, and suggestions for reform of the CJS oppression was essential before any academic attempt could be made to document and enumerate some aspect of the CJS crime issue as impinging on the Black community. Indeed, White researchers were apprehensive about conducting field research in Black neighborhoods. What is in question was not how the Black street people viewed White interviewers but how Whites could overlook oppressive CJS conditions suffered by locals in the course of daily pursuits. Indeed, should White scholars have helped locals to develop the formative skills necessary to conduct their own social surveys on issues best perceived by the victims of CJS oppression? Did White academics ever consider this angle for alleviating the suffering caused to citizens by CJS practices? "It's hard being Black. You ever been Black?" Boxer Larry Holmes once challenged a White reporter about his vantage point on race. "I was Black once," he continued, "when I was poor." Whites were always faced with this frustrating fact they could never reach that level of Blackness to get the idea of what local racism really meant.

It was a Black sociologist, W. E. B. Dubois, called the first Black Sociologist, who early attempted the first large-scale research survey, a research methodology beloved by countless White sociologists who used it to significant effect in their research projects. Dubois' research, aptly titled *The Philadelphia Negro* (1907), was first published in the Philadelphia record, and laid out the conditions of Blacks in that city whom he surveyed in the 1890s. With such a revelation of the miserable conditions uncovered, Dubois attempted to use the discipline, unlike White colleagues of his generation, to "contribute knowledge to the resolution of the social problems of race relations."[21] In his efforts on any other projects seeking racial equality and awareness by Whites, he was rewarded with total suppression and "made to feel unwelcome at sociology conferences organized by whites and his work was hardly ever published in major sociological journals."[22] Yet Dubois's *Philadelphia Negro* anticipated in every way the program of theory and research that later became known as the Chicago School of Sociology. His work represented the first true example of American social scientific research, preceding the work of Park and Burgess (at Chicago) by at least two decades.

> This work can be seen as the first major empirical study within the U.S. using a distinctively sociological approach . . . it anticipated in every way the programs and theories and research which later became known as the Chicago School.[23]

Anderson and Massey also claimed,

That were it not for the short-sighted racism of the University of Pennsylvania faculty and administration, which refused to acknowledge the significance of his criminological work by offering him a faculty appointment, the maturation of the discipline might have been advanced by two decades.[24]

Bharbra adds his comment: "Given the conditions of the time the research capacity of Black sociologists was at least as great as that of its White counterparts, albeit poorly resourced and supported."[25]

Most White academics mention Dubois as if he was the only exceptional Black academic because he successfully manipulated White survey protocols and knew how to discuss them intelligently. This in itself smacked racism by omitting the mention of many Black scientists (especially women scholars) of this period producing key research into White oppression on the Black community. Sociologists Bracey, Meier, and Rudwick have argued,

It is ironic that while Dubois was part of the mainstream of American sociology as the discipline was emerging at the turn of the century, he should have found himself relegated to the periphery of the profession at the end.[26]

Stephen Small points out that Dubois's frustration with the inefficiency of neutral, value-free academic-led research in achieving social change was met equally by his disappointment with White colleagues who showed little concern with the desperate condition of Black Americans facing Jim Crow segregation. His empirical research was, as Morris points out, in stark contrast to prevailing sociological methods of study. Dubois called this "car window" sociology. This was because most sociological studies were so superficial an analyst had merely to drive by without taking time or effort to understand the community being observed.[27] After all, what was the purpose of this research for Dubois and his Black colleagues if not to bring social and political justice to all Americans? In this pursuit, he was accused of being a leftist radical revolutionary. This tag allowed White schools and institutions to deny him access to research funds which came with it the failure of White colleagues to support him on the basis of open research opportunities for all academics.

If any sociologist needed the support and solidarity of fellow sociologists at the end of his life, Dubois was the man. Unfortunately, these were not forthcoming. His life had been one of continual threat by death vows that forced him to keep a gun in his home. Small reports that "he fled his office on a number of occasions to avoid being lynched (tired of all this, he eventually settled in Africa and freed of White threats of violence)." Katznelson argues,

The White establishment's failure to incorporate Dubois as more than an emblem of diversity has cost us a lot . . . the exclusion of other voices has evacuated the substantive gains that distinctive Black experiences and perspectives can bring.[28]

Both Democratic (Truman) and Republican (Eisenhower) administrations from 1949 to 1963 kept him constantly in court trials (he was always acquitted) under the direction of the fascist director of the FBI J. Edgar Hoover who attacked him for his antiwar (he was against the war with Japan), pro-Stalin, antinuclear weapons writings. He was called a "security threat" and his passport often confiscated, his foreign travels banned, and his life endlessly bugged and harassed by FBI agents. While he was made a member of the National Institute of Artists and Letters (its first Black member) in 1944, such recognition by fellow sociologists was never forthcoming. Through all these tribulations, and as a leading American intellectual, few scholars came to his aid. The author of over thirty authoritative books in the field, hundreds of courageous editorials over the years for the NAACP's magazine, *The Crisis*, and countless talks where his only supporters were students, trade union leftists, and churchgoers. Lanham wrote: "consequently, the trials and the publicity around them ruined his career." He was left scrabbling to earn enough money just to buy groceries. He was not a Soviet spy as Hoover had it, but an American using his First Amendment rights to protest. Thinking of their careers, sociologists everywhere stayed clear of him.[29]

Green and Driver called him a "giant of human creative enterprise . . . little known to Americans, and (to us) even more disconcerting was the failure of scholars especially sociologists to acknowledge Dubois who they kept in the shadows."[30] New Yorker writer Ian Frazier tells of when he went by Dubois' small rented house at 3059 Villa Avenue just off Jerome Avenue in the Bronx where

> the anchor business seems to be Osvaldo #5 Barber Shop, which advertises services for sending money to Africa . . . I wondered if I might find a plaque commemorating its former famous resident but the house is gone and 3059 Villa is now part of a fenced-in parking lot.[31]

Not even a "stolperstein" plaque on the sidewalk to honor him as a victim of a racist, repressive regime. No one has encouraged this idea either. How many war criminals can we spot in the way Dubois and his colleagues were abused and ignored over the years?

Ida B. Wells (1862–1931), who fled the South in the face of a lynch mob, is all but forgotten despite her landmark documentation against lynching (what Whites could ever explore this subject with proper field research?), Anna J. Cooper (1858–1964), Fannie Barrier Williams (1855–1944), E. Franklin Frazier (1894–1962), Charles Johnson (1983–1956), Ira A. Reid

(1901–1968), and G. E. Haynes (1880–1960) are a few pioneers who come to mind with concepts structured by Black sociological tradition with its emphasis on human behavior, inequality, and injustice. The prestigious University of Chicago Sociology Department was almost alone in producing high-quality Black sociologists of renown such as St. Clair Drake (1911–1990) and Horace Clayton (1903–1970) who received little attention from department chairs.

Another neglected Black scholar who comes to mind is Oliver Cox (1901–1974). Small writes of him, he was a significant but widely depreciated analyst of capitalism, race relations, and fascism. His output was impressive—five books and more than thirty articles published during his lifetime. "Political factors were important in his neglect, because of racism against Black scholars, because of his leftist thinking and because of the significant influence of Marxist ideology in his work."[32] He was also ignored by White colleagues because of his criticisms of the dominant sociological model of race relations, punitive White law enforcement attitudes on Black crime, and their consequent indifference to fascist-inspired violence toward Black communities.

In consequence, as was the case for so many marginalized Black thinkers, Cox was confined to teaching in small, little-known colleges. None of his major works were published by top-flight publishers having a long-enough reach and wide-enough distribution network to help extend his ideas. As a result, "the foremost White sociological writers of his day rarely cited his work . . . and he received no formal acclaim from any sociology department until being discovered in the mid-1970s by alert leftist scholars." Black students made Whites too edgy in the classroom. Few progressives got advanced degrees. In 1970–1979 only sixteen degrees were awarded to Black criminologists nationwide, thirty-three in the 1980s during a period when the War on Crime focused exclusively on Black-created crime in the streets that produced millions of offenders and arrestees, there was an enormous need for more compassionate scholars to research their plight. Whereas the American Society of Criminologists at the time boasted of 3,500 members, less than 1% identified themselves as Black academics, rarely as criminologists.[33]

We will never know how many sociological studies and crime reports are written in the past century by Black writers like Cox, teaching in very small schools that Whites dismissed as inconsequential and to their mind reflective of the current weak state of Black studies. They could have opened access to valuable university archives, or helped seek funds to financially sustain Black studies at Black colleges or enlist their own graduate students to help finish these half-written reports, or asked them to lecture their front-line staffs; even allocated adjunct positions to legitimately absorb them into the university system. These are academic war crimes on a substantial level:

White academics who collectively deprived the field and all future students of what this generation of unexposed Black sociologists might have given if Whites had the stomach to expand the field in ways and on key racial social injustices, they themselves could never have considered. These were social scientists who at that very moment were experiencing the worst of racial injustice, and the fear of being Black in the street so helpful in providing them with relevant experiences they brought to their studies. All of this we lost. The Black colleges and universities were an important bridge that never received money or other support to help enlighten us in this research.

Bhambra provides us with a perspective from which to draw applicable conclusions. He said,

> In the standard accounts of the history of sociology, the subject of slavery within segregated educational institutions from being a "European" invention to being regarded as an expression of American pragmatic optimism . . . it is little remarked however that the developing system in the U.S. was itself a segregated system within separate institutions for African Americans and Whites. (32)

Only until the civil rights movement, the urban riots, and the rise of Black power national leaders, did White American scholars wake up to the potential monetary windfall as Congress began providing funds to study the "Negro problem." This trend, which took place during the years of this study, brought many Whites into the research field, oblivious of what the Black culture meant to Blacks, but chose to study Black crime which seemed the most obvious and easiest to study (just pour over crime figures), availing themselves of job opportunities in the universities and of constantly flowing money from the government for their dubious studies on how to reduce crime in the alleged "dangerous" Black ghettoes. Mind you, most of these men knew little of what they spoke but were able to glean earlier negative profiles of Blacks to make their statements of intolerance. Nor could they improve on Monroe Work's 1900 essay (he was an associate of Dubois with an MA from the University of Chicago Sociology Department) on crime among Negroes in Chicago which was published by the American Journal of Sociology (possibly the first work of a Black scholar printed by that journal). Work exposed the extreme levels of segregation within Chicago housing and the miserable slum conditions which was a leading cause of crime among the Black population.[34]

Lee Brown evoked a serious charge against all White researchers attempting to generate data from studies and surveys developed from ghetto intrusion:

> Much of the research conducted by White criminologists of inner-city crime problems is suspect. Frequently the theoretical bases, research methods and data manipulation techniques that they employ are seriously flawed . . . with

techniques . . . designed and developed to further legitimize institutional instruments of racist and classic ideologies of the status quo . . . insensitive to African American culture and values.[35]

Young and Sulton followed this with damning contempt: "White criminologists bring with them professional habits and ideological baggage that are incompatible with what concerned minority investigators feel is satisfactory social science research . . . with questions and research methods." A more recent analysis from Rutgers University said much the same thing, causing us to wonder have any of these critical studies of White nationalistic outlook in social scientists changed over time:

> Since criminologists do not operate in a vacuum, any prejudgments, biases and beliefs acquired before their professional socialization may well persist and affect their approach to research over the course of their academic careers. Because American criminologists live in as society that racializes a number of problem behaviors, including crime, it is conceivable that widely held beliefs about race that predate graduate training will find their way into assumptions about the relationship between race and crime. Such preprofessional beliefs are transformed into "facts" when they meet with widespread agreement from other criminologists and thus come to be taken for granted when the criminal behaviors of individual black offenders are understood in terms of racial traits . . . such racialization in academic criminology can be used to justify increased control of individual Black criminals . . . to encompass whole communities.[36]

War crimes were often and repeated on the basis of sheer ignorance mixed with White supremacist ideology that placed Black scholars on a lower plane of academic achievement being unable to (a) conduct adequate research, (b) apply quantitative and methodological skills to create empirical studies, (c) develop cogent theories to underscore research findings, and most importantly (d) impart protest and indignation of intolerance in well-constructed studies as found in M. N. Work's publications.

These were years of critical awareness by Black scholars of the obvious failure of the White establishment to show sympathy and willingness to explore key Black issues fully understood within a broader sociological umbrella. The result was inevitable and disadvantageous to both White and Black scholars. The Black reaction to White sociological indifference to urban Black issues eventually led to the establishment of the Association of Black Sociologists in 1972. A collection of social scientists who had origins in the Black Sociology Caucus was created following the 1969 American Sociological Association meeting in San Francisco. Their platform demanded a more confrontative agenda on structural racism affecting Black communities, and the need to recognize the solid work of Black scholars who chose not to turn a blind eye to the many war crimes of the CJS (which received little contemporary appreciation by White sociologists).

Not that White criminologists did a better job studying Black crime. One difference between the two strands is highlighted by Brunsma and Wyse (2019) who note "White sociology treats knowledge as an objective process, claiming a value free approach which means a moral detachment from social issues and reinforces a separation of social activism from social thought." The two scholars note how elitism, power, knowledge production, and race are interconnecting from which flows the reproduction of White supremacy and ideas about Black crime. This possessive investment in White sociology reproduces racial inequality in publishing and writing via peer review and citation practices. Thus, we must examine who gets to produce knowledge and why, noticing the racist structure of White supremacy and its exclusionary practices for Black scholars.[37]

The American Journal of Sociology had indeed earlier ignored the *Philadelphia Negro*, rarely mentioned any work by Black sociologists (excluding the Work piece), marginalized Dubois' other contributions, and, worst of all, happily published and applauded many reviews where racist ideologies were obvious. Black academics took note:

> In our view, White criminologists intentionally present the relationship between race and crime in a superficial and nonscientific manner because it is consistent with their stereotypical view of the African American community. It supports their belief that Whites are superior to non-Whites and that race is the primary determinant of human traits and capacities.

For their part, Black criminologists questioned the usefulness of White-biased research data which asserted that Black men were more criminal than Whites.[38]

> Ideas advanced by White criminologists have consistently produced utterly impractical, obscenely costly, shockingly inefficient and wholly ineffective results . . . because many of them have careful avoided genuinely challenging new intellectual thrusts from minority scholars which would force them into a real confrontation with their own contradictions as myopic.[39]

In his study of the importance of race among Black sociologists, Evans found that Black social scientists didn't think highly of the White contribution to race relations. He reflected back to Thomas Merton's (1910–2003) notice in 1973 of a then-emerging "Black insiders" doctrine held by Black sociologists. From this view White sociologists were seen as "outsiders," as incapable of understanding or conducting research on matters concerning Blacks. As far back as 1948 Merton had famously written critically of this

> Self-fulfilling prophecy. To him this was a process through which an expectation, in this case fear of White academic rejection affected the outcome or situation in the way Blacks will behave. A False definition of the situation, will evoke a new behavior among Black activists making the original fear or false conception come true. Again, we witness an academic attack on Blacks for their largely true belief in the universality of White academic oppression as untrue, leading to a defensive response to that usefully ferments a mechanism of solidarity for minorities.[40]

Could a criminologist actually be dangerous to African American interests? One such man surely was James Q. Wilson. Professor of Criminology, Steve Cooper of Florida State University writes, "Not only have Wilson's works impacted academia, they have also fostered organizational change throughout the CJS. In particular his work has brought about significant change in the way our (authoritarian) police are managed."[41] As an example of high authoritarianism, Wilson wielded enormous influence in CJS circles. His resume is resplendent with achievements that show how he wormed his way into the center of the CJS to influence many criminology scholars to look to harsh sanctions against Blacks as a way to curb crime: twenty-six years at Harvard University in governmental public policy, a member of Reagan's attorney general's Task Force on Violent Crime (1981), chairman of the White House Task Force on Crime (1966), appointed by a democratic president, many national commissions on public policy and the police, author of twelve books on matters of crime and punishment, frequent writer to important criminology journals of the period, chairman of the National Advisory Commission on Drug Abuse Prevention (1972–1973) in Nixon's regime, chairman of the Council of Academic Advisers, member of the deeply conservative think tank, American Enterprise Institute, and board of directors member for numerous large corporations (he was very supportive of big business interests and small government), and President Reagan's go-to guy throughout the 1980s when advice was wanted on crime issues.

At the point when Reagan was elected Governor of California, Wilson's work shot up like a rocket with enormous popularity. Cooper again: "Wilson may well be one of the foremost criminologists of all time." Cooper ranks him in the top four for influence.[42] Where does Wilson's fascist ideas become dangerous to the interests of the Black community? He believed crime was an inherent characteristic of people including minorities who were uninhibited and anti-conformist and more likely to rationally choose to commit a crime (poverty had nothing to do with it, he says) for the excitement, risk, thrills, and challenge to the system.

His solutions? Mass incarceration, a proactive police community that made arrests with full force, a racist belief in the low intelligence and resistance to conformity inherent in Blacks. "His seminal work finds massive . . . acceptance and support from cops and researchers alike." Cooper finishes: "As our country seeks to get tough on crime, several of the policy recommendations made by Wilson and his colleagues are becoming increasingly attractive."[43]

How many war crimes can a right-wing criminologist generate with his racist polemic, fascist correctional doctrines and hardcore Police State suggestions? Is a man who makes a very nice living off Black suppression and legal injustice through anticrime theories a war criminal? Given the number of important government positions and advisements he held with regard to public policy on crime, he was very influential in changing policy, documentation for the worst must wait for any researcher to enumerate. There is no evidence he ever spent time in the Boston or Oakland ghettoes (although he lived nearby), no evidence he had any face to face relations or contact with Black street people or offenders, and I can find no connections with Black researchers, colleagues, or criminologists to help him widen his myopic opinion on a culture he chose to attack but for which he knew nothing. His view on drug usage was simply inane: "drug use is wrong because it's immoral . . . and destroys the soul!"[44]

Somewhere I remember reading a 1756 African profile of the White slavers they encountered in the Slave Trade kidnapping process: horrible in looks with red splotched faces, ugly long greasy straggly unkempt hair, were voracious eaters, overindulged in alcohol which exacerbated their violent natures, and wildly and indiscriminately sought any type of woman to appease their lecherous instincts. This is how Whites looked to Blacks although this never intrudes in White studies whereas the worst psychological and genetic aspects of Black lives are found in publications casting Blacks as brutes, unintelligent savages, and violent terrorists.

Historically, few Blacks have committed themselves to paper to record the hundreds of thousands of war crimes perpetrated on them by Whites. They didn't show their waking hours distressing over White misdeeds to the neighborhood unless an accomplished writer or social activist. Some with a southern education were nearly illiterate and couldn't write or were just literate enough but had no access to exposure (which Whites would want to listen?); the middle-class members avoided confronting White administrations and the White backlash retribution, they had something to lose, so it was far safer to just withhold comment. For Blacks to protest was to risk immediate possibly fatal reaction from Whites. Blacks did not have the ear of White criminologists who could have noted their complaints on CJS behavior and intolerance. During the Work Progress Administration days of the 1930s, when it came to researchers interviewing ex-slaves via oral testimony, the little we accumulated, showed those interviewed were very uneasy and suspicious of the intentions of White interrogators who owned the very process by which slave memories would be broadcast. In fact, the same class who had been the slave owners.

The audience for such reports was always White so Blacks felt little reason to position their views on equal Black–White relationships. White testimony about negative Black cultural activities overwhelmed in sheer numbers whatever was the Black contribution. Moreover, Blacks could not discuss racism without discussing the very lethal character of Whites, a most dangerous and unpopular line of thinking. Sociologists had neither insight nor cared to study this characteristic of Black oppression and so they left it alone. Keen observers of White behavior, Blacks saw them as a hierarchy holding limitless power, with inconsistent ideals of justice and human rights. Where were the criminologists to pick up on this line of thinking when assessing CJS behavior toward minorities?

Dangers abounded in White criminologists' methodological treatment and overview of Black crime. Not all possibilities for Black anger or reaction to their predicament were explored in discussing Black crime, only those most likely to ratify establishment status quo attitudes. Truth could be twisted, studies for government funding could reflect the need of researchers to maintain this status quo so that rewards were forthcoming—hardly so for criticism of government policy calling administrators racists and White supremacists. Pure truth is replaced by acceptable truth. As explained earlier, what did researchers living many miles away from the locales they study, really know about ghetto crime and its victims anyway? Just stay quiet and live off and derive benefit from the status quo that supports the White administration's brand of injustice.

Researchers didn't question overall government policy on overuse of the police or lengthy sentences or harsh punishments. To do risked withdrawal of funding. A suggestion or two on a policy that required minimal, inexpensive reform was enough. Don't challenge the system. Don't put harsh criticisms in Marxian terms. Don't suggest the CJS is a robust failure. Don't attack the Republican president's inhumane policies toward minorities and certainly don't suggest the administration was racist. One study of this approach to research found that a relatively narrow band of questions was used in studying crime of this period. Sixty-seven percent of all studies in 1975–1983 used roughly interchangeable research methods, mainly empirical, which kept producing the same toothless results. Fewer than 10% of the articles in the academic crime journals (by my count) were really experimental, radical, or asked challenging questions; the vast majority ran along very well-trod grooves.[45] Costs of alternative solutions were never calculated so researchers' conclusions remained blinded to the taxpayer ability to finance their wacky but expensive solutions with no awareness of any impact on community crime. The result was that little new burst forward to break the log jam of computerized commonplace social surveys that attempted only to out-quantify the competition.

War crimes? Maybe too severe a term to apply to White criminologists dismissing African American collegial contributions. What about simply intellectual atrocities? One of the earliest departments of sociology was developed with Rockefeller's money at the University of Chicago. That alone should have set Black knees to tremble. Rockefeller was never a friend to Black men and the Chicago's Sociology Department was not much better in its peeping tom approach to the ecology of the city by gazing at the lurid, kinky aspects of the city's neighborhoods and the stereotypical criminal scoundrels that highlighted the notoriety and lures for young White men seeking the vices in each of these neighborhoods. It was for this reason and Dubois's own suspicions about the racist intent of that department's controlling ideas on race that as a counterweight he sought to create an overlapping research center into Black studies that would include and prey upon the competitive natures of Harvard, Columbia, Johns Hopkins, and the University of Pennsylvania where the acting philosophy of the sociology department of the University of Chicago was purposely omitted. The hope was to enlarge this field and help establish Black studies and the Black academics who would be the main research beneficiaries on subjects necessary in order to fully comprehend Black crime and injustice and oppression of the White State from which crime was seen as a by-product. Possibly new sociological journals would arise with more diverse editorial boards that would offset racist tendencies found in the current periodicals. Social action against injustice as an outgrowth of this research might also develop.

How can it be otherwise when inner-city (pleasant term for ghetto) Blacks are deeply distrustful of Whites and refuse to participate in research projects or provide less than candid responses to questions posed by White scholars? Let's face it, Whites lack cultural familiarity, with too little personal experiences of this community, to understand how crime intercedes with history, languages, gestures, and facial expressions of this much-studied group. As a researcher in the 1990s in Harlem, I was often confronted by street people as either wanting drugs or their sister or was seen as a cop. No one took me seriously when I explained my purpose and after I did so, they considered me a cop on a mission.

While Black criminologists might be better equipped than their White counterparts to conduct research on ghetto social problems. It is the larger White society that, in the end, dictates whose views are going to be represented and hold intellectual sway. Duneier and others have pointed to this inherent ugly stubbornness to accept equality and skills by prominent White sociologists toward Black researchers in their care. Here we need only mention the unpleasant approaches taken by Gunnar Myrdal, W. Lloyd Warner, Arnold Rose, and Richard Steiner after 1940 to limit the progress of Black colleagues attempting to gain recognition. By this, we mean the budding achievements of Ralph Bunche, Horace Cayton, and St. Clair Drake were heavily dependent on White superiors for jobs, recognition, and income which never sufficiently materialized to boost their careers.

A quick glance at the references used by Young and Sulton from Howard University is useful in indicating serious and thoughtful Black research was being conducted during the War on Crime years. It causes us to suggest they should be positioned at the forefront in any intelligent discussion of the contribution Black academics were producing. However, most faced years of rejection by the White criminological community and omission of their work in books designed to present a contemporary view of Black crime.[46] According to one witness, White sociologists writing on Black/White relationships had few acquaintances among Black scholars. "Almost every written source instance of data recording used other White sources while giving no credit to Black assistance."[47]

Sociological journal editors showed little interest in the submissions by Black sociologists. In the first 40 volumes in the *American Journal of Sociology* only 4 Black of over 700 contributions saw their work published; none of the over 5,000 book reviews prior to 1940 were written by Blacks. This means a cloud of invisibility hung over the minority group who not only experienced blanket rejection but saw hopelessly racist sociological studies being published where attention was paid to Black genetic depravity versus White superior intelligence.[48]

What would we label as war crimes by academics? Unfortunately, we have no statistics, graduate study reports, or documentation to go by, only anecdotal impressions, often by grieved Black scholars in the course of their trying to publish their works. Certainly, the classification of war criminal could be applied to sociologists and criminologists who over the long term of their academic tenancy refused, rejected, minimized, disregarded, or disparaged minorities in the course of their academic pursuits, collegiate collegiality, or criminological evaluations of the Black culture and its alleged broad-based criminality.

The charge of war crimes against White academics is the result of traditional classic White thinking which contained all the elements of White nationalism. White racist social impressions fell into four categories: Blacks possessed an abundance of biological genetic criminal defects; Blacks possess innate violent Black behavior that deserves harsh legal sanctions; government funding for their benefit is wasted because they don't know how to use funds productively; and, let's face it, Blacks are simply funny to watch ad funny to listen to.

Repeat: Black people were a funny crowd. Gerald Suttles, in a classic book published by the University of Chicago Press, with a hardy approval of department director Morris Janowitz (who wrote the preface), studied Blacks on Chicago's near West Side in keeping with the study of the school's voyeuristic study of immigrant ethnic groups placed under a microscope. What did Suttles tell us? Negro dress, slang, dance, language, and grooming plus sex practices were revealed in an amusing anthropological way when he studied the local gang culture. He spent three years and used unpaid youth as field workers since he was afraid of walking near the nearby public housing. "Only after one plus year was I able to penetrate the private world of families, gangs and street corner groups (he remains unclear why it took so long and w/o attempting to tell us what he means by 'penetrate')." His view of the Negro gangs was patronizing and ethnocentric.

> They live in warrenlike passageways that made it impossible for cops to adequately gain surveillance . . . a group with a high unemployment rate and cultural deprivation, this group didn't inspire trust . . . and many of them have a disreputable character.[49]

Not much positive stuff here.

> It is a subculture where "insults and slight threats must be responded to with violence. Self-esteem can only be maintained by assaultive behavior . . . the current belief (1958) is that violence is the only moral way of coping with challenges to self-esteem."[50]

Respected sociologist Marvin E Wolfgang in his study of Philadelphia youth, 1949–1952 agrees that in his estimation, "homicide was mainly Black oriented, fueled by alcohol, committed usually between 8pm–2am on Saturday nights with over half the murderers and assailants having previous arrest records."[51]

White social scientists were unmerciful in their view of the animal qualities of Black people. In 1921, M. G. Wilson found that Black children could not exhale as much air as Whites making it difficult to "equal Western standards."[52] In the 1920s, well-recognized sociologist A. H. Stone had a perverted view: "It would be impossible to raise Blacks to the level of Whites because the differences between the races were so great a natural aversion existed between them."[53] Famed sociologist Robert E. Park at the University of Chicago (1930) saw Blacks as "docile, tractable and unambitious whereas mulattos were aggressive, restless, and enterprising with greater intellectual capacity."[54] His colleague Howard Odum, also at Chicago, wrote the "Inability of most Blacks to grasp the basic principles of family and home life," (often) where "disorder and filth were characteristic and books and art were nonexistent."[55]

Columbia University professor and politician, Daniel P. Moynihan, took a whole book in 1965 to probe Black family pathology: "Black women emasculate black men out of positions of strength leaving them with an inability to fit into the bourgeois society."[56] The Black family was written out of existence in Parson, and Bales studies of family socialization and references were not inserted while in a 600-page textbook on Urban Society, Gist & Fava devoted but 20 pages (4%) to Black urban life and not a single page to the Black family. Both Kephart (1966) and B. Sussman's 1959 source book on families leave them out altogether. Queen and Habenstein devote only one of the twenty-five chapters to Black families. In none of these works does the reader ever hear the voice or ideas from a Black academic or read much about the positive values and culture of the urban Black family.[57] We are only left with antisocial values that lead to crime.

One searches the social science and criminological journals in vain even in 1970 for contributions on urban issues by Black authors.

> Even on matters of book reviews, the White social science journals with their White editors are much more likely to ask a White expert on Black people and their customs to review books by or about Black people than turn to Black academics for comment. The very process made Blacks feel inferior while leaving the assumption we must turn to White scholars for scholarship on black life.

Applying White etiquette to research by Black academics also had built-in dangers. As an anthropologist, Zora Neale Hurston came to understand this while interviewing Black residents in small Florida and Alabama towns in 1927. Boyd wrote:

> She did learn valuable lessons on this trip: she developed the nuances of style which would serve her well as a creative writer and she discovered that the cultivated speech which she had acquired at Barnard College (Columbia University in New York) was a bar to attracting the confidence of rural African-Americans. From that point on, her speech and self-presentation were always "unabashedly Black and unapologetically southern." Whites could fall back on no such advantages.[58]

In line with this approach toward unmasking racist commentary in research studies of this period, I offer the following examples and citations. These are only a few but I believe representative of criminological thinking on War on Crime. Lest we forget none of the major criminologists of the period chose to condemn the actual War on Crime as a government attack against defenseless people with few advocates to challenge the view that Blacks were basically violent and criminally oriented.

David A. Schulz built on this with 146 pages of description with theories and conjectures about the sordidness of Black lives in urban housing project:

> It would be a serious mistake to leave the impression that the problems of the Negro male lower class derive mainly from a pattern of agonistic sexual development and broken unstable families. Yet this was one possible interpretation of the data thus far presented.

When police are in a Black neighborhood, writes James Mills, they have no difficulty spotting addicts on the street—"habitually dirty, clothes filthy, standing loosely as if his body were without muscles."[59]

James B. Conant's book *Slums & Suburbs* dealt with the tragic situation in Black ghettoes. The Black urban proletariat writes Conant

> Has little education, practically no skills . . . has never known normal family life . . . with a corresponding lack of socialization . . . this group is unfit for normal social life. They will just become victims of liquor, dope and disease in all forms of crime and anti-social behavior.[60]

Bit rough, I say. Wilson argues that over the past two decades a new and socially destructive class structure has emerged in the ghetto and this can be attributed not to racism but primarily to deindustrialization, whatever that means. "Individuals in the ghettoes are there as a result of their thinking and behaving," the ghettoes exist because they are populated by impulsive, foul-mouthed, aggressive, uneducated, oversexed, and crime prone males and females who share many of these characteristics and teach them to their offspring.[61] And Chambers: "It is well established that criminogenic conditions such as poverty, family instability, slum residence, and migration, conditions that the Chicago School sociologists used to construct their disorganization hypothesis, are indeed important factors to be considered when assessing crime."[62] Establishing the ghetto in a jungle motif, without real evidence, Eric Stewart and colleagues claim that "family and peers play a large part in producing violence in children and in adopting a street code associated with violence."[63]

Using a Chicago School ecological approach, Stark said "Black high crime rates are in large part the result of where Blacks live in northern cities . . . where a higher visibility of crime attracts and seen as rewarding . . ." and from the renowned criminologist Marvin Wolfgang: "Black militants who would burn cities harbor no better way of life than KKK who would burn crosses." Richard Stephenson, professor and Chairman of the Department of Sociology, Rutgers University and Frank Scarpitti, professor of sociology at the University of Delaware chimed in: "White boys are better controlled, more sociable, have higher ego strength and lower frustration levels thus lower delinquency rates. They have less direct expression of hostility." Evidence? Little is provided to back up these observations which are critical of Black boys by eminent social scientists. Robert Park, father of urban sociology and race relations at the University of Chicago believed negative traits of racial conflict and aggression in young Black men could be overcome by the "inevitable force of cultural assimilation and alter Black behavioral deviations from pre-defined norms."[64]

Charles Saunders brought up another valid concern in race relations research. A Canadian research assistant at McMaster University in Hamilton, Ontario, he called attention to the many dubious personality scales prevalent during the 1920–1950 period designed to measure attitudes and behavior. Saunders believed most scales, instruments, and techniques of measurement bore little relevance to Black people, especially as results too often suggest inherent inferiority of Black respondents no matter which measurement scale was being employed. Persistent use of these scales lasted until the 1960s when other social forces began to impose changes in the direction and purposes of race attitudes research. As the Black revolution increased in intensity, the interest in race attitudes research increased concurrently, says Saunders. There were nearly twice as many reports on Negroes listed in 1961 as in 1950 and in 1968 four times as many as in 1960.[65] Such abundant research however rarely studied the phenomenon of Black attitudes toward Whites or the CJS.[66]

Richard America, a prominent African American economist at Georgetown University concerned himself with the tendency of research foundations and university criminology departments who did have Black researchers, although few in number, to purposely keep them strikingly "in your face" visible for authenticity and legitimacy to key projects. Yet at the same time, these departments did what they could to constrain and separate these same academics from any part of a department's decision-making processes.[67]

Noted Harlem sociologist Kenneth B. Clark maintained a suspicious attitude of outside academics coming into the area to create usable documents: "It became clear in the early stages of our community project (his Haryou Study of teenagers in the area) that while usual methods of data collection and analysis would contribute to an understanding of the demographics of the community, the use of standardized questionnaires and interview procedures (used so often in criminological studies—me) would result in stylized and superficial verbal responses or evasions . . . which tended to perpetuate superficial and methodologically distorted social reality."[68] Clark recommended the formation of volunteer research assistants recruited from the young people of Harlem who were directly involved in the goals of creating a better Harlem community unlike outsiders of middle class but with a peripheral relationship with the community, unable to see direct benefit to themselves.[69]

In judging the criminological reports written between 1960 and 1990, I read about one hundred of them for the worth of new ideas. How many represented interesting experimental human rights studies of CJS violations to offenders? Projects which highlight examples of academic challenges to orthodox criminological thinking about class? How many attacked the CJS for instances of social injustice and social conflict where the agencies overstepped their bounds when it came to minorities? Did any of these try and expose CJS exploitation of the poor or harsh racial attitudes toward punishment? Did scholars study the processes, abuses, and practices of law enforcement, or were most simply repeating performances of studies on the barbaric nature of repeat offenders? I found the vast majority were mired in contradictions, confusing evidence, repetitions, indirection, and special pleading. I wondered where did these people get their ideas from? Previously written assignments? I assigned letter report card grades based on my own value system and awareness of CJS developments.

Out of every 100 papers, I found a scant 4% worthy of continued interest and clever use of what was available to curb crime (few on contentious subjects of race or the ghetto or Marxian analysis); 5–8% made a few substantive points that warranted follow-up study; the remaining 88% which trod familiar ideological and criminological ground provided no useful ideas, showed little concern for minority communities, and remained for the most part obsolete, badly written, and full of criminological jargon. It was not so many scholars having something to say and thus seeking publication as having journal space to fill and funding sources that permitted all sorts of digressions. There was complexity for sure, entanglements of formulas, equations, measurement issues, and impressive quantitative mappings but these provided little advice on how the metrics could solve crime, improve human relations between CJS agents, help minority clients gain some kind of justice, or rein in uncontrollable CJS agents. The term "war crimes" was mentioned no times. It was mine to invent. Four or five papers were excellent, the rest I would consign to purgatory. Consequently, I was brought face to face with the cruel reality: this stuff is rubbish!

Most of the authors, I would say 60–85%, continued to explore ideas developed in earlier papers, ad nauseum, with little change in viewpoint but plenty of microscopic manipulations of statistical applications. I counted seven Marxist-oriented papers which surprised me since few papers even bothered to cite Marxist academics in their papers or bibliographies. New ideas on race and social activism were noticeably absent. Joan Petersilia, a member of the

Rand Corp, distinguished criminologist. A highly respected scholar said in her 1990 presidential address to the American Society of Criminology:

> Our research is not perceived as sufficiently relevant or beneficial to the CJS . . . (and yet) the system has many problems that are verging on crisis because policies and operations are based on faulty assumptions or a narrow focus (which criminologists are not willing to challenge, my words).

Feuer claimed most criminologists as far back as 1940 (in time-honored professional fashion) tried to avoid embarrassment, ridicule, or loss of funding and employment by being labeled radical. They sat on the fence with writing that caused no concern or rebuke or reaction of any kind.[70] I estimate of the many research projects I read, maybe 2–3% dealt with racial issues that affected the CJS. Academics seemed fearful of discussing race in any but its most obvious forms for fear of being seen as racist or that a reader might misinterpret their conclusions. This was advanced by professors Holmes and Taggart who studied 966 articles published in criminology journals written between 1976 and 1988. They concluded, as did I, that the majority of papers focused on crime causation, social control theories, research design, and the use of multivariate statistics. Little attention was paid to racial issues within the CJS institution nor was there much scope for CJS efforts helping offenders succeed in experimental rehabilitation programs.[71]

Well, what can we say about White criminology for this period? Do we see war crimes committed by these scholars? Perhaps not in the sense of Black lives lost through violence and excessive brutality. But the academics, through their research, bolstered the notion in the minds of politicians, media, or public officials, as well as CJS agents of Black inferiority and criminality: prone to violence, indifference to being unemployed, disregarding family and paternal considerations, susceptible to overuse of drugs and alcohol, knee-deep in diversions and self-gratification, quite frankly a selfish individual willing to destroy his family and community in the process.

Much of the results suggest Binder and Geis' "folk tales and anecdotes." I found few opportunities presented for offenders or Black residents to critique how Whites see Black crime. Only 10% were qualitative but very few of these have a Black point of view. Were Black participants in these studies paid? Did they receive the results of the paper for comment? I find no evidence of this effect in these papers. Nor any real concern by the criminologists of possible damaging consequences to offenders under the microscope. Binder & Geis asked the legitimate question if the participants even had the opportunity to write a contrary opinion? Did White researchers provide their Black subjects full and early disclosure of their study results and the possible ramifications these would have on the Black community (where recommendations were for reduced project funding, increased jail sentences, need for more cops, lengthier prison sentences, increased terms and conditions to supervised probation orders, need for Blacks to undergo more and varied, further restrictions to an offender's lifestyle?). I found that this did not happen except in a minuscule number of cases.[72]

In the great debate over nature versus nurture, there was no doubting which side had the upper hand before 1940. The academics who founded and shaped sociology believed in racial essentialism. White people of Anglo-Saxon stock stood "scientifically proven" to be at the top of the evolutionary ladder, Black people at the bottom. The American statistician Walter Wilcox argued Blacks were so

> Far down the Darwinian scale that they would literally die out. Franz Boas of Columbia University believed Black people had smaller skulls placing them at a mental disadvantage not so much that Robert E. Park, one of the founders of the Chicago School, plagiarized black scholar Dubois when he needed. Keith Thomas hit the nail on the head when in 1995 he equated Blacks who lacked any sort of power specifically with crime and anti-social action, riots and worse.[73]

McElrath and Taylor presented an ironic line of reasoning when they said "criminologists and sociologists often address issues of inequality in their research, but gender and race-based discrimination throughout academia makes it senseless to preach about various social and racial injustices when our own discipline lacks equity or fairness."[74]

A key report evaluating criminological material for this period as recommended by peers comes from Marvin Wolfgang, R. M. Figlio, and T. P. Thornberry.[75] This study reviewed over 3,700 works in the field of criminology between 1945 and 1972. What did they find? About 2% of the titles were seen as important by over half the respondents while over 60% were never cited anywhere and made no impact in the field. Really important works totaled 10%. The authors concluded on page 172 that "the methodological sophistication and competency of most of these criminological reports was rated at dismally low." Overrepresented were typological studies of the offender, clinical testing, treatment modalities, observational case studies, legal issues, and prevention policies. Underrepresented were political crimes, drug use, gang behavior, and racial issues. Seventy-two percent of the scholars sought data that confirmed rather than tested or replicated their hypothesis, or the hypothesis was formed after data was collected.[76]

This is probably a good place to end the discussion of White social scientists and their reprehensible behavior toward their Black colleagues. We have cited many examples during the 1960–1990 period of how they thought, acted, and wrote about men and women of color with whom they kept at arm's length. These people were too emotional, too condemning, far from neutral, and too involved to make good sociologists. They did not accept how European-trained scholars went about the study of Black crime, CJS injustices, and the failure of the discipline to rise above racism when looking at police brutality. The result of so much distorted or fake news on the Black community led historian Robert Shapiro to see similarities in terms of the 1930s anti-Jewish views in Germany: The public generally didn't know what was going on in the Black districts, if they knew of police racism, they did nothing, or avoided information on Black life or misperceived what was really happening. All this was done to lessen the dissonance of what was really happening.[77]

One final ironic note to all the White supremacist researchers hyping Black crime and to all the White criminologists and sociologists who leant little support to Black academics seeking patronage, support, and encouragement. History of Philosophy Professor (Emeritus) at the University of Sidney, Stephen Gaukroger has just written something on the uses and abuses of the scientific method that caught my eye. The social sciences, as the bastion of empirical testing, has always remained highly problematic. So it was that in 2015, Gaukroger tells us an international team of 270 university researchers set out to replicate 100 psychological experiments that earned top billing in prestigious scientific journals. They determined they were simply unable to repeat 75% of the social psychology findings as did 50% of the cognitive psychology experiments. "This is not just a problem for psychology," warns Gaukroger, "but more generally for the idea of a scientific method that is taken to guarantee objective results. White criminologists may have been filled with certainty at what they were saying about the Black crime problem, but given such disturbing results, they should have leaned far more heavily on Black colleagues as a corrective to all their potentially misinformed racist conclusions."[78]

So, are we just racially insensitive and stupid, refusing to face facts on how Black professional criminologists were treated, or blindly prejudiced to convenience our interests? Taking the long view, we smell plenty of war crimes to be uncovered in this vast battlefield of false data. But like my old professor cautioned me, when doing research, leave something for someone else. It's all yours now.

NOTES

1. Gurminder K. Bhambra, Department of Sociology, University of Warwick, "A Sociological Dilemma: Race, Segregation and U. S. Sociology," *Current Sociology* 62, no. 4 (July 2014): 472–492.

2. Ibid., p. 473.

3. Julius Debro and Helen Taylor, University of Maryland Institute of Criminal Justice and Criminology, Study of the Status of Black Criminology in the United States, 1977, National Institute of Justice, University of Maryland, p. 12, 21 and 24; also Reza Barmaki, lecturer, University of Toronto, "Explanation of Blacks' Crime in America, 1630-1950," *Deviant Behavior* 41, no. 10 (2020): 1305–1329; and Debro, "Study on the Status of Black Crime in the U.S.," National Institute of Justice, University of Maryland, 1978.

4. Simon H. Tulchin and Ernest Burgess, *Intelligence and Crime: A Study of Penitentiary and Reformatory Offenders* (University of Chicago Press, 1939). Survey under the direction of Herman M. Adler, *Illinois State Criminologist as Far Back as 1920*, p. 15, 101 and 119.

5. Ibid.

6. Dubro, p. 24.

7. J. Thorsten Sellin, "The Negro Criminal A Statistical Note," *American Academy of Politics and Social Sciences* (1928): 52.

8. Albert Murray, "White Norms, Black Deviance," in Joyce A. Ladner's (Ed.), *Death of White Sociology: Essays on Race and Culture* (New York: Vintage, 1973), p. 100 and 105. Ladner is a prominent Howard University professor; also, Maurice Jackson, "Toward a Sociology of Black Studies," *Journal of Black Studies* 1 (1970): 131–140; Nathan Hare, "Challenge of a Black Scholar," *Black Scholar* 1 (1968).

9. Edward Byron Reuter, "The Superiority of the Mulatto," *American Journal of Sociology* 23 (1917): 83–85.

10. Michael Tonry, *Malign Neglect-Race, Crime and Punishment in America* (New York: Oxford UP, 1995), p. vii; and Peter Sorokin, *Fads and Foibles in Modern Sociology and Related Sciences* (New York: Henry Regnery, 1956), p. 103.

11. Taylor Debro, op cit., p. 12.

12. Frank Morn, *Academic Politics and the History of Criminal Justice Education* (Westport: Greenwood, 1995), p. 121 and 161.

13. Reuter, op. cit., *The American Race Problem* (New York: Crowell, 1966), pp. 333–334.

14. Op. cit., "The Superiority of the Mulatto," *American Journal of Sociology* 23 (1917): 83–85.

15. Taylor Debro, op. cit., p. 24; Michael J. Coyle, professor in the Department of Police Science and Criminal Justice, California State University (Chico: Abolish Criminology, 2017), p. 38.

16. Ibid., p. 39. Or…15/16 Michael J. Coyle, *Talking Criminal Justice Language and the Just Society* (Fairford: Routledge, 2013), pp. 38–39.

17. Debro and Taylor, op. cit., p. 15 and 30.

18. Bhambra, op. cit., p. 477.

19. Donald Goines, *White Man's Justice, Black Man's Grief* (Los Angeles: Holloway House, 1975), p. 69 and 87.

20. John Gifford, *Pimping Fictions: African American Literature and the Untold Story of Black Pulp Fiction* (Philadelphia: Temple UP, 2013), p. 51.

21. Stephen Small, *Racialized Barriers, The Black Experience in the U.S. and England in the 1980s* (London: Routledge, 1994), p. 31.

22. Ibid., p. 32; and "W. E. B. Dubois," in John Scott (Ed.), *Fifty Key Sociologists-The Formative Theorists* (London: Routledge, 2007), pp. 36–37.

23. Elijah Anderson and Douglas S. Massey, *Problem of the Century-Racial Stratification in the U.S.* (New York: Russell Sage Foundation, 2001), p. 3.

24. Ibid.

25. Bhambra, p. 8.

26. John H. Bracey, Jr., August Meier and Elliott Rudnick, "The Black Society, First Half Century," in Joyce Ladner's (Ed.), *Death of White Sociology*, op cit. See also their earlier *Black Nationalism in America* (New York: Macmillan, 1970).

27. Aldon D. Morris, professor of sociology at Northwestern University, "Scholars' Work has been Systematically Ignored," about Dubois in Harvard Gazette, 29 October 2018 and in the same paper given in a symposium at the same time.

28. Ira Katznelson, "DuBois Century," *Social Science History* 23, no. 4 (1999), pp. 469–470. See his more recent *When Affirmative Action was White: An Untold Story of Racial Inequality in the 20th Century* (New York: Norton, 2006). Katznelson is Professor of Political Science at Rutgers University.

29. Drew Lanham, "When W.E.B. Dubois was Un-American," *Bostonreview.net*, 13 January 2017.

30. Dan S. Green and Edwin D. Driver, "W.E.B. Dubois-A Case in the Sociology of Sociological Negation," *Phylon* 37, no. 4 (1976): 308.

31. Ian Frazier, "Old Hatreds," *The New Yorker*, 26 August 2019.

32. Bhambra, op. cit.; Monroe N. Work and his studies mentioned in Jonathan Grossman (U.S. Department of Labor Historian) in his "Black Studies in the Department of Labor, 1897-1907," *Monthly Labor Review*, June 1974.

33. Everette B. Penn, *On Black Criminology, Past, Present and Future* (Prairie View A & M, University of Texas, 2000), p. 317 and 325.

34. Everette B. Penn, *On Black Criminology, Past, Present and Future* (Prairie View A & M, University of Texas, 2000), p. 317 and 325.

35. Lee Brown, "Crime and Criminal Justice in the Black Community," *Journal of African American Issues* 11 (1974): 87–88.

36. Vernetta Young and Anne Thomas Sulton, "Excluded: The Current Status of African American Scholars in the Field of Criminology and Criminal Justice," *Journal of Research in Crime and Delinquency* 28, no. 1 (1991): 105.

37. Davarian L. Baldwin, "Recorded in Black Belts and Ivory Towers: The Place of Race in the U.S. in Social Thought 1892-1948," *Critical Sociology* 30, no. 2 (2004): 400 and 406.

38. Clemmont E. Vontress, "Patterns of Segregation and Discrimination-Contributing Factors to Crime Among Negroes," *Journal of Negro Education* 31 (1962): 108; Brown, op. cit.

39. Young and Sulton, op. cit., p. 102.

40. Art Evans, "Importance of Race Among Black Sociologists," *Sociological Quarterly* 21 (1980): 23.

41. Steve Cooper, see Florida State University's Criminology website for his paper on James Q. Wilson, "Wilson Had a Huge Influence on America's Commitment to Mass Incarceration."

42. Ibid.

43. Ibid.

44. James Q. Wilson, op. cit., *Thinking of Crime*, p. 231.

45. Mitchell Duneier, *Ghetto: The Invention of a Place, the History of an Idea* (New York: Farrar, Straus and Giroux, 2016), p. 29, 33, 38 and 52; St Clair Drake, Black Metropolis Revisited, box 39, the Drake Papers, Schomburg Center for Special Research in Black Culture, NYPL; and Henri Peretz, "The Making of Black Metropolis," *Annals of American Academy of Politics and Social Sciences* (2004): 171; Kenneth B. Clark, *The Dark Ghetto: Dilemma of Social Power* (New York: Harper & Row, 1965), p. 148; and Ralph Ellison, *An American Dilemma: A Review of Myrdal's American Dilemma* (1944) in Joyce Ladner's *Death of White Sociology*, op cit., pp. 94–95.

46. Young and Sulton, op. cit., p. 102 and 100; George Napper, "Perceptions of Crime and Implications," in Robert Woodson (Ed.), *Black Perspective on Crime and the Criminal Justice System* (Boston: Hall, 1977); Benny Primm, "Drug Use: Special Implications for Black Americans," in *National Urban league State of Black America* (New York: NAACP, 1987), p. 145 and 158.

47. James E. Blackwell and Morris Janowitz (Eds.), *Black Sociologists-Historical and Contemporary Perspectives* (Chicago: Chicago UP, 1974), p. 133.

48. Ibid., pp. 134–135.

49. Gerald Suttles, *The Social Order in the Slums* (Chicago: Chicago UP, 1968), p. 9.

50. Ibid., pp. 4–6.

51. Marvin E. Wolfgang, *Patterns in Criminal Homicide* (Philadelphia: University of Pennsylvania Press, 1958), pp. 116–119.

52. M. G. Wilson and D. J. Edwards, "Vital Capacity of Lungs and its Relations to the Exercise of Tolerance in Children with Heart Disease," *American Journal of Diseases of Children* 22 (1921): 443.

53. Alfred H. Stone, "Is Race Friction Between Whites and Blacks Growing and Inevitable," *American Journal of Sociology* 13 (1908): 677; and John Van Eurie, *White Supremacy and Negro Insubordination* (New York: Van Eurie and Horton, 1870), especially chapter III.

54. Robert E. Park, "The Mentality of Racial Hybrids," *American Journal of Sociology* 36 (1931): 534; also Barbara Ballis Lal on "Black and Blue in Robert E. Park's Perspective on Race Relations in Urban America," *British Journal of Sociology* 38, no. 4 (1987): 546–566.

55. Howard W. Odum, *Social and Mental Traits of Negroes* (New York: Longmans, Green, 1912), see chapter 4 for a fuller attention to this persecution.

56. Murray, op. cit., Ladner's *Death of White Sociology*, p. 102 and 105; also discussed in S. Daniel Moynihan's *The Negro Family: A Case for National Action*, Office of Policy Planning and Research, U.S. Department of Labor, March 1965.

57. Talcott Parsons and Robert F. Bales, *Family, Socialization and the Interactive Process* (New York: Free Press, 1955); N. D. Gist and S. F. Fava, *Urban Society*

(New York: Free Press, 1965); A. F. Stone, "The Mulatto Factor in the Race Problem," *Atlantic Monthly*, November 1908, p. 658; Robert Kephart, *The Family, Society and the Individual* (New York: Houghton Mifflin, 1966), Marvin B. Sussman (Ed.), *Sourcebook in Marriage and the Family* (New York: Houghton Mifflin, 1973), and Stuart A. Queen and Robert W. Habenstein, *The Family in Various Cultures* (Philadelphia: J. B. Lippincott, 1967).

58. Andrew Billingsley, "Black families and White Social Science," in *Ladner's Death*, op. cit., p. 442; and V. Boyd, *Wrapped in Rainbows: The Life of Zora Neale Hurston* (New York: Scribner's, 2003), p. 142.

59. David A. Schulz, *Coming Up Black-Patterns of Ghetto Socialization* (Englewood Cliffs: Prentice-Hall, 1969), p. 147; James Mills, *On the Edge* (Garden City: Doubleday, 1975), p. 98.

60. James B. Conant, *Slums & Suburbs* (New York: McGraw-Hill, 1961), p. 76.

61. Wilson, already cited in the Cooper reference, quote found in his *Thinking of Crime*, p. 231.

62. James A. Chambers, *Blacks and Crime, a Function of Class* (Westport: Prager, 1995).

63. Eric Stewart, Ronald Simon and Rand Congi, "Assessing Neighborhood Social Psychological Influences on Childhood Violence in a Sample," *Criminology* 40 (2006): 802.

64. R. M. Stephenson and Frank R. Scarpitti, *Group Interaction as Therapy—The Use of the Small Group in Corrections* (Westport: Praeger, 1974).

65. Charles Saunders, "Assessing Race Relations Research," *Journal of Black Studies & Research* 1 (1970): 17–25.

66. Herbert M. Greenberg, "Development of an Integration Attitude Scale," *Journal of Social Psychology* 54 (1961): 105–109.

67. Richard F. America, "The Case of the Racist Researcher," in Ladner, op cit., p. 457; and Robert M. Shapiro, "Why Didn't the Press Shout? American and International Journalism During the Holocaust," paper given at the Yeshiva Conference, 1995, New York.

68. Kenneth B. Clark, "Introduction to an Epilogue," in Ladner, pp. 401–408; also, Haryou (Harlem Youth Opportunities Unlimited, financed by the New York Mayor and Presidential Committee on Juvenile Delinquency in 1962, published findings in 1964 Youth in The Ghetto, a Study of the Consequences of Power Lessons and a Blueprint for Change, 620pp.

69. Ibid.

70. Joan Petersilia, "Policy Relevance and the Future of Criminology," the Presidential address to the American Society of Criminologists, *Criminology* 29 (1991): 1–15; Louis S. Feuer, "The Economic Factor in History," *Science and Society* (1940): 174.

71. Malcom Holmes and William Taggart, "A Comparative Analysis of Research Methods," *Journal of Criminology and Criminal Justice* 7, no. 2 (1990): 180.

72. Arnold Binder and Gilbert Geis, *Methods of Research in Criminology* (New York: McGraw-Hill, 1983), p. 12 and 18.

73. Keith Thomas, "New Ways Revisited: How History's Borders have Expanded in the Past 40 Years," *The Times Literary Supplement*, 13 October 2006, p. 16.

74. Karen McElrath and Dorothy Taylor, "Gender and Earnings in Academic Criminology," *Journal of Criminal Justice Education* 7, no. 1 (1996): 41 and 43.

75. Marvin Wolfgang, Robert M. Figlio and T. Sellin, *Delinquency in a Birth Cohort* (Chicago: University of Chicago Press, 1972), p. 172.

76. Roy D. King and Emma Wincup, *Doing Research on Crime and Justice* (New York: Oxford UP, 2000), pp. 1–11.

77. Shapiro, op. cit., pp. 54–55.

78. Reported in The Times Literary Supplement, "How Psychology Failed the Test," review of a book by Henry M. Cowles, *The Scientific Method, An Evolution of Thinking from Darwin to Dewey* (Cambridge: Harvard UP, 2020), reviewer was Stephen Gaukroger, 1 January 2021, p. 10.

Chapter 8

Results of the Harlem Survey
(on the American Criminal Justice System)

By the mid-1960s, James Baldwin had become the most eloquent voice of the civil rights movement and many saw him as the de facto mayor of Harlem. In 1963, one theater critic claimed "his pictures of Harlem life are as fresh today (1963) as they were when they were first set down." A loving tribute of Hughes came from the editor of his plays, Webster Smalley:

> His primary interest is in the "little people" . . . he prefers to write about those of his race who live constantly on the edge of financial disaster, who are used to living precariously, occasionally falling over the edge and crawling back up, and who have no time to be pretentious . . . he writes to express truths he feels need expressing about characters he feels need to be recognized.

He thus seems like a fitting individual to listen to when he talks about this period under study and the treatment of Harlem residents by the CJS.

Here is Hughes speaking about police excesses he witnessed many times:

> Rare is the Harlem citizen, from the most respectable church member to the most shiftless adolescent who does not have a long tale to tell of police incompetence, injustice or brutality. I myself have witnessed and endured it more than once.

There is a constant referral to police brutality in his stories, a recurring theme between him and the cops and suggests they were a "very present danger to the Black community in this period . . . the menace of the criminal law as a regulatory force by the CJS sustains White privilege and White oppression."[1]

As a member of the CJS, FBI director J. Edgar Hoover was less literate in his view of Baldwin, calling him un-American, a pervert, a danger to national security, and a radical. Hoover wasted plenty of taxpayer money as his agency assembled 2,000 pages of hysteria on Baldwin before the dossier was officially closed in 1974.[2]

But there are other voices of protest. Here are many that originated in the present survey (an example of the survey instrument can be found at the end of this chapter) taken of Harlem residents for this study. It was part of a study where college students of Harlem mostly interviewed family members from the 1960s generation who had witnessed the CJS in full command during the War on Crime years. Here are the sentiments of one such interviewee, the man is Black and aged fifty, a resident of Harlem. Like the others he does not remember this era fondly:

> I was forever being bothered by the New York City cops. A few times they took my money to avoid me being arrested. A friend was arrested on day for using his sister's train ticket and instead of being brought to the station or put behind bars he was locked in a bathroom for almost an entire day and threatened by White police to be sent to Rikers Island. Living life in a poor minority family of the 1960s in the ghetto, my life was full of racism and hate. This has clearly shaped my perception of the CJS which I regard as a supreme governmental failure. Me and my friend were harassed by the NYPD police on a regular basis and regularly stopped from the ages of 16–21. Often, we just stood quietly on one particular corner which always seemed to attract the cops who wrongly believed we were selling drugs. Their usual annoying searches always found nothing. We felt we had a right to stand there in our neighborhood. Cops seemed to feel they owned the area and that included the corner we had chosen.[3]

> I believed the CJ agencies were bad because they took advantage with their power. Also, they didn't show any remorse towards darker skin. All my life it seems I had witnessed unfair police arrests.[4]

This has been a study of the dark side of America's CJS during the War on Crime years (1960–1990). We have noted the many ways in which war crimes were committed by different sectors of the CJS, especially the cops. We have given voice to a broader class of academics fighting crime in the streets: criminologists and sociologists, CJS agency administrators, practitioners and other key personnel, the many politicians and government funding agencies, and researchers and journalists of all kinds who had their own take on crime issues. The one group so far left out, the one closest to the scene, and the one most in a position to judge the system during these years was the Black community itself. It was also the one group that most often felt the severe blow of racial injustice and agency intolerance toward civil rights. Black urban citizens own the most critical attitude toward the CJS and it is this group we now listen to as we complete the survey of these War on Crime years.

Images of Harlem for the 1960s and 1970s are routinely negative, and generally provide an unflattering portrayal of the city . . ." dirty, dangerous, and morally suspect . . . chaotic, decay, and division solidified.[5] Hollywood crime and cop films of this period only made Harlem seem worse due to the gratuitous violence depicted in Shaft (1971), Superfly (1972), Across 110th Street (1972), Cotton Comes to Harlem (1970), Mean Streets (1973) and Death Wish (1974).

All the CJS agencies which impacted Harlem and New York have hitherto been examined, recalling the many ways in which each committed war crimes on people toward whom they showed little regard. No records were kept on how nasty the CJS could be toward the urban Black population, no evidence exists to reveal the extent and regularity of these infractions, certainly no data on disciplinary action taken to reduce behavior that went against even police department codes of conduct. It makes it impossible to statistically, empirically, and scientifically label, with a general view toward accounting for their regularity, these behaviors we deem as war crimes. We can only speculate on the basis of what witnesses have candidly told us for this survey. We understand that such unscientific observations make the case against the police, or corrections, for any area in the country, difficult to prove. Nor can we attach any names to the perpetrators involved. And if we could, what sort of justice do we think could come of it? In those bygone days, there were very few Black citizens who dared to raise a voice of protest or indignation, fearful of the repercussions that would follow by cops who knew where these people and their families lived and who knew how best to exact revenge on whistleblowers.

This study has taken the time to look at and listen to people who lived in the period. People who prepared to share their views of the CJS in as objective way as possible, given that many of them were victims of the CJS at the time. The study includes opinions and observations to thirty-six questions asked of the respondents as they saw these agents. In 2015, I selected willing students from several criminology classes at John Jay College where I taught. Each of them was called upon to ask senior family members who had lived through this period if they would respond to questions about the behavior of the CJS during the years 1960–1990, as best they could remember. The ages of the 172 interviewees who make up this investigation range from 45 to 92, and all were interviewed by junior members of their families who were criminology students. There was the hope that some of the students would realize how much valor and courage it took these older members to live through what was a very intense and harrowing period for the Black residents of New

York. What follows are the general results and statistics for the 112 men and 60 women interviewed. The second series of interviews were conducted with Latino residents but this was put aside because police and CJS reactions toward them were less murderous, less nationwide; a second report on these findings will be published at a later date. But the Black study will provide us with as close and meaningful a look at the results of CJS behavior for one city as has presently been published.

The first block of questions (a sample of the questionnaire can be found in the appendix) are composed of broad social and political issues that centered on family life and neighborhood conditions. This was designed to provide a backdrop to the kind of world respondents lived in as they attempted to adjust to the many invasive and dangerous CJS intrusions into their lives during these crime years. A second block focuses more sharply on the police tactics and their Gestapo-like intrusions and interrogations which took place on a daily basis. Here the community under study is defined broadly as the Black neighborhoods of the five boroughs as far East as Nassau County. The final block represents a self-determined attitudinal report card of citizen grades of the CJS, for better or worse. This has been split between both men and women for comparative purposes: Who was most angered, who rated these agencies the lowest, men or women? In some cases, women displayed surprising belligerence despite the much larger number of men who were chosen for victimization, harassment, and police brutality.

Results indicate a broad-based disavowal of the American political system. Seventy-two percent of the men and 74% of the women uniformly claimed that while they belonged to a political party (Democratic Party), when it came to actual voting, men were less likely to take an interest, Democrat or otherwise, but 45% voted regularly in elections (49% for women)! Both groups were beneath national averages for the elections of this period as men showed less faith that voting would lead to improvements in their lives despite selecting Democratic representatives. There was little evidence of the weight of political parties on local residents which probably led to an underrepresentation. And if turnout was low, one could expect this group to be ignored by the government. There was little verbal evidence that party affiliation or allegiance brought any local advantages or comfort by way of a lessening of police harassment.

Residents in prison were ignored in the census. If he was a felon he was disenfranchised from voting and did little to encourage people around him to vote, "if I can't vote, I won't participate," said one.[6] Burch again: "High rates of imprisonment through CJS interaction before a general election lowers voter turnout and excludes people with a declining participation rate. It also keeps any Democratic Party campaign from extending into the community to seek potential voters."[7]

We can only speculate on what such a low turnout of Black voters would mean, if Blacks everywhere came out in the same puny numbers to support liberal political issues of the day. Concurrently, it is hardly surprising that the level of admiration for political figures of the day was also very low. Those who were nominated as role models attracted few admirers and not many votes—Dr. M. L. King headed the list with a paltry 14%, Malcolm X received 10%, President John F. Kennedy 5%, David Dinkins 2.5%, and Robert Kennedy 2% with a sprinkling of support for Mandela, Jesse Jackson, James Baldwin, Che Guevara, Fred Hampton, Angela Davis, Rosa Parks, Charlie Wrangel, and Shirley Chisholm.

When asked how they handled malicious police behavior, several claimed they tried to either join, help organize, or create community action groups whose objective was to stand up to bad police behavior, help lessen local crime, attempt to provide alternative leadership, or make a minimal display of objection. Most admitted they did next to nothing to prevent a more severe police response that would only make matters worse. Burch noted how CJS behavior could affect local elections. "Punitive interactions between citizens and the CJS matter for politics. The government, by punishing citizens, affected politics not by deciding who holds office but by shaping the contours of the polity. It defines who belongs to the political community."[8] And so few looked to politicians for relief. Brager bemoaned how so little of this action came to fruition or made a dent in police relations with the community. He comments: "Delinquency and crime can only be lowered if residents partici-pated in decision-making matters that affect their interest and increase their sense of identifying with the community and social order." But this rarely happened. The CJS was not about to surrender any authority or show coop-eration to groups whose efforts were designed to undermine or torpedo their tyrannical grip on the community."[9]

What Brager reports as the weaknesses of any community-based programs occurred when lower-class residents did not become participants: local orga-nizations failed to entice a significant number of these people, being com-posed of already entrenched bourgeois groups whose positions of power felt threatened, a dominance of incumbent leadership who supported middle-class values that made residents feel inferior, structural obstacles to indigenous participation, status quo attitudes that claimed "they were not really inter-ested," or "not ready to lead," or "controlled by left-wing agitators," or "have bizarre or costly and unworkable views on how to reform the organization."[10] I personally found many small-scale storefront operations trying to make tiny improvements to help youth overcome truant behavior, or drug addicts break the habit, but outsiders (White middle-class suburbanites with social work experience and years of working in bureaucratic agencies to oversee human tragedies and personal issues) seem to have had a major grasp on funding

and political support and were overwhelmingly appreciated by outside bene-
factors (i.e., Ford Foundation, John D. MacArthur Foundation, Rockefeller,
Lily), for their predictable, nonthreatening, and conformist approaches
against radical action, local militancy, and antipolice demonstrations.

Although two-thirds of the survey believed they faced racial issues from
police on a daily basis, almost half believed they lived in a dangerous neighborhood—no doubt in part because of unpredictable police behavior (men
curiously found their neighborhood a fun place in 30% of the cases, "it was
just me hanging with my boys," while 60% of the women held a benign
view), when it came to being a recent (less than a year) victim of crime 37%
of the women and 50% of the men spoke of this, mainly minor in nature.
Quite surprising, despite the raging crime and/or police violence that surrounded these neighborhoods, most tried to put on a happy face. A majority
of 65% of the women and perhaps 37% of men said yes, they lived basically happy lives, free from family responsibilities, and devoting plenty of
time to friends and mischievous activities. They tried to dismiss what police
intervention might mean and claimed the issue didn't occupy much of their
thinking, but they knew it existed and that it could be both capricious and
spontaneous. Half the survey claimed family life was pleasant, secure, and
stable, while the other half spoke of instability, domestic abuse, and drugs;
49% of all families received some sort of government support (i.e., housing,
food, cash) and 55% had faced lengthy unemployment within the past three
years. This then was the overall social picture portrayed by the Black residents of the questionnaire.

The civil rights era brought considerable urban unrest. Written media
perspectives were always of a White man. "I cannot lie and defend what is
wrongdoing. The cops during the 1960s and 1970s were very aggressive and
violent toward African American men because of the main reason that we
all know was racism."[11] Black American demands for parity and justice met
with resultant oppression from government agencies such as the CJS. "Once
I had a case and the lawyer didn't take it because of racial tension between
us."[12] The battlefields tended to be concentrated in the main cities where the
percentage of African Americans was above 15% and had withstood decades
of grievances from bad policing and unforgiving brutality and war crimes.
Police were the main conduits through which the system attempted to control
and suppress lawful demands and, when not granted, navigate the upheaval
in violent directions. It is against this backdrop of resolve that police as the
main supporters of law enforcement were tasked with keeping law and order
in the ghettoes by any means possible as Malcolm X would say. "Police did
what they wanted. Police were violent. Jails and prisons were mostly filled
with Blacks. There weren't many community helpers that I knew of. The CJS
was simply corrupt."[13] Which members of the CJS were appreciated for the

sympathetic work they did helping neighbors? And which were awarded the lowest marks for behavior that fell wide of the mark in terms of inhumanity and disgrace? This survey offers some suggestive answers into how African Americans in New York City perceived the police with their endless stop and frisk and the broader functions of the CJS as they blended into a broader pattern of repression (i.e., lawyers, district attorneys, courts and judges, jail guards, prison staffs, and rehabilitation personnel). "I was never arrested. I got stopped a few times but was always able to talk my way out. Money helped at times. If they took money from me they never bothered me again."[14]

The need for fair and tolerant police that would preserve order in the communities was clearly evident. Our survey of the 172 Black residents of NYC made that apparent. Seventy-four percent had actually witnessed a crime in the past two years while 37% of them had themselves been victims (50% of the men), and 47% had witnessed some kind of a riot, flare-up, or demonstration. The political turbulence of the period, along with War on Crime zealots from the CJS pitted citizens (young and old) against one another, against local merchants, against the media, and against the police and other representatives of the CJS. If this investigation is any indication, tension and daily conflict between residents of all ages and the police were ongoing, with serious consequences for the legal and human rights of individuals and the safety and security of their communities. NYPD seemed to occupy a major part of the problem instigating urban unrest while under the cloak of investigating criminal activity.

Respondents were asked to evaluate the quality of the arrests made by NYPD in their neighborhoods; they were awarded little praise. The average arrest was seen as fair and proper by 15% of the women and 13% of the men. Often the target of police suspicion, most men felt the arrests were unjustified—either wrong-headed or were stopping residents for trivial offenses. "I was stopped and frisked many times and occasionally arrested but these never went anywhere. They did ruin my day and waste my time."[15] This view was supported by a feeling from 70% of the men that police harassment and random stops occurred on a daily basis (much less (about 14%) for women who were never treated with the same animosity as their men).

The findings are supported by Goodman's returns elsewhere. He found that 56% believed police generally were not doing a good job at preventing crime in the Black community; 50% knew of the regularity of police brutality; 57% felt police were more harm than help, "occupiers sent to pacify the natives," while 69% just "want to keep the Black man down."[16]

During daily stops, cop brutality took place regularly and without warning—a stick in the ribs, a slap at the knees. Two of every three interviewees claimed when they themselves had not been made victim they had witnessed police brutality (64%) in the past two years, sometimes against relatives or friends, sometimes just random males in the street. Such behavior must have been deeply traumatic for the general population although neither anecdotal figures nor official reports can support this contention which cannot reasonably be measured. One major police transgression which the respondents, against usual police denials, claimed to have seen was the bringing of drugs into the neighborhood (witnessed by 41% of the survey) to sell, plant as evidence, use personally, lure women into physical contact, buy witness testimony, or just use as a medium of currency for myriad of needs. About half were unsure but held out the possibility police were capable of doing these things and some had heard rumors to the effect at various times. Thirty-four percent of respondents claimed police accepted bribes from prostitutes, drug dealers, or potential suspects so as to avoid arrest. Thirty-five percent believed there existed a quota for arrests.

All these figures appear to represent sharp indicators of extremely bad behavior if not downright war crimes by police as witnessed by residents of this survey. They do not suggest the police notion of "just a few rotten apples" 'but suggest a serious degree of universality in how police treat citizens of this community. Anything above 15% return I would suggest bears witness to a dangerous condition of poor training, bad police management, and acceptance of a reign of terror which is incompatible with proper police procedure. NYPD stands as the culprit and probably deserves a serious reduction in finances and forces to offset the many dangers their practices represent to the Black neighborhoods of New York.

Intimidation by police was another common trait cited by interviewees. Residents were asked how often they protested when police misbehaved. Not often: an occasional loud remark or protest sign or surly crowd gathering was the sum total of what could be summoned to challenge widespread police illegalities. Nevertheless, 45% of surveyed residents claimed at least at one point in their lives they had exercised their civil rights in protesting against CJS abuses in their neighborhoods. Most respondents made it quite clear you were taking your life in your hands if you challenged cops as many White cops were trigger-happy and easily coaxed into employing physical and violent behavior (most cases of intimidation and physical assault were thrown out of court but go tell that to the man nursing a broken arm) while making arrests.

At this juncture it is relevant to recall a recent Black cop's repeated kind of abusive behavior already documented toward ghetto citizens of New York. Ex-Black cop Redditt Hudson remembers:

> On any given day, in any police department in the nation, 15% of officers will do the right thing, 15% will abuse their authority at every opportunity (and exert an outsize influence). The remaining 70% could go either way depending on the culture of the department in which they are working . . . if their command ranks

are racist or allow institutional racism to persist, or if a number of officers in their department are racist, they may end up doing terrible things . . . no matter what an officer has done to a black person, that officer can always cover himself in the running narrative of heroism . . . there are officers who willfully violate the human rights of the people in the communities they serve . . .[17]

We agree with these findings as they relate to this survey.

The final portion asked respondents to simply give a letter grade for performance and duty to the community for various components of the CJS as experienced for these years. Everyone understands the grading system and that there is a significant difference between an A from an F. This is pretty clear to almost everybody. Grades were assigned on a point system where As were given the number 5, Bs were 4, and so on. Male respondents were analyzed separately to see if one or the other gender was particularly exasperated by the CJS agents. These grades are presented so that readers can form their own opinion about what potential war crimes might have occurred on a regular basis against minority residents of NYC for the War on Crime years. And how citizens chose to interpret this war crime behavior. Many opinions came from people who had only the occasional brush with the system and could only repeat things they had heard from others. Still, at least 38% of the respondents, that's three in ten, a sizeable number, had experienced firsthand the CJS seen from the inside (as temporary captives in jails or long-term prisoners or in a drug treatment facility, or exposed to courts processing their cases on a regular basis, or time spent in the bowels of a police precinct undergoing questioning and interrogation).

So how did the CJS come out for their overall performance for this period when graded by NYC Black residents? The results make for dismal reading. They are, in fact, a monstrous and condemnatory indictment of the whole CJS for these thirty years as experienced by those at the pointed end of the sword. "Police were very corrupt and targeted minorities who were sentenced for long periods of time to slow any progress."[18] These were the grades contrasted by gender for seven components of the CJS: police, corrections, rehabilitation agencies, probation services, criminal attorneys combined with district attorneys, and the Criminal Courts. As seen in table 8.1, women tended to give the system a slightly better grade for each of the agencies than did the men who, as a group, were the biggest victims. The point spread between lowest and highest scores out of a score of 5.00 is but .86 (under 1.00) for the women and .92 for the men suggesting very slight disagreements in the grade which in all cases receives traditional letter grades of D for women and D or less for the men. Polling the results of all seven categories gives men an average score of 2.2 and 2.6 for women (no statistical significance). The gap is but .4 showing again a basic agreement on the rating of the CJS between both groups. These are grades that speak to the enormous dissatisfaction NYC Black population has for their local CJS representatives.

Police and corrections permitted the most unrestrained, arbitrary violence in their work and as a result earned the worst scores. Men believed them the worst of all the CJS agencies, women rated them close to a failure mark. "Abusive, rude, racist, violent, corrupt" were some terms used by one respondent about the police because as another witness[19] put it "no one likes them." "They're always harassing Black people" was[20] a common comment, while one woman[21] wrote: "I believe police target minorities deliberately and always use too much force for the circumstances." Corrections (jails, detention centers, prisons, concentration camps) sat at the bottom of the stack and drew the worst grades from everyone. Some women found "horrible conditions not unlike a zoo" when they visited their male relatives or husbands,[22] "I found they treated the men like caged animals." Some of the male respondents spoke from genuine experience. "They treated us like slaves," "conditions were cruel and inhuman," "terrible treatment with no good outcomes,"[23] "staff were cruel and brutal and treated us horribly."[24] Criminal Courts ran into their fair share of criticisms and received grades in the lowest third. "Punishments and sentences way too long" were the normal responses. Trials were seen as unfair, jails were used too often, money seemed the only way to get justice, sentences were routinely bad, and anyway it took too long to hear a case before the bad sentences were applied. Advocates who worked for free for the defendants drew faint praise. "If you have a public defender, you are sure to lose your case," said one cynical interviewee.[25] "Lawyers disregard minorities, and didn't care if they won or loss,"[26] "I felt like an outcast and got no real help,"[27] "I found them uncaring, they didn't bother to use many local resources and lacked enthusiasm to fight my case,"[28] "some seemed really wanting to help but either lacked compassion or gave really bad advice, or bother."[29]

Table 8.1   Report Card Ratings of CJS (Total = 5.0)

	Bl Men	Bl Women	L Men	L Women
Community Programs	2.6	2.8	-	-
Rehabilitation Agencies	2.5	2.5	3.1	3.8
Probation Services	2.4	2.9	3.2	3.7
Lawyers	2.2	2.6	3.1	3.3
Criminal Court	1.9	2.5	2.6	2.3
Police	1.8	2.5	1.9	2.6
Corrections	1.7	2.1	1.8	2.8
OVERALL AVERAGE CJS RATING	2.2	2.6	2.6	3.1

Source: Table created with data from author study.

Local politicians worked to undercut attempts at community organizations trying to help ex-offenders and drug addicts. They felt threatened and saw such groups as subversive trends trying to extend welfare services that would require budgets and monies subtracted from the status quo official city agencies. Mayors were keen on keeping such efforts as limited as possible, also feeling competition although few of this group offered any kind of services that could help reclaim individuals from a criminal lifestyle. Fisher reports before the 1960s this was a persistent force in urban areas with thousands of grassroots active in America. Acorn as a community action group maintained a membership of over 25,000 in 19 states by 1968. CJS agencies and urban renewal projects by the federal government under the Nixon Republicans eventually brought this force to heel through underfunding and legal constraints that left a large gap in services for ex-offenders after 1970. "Republicans knew its mandate didn't reside in poor, inner cities or Black constituents" and this sector of rehabilitation was soon starved out of any useful purpose.[30] Residents from this service recognized and felt this loss gravely.

Thus, top marks, which translated to a middle D, were reserved for these woebegone rehabilitation agencies, probation services, and community programs which made fitful starts at trying to rescue the victims cast out by the CJS. Sadly, too few respondents said they knew of the existence of any of these near them or that their outreach programs were very limited in number, accepted too few referrals, were notoriously underfunded, and had few concrete resources such as cash to help residents get over immediate troubles (i.e., rent, food, carfare). Had government agencies spent more money, advertised their presence to a greater degree, and devoted more personnel and resources, residents believed crime might have been sufficiently reduced and their hostile view of police might have improved. Probation officers were usually given ok marks but one respondent saw deeper meaning in this service: "The PO may appear to be helping but this allows the CJS to remain in power over the individual for as long as he's on probation, even afterwards."[31] Drug addicts were the toughest to reclaim and doubtless much time and attention was spent attempting to rehabilitate them when community resources were themselves starved of assets. "Some good people worked there," claims,[32] and "I knew of a few drug users that benefited, but often these agencies refused too many, and these fell through the grating and ended up back in jail after police rousing. They were bogus and did little good."[33] "They were scarce, hard to find, didn't try hard enough, and many were uncaring. There were too few to evaluate and never had enough jobs to offer which was the big thing if you wanted to help someone."[34] It was clear that if agents of the CJS had provided decent contacts with respondents, grades would have been measurably higher. But the vast majority of this survey had tasted real physical pain, loss of identity, career frustration, and damage to family and ego that resulted from too many years behind bars. And many had battle scars to show where police brutality and their war crimes had touched them physically. "The police do more than they're supposed to with force. They see a dark-colored person and treat them unfairly."[35] "Everyone in the CJS targeted Black people at the time."[36]

Let's remember what's not being graded is a baby's highchair, a used car, or hair spray. This is an exercise in grading an institution with its sub-parts that can physically abuse, murder, imprison, traumatized, destroy a person's livelihood and future prospects, decimate a ghetto communities' human resources, or seriously impinge on and destroy family relationships. Human lives are at stake. If a community awards pitifully low grades and evaluations for its CJS, we must be alarmed for the citizens. These are grades for an institution whose performance of rampant injustice took place many years ago. This only serves to warn us of the many lives theoretically destroyed and the sadness for what might have happened should these communities been allowed to thrive. That our position of war crimes is specu-lative we acknowledge but what if it really happened? Without evidence either way we only have witnesses of the time to explain their side of the story. And here we offer one set of witnesses with their appraisal. We also offer some of the comments by people who were oppressed by NYPD at the time. We are less concerned with the environmental aesthetics of liv-ing in New York than with basic civil liberties and juridical fairness. The community struggle against Eurocentric, White nationalist and supremacist cultural values is apparent from the way residents gave their oppressors an essential mark of failure in their performance. "I took part in marches fighting for better rights and treatment but police just wouldn't do their job correctly. Witnessing crimes and being embarrassed by police mistreatment made change necessary."[37] To my mind, the dark side of the CJS made itself clearly apparent in the many provocative encounters they had with the Black community. Police saw Blacks as lazy, criminal, endlessly unemployed, irresponsible, thieves, redolent in drug mannerisms, and uncaring about the future. Because of this frightful racist belief in the worthiness of Black people of all ages, police gave in to their worst instincts. What occurred was an endless series of war crimes that left victims gasping for breath. It is an ugly picture that appears.

> "We seemed like enemies to the police and the CJS. Police encounters were always unpleasant. We knew them. Lawyers were worthless because people of color would most likely go to jail. All the time the focus was on race. It all ended in prison where you were lucky if you left there alive."[38] "Courts favored White people more and seemed to give prison sentences only for Black people."[39]

"Back then the police had a field day with our lives. Remember there were no cell phones to record things."[40]

One woman[41] remembered a cop giving her thirteen tickets based on false allegations. She then went to court to report the baseless incidents and the judge dropped all the tickets, telling her "it will not happen again." But, of course, it did, and she was back without a successful outcome. This was the banner that typified the entire Black community of New York City from 1960 to 1990.

To some degree, this study traverses already known territory. The quotes used have appeared elsewhere in conjunction with a steady drumbeat of complaints about police and CJS brutality. We merely raised the ante by describing this kind of behavior, in the context of the then–War on Crime, as shocking war crimes themselves. This raises the ante by recognizing what earlier social scientists have failed to do—apply basic standards of humanity and human rights to the CJS which should have followed these already established international rules. We have tried to combine historical data, personal testimonies, and ethical guidelines to better judge this period of state-owned repression of the Black community. This reckoning of what the CJS did during these years in a period of acute civil rights turmoil was not rectified at the time. Government employees, especially cops, were aided by numerous vested interests in hiding their crimes while ignoring their victims. We have tried to give this imbalance the justice and recognition it deserves. Sadly, it is far too late to rectify that imbalance. The most that can be done, as journalist Deborah Lipstadt reminds us in a similar case of postwar Nazi ability to escape justice, is to at least recognize and acknowledge it.[42]

NOTES

1. D. Quentin Miller, *A Criminal Power, James Baldwin and the Law* (Columbus: Ohio State University, 2012), p. 3, 21, 50, 64 and 87; theatre critic of the Long Beach Press-Telegraph, 1963; Webster Smalley (ed.), *Five Plays by Langston Hughes* (Bloomington: Indiana UP, 1963), p. vii; and Jame Baldwin, *Nobody Knows My Name* (New York: Laurel Books, 1961), p. 62.

2. Douglas Field book review of William J. Maxwell's *FB Eyes, How J. Edgar Hoover Ghost Readers Framed African American Literature* (Princeton: Princeton UP, 2015), The Times Literary Supplement, 29 May 2020, p. 13.

3. Man respondent comments from the survey #111, interviewed 21 February 2015.

4. Woman respondent comments from the survey #44, 4 February 2015.

5. Vincent Cannato, *The Ungovernable City, John Lindsay and his Struggle to Save New York* (New York: Basic Books, 2001), pp. 6–7.

6. Man respondent, #13, 16 September 2015.

7. Traci Burch, *Trading Democracy for Justice. Criminal Convictions and the Decline of Neighborhood Political Parties* (Chicago: Chicago University Press, 2013)), p. 7, 8, 10 and 14.

8. Ibid., p. 171.

9. George Brager, *Community Organizing* (New York: Columbia UP, 1987), p. 68.

10. Ibid., pp. 70–75.

11. Man respondent, #61, 21 February, 2015.

12. Man respondent, #74, 13 October 2015.

13. Woman respondent, #37, 21 February 2015.

14. Man respondent, #112, 3 March 2015.

15. Man respondent, #83, 12 April 2015.

16. Peter Goldman, *Report from Black America* (New York: Simon & Schuster, 1970), p. 147 and 149.

17. Redditt Hudson, "Being a Cop Showed me Just How Racist and Violent Police Are," *Washington Post*, 6 December 2014.

18. Man respondent, #22, 7 October 2015.

19. Woman respondent, #49, 4 April 2015.

20. Male respondent, #82, 16 November 2015.

21. Woman respondent, #28, 3 March 2015.

22. Woman respondent, #9, 9 April 2015.

23. Man respondent, #93, 1 November 2015.

24. Man respondent, #70, 4 March 2015.

25. Man respondent, #38, 27 October 2015.

26. Man respondent, #77, 8 February 2015.

27. Man respondent, #53, 26 September 2015.

28. Man respondent, #8, 3 October 2015.

29. Woman respondent, #42, 16 November 2015.

30. Robert Fisher, *Let the People Decide—Neighborhood Organizing in America* (New York: Thwayne Publ., 1994), pp. xii, 126–130 and 138.

31. Man respondent, #34, 18 November 2015.

32. Woman respondent, #66, 4 March 2015.

33. Woman respondent, #49, 25 September 2015

34. Man respondent, #115, 3 November 2015.

35. Man respondent, #94, 3 October 2015.

36. Man respondent, #14, 24 September 2015.

37. Man respondent, #13, 8 February 2015.

38. Woman respondent, #41, 17 March 2015.

39. Man respondent, #94, 27 October 2015.

40. Woman respondent, #26, 30 November 2015.

41. Woman respondent, #59, 6 March 2015.

42. Deborah Lipstadt, "The Triumph of Deaths, How Many Nazis Escaped Prosecution?" a book review of European historian, Professor Mary Fulbrook's *Reckoning-Legacies of Nazi Prosecution and the Quest for Justice* (Oxford UP, 2019) in The Times Literary Supplement, 1 March 2019, p. 13.

Conclusion

The high rates of Black arrests and incarceration from 1960 to 1990 as portrayed in this turbulent study did not just happen. They were the end result of deliberate government policies and a zealous CJS. Republicans allied with Southern Democrats, as well as many Northern Democrats all played their part. There were exceptions but most of them took no notice of how their anticrime policies and apprehensions would injure and derail Black political objectives while ignoring Black family and community life all of which suffered every time a Black man was stopped and detained by police. Maybe that was the point. Because thousands of Black men spent much of their time behind bars, perhaps one in three at some point in this era, in jails, camps, detention centers, drug clinics, and prisons while White politicians did what they could, fortified with White nationalist rhetoric, to derail Black economic and political gains. Republicans and Southern Democrats must have really hated Black people for they were willing to sacrifice core beliefs and accept deficit government spending on anticrime programs, expanded government, and bloated bureaucracy, fattened by large budgets and minimum supervision. Sadly, we have no significant memoirs, secondary literature, diaries or interpretative art from the period to adequately document either the memories of persecuted Black residents or the CJS personnel who pursued racist activities.

Repressed ghettoes felt the worst of it. Some Whites cared little if Black people even deserved a future. Morality was flexible, and Black dissidents were not always greeted with enthusiasm by White revolutionaries much less the great White public at large. Even to this day, there is one topic few Whites of this period talk about: Their participation in any form to the widespread racism and brutality of the period. There is still little effort to engage in adequate reckoning with the enormity of crimes in which so many Whites were engaged.[1]

Perpetual bondage backed by a zealous CJS capable of perpetuating war crimes that were completely unaccountable ruled the day. Some parts of the country were worse than others, and traditionally the Deep South was the worse for more arrests, punitive sentences, long incarcerations, and miserable prison conditions. But everywhere, Black communities were treated by police as free-fire zones in a war against crime. The 1930s and 1940s had seen police departments recruited by big businesses to fight trade unions and labor discontent with brute force. By 1960 this was a thing of the past while civil rights disorder, racial segregation, and the Watts riots turned police attention to Black defiance and these they fought with relish.

In place of humane negotiations or purposeful human-oriented rehabilitation projects and community improvement programs, police oppression was the best politicians could do to repel Black demands for equality and social justice. This is why the label of "war crimes" as it applies to CJS behavior is used so often in this analysis. CJS practitioners had the wrong skill set, experiences, cultural misunderstanding with an empty attitude when attempting to "help." Moreover, personal ambition and the conservative nature of the CJS continually got in the way of proper service to the Black community. Then there were those unqualified individuals with stark racist attitudes who saw Whites as superior and Blacks as inferior. They were the wrong people to put in charge and when it happened, as it so often did, the results led to terrible consequences. CJS officials too often disregarded human rights violations leaving CJS agents free rein in pursuing Black offenders. In my view, two-thirds of CJS appointments in this period should never have been made by administrators and upper management possessing terrible intuition at divining who would make a good CJS agent.

It is an underlying proposition of this study that the expanding American State for a period that featured a War on Crime was an agent of crime causation. While crime can be seen as a social judgment about behavior emanating from an authority with political power to legislate and punish, it can also be seen as responsible for creating the conditions and administrative decisions that produce crime itself. Berk and Brackman are of the belief that the really important anticrime decisions were not made by politicians no matter how tough they were on crime but by agents of the CJS (i.e., wardens, judges, cops, prosecutors) who would commit crime in pursuit of curbing it. It has also been pointed out this was an undemocratic CJS venture completely as "criminal legislation was conducted with little public interest or participation by citizens who were both unorganized and disinterested."[2]

More importantly here, how likely was it that in attempting to curb crime, officials of the CJS overmanaged, overindulged, and overutilized their powers to cause undue and ill-considered harm on individuals arbitrarily labeled criminals? How likely was it that in such a zeal to punish prejudged people, fascist-leaning police and court officials (i.e., judges, lawyers, and prosecutors) used brutal, unconstitutional, and abusive methods of crime fighting that caused them to shift away from crime fighting to the state protecting those agents whose behavior had transformed them into war criminals? Such abusive behavior on the part of the police discloses as much about the White nationalist war mentality and methods of retribution of those responsible for the maintenance of authority and about the pattern of incidence of state-sponsored war criminality than about the prevalence of street crime itself. The remainder of the study has attempted to present the many different ways these CJS representatives committed war crimes that went unaccountable. Indeed, in this endeavor, the CJS was a criminal organization that waged a war of aggression in violation of human rights.

Many of these representatives of the state with their multiple ways of mistreating Black citizens were highly educated and respected people like congressmen, academics, and professional types. "All of them have in common," says Dr. Cohen who was a survivor of a Nazi concentration camp,

> a callous lack of consideration and human regard for, and an unprincipled willingness to abuse their power over the poor, unfortunate, defenseless creatures who had been deprived of their rights by a ruthless and criminal government . . . and who obeyed the dictates of political leadership rather than the ethics of their profession. Knowledge, wealth or cultural accomplishments are not the slightest guarantee that the individual who has acquired them is at the same time a man of high character.[3]

Eight years into Richard Nixon's administration, at the height of his War on Crime, Max Belli, a prominent criminal lawyer in San Francisco, had much to say about the CJS he battled in the many court trials he waged. His insider views provide a lengthy, damning rebuke. Here he is in 1976:

> The CJS was lopsided; the system from the cops to the judges, had already determined in advance which criminals would be vacationing in Acapulco and which would be spending time in San Quentin, Folsom or Alcatraz (California's worst prisons). The police (as well as the judges) were adequately equipped to handle the guy who stole a rutabaga from a Third Street market but they didn't have the smarts to do anything about the Stanford graduate who was floating a phony stock scheme, swindling not one but hundreds. State and federal

prosecutors barely lifted a finger against the corporate plunderers who stole from the People at large on the grandest scale . . . as far as I could see the Courts were trampling on the rights of the accused in a way that didn't square with the constitutional law, I learned in law school. For most of the nation's history it has been far too easy for local, state and federal officers to ignore constitutional guarantees and almost as easy for the courts to go along with them as judges were on the side of the law and against those who broke it. Never mind the niceties of the constitution. The constitutional freedom against self-incrimination? The constitutional right to a free trial? They meant nothing.[4]

Criminal defense lawyer Cochran had his own take on how the aggressiveness of the police was seen by different constituents of Los Angeles where he worked:

Most people welcomed the increasing militarization of the police . . . which was good, as far as the White majority was concerned, because it kept the police out of sight until you called them and then they came pretty quickly. More importantly, it allowed Los Angeles to police its vast area with very few officers which meant very cheaply. Latinos and African Americans took a different view of this process since they were treated differently by the police from the start.[5]

In this war, ill-tempered militaristic cops and swat teams were assigned to oversee Black offenders. Militaristic cops with keen authoritarian personalities, some of them developed while in combat situations in Vietnam, were seen as perfect for taming Black criminals and drug addicts. Two-thirds of these appointments probably should never have been made as agreed by the people of Harlem who we interviewed about their experiences with the local CJS. The wrong people were in charge of hiring the worst candidates to eventually do a miserable job at reducing the incidents of crime in the neighborhood. It is tempting to conclude that we lived in a world governed by genocidal and callous politicians too stupid to appreciate the cumulative destruction of African American careers, job development, family life, and community bonds for men having political ambitions of their own.

We have addressed the faults and failures of LEAA which was set in motion to help bring relief and innovative projects to Black communities. It was developed as a streamlined process for funding agencies and local programs for the benefit of Black neighborhoods. This never happened. White politicians and administrators got their hands on the reins and steered vast sums of money to pet projects, favorite friends, and ideas they hoped with springboard them to fame and success.

None of this occurred because, again, the wrong people were in charge of hiring and administering. Certainly, the worst types of hacks were available for hire. Zimbardo tells us,

> If a system of death camps were set up in the United States of the sort seen in Nazi Germany, one would be able to find sufficient personnel for those camps in any medium sized American town. This is because most people under particular circumstances have the capacity for extreme violence and destruction of human life if obsessed with the lesson of national security.[6]

One might easily add police officers to this group. Professor Erwin Staub (emeritus University of Massachusetts who studied mass violence and genocide) underscored Zimbardo's observation with one of his own: "Great evil that arises out of ordinary thinking is created by ordinary people and is the norm, not the exception. It evolves with a progression along a continuum of destruction . . . if demanded by a higher-level authoritarian system."[7]

LEAA has already been described as inept and badly directed. In fact, many police departments might well have been forced to devise benign and more community-oriented plans with Black community leaders had they not been overwhelmed with LEAA's federal money earmarked for riot control, swat teams, and tactical squads against Black power groups. Monies were also handed out for computer systems that helped in cataloging the names of most local residents for purposes of linking them to suspected leftist political activities. All encouraged by LEAA.

The era realized the growing power of the state with its transparent cruelty toward its citizens, notably its Black ones. An almost universal knee-jerk simple answer by politicians of both parties to the perceived drug and crime response was to militarize the police and weaponize the CJS. To this extent, White nationalists who supported such policies were satisfied. For over fifteen years we witnessed a steady expansion of law enforcement brutality as if that alone would end crime, the heel on the neck approach. As it turned out, there was the accompanying widening of state intervention in the daily lives of Black citizens who deserved instead governmental support in satisfying demands for social justice and civil rights.

These men we are discussing, who caused so much suffering and grief in the Black ghettoes, were neither exceptionally smart nor exceptionally stupid. Cohen reminds us that of the 21 major Nazi criminals who were tried at Nuremberg in 1945, 17 had intelligence over 120 (80%).

> Lack of intellect was not necessary in order to join the SS . . . accepting their ideology of hate was a more influencing factor. The United States, which has

produced so many thousands of infantile young men, was itself emotionally immature . . . many of these men with an intellectual age of about ten years.[8]

It is the hope that this study will help clarify some of the serious issues at stake when a CJS decides to wage an all-out war on citizens who represent a demographic that is exploited to their disadvantage. In such situations, what is wanted is a wholesale house cleaning of the entire bureaucracy and replacement of its guardians by people with a different set of morals and peaceful, conciliatory attitudes, if the country is to survive the terrors and horrors that took place to the American Black population between 1960 and 1990.

NOTES

1. See the similar case for Germans after the war in Mary Fulbrook's analysis, "Peace with Dishonour,' in The Times Literary Supplement, 24 December 2021, p. 12.

2. Richard A. Berk, Harold Brackman and Selma Lesser, *A Measure of Justice: An Empirical Study of Change in California Penal Code* (New York: Academic Press, 1977), p. 257 and 236.

3. Dr. Ellie A. Cohen, *Human Behavior in the Concentration Camp* (New York: Grosset & Dunlap, 1953), p. 237, 267 and 281.

4. Max Belli, *My Life on Trial: An Autobiography* (New York: Morrow, 1976), p. 82–83.

5. Johnnie Cochran, Jr. with Tim Rutten, *Journey to Justice* (New York: Ballantine, 1996), p. 77.

6. Philip G. Zimbardo, *The Lucifer Effect* (New York: Random House, 2007), p. 190, 195 and 281.

7. Op. cit., p. 286.

8. Cohen, op. cit., p. 221 and 237.

Appendix

Criminal Justice Historical Witness Survey

Age_____ Gender_____ BP_____ Political Party_____Occup:

Ethnicity___When you were 21: Did you vote____Crime victim_____
 Where were you living_____

-Witness police brutality?_____Did you protest against this? YES NO How?

--Witness a riot?_____ Witness a crime?_____Face unemployment?_____
 Have drug problem?___

---Do you believe police brought DRUGS into your neighborhood? YES NO
 DK

---Were most police arrests in your area:

FAIR_____UNFAIR_____BOGUS___ILLEGAL___CHEAP____

---Were police then on a QUOTA system when making arrests? YES NO DK
 How do you know?

---Did you see police take money to NOT make an arrest (from drug sellers,
 prostitutes)? YES NO DK

---Did police stop/harass you on a regular basis when you were 16–21?
 _____

---Ever arrested where you saw the system from the inside? YES NO what
 did you see?

REPORT CARD GRADE (A tops to F failure) for these criminal justice
 agencies when you were 21:

POLICE_____

why?_____

CRIMINAL COURTS_____ why?
_____

CORRECTIONS (jails, juvenile detention, prisons) _____

why?_____

PROBATION SERVICES_____

why?_____
LAWYERS/PUBLIC DEFENDERS? _____
why?_____
REHAB DRUG AGENCIES_____
why?_____
COMMUNITY GROUPS TO HELP EX-OFFENDERS_____
why?_____
At age 21 was your neighborhood: fun_____ dangerous_____ boring_____
   ugly_____ OTHER:
Did your family ever receive any GOVERNMENT AID? YES NO what kind:
What POLITICAL LEADER(s) did you admire at age
21_____
Was RACE a major problem for you? YES NO
Explain_____
Were your TEENAGE years happy ones? YES NO
Explain_____
What was your FAMILY LIFE like for you then?
Did you ever join a protest, demonstrate, or challenge the system? YES NO
   How? _____
YOUR OWN COMMENTS:

Bibliography

Adorno, Theodor W., and Elise Frenkel-Brunswick, Daniel L. Levinson, and R. N. Sanford. *The Authoritarian Personality* (New York: Harper & Row, 1950).

Alex, Nicholas. *New York City Cops Talk Back: A Study of a Beleaguered Minority* (New York: Wiley, 1971).

Alexander, Michelle. *The New Jim Crow-Mass Incarceration in an Age of Colorblindness* (Seattle: New Press, 2012).

Alpert, Geoffrey P. Police Use of Deadly Force: The Miami Experience. In Roger G. Dunham and G. P. Alpert (eds.), *Critical Issues in Policing: Contemporary Readings* (Prospect Heights: Waveland, 1989).

America, Richard F. The Case of the Racist Researcher. In Joyce A. Ladner (ed.), *The Death of White America* (New York: Random House, 1973).

Anderson, Elijah. *Code of the Street, Decency, Violence and the Moral Life of the Inner City* (New York: Norton, 2000).

———. *Problems of the Century: Racial Stratification and the United States* (New York: Russell Sage, 2001).

Arendt, Hannah. *Eichmann in Jerusalem* (New York: Viking Press, 1963).

———. *Origins of Totalitarianism* (New York: Harcourt, Brace, Jovanovich, 1968).

Armstrong, Andrea. *Prison Conditions* (New York: Oxford University Press, 2017).

———. Race, Prison Disciple & the Law. *University of California Irvine Law Review* 101 (2015): 759–782.

Ash, Timothy G. *The File: A Personal History* (New York: Vantage, 1977).

Bailey, W. C. Correctional Outcomes: An Evaluation of 100 Reports. *Journal of Criminal Law, Criminology and Police Science* 57 (1966): 153–160.

Baldwin, Davarian L. Recorded in the Black Belt and Ivory Towers: The Place of Race in the United States Social Thought 1892–1948. *Critical Sociology* 30, no. 2 (2004): 397–450.

Baldwin, James. *Nobody Knows My Name* (New York: Laurel, 1961).

Balko, Radley. *Rise of the Warrior Cop: The Militarization of American Police Forces* (New York: Public Affairs, 2013).

Barmaki, Reza. Explanations of Blacks' Criminality in America, 1630–1950. *Deviant Behavior* 41, no. 10 (2010): 1305–1329.

Bauman, Zygmunt. *Modernity and the Holocaust* (Ithaca: Cornell University Press, 1985).

Bayley, D. H., and H. Mendelson. *Minorities and the Police* (New York: Free Press, 1969).

Becker, Andrew, and G. W. Schulz. Cops Ready for War. *Daily Beast*, 2 February 2011.

Bell, Derrick A. Racism in American Courts-Cause for Black Disruption or Despair. *California Law Review* 61 (1973): 165.

Belli, Max. *My Life on Trial: An Autobiography* (New York: Morrow, 1976).

Benner, Lawrence A. Tokenism and the American Indigent: Some Perspectives on Defender Services. *ACLU Newsletter*, Spring 1975.

Bennett, L. A. Should We Change the Offender or the System? *Crime & Delinquency* 19 (1973): 332–342.

Berk, Richard A., Harold Brachman, and Selma Lesser. *A Measure of Justice: An Empirical Study of Changes in California's Penal Code* (New York: Academic Press, 1977).

Bhambra, Gurminder K. A Sociological Dilemma-Race, Segregation and U.S. Sociology. *Current Society* 62, no. 4 (2014): 472–492.

Billingsley, Andrew. Black Families and White Social Sciences. In Joyce A. Ladner (ed.), op. cit.

Binder, Arnold, and Peter Scharf. *The Badge and the Bullet-Police Use of Deadly Force* (New York: Praeger, 1983).

Binder, Arnold, Peter Scharf, and Gilbert Geis. *Methods of Research in Criminology* (New York: McGraw-Hill, 1983).

Bing, Stephen R., and Stephen Rosenfeld. *The Quality of Justice in the Lower Criminal Courts of Metropolitan Boston* (Westborough: NextStage Vintage, 1970).

Black, Donald. The Social Organization of Arrest. *Stanford Law Review* 23, no. 6 (1971): 1087.

Blackwell, James E., and Morris Janowitz (eds.). *Black Sociologists-Historical and Contemporary Perspectives* (Chicago: Chicago University Press, 1974).

Blauner, Robert. Internal Colonialism and Ghetto Revolt. *Social Problems* 10, no. 4 (1969).

Boardman, Roger. The New Negro Mood. *Fortune Magazine*, June 1960.

Borchard, Edwin. *Convicting the Innocent-Errors of Criminal Justice* (New Haven: Yale University Press, 1932).

Boyd, V. *Wrapped in Rainbows: The Life of Zora Neale Hurston* (New York: Scribners, 2003).

Bracey, John H., Jr. *Black Nationalism* (New York: Macmillan, 1970).

Bracey, John H., Jr., August Meier, and Elliot Rudnick. Black Society's First Half Century. In Joyce A. Ladner (ed.), op. cit. (1973).

Brager, George. *Community Organizing* (New York: Columbia University Press, 1987).

Brakke, Paul. *The Price of Justice in America-Commentaries on the Criminal Justice System: Ways to Fix What's Wrong* (Columbia: Changemakers, 2017).

Brandel, Steven G. *Police in America* (Beverly Hills: Sage, 2020).

Breitman, George. *The Last Years of Malcolm X, Evolution of a Revolutionary* (New York: Pathfinder, 1970).

Brooks, Rosa. Tangled Up in Blue. In *The Times Literary Supplement*, 10 July 2021.

Brown, Lee. Crime and Criminal Justice in the Black Community. *Journal of African American Issues* 11 (1974): 3–11.

Browning, Christopher R. *Ordinary Men* (New York: Harper/Collins, 2017).

Buck, Marilyn. The Struggle for Status Under International Law, U.S. Political Prisoners and the Political Offense Exception to Extradition. In Joy James (ed.), *Imprisoned Intellectuals, American Political Prisoners Write on Life, Liberation and Rebellion* (Lanham: Rowman & Littlefield, 2002).

Burch, Traci. *Trading Democracy for Justice, Criminal Convictions and the Decline of Neighborhood Political Parties* (Chicago: Chicago University Press, 2013).

Burnham, David. Police Violence and a Changing Pattern. *New York Times*, 7 July 1968.

Burns, Robert P. *Kafka's Law, The Trial of American Criminal Justice* (Chicago: Chicago University Press, 2014).

Burwell, William R. *Police Brutality and Authoritarianism: A Locus of Control* (Chicago: Illinois Institute of Technology, 1983).

Butler, Paul. *Chokehold, Policing Black Men* (New York: New Press, 2018).

Calahan, Margaret W., and Lee Anne Parsons. *Historical Corrections Statistics, 1850–1984* (Rockville: Westat, 1986).

Cannato, Vincent. *The Unforgiveable City-John Lindsay and His Struggle to Save New York* (New York: Basic Books, 2001).

Carbery, Genievieve. Alcohol More Dangerous Than Cocaine. *Irish Times*, 11 February 2010.

Carle, Robert. Police Unions and the Conservative Conscience. *americaninterest .com*, 2020.

Carlson, H., and M. S. Sutton. The Effects of Different Police Roles on Attitudes and Values. *Journal of Psychology* 91 (1975): 57–64.

Cellars, Emanuel. *Congressional Hearings Before the Subcommittee, 92nd Congress, 1st Session* (Washington DC: USGPO, May–June 1971).

Census of Nation's Jails. *The 1972 Survey of Inmates of Local Jails* (Washington DC: USGPO, May 1975).

Chadwick, Bruce. *Baseball's Home Town Teams, The Story of the Minor Leagues* (New York: Abbeville, 1994).

Chafe, William, and William Gavins. *Remembering Jim Crow: African Americans Tell About Life in the Segregated South* (New York: New Press, 2011).

Chambers, James A. *Blacks & Crime: A Function of Class* (Westport: Praeger, 1995).

Chasin, Alexander. *Assassin of Youth, a Kaleidoscopic History of Henry Anslinger's War on Drugs* (Chicago: Chicago University Press, 2014).

Chevigny, P. *Police Power* (New York: Pantheon, 1969).

Chung, Ed with Betsy Pearl, and Lea Hunter. *The 1994 Crime Bill Continues to Undercut Justice Reform. Here's How to Stop It* (Washington DC: The Sentencing Project, March 2019).

Churchill, Ward, and Jim Vanderwall. *Prisoners of War-The Legal Standing and Members of National Liberation Movements in Cages of Steel-The Politics of Imprisonment in the United States* (Washington: Maison-Neuve, 1992).

Clark, Kenneth B., and Jeanette Hopkins. *A Relevant War Against Poverty: A Study of Community Action Programs and Observable Social Change* (New York: Harper & Row, 1969).

———. *Dark Ghetto-Dilemmas of Social Change* (New York: Harper & Row, 1965).

———. *HARYOU: Harlem Youth in the Ghetto, a Study of the Consequences of Power Lessons and a Blueprint for Change* (Harlem Youth Opportunities Unlimited, 1962).

———. Introduction to an Epilogue. In Joyce A. Ladner, op. cit.

Clark, Robert S. *The Criminal Justice System, an Analytical Approach* (Boston: Allyn & Bacon, 1982).

Cochrane, Johnnie, Jr., and Tim Rutten. *Journey to Justice* (New York: Ballantine, 1997).

Cohen, Ellie A. *Human Behavior in a Concentration Camp* (New York: Grosset & Dunlap, 1953).

Colaianni, Paul. *Dealing with Selfish People That Don't Care If They Hurt You* (Arlington: The Overwhelmed Brain Workbook Website, Private, 2013).

Comey, James. *BBC News Magazine Website*, 18 July 2016.

Conant, James B. *Slums & Suburbs* (New York: McGraw-Hill, 1961).

Constas, Helen. Max Weber's Two Conceptions of Bureaucracy. *American Journal of Sociology* 63 (1958): 400–409.

Conyers, John. *Oversight Hearings Before a Subcommittee on the Judiciary and Crime* (Washington DC: USGPO, 1981).

Corley, Cheryl L. President Johnson's Crime Commission Report 50 Years Later. *Chicago NPR*, 6 October 2017.

Corley, John A. (ed.). *The 1967 Presidential Crime Commission Report Its Impact 25 Years Later* (Highland Park: North Kentucky University, 1994).

Cray, Ed. *The Enemy in the Streets-Police Malpractice in America* (New York: Anchor, 1992).

Cunningham, David. *Klansville USA. The Rise and Fall of the KKK in the Civil Rights Era* (New York: Oxford University Press, 2013).

———. What Policing Responses to White Power in the 1960s Can Teach Us About Dismantling White Supremacy Today. *conversation.com*, 2021.

Currie, Elliott. *PBS Website New River Interview, Failure of the War on Crime*. Host Ben Wattenberg, 2000.

Dahl, James, James Intagliata, John K. Wing and Kevin Baker. *Improved Social Services of the City of New York, Workshop Executive Training Program* (Washington DC: Department of Justice, 1978).

Davey, Joseph D. *The Politics of Prison Expansion: Winning Elections by Waging War on Crime* (Westport: Praeger, 1998).

Davidowicz, Lucy. *The Holocaust and the Historians* (Cambridge: Harvard University Press, 1981).

Davies, Allyson Ross. Assessing Outcomes of Medical Crime, Some Lessons for Criminal Offender Rehabilitation. In Lee Sechrist (ed.), p. 286.

Davis, Angela Y. *Autobiography* (New York: International Publishers, 1974).

———. Political Prisoners, Prisons and Black Liberation. In Joy James (ed.), *The Angela Davis Reader* (New York: Wiley/Blackwell, 1998).

———. Race and Criminalization: Black Crime and the Punishment Industry. In Wahneema Lubiano (ed.), *The House that Race Built, Black America, U.S. Terrain* (New York: Pantheon, 1997).

Debro, Julius, and Helen Taylor. *Study of Status of Black Crime in the United States* (College Park: National Institute of Justice, University of Maryland, 1977).

Denziger, Steven R. *The Real War on Crime, Report on the National Criminal Justice Commission* (Washington DC: USGPO, 1996).

Donley, Genie A. *The Gathering Storm. The Role of White Nationalism in U.S. Politics* (Cleveland: Cleveland SU Online, 2018).

Drake, St. Clair. *Black Metropolis Revisited* (New York: The Drake Papers).

Duffee, David E., and F. A. Hussey. The Community Context of Probation in Planning. In *Probation, Parole and Community New Services, Policy, Structures and Processes* (Scranton: Harper & Row, 1980).

Dunbar, Tony. *Delta Time: Journey Through Mississippi* (New York: Pantheon, 1990).

Duncier, Mitchell. *Ghetto to Invention of a Place: The History of an American Idea* (New York: Farrar, Straus & Giroux, 2016).

Editor Jail Management. *Who's Who in Jail Management*, 5th edition (Washington DC: American Prisons Association, 2007).

Ellison, Ralph. An American Dilemma: A Review of Myrdal's American Dilemma. In Joyce A. Ladner (ed.), op. cit., (1973).

Elsner, Alan. *Courts of Injustice: The Crisis in American Prisons* (Saddle River: Prentice-Hall, 2004).

Elwell, Frank. *Sociology of Max Weber* (Claremore: Rogers SU Website, 1996).

English, T. S. *The Savage City: Race, Murder and a Generation on Edge* (New York: Morrow, 2011).

Erickson, Charles L. *The Perils of Probation* (Springfield: Charles C. Thomas, 1980).

Evans, Art. Importance of Race Among Black Sociologists. *Sociological Quarterly* 21 (1980): 23–34.

Fagan, Ginger Ann. *The Relevant Lawyers, Conversations Out of Court on Their Clients, Their Practice, Their Politics and Their Lifestyle* (New York: Simon & Schuster, 1972).

Fairclough, Adam. *Martin Luther King, Jr.* (Athens: University of Georgia Press, 1995).

Falco, Mathea. *Drugs and Crime Across America: Police Chiefs Speak Out, Nation, Survey Among Chiefs of Police* (Washington DC: Peter Hart, 2004).

Farrell, Stephen. *Rethinking What Works With Offenders and Probationers: Social Content and Desistance From Crime* (New York: Routledge, 2002).

Farrell, Victoria L. The Effectiveness of Training for Correctional Officers in the Performance of Their Job. In *Scholar's Archive for Criminal Justice* (Albany: SUNY, 2015).

Fayer, Roland C. An Empirical Analysis of Racial Differences in Police Use of Force. *Journal of Political Economy* (2016).

Feely, Malcolm M. How to Think About Criminal Court Reform. *Boston Law Review* 98 (2018): 673.

Ferner, Matt. Here's How Often Cops Are Arrested for Breaking the Law They're Paid to Uphold. *Washington Post*, 24 June 2016.

Feuer, Louis S. Economic Factors in History. *Science & Society* (1940).

Field, Douglas. *FB Eyes, How J. Edgar Hoover's Ghost Readers Framed African American Literature* (Princeton: Princeton University Press, 2011).

Fisher, Robert. *Let the People Decide-Neighborhood Organizations in America* (New York: Thwayne, 1994).

Fitzgerald, Kelly. *Why Alcohol is the Deadliest Drug.* Addiction Center of New Jersey, December 2017.

Flamm, Michael W. *Law and Order, Street Crime and Civil Unrest and the Crisis of Liberalism in the 1960s* (New York: Columbia University Press, 2005).

Fogel, David. *The Emergence of Probation as a Profession in the Service of Public Safety: The Next Ten Years* (Washington DC: USGPO, 1984).

Frankel, Marvin E. *Criminal Sentences: Law Without Order* (New York: Hill & Wang, 1973).

Freed, David J., and Patricia M. Ward. Bail in the United States: 1964. In *Proceedings of the National Conference on Bail and Justice*, 27–29 May 1964 (Washington DC: Department of Justice, April 1965).

Friedman, Leon (ed.). *Southern Justice* (New York: Pantheon, 1966).

Friedrich, Robert J. *Police Shootings in Pennsylvania: An Analysis of Two Decades of Deadly Force.* Ph.D. dissertation (Philadelphia: Temple University, 1995).

Fulbrook, Mary, Peace with Dishonour, in The Times Literary Supplement, 24 October 2021, p. 12.

Fyfe, James J. Geographic Correlates of Police shootings, a Microanalysis. *Journal of Research in Crime & Delinquency* 17 (1980): 101–113.

———. Race and Extreme Police Citizen Violence. In R. L. McNeeley and Carl E. Pope (eds.), *Race, Crime and Criminal Justice* (Beverly Hills: Sage, 1981).

———. *Readings on Police Use of Deadly Force* (Washington DC: Police Foundation, 1982).

Galvin, James, Jane Maxwell, and Frank Kellum. *Shock Probation and More.* Draft Report From National Probation Reporting Study, National Council on Crime & Delinquency, 16 June 1981.

Gaukruger, Stephen. How Psychology Failed to Test. *The Times Literary Supplement*, 1 January 2021.

Geller, William A., and Hans Toch. *Police Violence: Understanding and Controlling Police Abuse of Force* (New Haven: Yale University Press, 1976).

Geller, William A., Hans Toch, and Kevin Karales. *Split-Second Decisions-Shootings Of and By Chicago Police* (Chicago: Chicago Law Enforcement Study Group, 1981).

Gendreau, Paul, and James Bonita. Reexamining the Cruel and Unusual Punishment of Prisons and Prison Life. *Law & Human Behavior* 14 (1990): 347.

Gibbons, D. C. Differential Treatment and Interpersonal Maturity Levels Theory: A Critique. *Social Science Review* 44 (1970): 22–33.

Gilford, John. *Pimping Fictions-African American Literature and the Untold Story of Black Pulp Fiction* (Philadelphia: Temple University Press, 2013).

Gist, N. D., and S. F. Fava. *Urban Sociology* (New York: Free Press, 1965).

Goines, Donald. *White Man's Justice, Black Man's Grief* (Los Angeles: Holloway House, 1975.)

Goldman, Peter. *Report from Black America* (New York: Simon & Schuster, 1970).

Gonzalez van Cleve, Nicola. *Crook County, Racism and Injustice in America's Largest Criminal Court* (Stanford: Stanford University Press, 2016).

Green, Dan S., and Edwin D. Driver. W.E.B. DuBois-A Case in the Sociology of Social Negation. *Phylon* 37, no. 4 (1976): 308–333.

Greenberg, Herbert M. The Development of an Integration Attitude Scale, *Journal of Social Psychology* 54 (1961): 103–109.

Grier, William K., and Price M. Cobbs. *Black Rage* (New York: Basic Books, 1968).

Griffin, John Howard. *Black Like Me* (New York: Houghton Mifflin, 1961).

Hadjor, Kofi B. *Another America*: *The Politics of Race and Blame* (Boston: South End Press, 1995).

Hagan, John L. *Crime and Disrepute* (Thousand Oaks: Sage, 1994).

———. *Modern Criminology, Crime, Criminal Behavior and Its Control* (New York: McGraw Hill, 1987).

———. *Who Are the Criminals? The Politics of Crime Policy from the Age of Roosevelt to the Age of Reagan* (Princeton: Princeton University Press, 2010).

Halleck, Seymour L. *Psychiatry and Dilemmas of Crime: A Study of Causes of Punishment and Treatment* (New York: Harper & Row, 1967).

Haney, Craig. *From Prison to Home: The Effect of Incarceration and Re-Entry on Children, Families and Communities. The Psychological Impact of Incarceration With Implications for Post-Prison Adjustment* (Washington DC: Health & Human Services, 2001).

Hare, Nathan. Challenge of a Black Scholar. *Black Scholar* 1 (1968): 58–63.

Haring, Sid, Tony Platt, Richard Speigelman, and Paul Takagi. The Management of Police Killings. *Crime and Social Justice* 8 (1977).

Harriot, Michael. White Men Can't Murder. Why White Cops Are Immune to the Law. *The Root*, June 2017.

Havenstrite, Alfred L. *About Probation Practices in Texas, Criminal Justice*. Monograph (Huntsville: Sam Houston State College, 1969).

Hayes, Chris. *A Colony in a Nation* (New York: Norton, 2017).

Hayward, Clarissa Role. *Justice and the American Metropolis* (Minneapolis: University of Minnesota Press, 2011).

———. Responsibility and Ignorance on Dismantling Structural Injustice. *Journal of Politics* 79, no. 2 (2012): 396–408.

Henderson, Joel H., and David R. Simon. *Crime of the Criminal Justice System* (London: Routledge, 1994).

Henick, Peter, and Randy Furst. Cops-Same Role, New Tactics. In Arthur Niederhofer and Abraham S. Blumberg (eds.), *The Ambivalent Force-Perspectives on the Police* (New York: Ginn, 1970).

Henry, Stuart, and Mark Lanier. *What is Crime? Controversies Over the Nature of Crime and What to Do About It* (New York: Rowman & Littlefield, 2001).

Heppner, Robert. *The Untherapeutic Community: Organizational Behavior in a Failed Addiction Treatment Program* (Lincoln: University of Nebraska Press, 1983).

Hinton, Elizabeth. *From the War on Poverty to the War on Crime: The Making of Mass Incarceration in America* (Cambridge: Harvard University Press, 2017).

Hirsh, Andrew, and Kathleen J. Hanrahan. *Abolish Parole? Summary Report* (Washington DC: National Institute of Law Enforcement and Criminal Justice, September 1978).

Holmes, Malcolm, and William Taggart. A Comparative Analysis and Research Method. *Journal of Crime and Criminal Justice* 7, no. 2 (1990): 421–437.

Holmes, Thomas, and Richard Rahe. Stress Readjustment Rating Scale-43 Life Events. *Journal of Psychosomatic Research* 11, no. 2 (1967).

Hudson, Radditt. Being a Cop Showed Me Just How Racist and Violent Police Are. *Washington Post*, 6 December 2014.

———. The Hell of Being a Black Cop. *New Republic*, 31 August 2000.

Jackson, Maurice. Toward a Sociology of Black Studies. *Journal of Black Studies* 1 (1970): 131–140.

Jacobs, J. B., and S. B. Magdovitz. At Leep's End: A Review of Law Enforcement Education Program. *Journal of Police Science and Administration* 5, no. 1 (1977): 1–18.

James, Joy. *Imprisoned Intellectuals Write-Life, Liberation and Rebellion* (New York: Rowman & Littlefield, 2003).

Johnson, Marilyn. *Street Justice: A History of Police Violence in New York City* (Boston: Beacon Press, 2003).

Johnson, Vida. KKK in the Police Department, White Supremacy Police and What to Do About It (Lewis & Clark Law Review. *Georgetown Law School* 23, no. 1 (2019): 205–261.

Kamisac, Yale. When the Cops Were Not Handcuffed. *New York Times Magazine*, 7 November 1965.

Kasselbaum, G. *Prison Treatment and Parole Survival* (New York: Wiley, 1971).

Katzenbach, Nicholas. *The Challenge of Crime in a Free Society, President's Commission on Law Enforcement and Administration of Justice* (Washington DC: USGPO, 1967).

Katznelson, Ira. DuBois Country. *Social Science History* 23, no. 4 (1999): 459–474.

———. *When Affirmative Action Was White-An Untold Story of Racial Inequality in the 20th Century* (New York: Norton, 2006).

Kay, Harris M. Rethinking Probation in the Context of a Justice Novel. In Patrick D. McAnany, Doug Thomsen, and David Fogel (eds.), *Probation and Justice: Reconsideration of a Mission* (Cambridge: Oelgeschlager, Quinn & Hain, 1984).

Keller, Clarence. *Crime in the United States, 1974 Uniform Crime Reports* (Washington DC: NIJ, 1975).

Kephart, Robert. *The Family, Society and the Individual* (New York: Houghton Mifflin, 1966).

Kimberly, Kindy, and Dan Keating. For Women, Heavy Drinking Has Been Normalized and That's Dangerous. *Washington Post*, 23 December 2016.

King, Martin Luther, Jr. *Autobiography* (New York: Warner, 1998).

King, Roy D., and Emma Wincup. *Doing Research on Crime and Justice* (New York: Oxford University Press, 2000).

Kleinknecht, William. *The Man Who Sold the World, Ronald Reagan and the Betrayal of Main Street America* (New York: Perseus, 2009).

Klinger, David A. *Deference or Deviance, A Note on Why Hostile Suspects Are Arrested, Talk at the Annual Meeting of the American Society of Criminologists*, New Orleans, November 1994.

Knoohuizen, Ralph, Richard P. Fahey, and Deborah J. Palmer. *The Police and Use of Lethal Force* (Chicago: Chicago Law Enforcement Study Group, 1972).

Koehl, Matt (ed.). *White Power, The Newspaper for White Revolution, National Socialist White People's Party, Arlington 1971–1973*.

Kohler-Hausmann, Issa. *Misdemeanorland: Criminal Courts and Social Control in the Age of Broken Windows* (Princeton: Princeton University Press, 2018).

Lal, Barbara Balli., Black and Blue in A. E. Park's Perspective on Race Relations in Urban America. *British Journal of Sociology* 38, no. 4 (1987): 546–566.

Lanham, Drew. When W.E.B. DuBois Was Un-American. *bostonreview.net*, 13 January 2017.

Latzer, Barry. *Rise and Fall of Violent Crime in America* (New York: Encounter Books, 2017).

Lefkowitz, Joel. Psychological Attributes of Police: A Review of Research and Opinion. *Journal of Social Issues* 31, no. 1 (1975): 3–26.

Lemert, Edwin M. *Offenders in the Community* (Lexington: Lexington Books, 1978).

Lerner, Max. *America as a Civilization* (New York: Simon & Schuster, 1957).

Leuci, Robert. *All the Centurions: A New York City Cop Remembers His Years on the Street, 1961–1981* (New York: Morrow, 2004).

Lewis, Gregory, and Rahul Patkak. *When Warriors Put on a Badge* (Athens: Georgia State University, 2017).

Lichtenberg, Judith. The American Prison System is Inhumane, Here's Why. *Theweek.com/article 651722*, 30 September 2016.

Lincoln, Eric. *The Black Muslims in America* (Boston: Beacon Press, 1973).

Lindeman, Alfred R. *The Addict and the Law* (Bloomington: Indiana University Press, 1965).

Lipstadt, Deborah. The Triumph of Deaths. How the Nazis Escaped Prosecution. *Times Literary Supplement*, 1 March 2019.

Liptak, Adam, Alma Cohen, and Crystal Yang. Black Defendants Get Longer Sentences From Republican-Appointed Judges. *New York Times*, 28 May 2018.

Loader, Ian. To Reduce Harm. *Times Literary Supplement*, 14 August 2020.

Lowe, V. I. *Overview of Activities Funded by LEAA* (Washington DC: USGPO, 1977).

Ludwig, Edward G., and John Collette. Bias in Bureaucratic Decision-Making. *Journal of the National Medical Association* 65, no. 6 (1973): 487.

Lundman, Richard J. Routine Police Arrest Practices: A Commonweal Perspective. *Social Problems* 22 (1974): 127–141.

MacCommick, Austin. *Committee Report on the Investigation of Penitentiaries* (Houston, Texas, 1947).

MacNamara, Donal E. J., and Fred Montanio (eds.). *Incarceration, The Sociology of Prisons* (Beverly Hills: Sage, 1978).

Malcolm, Andrew M. Violent Raids Against the Innocent Found Widespread. *New York Times*, 25 June 1973.

Marable, Manning. *Race, Reform and Rebellion: The Second Reconstruction in Black America, 1945–1982* (Jackson: University Press of Mississippi, 1984).

Martinson, D. O. What Works? Answers About Prison Reform. *The Public Interest* 35 (1974).

Maurer, Mark, and Sabrina Jones. *The Race to Incarcerate* (New York: New Press, 2013).

McAdam, Doug. *The Political Process and Development of Black Insurgency, 1930–1970* (Chicago: Chicago University Press, 1999).

McAnany, Patrick D., Doug Thomsen, and David Fogel. *Probation and Justice: Reconsideration of a Mission* (Cambridge: Oelgeschlager, Quinn & Hain, 1984).

McCann, E. Michael. Don't Exempt Political Corruption from Effective Prosecution. *Wisconsin State Journal*, 19 October 2015.

McElrath, Karen, and Dorothy Taylor. Gender and Earnings in Academic Criminology. *Journal of Criminal Justice Education* 7, no. 1 (1986): 35–44.

McGonigal, Jane. *Our Puny Human Brains are Terrible Thinking About the Future, Future Tense*. Arizona State University, 13 April 2017.

McIver, Robert M., and Leon Bramson. *Community, Society and Power* (Chicago: Chicago University Press, 1971).

McKenna, Abby. *Is Cocaine or Alcohol Worse?* (Denver, CO: Raleigh House, 2018).

McLuckie, Lori Lynn. Correctional Officers Fail to Live Up to Glorified Billing Inmate Says. *Denver Post*, 1 November 1998.

Mechie, Calum. Still Orwell's England? *Times Literary Supplement*, 18 December 2010.

Merton, Robert K. Bureaucratic Structure and Personality. *Social Forces* 18 (1940): 560–568.

———. Social Structure and Anomie. *American Sociological Review* 3 (1938): 672–682.

Miller, Jerome G. *Search and Seizure, African American Males in the Criminal Justice System* (Cambridge: Cambridge University Press, 1996).

Miller, Quentin D. *A Criminal Power, James Baldwin and the Law* (Columbus: Ohio SU, 2012).

Mills, C. Wright. *The Causes of WW3* (New York: Simon & Schuster, 1958).

Mills, James. *On the Edge* (Garden City: Doubleday, 1975).

Milton, Catherine H., Jeanne W. Halleck, James Lardner, and Gary L. Abrecht. *Police Use of Deadly Force* (Washington DC: Police Foundation, 1979).

Monk, R. C. *Taking Sides: Clashing Views and Controversial Issues in Crime and Criminology* (Guilford: Dushkin, 1996).

Moore, Leonard. *Black Rage in New Orleans: Police Brutality and African American Activism From World War 2 to Hurricane Katrina* (Baton Rouge: Louisiana University Press, 2010).

Morn, Frank. *Academic Politics and the History of Criminal Justice Education* (Westport: Greenwood, 1995).

Morris, Aldon D. Scholar's Work Has Been Systematically Ignored. *Harvard Gazette*, 29 October 2018.

Morris, Ronald L. *Harlem Survey of Resident Perspectives of the Criminal Justice System* (New York: John Jay College of Criminal Justice (CUNY), Unpublished, 2018).

———. *Survey of 100 Probationer Complaints About Their Probation Officers* (San Rafael: Marin County (CA) Probation Department, Unpublished, 1976).

Moynihan, Daniel. *Maximum Possible Misunderstanding* (New York: Free Press, 1969).

———. *The Negro Family. A Case for National Action* (Washington DC: Office of Policy Planning and Research, Department of Labor, March 1965)

Murakawa, Naomi. The Origins of the Carceral Crisis: Racial Order as Law and Order in Postwar American Politics. In Joseph Lowndes, Julie Novikov, and Dorian T. Warner (eds.), *Race and Political Development* (New York: Routledge, 2008).

Murray, Albert. White Norms, Black Development. In Joyce A. Ladner (ed.), op. cit.

Napper, George. Perceptions of Crime and Implications. In Robert Woodson (ed.), *Perspectives on Crime and the Criminal Justice System* (Boston: Hall, 1977).

National Conference on Alternatives to Incarceration. *Summary Report on the Alternatives to Prison* (Boston: NCAC, 1975).

Navasky, Victor, and Darrell Paster. *Law Enforcement-The Federal Role, the Twentieth Century Fund Task Force on LEAA* (New York: McGraw-Hill, 1976).

Nixon, Richard. *Special Message to Congress on Control of Narcotics and Dangerous Drugs*. presidency.ucsb.edu/documents, 14 July 1969.

Nutt, David. Independent Scientific Committee on Drugs. *Lancet*, June 2019.

Odum, Howard W. *Social and Mental Traits of Negroes* (New York: Longmans, Green, 1912).

O'Leary, Vincent, and Edward Ryan. *A Study of Conflict Resolution in Criminal Justice, School of Criminal Justice* (Albany: SUNY, 1969).

Oshinsky, Drury M. *Worse Than Slavery: Parchman Farms, the Ordeal of Jim Crow Justice* (New York: Free Press, 1997).

Packer, Herbert J. *A Special Supplement-Negro Crime Programs and What It Means* (New York: New Book, 22 October 1970).

Palmer, Ted. *The Re-Emergence of Correctional Intervention, Developments Through the 1960s and Prospects* (Beverly Hills: Sage, 1992).

Park, Robert E. The Mentality of Racial Hybrids. *American Journal of Sociology* 36, no. 4 (1931): 534–551.

Parratt, Spencer. A Police Service Rating Scale. *Journal of Criminal Law and Criminology* 26 (1938).

Parsons, Talcott, and Robert F. Bales. *Family, Socialization and the Interactive Process* (New York: Free Press, 1955).

Parten, M. *Surveys, Polls and Samples* (New York: Harper, 1950).

Patterson, Lyman Ray. Should Lawyers Judge the Judges. *Judicature* 59, no. 10 (1976): 457–467.

Pawelczynska, Anna. *Values on Violence in Auschwitz, a Sociological Analysis* (Berkeley: California University Press, 1979).

Payan, Tony. *A War that Cannot Be Won* (Boston: Atlantic Press, 2013).

Pegues, Corey. *Once a Cop* (Dallas: Atrio Books, 2016).

Pell, Eve (ed.). *Maximum Security: Letters from California Prisons* (New York: Dutton, 1972).

Penn, Everette B. *On Black Crime, Past, Present, Future* (Prairie View: Prairie View A & M, 2000).

Peretz, Henri. The Making of Black Methodology. *Annual Academy of Social Sciences* (2004): 168–175.

Perlman, Liv. *American Justice on Trial* (New York: Regent, 2016).

Petersilia, Joan R. Policy Relevance and the Future of Crime, presidential address, American Society of Criminologists. *Criminology* 29 (1991): 1–15.

———. *Racial Disparities in the Criminal Justice System* (Santa Monica: Rand, 1983).

Phelps, Michelle. Rehabilitation in the Punitive Era: The Gap Between Rhetoric and Reality in the United States Prisons. *Law & Society Review* 45, no. 1 (2011): 33–68.

Philliger, Susan. Thy Brother's Keeper, A Review of the Literature of the 1960s. *Justice Quarterly* 4 (1987).

Piven, Herman, and Abraham Alcabes. *Pilot Study of Correctional Treatment and Manpower.* Department of Education & Welfare, Office of Juvenile Delinquency and Youth Development (Washington DC: USGPO, 1969).

Pizarro, J., and Vanja M. K. Stenius. Supermax Prisons: Their Rise and Current Practices and Effects on Inmates. *The Prison Journal* 84 (2004): 248–264.

Pound, Roscoe, and Felix Frankfurter. *Politics and Criminal Prosecution* (New York: Minton, Balch, 1922).

Prassel, Frank R. *Introduction to the American Criminal Justice System* (New York: Harper & Row, 1975).

Queen, Stuart A., and Robert W. Haberstein. *The Family in Various Cultures* (Philadelphia: J. B. Lippincott, 1967).

Reiss, Albert. Police Brutality, Answers to Key Questions. *Trans-Action Magazine* 5 (1968).

———. *Community and Crime* (Chicago: Chicago University Press, 1987).

Reuter, Edward Byron. The Superiority of the Mulatto. *American Journal of Sociology* 23, no. 1 (1917): 83–106.

Ringelblum, Emanuel. *Notes from a Warsaw Ghetto* (New York: Schocken, 1974).

Ritzer, Arthur, and Lars Trautman. The Conservative Case for Criminal Justice Reform. *The Guardian/U.S. News*, 5 August 2018.

Robin, Gerald D. *Introduction to the Criminal Justice System* (New York: Harper, 1980).

———. Justifiable Homicide for Police Officers. *Journal of Crime, Criminology and Police Science* 54 (1963): 225–231.

Robison, J., and G. Smith. The Effectiveness of Correctional Programs. *Crime & Delinquency* 17 (1971): 67–80.

Rodriguez, Isidero. Does Community Supervision Have a Future? *thecrimereport .org*, 3 January 2019.

Rosenberger, Leif R. *America's Drug War Debacle* (Brookfield: Ashgate, 1996).

Ross, J. I., G. Barak, J. Ferrell, D. Kauzlarich, M. Hamm, D. Friedrichs, R. Matthews, S. Pickering, M. Presdee, P. Kraska, and V. Kappeler. The State of State Criminal Research: A Commentary. *Humanity & Society* 23, no. 3 (1995): 273–281.

Ross, Luana. *Investigating the Savage: The Social Construct of Native American Criminality* (Austin: University of Texas Press, 1998).

Rudovsky, David. Criminal Justice: The Accused in Norman Dorsen. In *Our Endangered Rights* (New York: Pantheon, 1984).

———. *Impressions from a Lawyer with the Defender Association* (Philadelphia: Defender Association, 1982).

Rudovsky, David, Michael Avery, and Karen Blum. *Police Misconduct: Law and Litigation* (Eagan: Clark Boardman, 2006).

Russell-Brown, Katheryn. *The Color of Crime: Racial Hoaxes, White Fear, Black Protectionism, Police Harassment and Other Macroaggressions* (New York: New York University Press, 1998).

Ruthmiller, Mike, and Ivan E. Goldman. *Los Angeles's Secret Police: Inside LAPD's Elite Spy Network* (New York: Pocket Books, 1992).

Sacks, Mary. Police Repression of Negroes from 1951 New York City's Black Population to the 20th Century. *Journal of Urban History* 31 (2015).

St. John, Victor. Probation and Race in the 1980s: A Quantitative Examination of Felonious Rearrests and Minority Threat Theory. *Race & Social Problems* 11 (2019): 243–252.

Sances, Michael W. Do DAs Represent Their Voters? Evidence from California's Era of Criminal Justice Reform. *Political Science* 2 (2021): 169–197.

Saunders, Charles. Assessing Race Relations Research. *Journal of Black Studies and Research* 1 (1970): 17–25.

Savelsberg, Joachim. Knowledge, Domination and Criminal Punishment. *American Journal of Sociology* 99, no. 4 (1994): 911–943.

Scharf, Peter. Empty Bars, Violence and Crisis of Meaning in Prison. In Michael C. Braswell, Reid H. Montgomery, Jr., and Lucien T. Lombardo (eds.), *Prison Violence in America* (Cincinnati: Anderson, 1994).

Schlesinger, S. R. *Justice, Expenditures, Employment in the United States, 1971–1979* (Washington DC: Department of Justice, 1984).

Schulz, David A. *Coming Up Black-Patterns of Ghetto Socialization* (Englewood Cliffs: Prentice-Hall, 1969).

Schwartz, Herman. *Right Wing Justice: The Conservative Campaign to Take Over the Courts* (New York: Nation Books, 2004).

Scott, John. *W.E. B. DuBois, Fifty Key Sociologists: The Formative Theorists* (London: Routledge, 2007).

Sebulo, Leanne C., and Karen T. Gibson. Black and Blue: Police and Community Relations in Portland's Albina District, 1964–1985. *Oregon Historical Quarterly* 114, no. 1 (2013): 6–37.

Sechrist, Lee, Susan O. White, and Elizabeth D. Brown (eds.). *The Rehabilitation of Criminal Offenders: Problems and Prospects—A Panel Discussion on Research and Rehabilitation Techniques* (Washington DC: National Academy Press, 1979).

Sellin, Thorston. The Negro Criminal: A Statistical Note. *Annals of the American Academy of Politics* 140 (1928): 52–64.

Serpas, Frank. *The Spatial Ecology of Crime in New Orleans-Patterns of Certain Crimes and Their Occurrences Among Socio-Economic Areas.* MS thesis (New Orleans: Urban Studies, University of New Orleans, 1981).

Shapiro, Robert M. (ed.). *Why Didn't the Press Shout? American and International Journalism During the Holocaust?* Papers given at the Yeshiva University Conference, NY, October 1995.

Siegel, Larry L., and John L. Worrall. *Police and Law Enforcement: Introduction to Criminal Justice* (Boston: Cengage Learning, 2013).

Sikes, Melvin P. *The Administration of Injustice* (New York: Harper & Row, 1975).

Simon, Herbert A. *Administrative Behavior.* Ph.D. dissertation in Economics, p. 384 (Chicago, 1947).

Skocpol, Theda. Bringing the State Back In: Strategies of Analysis in Current Research. In Theda Skocpol, Peter Evans, and Dietrich Rueschemeyer (eds.), *Bringing the State Back In* (New York: Columbia University Press, 1985).

Sludden, Richard D., and Robert A. Shearer. *An Examination of Probation Officer Ideologies and Personality Types* (Warrensburg: Central Missouri State University, 1992).

Small, Stephen. *Racialized Barriers, The Black Experience in the United States and England in the 1980s* (London: Routledge, 1994).

Smalley, Webster (ed.). *Five Plays by Langston Hughes* (Bloomington: Indiana University Press, 1963).

Smith, Clive Stafford. Judge Dread and Witty: Its Purpose. United States Justice is Not Fit for Its Purpose. *Times Literary Supplement,* 1 December 2018.

Smith, Douglas A., Jody R. Klein, and Christy A. Visher. Street Level Justice-Situational Determinants of Police Arrest Decisions. *Social Problems* 29 (1981): 167–177.

Smith, Robert L. *A Quiet Revolution: Probation Subsidy* (Washington DC: Department of HEW, 1970).

Smyicka, J. *Probation and Parole-Crime Control in the Community* (New York: Macmillan, 1984).

Sniffen, Michael J. *Knock at the Door Strikes Terror into These Families,* 26 June, AP, p. 53 (Associated Press, 1973).

Sorenson, Jan. Scholarly Production in Criminal Justice: Top Ten Criminal Justice Journals. *Journal of Criminal Justice* 22 (1954): 535–547.

Sorokin, Pitrim. *Fads and Foibles and Modern Society in Related Science* (New York: Henry Regnery, 1956).

Spencer, Jack W. *Discourse and Textual Processes in a Probation Department: An Analysis of Written and Interactional Communication.* Ph.D. dissertation (Bloomfield: Indiana University, 1983).

Spohn, Cassie C. *How Do Judges Decide: The Search for Fairness in Justice and Punishment* (Thousand Oaks: Sage, 2002).

Stahl, David, Frederick Sussman, and Neil Bloomfeld. *The Community and Racial Crisis* (New York: Practicing Law Institute, 1966).

Stamper, Norm. *Breaking Ranks: A Top Cop's Exposure of the Dark Side of American Policing* (New York: Nation Books, 2005).

Stanley, Stephen, and Mary Baginsky. *Alternatives to Prison: An Examination of Noncustodial Sentencing on Offenders* (London: Peter Owen, 1984).

Staples, Robert. White Racism, Black Crime and American Justice. *Phylon* 36 (1975): 14–22.

Stender, Fay. *Congressional Hearings, Part II* (Washington DC: USGPO, 1971).

Stephenson, R. M., and Frank Scarpitti. *Group Interaction as Therapy: The Use of the Small Group in Corrections* (Westport: Praeger, 1974).

Stern, Vivien. *Failures in Penal Policy* (Manchester: Statistical Society, 1987).

Stevens, Francis, and John Maxoy. Representing the Unrepresented: A Decennial Report. *Mississippi Law Journal* 44 (1973): 333.

Stewart, Eric, Ronald Simon, and Rand Congi. Assessing Neighborhood Social Psychological Influences on Childhood Violence in a Sample. *Criminology* 40, no. 4 (2002): 801–830.

Stojkovic, Stan. The President Crime Commission Recommendations for Corrections: The Twilight of the Idols. In John Conley (ed.), *The President's Crime Commission 25 Years Later* (New York: Routledge, 1994).

Stone, A. F. Is Race Friction Between Whites and Blacks Growing and Inevitable? *American Journal of Sociology* 13 (1908): 676–697.

———. *The Mulatto Factor in the Race Problem* (Boston: Atlantic Monthly, November 1908).

Sussman, Marvyn B. (ed.). *Sourcebook in Marriage and Family* (New York: Houghton Mifflin, 1973).

Suttles, Gerald. *The Social Order in the Slums* (Chicago: Chicago University Press, 1968).

Sykes, Gresham, and David Matza. Techniques of Police Neutralization: A Theory of Delinquency. *American Journal of Sociological Review* 22, no. 6 (1957): 664–670.

Tackett, Michael. Probation on the Defensive in the Drug Wars. *The Chicago Tribune*, 4 November 1990.

Tagaki, Paul. A Garrison State in a Democratic Society. In *Crime & Social Justice*, pp. 27–38 (Berkeley, 1974).

Tarrow, Sidney. Contentious Politics. In Dunatella Della Porta and Marion Diani (eds.), *Oxford Handbook of Social Movements* (New York: Oxford University Press, 2015).

————. *Power in Movements and Contentious Politics* (Cambridge: Cambridge University Press, 1998).

Teasley, C. E., and L. Wright. The Effects of Training on Police Recruit Attitudes. *Journal of Police Sciences and Administration* 1, no. 2 (1973): 241.

Thomas, John Clayton. The Personal Side of Street Level Bureaucracy-Discard or Neutral Competence. *Urban Affairs Review* 21, no. 1 (1986): 84–100.

Thomas, Keith. New Ways Revisited-How History's Borders Were Expanded During the Past 40 Years. *Times Literary Supplement*, 13 October 2006.

Thompson, Heather Ann. Racial History of Criminal Justice in America. *DuBois Review* 16 (2019): 221–241.

————. Why Mass Incarceration Matters: Rethinking Crisis Decline and Transformation in Postwar American History. *Journal of American History* 97, no. 3 (2010): 703–734.

Tilly, Charles. *Popular Contention in Great Britain, 1758–1834* (Boulder: Paradigm, 1995).

————. War-Making and State-Making of Organized Crime in Bringing Back the State. In Peter Evans, Rueschmeyer and Skoepel (eds.), op. cit.

Timasheff, N. S. *Probation in the Light of Criminal Statistics* (New York: Macmillan, 1949).

Toch, Hans. *Violent Men: An Enquiry into the Psychology of Violence* (Chicago: Aldine, 1969).

Tonry, Michael. *Malign Neglect, Race, Crime and Punishment in America* (New York: Oxford University Press, 1995).

————. *Punishing Race, a Continuing American Dilemma* (New York: Oxford University Press, 2012).

Trebach, Arnold S. *The Rationing of Justice: Constitutional Rights and the Criminal Process* (New Brunswick: Rutgers University, 1964).

Tulchin, Simon H., and Ernest Burgess. *Intelligence and Crime: A Study of Penitentiary and Reformatory Offenders* (Chicago: Chicago University Press, 1939).

United Crime Reporting Program. *U. S. Crime Rates, 1960–1990*. diastercenter .com.

Van Eurie, John H. *White Supremacy and Negro Subordination or Negroes: A Subordinate Race and Slavery Its So-Called Normal Condition* (New York: Van Eurie and Horton, 1870).

Van Velde, Richard W. *Report on the Task Force on Criminal Justice Research and Development* (Washington DC: USGPO, 1971).

Varon, Jay N. A Re-Examination of the LEAA. *Stanford Law Review* 27, no. 5 (1975).

VERA Institute of Justice Staff. *Prosecuting Police Misconduct-Reflections on the Role of the United States Civil Rights Division* (New York: Vera Institute, 1995).

Vontress, Clemmont E. Patterns of Segregation and Discrimination: Contributing Factors in Crime Among Negroes. *Journal of Education* 31 (1962): 108–116.

Wacquant, Loic. *Punishing the Poor: The New Liberal Government of Social Insecurity* (Durham: Duke University Press, 2009).

Waldo, G. P., and Stanley Dinitz. Personality Attributes of the Criminal: An Analysis of Research Studies 1950–1965. *Journal of Research in Crime & Delinquency* 4, no. 2 (1967): 185–202.

Wambaugh, Joseph H. *The New Centurions* (Boston: Little, Brown, 1970).

Ward, Geoff. Living Histories of White Supremacy Policing Toward Transformative Justice. *DuBois Review* 15, no. 1 (2018): 167–184.

Watson, Bruce. John Howard Griffin Gives Readers an Unflinching View of the Jim Crow South: How Has His Book Held Up? *Smithsonian Magazine Online*, October 2011.

Watson, Nelson A. The Defenders: A Case Study of an Informal Police Organization. *Social Problems* 15 (1967): 127–147.

Wayson, B., and G. S. Funke. *What Price Justice?* (Rockville: National Institute of Justice, 1989).

Weber, Max. *Capitalism, Bureaucracy and Religion: A Selection of Texts* (London: Allen & Unwin, 1983).

Weitz, Don. *Notes on Psychiatric Fascism.* www.antpsychiatry.org, 2001.

Welch, Ronald. Developing Prisoner Self-Help Techniques: The Early Mississippi Experiment. *Prison Law Monitor* 2, no. 5 (1979): 105–118.

Wells, Bob. United States Police are Killing People With War Crimes Ammunition. *San Francisco Bayview News*, 25 January 2016.

Westley, William A. *The Police: A Sociological Study of Law, Custom and Morality.* Unpublished Ph.D. dissertation (Chicago: Department of Sociology, University of Chicago, 1951).

———. Violence and Police. *American Journal of Sociology* 59, no. 1 (1962): 167–177.

———. *Violence and Police: A Sociological Study of Law, Custom and Morality* (Boston: MIT Press, 1970).

Whitboune, Susan Krauss. Psychopaths Don't Care if They Hurt You, This is Why. *Psychology Today*, June 2017.

Whitehead, John T. *Burnout in Probation and Corrections* (New York: Praeger, 1989).

Wice, Paul B., and Mark Pilgrim. Meeting the Gideon Mandate: A Survey of Public Defender Programs. *Judicature* 58, no. 8 (1975): 400.

Wicker, Tom. *A Time to Die* (New York: New York Times/Quadrangle, 1975).

Wilson, Amos N. *Blueprint for Black Power: A Moral, Political and Economic Imperative for the 21st Century* (New York: afrikanworldinfosystems, 1998).

———. *The Falsification of Afrikan Consciousness, Eurocentric History, Psychiatry and the Politics of White Supremacy* (New York: afrikanworldinfosystems, 1993).

Wilson, James Q. *Thinking of Crime* (New York: Vintage, 1977).

Wilson, M. G., and D. J. Edwards. Vital Capacity of Lungs and Its Relation to the Exercise of Tolerance in Children with Heart Disease. *American Journal of Diseases of Children* 22 (1921): 443–454.

Winter, Sylvia. *Long Road to Justice, Civil Rights at Fifty* (Washington DC: Leadership Conference on Civil Rights and Human Rights, 2015).

Wolfgang, Marvin E. *Patterns in Criminal Homicide* (Philadelphia: Pennsylvania University Press, 1958).

Wolfgang, Marvin E., Robert M. Figlis, and T. Sellin. *Delinquency in a Birth Cohort* (Chicago: Chicago University Press, 1972).

Worden, Robert E. The Causes of Police Brutality-Theory and Evidence on Police Use of Force in Geller & Toch. *Police Violence*, op. cit.

Work, Monroe N. His Contributions in Jonathan Grossman's Black Studies in the Department of Labor, 1897–1907. *Monthly Labor Review* 97 (1974): 17–27.

Wright, Bruce. *Black Robes, White Justice: Why the Justice System Doesn't Work for Blacks* (Secaucus: Lyle Stuart, 1987).

Young, Iris Marion. *Justice and Politics of Difference* (Princeton: Princeton University Press, 2011).

———. *Responsibility for Justice* (New York: Oxford University Press, 2011).

Young, Veneta, and Anne Thomas Sutton. Excluded: The Current Status of African American Scholars in the Field of Criminology and Criminal Justice. *Journal of Research in Crime & Delinquency* 28, no. 1 (1991): 101–116.

YouTube Video Presentations. Police Training Films of the 1930s, 1940s and 1950s (Various).

Zimbardo, Philip E. *The Lucifer Effect* (New York: Random House, 2007).

Index

About the Author

Ronald L. Morris was an active combat soldier in the War on Crime, 1968–85. He was an adult supervising probation officer, seeing action on the Watts/ South Central Los Angeles, Marin County (CA), New York City (Lower Manhattan and Staten Island) plus Inner London Service UK battle campaigns. He is an adjunct professor of criminology at John Jay College of Criminal Justice (NYC), a family court adviser (Staten Island Family Court), and author (*Wait Until Dark: Jazz and the Underworld, 1880–1940*), and was an anti-Viet Nam protester, a social worker striker in Los Angeles, and observer to the Watts Riots of 1965. He now lives in Flemington (NJ) with wife and 20,000 lovable antique/vintage books available for sale.

www.ingramcontent.com/pod-product-compliance
Lightning Source LLC
Chambersburg PA
CBHW022304280326
41932CB00010B/977